Autonomous Driving Network

Aiming to outline the vision of realizing automated and intelligent communications networks in the era of intelligence, this book describes the development history, application scenarios, theories, architectures, and key technologies of Huawei's Autonomous Driving Network (ADN) solution.

In this book, the authors explain the design of the top-level architecture, hierarchical architecture (ANE, NetGraph, and AI Native NE), and key feature architecture (distributed AI and endogenous security) that underpin Huawei's ADN solution. This book delves into various key technologies, including trustworthy AI, distributed AI, digital twin, network simulation, digitalization of knowledge and expertise, human-machine symbiosis, NE endogenous intelligence, and endogenous security. It also provides an overview of the standards and level evaluation methods defined by industry and standards organizations and uses Huawei's ADN solution as an example to illustrate how to implement AN.

This book is an essential reference for professionals and researchers who want to gain a deeper understanding of automated and intelligent communications networks and their applications.

Wenshuan Dang is a Chief Strategy Architect of Huawei Technologies Co., Ltd., Director of Huawei Future Network Research Department, and Director of Huawei ADN Research Project Execution Team. He leads research on architectural innovation in ICT, plans strategic initiatives, and promotes strategy implementation and communication. He currently focuses on cloud computing, 5G evolution and its applications, 6G networks, AI and its applications in various industries, ICT technologies and subsystems for autonomous driving vehicles, and solutions for vertical industries.

River Huang is the CTO of Huawei's ADN domain. With 22 years of experience in managing and designing network products and solutions, he has led the architecture research and design of various products and solutions, including the general software platform for network products, core routers, SDN, and fixed network management, control, and analysis platforms. He is now responsible for developing and implementing the ADN strategy as well as designing the top-level architecture and technology roadmaps for ADN products, platforms, and common components.

Yijun Yu is the Director of Huawei ADN Research Department and a senior research expert in autonomous systems. With 18 years of experience in wireless network research, innovation, product development, and design, he has led innovative research on many key 4G/5G technologies, including wireless, core network, network management, SDN/NFV/cloud computing, and other service domains. He is now responsible for innovative research on Huawei's ADN solution.

Yong Zhang is a chief research expert of Huawei's ADN solution. With 22 years of experience in R&D and planning of management software products for communications networks, he has led the architecture research and design of network management systems for optical networks and FMC networks. He is now responsible for ADN L5 topic research and focuses on the basic theories, reference architecture, evolution pace, and key technologies of L5.

Autonomous Driving Network
Network Architecture in the Era of Autonomy

Wenshuan Dang, River Huang, Yijun Yu,
and Yong Zhang

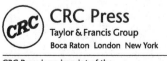

CRC Press
Taylor & Francis Group
Boca Raton London New York

CRC Press is an imprint of the
Taylor & Francis Group, an **informa** business

人民邮电出版社
POSTS & TELECOM PRESS

Designed cover image: by Pasko Maksim (Shutterstock No. 402161899)

First edition published 2024
by CRC Press
2385 NW Executive Center Drive, Suite 320, Boca Raton FL 33431

and by CRC Press
4 Park Square, Milton Park, Abingdon, Oxon, OX14 4RN

CRC Press is an imprint of Taylor & Francis Group, LLC

© 2024 Wenshuan Dang, River Huang, Yijun Yu, and Yong Zhang

English Version by permission of Posts and Telecom Press Co., Ltd.

ISBN: 978-1-032-65506-2 (hbk)
ISBN: 978-1-032-66288-6 (pbk)
ISBN: 978-1-032-66287-9 (ebk)

DOI: 10.1201/9781032662879

Typeset in Minion
by codeMantra

Contents

Foreword I

Autonomous systems resulting from the convergence of ICT and AI represent a bold step toward AGI. In this transition, Autonomous Networks are emerging as the answer to the exploding needs for new services, increased trusted connectivity, and seamless integration of everything between sensors and the cloud.

After a brief overview of the vision of Autonomous Networks, this book provides a detailed technical description of their implementation by Huawei's pioneering ADN (Autonomous Driving Network) solution. It explains the proposed solution in terms of recent developments in autonomous systems theory and proposes reference architectures enabling self-fulfilling, self-healing, and self-optimizing operations. It describes the objectives and principles of their design, as well as their hierarchical organization with the types of components involved. ADN relies heavily on the use of AI techniques to improve predictability, critical situation analysis, and resource optimization.

This book enlightens readers by answering questions about the what, how, and why of the evolution of Autonomous Networks; explaining the underlying issues; and encouraging service providers and enterprises to accelerate their deployment and use. It describes ADN application scenarios for different types of networks and reviews key ADN technologies. These include trustworthy AI, simulation technology, and digital twins, as well as human-machine symbiosis technology, whose integration and effective use pose significant scientific and technical challenges.

This book is an important technical contribution that will teach readers a great deal and raise their awareness of the crucial role that Autonomous Networks, and in particular ADN under Huawei's visionary leadership, are called upon to play in building tomorrow's intelligent world.

Joseph Sifakis
Turing Award 2007, Member of the French Academy of Sciences,
Member of the French Academy of Engineering, Member of Academia Europaea,
Member of the American Academy of Arts and Sciences, Member of the National
Academy of Engineering, Foreign member of the Chinese Academy of Sciences

Foreword II

Autonomous Networks (AN), a product of the mutual development between network and digital technologies, has become an indispensable capability for future networks. It will help coordinate network devices and management systems, improve network intelligence, enable intelligent services, and promote transformation toward digital, automated, and intelligent infrastructure. As such, it will accelerate the progress of building a Digital China with strong, capable networks.

China Communications Standards Association (CCSA), one of the parties that initiated and promoted AN, has been collaborating with industry partners such as TM Forum since 2021 to promote AN standards, which are key to advancing the AN industry and developing innovative technologies. It has also established a standards coordination mechanism based on TC7 (AN meetings) and an industry promotion system based on TC610 (AN working groups) that together will jointly promote the development of the AN industry and standards.

In response to the AN development trend around the globe, China has started to pilot AN on a large scale and systematically deploy it on live networks. Various organizations in the country work together to develop industry standards, and CSPs accelerate planning and deployment of AN based on the innovative use cases jointly developed by vendors. CCSA has proposed a systematic approach for improving network automation and intelligence, aiming to advance technological research and development. It has also defined more than 20 industry standards and initiated 10 standards research topics. To build a converged AN ecosystem, China Academy of Information and Communications Technology (CAICT) and CCSA have jointly launched the Autonomous Network Pilot Program to promote industry development and collaborate with CSPs, which have set strategic goals of reaching L4 by 2025.

As a landmark on the journey toward fully automated and intelligent networks, AN calls for converged innovation and collaborative development of cutting-edge technologies, as well as the formation of advanced standards through global efforts spanning different domains. Standards organizations need to work closely with each other in order to efficiently develop practical standards for the industry and their members. Instead of simply focusing on specific technologies, AN standards are a comprehensive system covering the target architecture, levels, evaluation indicators, and CSPs' O&M practices. Developing such a standards system requires that all industry partners apply these standards in all industry procedures and actively provide feedback. In this way, standards can be improved to better suit real-world applications, facilitate scientific and technological innovation, and enable epoch-making breakthroughs.

Autonomous Driving Network - Network Architecture in the Era of Autonomy shares Huawei's systematic thoughts and ideas about the evolution toward L5 AN from a technological perspective, helping the AN industry to develop and evolve long into the future. I sincerely hope that this book can encourage all industry partners to jointly explore and develop systems for AN standards and technologies. By doing so, we can use standards to fully promote innovation, harness the resources and efforts of all parties, and facilitate industry evolution and technology upgrades according to the AN levels, thereby promoting AN development.

Ku Wen
Chair of the Board of
China Communications Standard Association

Foreword III

The emergence of 5G and other next-generation information technologies is expediting today's innovations and breakthroughs. As computing power and networks become more deeply integrated, new information infrastructures are enabling digital upgrade and reconstruction of production organizations, objects, tools, and modes in various industries – this in turn is facilitating digital transformation across society as a whole. One of the major driving forces powering the industrialization of digital technologies and the digitalization of various industries is AN, which offers a Zero-X (zero-wait, zero-trouble, and zero-touch) and Self-X (self-configuration, self-healing, and self-optimizing) experience.

As one of the parties that initiated and pioneered the concept of AN, China Mobile is dedicated to strengthening its leading advantages in the network field, facilitating the innovation, capability development, and large-scale application of the AN system, enabling the transformation of social production modes, and promoting "intelligent network revolution and digital transformation" in various industries. Through our relentless efforts, we made many significant achievements in 2022 – for example, we realized an average AN level higher than L2.8, we automated more than 80% of core O&M capabilities, and we developed more than 170 AI O&M capabilities, which were requested more than 4 billion times a day.

Despite these achievements, we still face many challenges in the course of developing AN. For example, no mutually agreed system has yet been established for measuring service value – the industry has long faced difficulty in measuring the service value delivered by AN and leveraging such value to improve digital intelligent capabilities. In addition, further innovative technological breakthroughs are yet to be made. The first such breakthrough is computing-network collaborative autonomy – calculating the optimal "computing+network" route in real time based on the computing power and traffic characteristics in different service scenarios to fulfill the vision of "computing as the core" and "computing enhanced by network". The second breakthrough is full-stack AI deployment – collaboratively improving the AI capabilities of networks and network management systems to achieve full-stack intelligence and use intelligence to improve quality. The third is digital twin – developing virtual images of physical networks to achieve holographic real-time network awareness and spatiotemporal mirroring, facilitating intelligent decision-making and efficient innovation.

In the post-information era, the global communications industry demonstrates the potential of making the impossible possible. Industry partners need to work together to accelerate the digital intelligent transformation toward networks oriented to "connection+computing power+capability". This book shares Huawei's latest research progress and achievements in the field of AN with industry partners, offering a valuable reference for academic research, innovative practices, and standards formulation of AN. We hope that industry partners can work together closely to speed up the development of innovative AN theories and technologies and advance the AN industry in the digital era.

Huidi Li
Vice President of China Mobile Limited

Foreword IV

Huawei has been dedicated to discovering the fields that AI can benefit since it decided to develop Ascend AI chips in 2017. Machine vision, voice and semantic recognition, and autonomous driving are undoubtedly among these fields. I have been engaged in discussions on autonomous driving for a long time and learned that the industry has defined five autonomous driving levels, with unmanned driving as the highest one. Based on Huawei's over 30 years of experience in helping CSPs improve O&M efficiency and reduce O&M workload, I had an innovative idea: using AI to implement "autonomous driving" for networks, which is what I call "autonomous driving networks (ADN)". This game-changing concept has become an ultimate goal for CSPs to deploy intelligent networks.

As such, Huawei has set up an ADN research project team to continuously make groundbreaking achievements in terms of the definition and key technologies of ADN.

This book provides a collection of the team's research findings to inspire greater discussion across the industry.

Eric Xu
Chairman of the Board and Rotating Chairman
of Huawei Technologies Co., Ltd.

Preface

COMMUNICATIONS NETWORKS HAVE WITNESSED tremendous progress over nearly a century and a half since Alexander Graham Bell patented the telephone in 1876. Today, they are deeply integrated into all aspects of our work and lives – people day and night are enjoying the services and Internet applications supported by communications networks all over the world. In addition to providing consumer services (e.g., voice communication, online shopping, mobile payment, live streaming, online education, and telemedicine), communications networks have become an information foundation in numerous fields, including electric power, finance, manufacturing, energy, government affairs, healthcare, education, transportation, and chemical industries. As such, these networks have become so deeply integrated into our lives that we barely realize how indispensable they are until they fail. At the same time, though, these networks have reached an unprecedented level of complexity. Worldwide, CSPs have deployed more than 7 million physical sites, 10 million logical sites, 30,000 IP core devices, 200,000 IP aggregation devices, 1 million IP access devices, 150,000 optical transmission network (OTN) backbone devices, 260,000 OTN metro devices, and 70,000 OTN access devices by the end of 2022. Of note is the fact that about 80% of these large-scale networks were built within just two decades. Take China Mobile as an example. Within this time span, China Mobile upgraded its networks from 2G and 3G to 4G and then to 5G, all of which still coexist today. The general demand to upgrade communications networks will continue to grow relentlessly as it has in the past, driving mobile, optical, and data communications networks to evolve toward 5.5G, F5.5G, and Net5.5G. Two decades was a short time in which to achieve such tremendous progress in terms of both technology and scale, leaving us with barely enough time to optimize networks or fully adapt them to the technological changes. Rapid development came at the cost of increasing network complexity, which has created numerous challenges to CSPs' business development. There are three prominent challenges.

The first is service agility and continuous innovation. Fast-growing network technologies create numerous opportunities for CSPs to develop new services for consumers (e.g., high-bandwidth and low-latency XR, home-company hybrid office, and high-quality videos for online-offline remote education) and vertical industries (e.g., highly reliable and low-latency private mobile network services). Such services are becoming business and revenue growth engines for CSPs. In response to fast-growing digital services, many CSPs have adapted their strategy to quickly develop innovative technologies and services in addition to seizing new market opportunities, aiming to achieve business success. Things would be easier if it were just a case of providing innovative services on new networks. However, CSPs must also continue to provide existing services, meaning that different network generations (2G, 3G, 4G, and 5G) will coexist for a long time. Changes that have to be made to existing networks and services during service innovation might slow down the rollout of innovative services and compromise the benefits they will bring.

The second challenge is on-demand real-time user experience assurance. Over the next 5–10 years, new intelligent devices will emerge more rapidly. Such devices include those for the consumer market (e.g., drones, VR/AR glasses, and robots) and digital industry sector (e.g., automated guided vehicles [AGVs], medical devices, and heavy machinery). The result of this is that there will be a higher requirement for on-demand real-time user experience assurance. Communications networks, which function as the public infrastructure serving different users and devices at different sites, are ultra-complex time-varying systems where user requirements and distributions, environments, and device status constantly change. They are also where upgrades, capacity expansion, reconstruction, service provisioning, and service changes constantly happen. Such time-varying complexity may cause user experience to become uneven with wider gaps – user experience will also become more difficult to measure. The current passive response approach is implemented based on post-event analysis and average statistics. The key to future network innovation lies in precise awareness for various types of devices and applications, service level agreement (SLA) assurance, and improvements on user experience and loyalty.

The third challenge is the network O&M challenge caused by issues surrounding the architecture, processes, and skills. Despite continuous network upgrades over the past two decades, the O&M systems employed on communications networks have barely changed because these networks – as key infrastructure – must continue to provide existing services. O&M complexity is increasing along with network complexity to a level that exceeds human capabilities and has become a problem that cannot be addressed by simply increasing the number of O&M engineers. A diverse range of new services requires upskilling of O&M engineers. As networks become more complex, the upskilling process becomes more challenging and inefficient, widening the gap between the talent supply and demand. These architectural, process, and skill issues faced by network O&M have become a major bottleneck for network development.

The entire communications industry has long been striving to overcome these challenges. In 2006, Huawei proposed the All IP-based Fixed Mobile Convergence (FMC) architecture and has since released a series of solutions based on the Single strategy to help CSPs simplify networks and reduce operating expense (OPEX). In 2011, Huawei launched the cloud-based SoftCOM architecture and a series of solutions based on the All Cloud strategy to help CSPs improve user experience and achieve Real-time, On-demand, All-online, DIY, and Social (ROADS). Although these innovative architectures have played an active role in tackling the major challenges faced by communications networks, we are still on our way to achieve our goals due to the obstacles caused by high network complexity.

Fortunately, the development of AI technologies opens up new possibilities. It introduces a data-centric machine learning approach that is a state-of-the-art thinking pattern completely unlike rule-based systems used by traditional communications networks. Such systems operate based on rules and models designed by professionals and are relentlessly tuned to better suit real-world requirements, but they cannot adapt to the increasing network and service complexity in uncertain network environments – this is where AI technologies demonstrate unique advantages. In 2017, Huawei proposed the concept of SoftCOM AI, introducing AI technologies into communications networks. And the following year, Huawei proposed the concept of ADN to achieve the long-term vision of building "self-fulfilling, self-healing, self-optimizing, and autonomous networks", enabling new services, delivering a superior customer experience, and maximizing resource and energy efficiency. This "Self-X and Zero-X" vision will deliver a "zero-wait, zero-touch, and zero-trouble" experience for users and a "self-serving, self-fulfilling, and self-assuring" network O&M experience for CSPs' network planning, construction, and maintenance engineers. Over the past 5 years, Huawei has successfully applied AI in more than 100 communications network scenarios and made tremendous breakthroughs in experience assurance, fault management, and network energy saving, demonstrating the unique value of AI in the field of communications. These innovative practices led to the release of Huawei's Intelligent series solutions in the autumn of 2022. Even so, we remain fully aware that communications networks are large and complex systems that involve many special scenarios and face numerous technological challenges. New challenges will become more complex and daunting due to the differences in services and technologies across different domains (e.g., mobile, optical, and data communications networks), in wide-area coverage across different geographical regions with different population distributions, and in mobility and traffic changes caused by users. It is essential to remember that communications networks are crucial infrastructure that must be guaranteed to function properly 24/7 – any problems that occur locally may cause faults that impact the entire network.

We believe that continuously launching innovative AI and communications network technology research across different fields in terms of basic theories, network architectures, key technologies and algorithms, and business models is key to fully applying AI on communications networks that are highly complex and overcoming the major challenges they face. Such research requires the joint efforts of academia, CSPs, and device vendors. By sharing Huawei's latest research progress with the industry in this book, we hope that more academic researchers and industry experts can join us in fulfilling our ADN vision and promote the sustainable and healthy development of the communications industry.

Wenshuan Dang
Chief Strategy Architect of
Huawei Technologies Co., Ltd.

Introduction

THE IMPETUS TO IMPROVE productivity is deeply rooted in our DNA. Over the past few centuries, each technological revolution – namely, the industrial revolution, electric power revolution, and information technology revolution has led to significant growth in productivity and elevated our civilization to the next level. Today, the fourth industrial revolution, dominated by Artificial Intelligence (AI), 5G, cloud computing, and other cutting-edge technologies, is reshaping the world before our eyes, into one where all things are sensing, connected, and intelligent.

A wide range of information and communications technology (ICT) services, including 5G, cloud, video, Internet of Things (IoT), and AI, are generating information flows as the foundation of a more intelligent world. Intelligent World 2030 is just around the corner. A seamless intelligent network that covers land, sea, and air is the future and will provide ubiquitous cloud-edge-device convergence services in all production scenarios, achieving fully autonomous communications networks. Such communications networks will continue to play a leading role in promoting global development and accelerating the advent of a more intelligent world.

The large-scale deployment and rapid commercial use of 5G, together with the fast-growing digital economy, unleash the potential of the digital era. New digital technologies are emerging and iteratively evolving at an unprecedented speed. Enterprises embrace continuous adjustment and transformation to seize the opportunities created by the pace of change. New scenarios, new services, and new customers raise more advanced requirements on network performance – including availability, bandwidth, latency, and reliability – and require new network features, such as online self-subscription, on-demand minute-level provisioning, differentiated and deterministic service level agreement (SLA) assurance, private network with high data security, preventive maintenance, and simplified and visualized management.

Against this backdrop, the concept of Autonomous Networks (AN) was proposed in 2019 to apply numerous intelligent technologies in the telecom industry in order to achieve intelligent automation. AN completely changes the way we produce, operate, and think, and the skills we need in the industry. All industry partners, including industry organizations, standards development organizations (SDOs), communications service providers (CSPs), and vendors, have quickly and actively responded, launching many innovation projects in all network domains. An industry consensus has been reached on the vision, target architecture, and level standards. Multiple SDOs are collaborating to define industry standards, and CSPs are accelerating the AN deployment and practices.

DOI: 10.1201/9781032662879-1

At the forefront of implementing and contributing to AN, Huawei released the Autonomous Driving Network (ADN) solution, aiming to build a self-fulfilling, self-healing, and self-optimizing autonomous network through connectivity and intelligence. ADN encompasses numerous technologies, such as native intelligence, big data and knowledge, intent application programming interface (API) interaction, single-domain autonomy, and cross-domain collaboration. This solution enables Huawei to jointly develop self-configuration, self-healing, and self-optimizing network capabilities with CSPs and enterprises, delivering a zero-wait, zero-touch, zero-trouble experience for consumers and business customers.

This book summarizes the latest trends and progress of network automation and intelligence and shares Huawei's ADN solution in terms of the latest theories, architectures, technologies, and methodologies of network automation and intelligence. This book will also answer the "what," "why," and "how" questions about AN evolution, helping you understand AN and encouraging CSPs and enterprises to accelerate AN deployment.

Part I describes how the concepts of AN and ADN were proposed and explores four key application scenarios to help you understand the need for AN.

- Chapter 1 Birth of ADN. This chapter summarizes the architectural evolution, key driving forces for network automation and intelligence, and industry ideas of communications networks and introduces the birth, general vision, level definitions, and development of ADN. This is the background knowledge that you need to understand the significance of AN and the correlation between AN and ADN.

- Chapter 2 Application Scenarios of ADN. This chapter outlines four key application scenarios of ADN, namely emergency assurance of integrated terrestrial and non-terrestrial communications, all-wireless enterprise local area network (LAN), secure, reliable, and immersive remote office, and remote control of deterministic wide area network (WAN).

Part II explains the AN architecture and technologies by exploring ADN achievements in terms of basic theories, reference architecture, and key technologies.

- Chapter 3 Fundamental Theories of ADN. This chapter reviews fundamental theories of ADN, including network adaptive control theory, network cognitive theory, and user and environmental model theory.

- Chapter 4 Reference Architecture of ADN. This chapter describes the reference architecture of ADN, including the design objectives and principles, and the design of the top-level architecture, hierarchical architecture (including the ANE, NetGraph, and AI Native NE), and key feature architecture (including distributed AI and endogenous security).

- Chapter 5 Key Technologies of ADN. This chapter introduces eight key technologies of ADN from multiple perspectives, including background and motivation, technology insight, key technical solutions, and technology prospect. These technologies encompass trustworthy network AI, distributed network AI, network digital twin, network simulation, digitalization of network knowledge and expertise, network human-machine symbiosis, NE endogenous intelligence, and network endogenous security.

Part III provides the industry standards and an ADN level evaluation method. Huawei's ADN solution is used as an example to illustrate how to implement AN.

- Chapter 6 Industry Standards. This chapter presents an overview of the standards (both in China and internationally) in the AN industry, including the responsibilities and latest achievements of industry organizations and SDOs, and cross-organization standards collaboration.

- Chapter 7 Level Evaluation of ADN. This chapter uses an ADN level methodology and an example to explain how to explicitly define level standards in detail, and how to objectively, comprehensively, and quantitatively evaluate the ADN level of each product domain.

- Chapter 8 ADN Solution. This chapter provides an overview of Huawei's ADN solution for wireless, core, IP, enterprise campus, data center, all-optical access, all-optical transport networks, and digital and intelligent O&M.

Part IV is Summary and Outlook. ADN has made tremendous achievements in terms of theory, architecture, technology, and standards, unlocking the potential of AN. All industry partners need to keep working together to explore and develop AN despite all the uncertainties ahead.

CHAPTER 1

Birth of ADN

I N MAY 2019, TELEMANAGEMENT FORUM (TM Forum)[1] released *Autonomous Networks: Empowering Digital Transformation For The Telecoms Industry* with BT Group, China Mobile, Orange, Telstra, Huawei, and Ericsson.

In this very first whitepaper, the concept of Autonomous Networks (AN) was proposed to business leaders, including chief x officers (CXOs) of CSPs and vertical industries, opinion leaders in the telecom industry (industry associations, research institutes, senior experts, and analysts), policymakers and think tanks in the telecom industry, and business owners of telecom device vendors and operations support system (OSS)/business support system (BSS) vendors.

The whitepaper described the industry consensus on the definition, vision, reference architecture, and level standards (L0 to L5) of AN. Core concepts, including single-domain autonomy, hierarchical closed loops, and intent-driven, were also described. In addition, the whitepaper offered an architecture blueprint for CSPs' digital transformation and a top-level architecture for industry practices and collaboration.

AN is designed to integrate network and digital technologies in order to help CSPs and vertical industries implement digital transformation, stimulate business growth, and improve operations efficiency. It delivers a zero-wait, zero-touch, zero-trouble experience to vertical industries and consumers and offers self-serving, self-fulfilling, and self-assuring network capabilities for CSPs and enterprises throughout the entire lifecycle, achieving intelligent network operations.

Huawei is a technological pioneer in the communications industry with a nose for the latest industry trends and cutting-edge technologies. In September 2018, Huawei proposed the concept of autonomous driving network (ADN) at the Ultra-Broadband Forum (UBBF) held in Geneva, Switzerland. The connotation and denotation of ADN are highly consistent with those of AN proposed by TM Forum later. And the following year, in October 2019, Huawei announced ADN as the brand name of its AN solution and globally released the ADN solution, becoming the world's first telecom device vendor with its own AN brand and comprehensive AN solution.

DOI: 10.1201/9781032662879-2

1.1 ARCHITECTURE EVOLUTION OF MODERN COMMUNICATIONS NETWORKS

In 1876, Alexander Graham Bell invented the telephone, marking the beginning of using electrical signals to transmit voice in human history. A telephone is a simple device that connects a transmitter and a receiver by two wires. Since then, fixed-line telephone networks remained the only kind of communications network for about a century until the 1980s. In the 1990s, the fixed-line telephone service reached its peak, and the mobile phone service started to take off at an unexpected speed, reshaping the landscape of communication services.

Over the past three decades, IT has been introduced to the communications technology (CT) industry, continuously extending the boundaries of the telecom industry. This resulted in the rapid development of communications networks and two major architectural revolutions from traditional voice and data communications to IP Native, and then from IP Native to Cloud Native. The next decade will witness more incredible breakthroughs and applications of IT technologies (represented by AI, digital twin, security technologies, blockchain, and others) in the CT industry. The architecture of communications networks will transform toward AI Native, providing an ICT infrastructure that involves multiple technologies and industries, including fixed broadband network, mobile broadband network, IP network, cloud computing, and AI. These technologies and industries will benefit each other during the course of their own development. Related technologies and industries develop independently, affect each other, and promote each other. Figure 1.1 shows the architecture evolution of modern communications networks.

Around 2000, IP technologies had reached maturity and were introduced to communications networks deployed using optical fibers and network cables, driving the evolution toward carrier-grade IP networks. Such networks featured a flexible networking mode, high bandwidth, low cost, and easy management, and therefore were rapidly used in a wide scope of applications. Around 2006, IP Native became an industry consensus and a crucial component of communications networks, laying a solid foundation

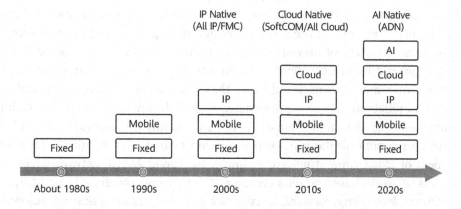

FIGURE 1.1 Architecture evolution of modern communications networks.

for achieving connectivity of everything. The IP Native network architecture has the following advantages:

- Uses unified network interconnection protocols to greatly simplify network element (NE) data transmission, processing, and usage, implementing information-based network systems.

- Reduces network layers and processing complexity.

- Improves network performance, cuts costs, enhances scalability, and simplifies management.

- Facilitates network evolution in the long run.

In the IP Native era, unified IP protocols were used – instead of many different network interconnection protocols – to greatly improve NE connection efficiency and to implement network convergence and information-based systems, marking a tremendous architectural transformation at the network level. IP technologies, initially developed for the Internet, have become an essential component of network infrastructure and profoundly changed the technical architecture of fixed and mobile networks. Since the first decade of the 21st century, Huawei has become a pioneer in ICT infrastructure, specializing in network architecture evolution. Huawei is a company with successful global businesses in all the following industries: fixed broadband network, mobile broadband network, and IP network. Huawei proposed the All-IP fixed mobile convergence (FMC) network architecture and a series of related solutions based on its "Single" strategy, helping CSPs simplify networks and reduce operating expense (OPEX). By doing so, Huawei has successfully built its advantages in network architecture.

In 2011, the Cloud Native network architecture was first proposed in the telecom industry as technologies, services, and O&M further developed, sparking a new round of network architecture transformation and opening up the Cloud Native era for communications networks. This architecture requires a transformation toward cloud communications networks and can better support enterprises' digital transformation and cloud services. Cloud communications networks can integrate multiple hardware and software platforms into a cloud platform, solving the problem of high management and maintenance costs caused by using a variety of network devices. Hardware resources are pooled in a fully distributed software architecture with fully automated operations, so that resources can be shared to the maximum extent. In addition, the cloud platform features high scalability, flexibility, and reliability, achieving automated service deployment, resource scheduling, and troubleshooting. The Cloud Native network architecture introduces many revolutionary changes for communications networks to support cloud services during the vigorous development of cloud computing. For example, the Cloud Native network architecture reconstructs networks based on data centers (DCs) to deeply integrate IT and CT, facilitating software decoupling, forwarding-control separation, resource sharing, autoscaling, and centralized scheduling. The evolution toward Cloud Native – an initial level of system automation – is considered as a device-level transformation. It solves the structural problem of traditional communications networks where capacity can be increased only by adding devices. Network infrastructure that involves the fixed broadband network, mobile broadband network, and IP network lays a solid foundation for the development of cloud computing, which has developed into a mature industry, delivering various benefits to the development of fixed, mobile, and IP networks. Huawei has become a technology provider that is involved in both the network industry and cloud computing industry. In addition to proposing a cloud-based SoftCOM architecture, further strengthening Huawei's advantages in network architecture, Huawei also launched a series of All-Cloud solutions to help CSPs improve user experience and achieve ROADS.

In the future, more IT technologies will be introduced to the CT industry, which will have a profound impact on the development of communications networks. Control and knowledge closed loops based on technologies such as network AI and digital twin will become the major driving forces for communications networks to achieve full autonomy. This will fundamentally solve the structural problem caused by network scale and complexity, facilitating the evolution of communications networks toward AI Native. Autonomous NEs, network management systems, and operations systems are the prerequisites for achieving an autonomous communications system. Full network autonomy requires many fundamental theories and technologies, including network digital twin modeling and simulation, object-driven automatic closed loop and collaboration, network self-awareness, network environment awareness and modeling, self-fulfilling, self-healing, self-optimizing, autonomous network technologies, network adaptive learning, and self-evolution. Their development requires close collaboration between the academia and industry in many fields, including software engineering, computing platform and infrastructure, AI-based network cognition system, system and control theory and application, human-machine interaction, information security, and network security design. NEs and network functions will be redesigned in the AI Native era. With the powerful data analysis and information extraction capabilities of AI, massive network data can be collected and analyzed to detect and predict network status and make decisions. This will allow CSPs to diagnose network quality, optimize service performance, reduce the operations load, and improve user experience. As we can see, the development of networks and cloud computing has resulted in many breakthroughs in AI technologies and promoted their application in the CT industry, while their development will also benefit networks and cloud computing. In 2017, Huawei proposed the concept of SoftCOM AI to introduce AI technologies into communications networks. And the following year, Huawei proposed the concept of ADN to help CSPs achieve their long-term vision of building self-fulfilling, self-healing, and self-optimizing autonomous networks, enabling new services, delivering a superior customer experience, achieving fully automated O&M, and maximizing resource and energy efficiency.

Network architecture evolution has been and will always be essentially a development process where the latest IT practices are continuously introduced into the CT industry and where IT and CT benefit each other. IP Native made it possible to realize an information-based communications system, and Cloud Native realized an automated communications system. In the AI Native era, the communications system is evolving to a higher level of automation and intelligence. With further convergence of fixed broadband network, mobile broadband network, IP network, cloud computing, and AI technologies across various industries, CT and IT will continue to complement each other, strengthening the capabilities of ICT infrastructure providers and resulting in more, greater, and unique contributions to the digital intelligent transformation in all industries. Huawei will continue to promote network architecture evolution by leveraging its unique advantages in five key industries and technologies: fixed broadband network, mobile broadband network, IP network, cloud computing, and AI.

1.2 DRIVING FORCES OF NETWORK AUTOMATION AND INTELLIGENCE

Two decades ago, IP technologies reconstructed the forwarding architecture of communications networks. One decade ago, cloud technologies profoundly changed the service architecture, including the network topology, traffic direction, and core network service implementation. Over the next decade, many AI technologies will be applied on communications networks to facilitate the evolution toward AI Native. Network automation and intelligence are key to overcoming the following challenges that have occurred on telecom networks in recent years:

CSPs' OPEX keeps increasing every year. The revenue growth in the telecom industry has been struggling to outrun the OPEX increase in these years. The OPEX proportion remains high, and reducing the total cost of ownership (TCO) is impossible without structural OPEX optimization. According to the annual report of a major European CSP, the OPEX-to-revenue ratios from 2017 to 2021 were 68.4%, 68.1%, 66.9%, 67.2%, and 66.6%, respectively. From 2015 to 2020, the average revenue growth of about 100 leading global CSPs was lower than the OPEX increase, with the average OPEX accounting for nearly 70% of the total revenue. CSPs must reduce OPEX by improving O&M efficiency.

Network operations rely heavily on manual intervention. Network O&M still depends on human experience and skills, creating a huge demand for more O&M experts. (For example, China Telecom has launched a talent project to train a large number of cloud experts.) 70% of major faults that occur on telecom networks are caused by human factors due to the increasing network complexity. Humans alone will not be able to quickly operate and maintain a large number of real-time cloud services in the future – where machines must come into play.

Customer experience is difficult to manage. Because there is a lack of methods for visualizing telecom service experience or full-lifecycle management based on user experience, most CSPs adopt a complaint-driven user experience management mechanism. Problems that are not reported in user complaints cannot be rectified until they are detected by the network monitoring center. Take home broadband as an example. Fifty-eight percent of experience problems are found only when complaints are raised, and most are difficult to solve because they cannot be reproduced, resulting in a high churn rate.

Emerging services create new challenges for network performance. As various industries further promote digital transformation, more social and business activities are shifting from offline to online, resulting in a wide range of new digital services and markets. This trend is considered as a critical juncture for achieving new breakthroughs in the ICT industry. For example, the 2B market demonstrates tremendous potential. Many vertical industries are emerging, including smart city, smart factory, and smart healthcare, creating a daunting challenge for the ICT industry: how to quickly replicate differentiated network applications across these industries at scale.

CSPs must develop an innovative network architecture to overcome these closely related challenges. Many CSPs have reached a consensus to transform the network architecture toward automation and intelligence. In April 2021, TM Forum conducted a survey on 60 CSP respondents from 46 companies or departments [1] and found that most CSPs believe that network automation and intelligence have become an industry trend.

- Ninety-four percent of respondents said they were implementing network **automation** or would do so. And 38% of respondents said they were promoting automation as much as possible in current network domains. And 56% said their organization had defined a comprehensive vision of automation.

- Eighty-eight percent of respondents said they would (54%) or were very likely to (34%) deploy AI-based networks at scale within 10 years to improve the level of **intelligence**. AI and other intelligent technologies have gained popularity and will be widely promoted over the next decade.

CSPs are shifting their focus from refined and efficient network operations (which are still important) to meeting new requirements for telecom networks from the business and service perspectives. However, the above challenges are not the ultimate driving forces of network automation and intelligence. According to TM Forum's survey report, the key

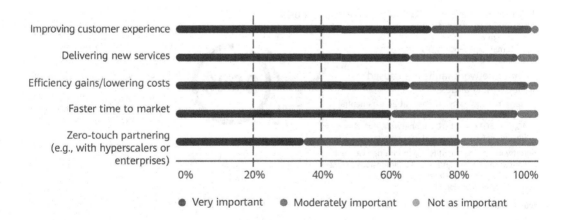

FIGURE 1.2　TM Forum: key driving forces of AN.

driving forces of AN include improving customer experience, delivering new services, efficiency gains/lowering costs, and faster time to market (TTM), as shown in Figure 1.2.

Four key driving forces of network automation and intelligence are summarized based on the report.

- Network O&M efficiency. Inefficient network O&M is the main reason for high OPEX, heavy dependency on manual operations, and poor customer experience.

- New scenarios and services require large-scale deployment of more intelligent network applications.

- Cutting-edge technologies, including AI, digital twin, and security technologies. They are the foundation of a fully automated and intelligent network. These technologies are described later in Chapter 5 Key Technologies of ADN.

- Social responsibility and sustainable development. As ICT infrastructure, networks will become a new type of indispensable resource, just like water and electricity.

1.2.1 Network O&M Efficiency

The evolution of telecom networks has led to many O&M changes but has not fundamentally solved all O&M problems. A Gartner survey report summarizes the network O&M problems, as shown in Figure 1.3. Seventy-five percent of network problems are detected by end users and reported to CSPs through complaints. Such a complaint-driven mechanism cannot guarantee customer experience or satisfaction. The report also shows that 37% of network faults are caused by network changes. Network O&M has far exceeded human capabilities due to the increasing network complexity. O&M personnel have to spend 90% of their time on locating problems, resulting in low O&M efficiency.

To solve these problems, CSPs must analyze them from multiple perspectives, including the size of the O&M organization, process, and support systems.

First, the complexity of network O&M has soared at an exponential rate and far exceeded human capabilities due to the increasing network complexity.

75% of network problems are detected by end users.
- Network faults are difficult to detect and prevent in advance.
- Customer experience and satisfaction are difficult to ensure.

37% of network faults are caused by network changes.
- Network complexity increases at an exponential rate. Four generations of wireless networks (2G, 3G, 4G, and 5G) coexist. 10 core network domains (including CS, PS, IMS, and IoT) coexist.
- Network management is beyond human capabilities. People can understand only 3.5 dimensions (X/Y/Z and 0.5 time axis in the past). Network management involves N dimensions.

Source: Garter

75%

90%

37%

O&M engineers spend **90%** of their time identifying fault causes.
- The causes of network problems are difficult to identify. Cross-domain problems are difficult to demarcate.
- Root cause locating is complex and relies heavily on expertise.

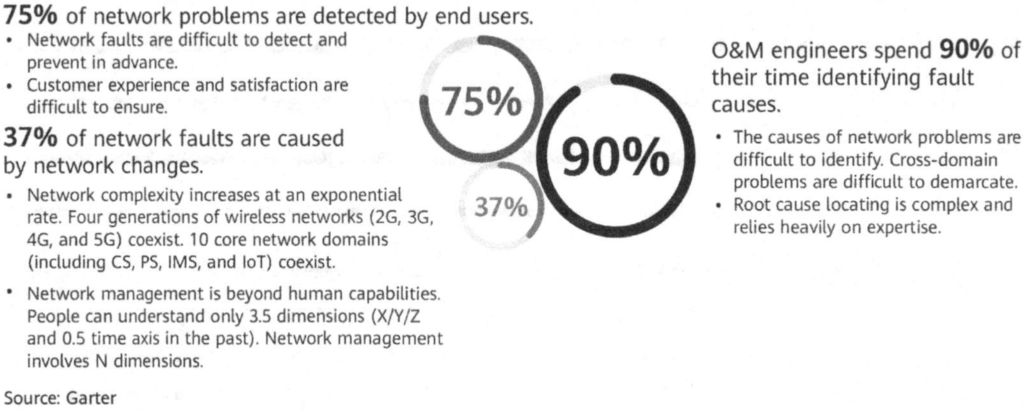

FIGURE 1.3   Network O&M problems.

Network O&M, which is hardly perceptible to users, requires numerous O&M engineers and complex system collaboration during service design, rollout, provisioning, and maintenance for many network domains from the access network to the metropolitan area network (MAN), backbone network, and core network. In terms of service, technology, and role, network O&M engineers face many challenges.

- Service: Telecom network management involves managing the experience of many different services and customers. A telecom network offers various customer services, including home broadband, mobile phone, and enterprise private line services. Different services of different customers create different constraints for achieving automated operations. The network system must be able to understand the motivations and intents of different customers and services.

  Even a single network domain can be complex. For example, in the wireless domain, 2G, 3G, 4G, and 5G coexist and serve different customers. Manually adjusting wireless parameters of 3G and 4G networks is possible. However, the number of parameters to be adjusted in 5G increases to 2000, which is far beyond human capabilities and requires automated, accurate adjustment.

  Customers in different vertical industries also have differentiated network requirements. It is impossible for O&M engineers to learn the knowledge of each of these industries.

- Technology: Telecom networks involve multi-network and hypernetwork technologies, including centralized structured networks (such as DC), regional IP and campus networks, fixed access networks using fiber to the x (FTTx) with numerous terminals, and wireless networks.

  A hyper-distributed air-space-land-sea network will emerge in the near future. As 5G becomes a crucial ICT infrastructure, the network will evolve toward a large, complex, and hyper-distributed network. Deeper integration between the hyper-distributed one and computing technologies will make network architecture evolution and integration a daunting challenge for the entire industry.

- Role: Telecom network O&M involves a large number of different and complex roles throughout the entire lifecycle. For example, a CSP needs design, supervision, construction, and monitoring personnel for network planning and construction. All these roles interact with the system, making O&M even more complex and error-prone.

  Automation and intelligence technologies need to be introduced in order to transform O&M, enable the network to better simplify and solve problems, and liberate humans from labor-intensive O&M work.

Second, the network scale keeps increasing. The workforce is mainly invested in simple and repetitive tasks, instead of high-value work (such as marketing, network planning, risk analysis, and optimization). CSPs cannot keep hiring more people due to limited OPEX, resulting in passive complaint handling instead of proactive O&M.

According to *The Mobile Economy 2022* [2] released by the Global System for Mobile Communications Association (GSMA), the total number of global IoT connections had reached 15.1 billion by 2021 and is expected to increase to 23.3 billion by 2025. Communications networks will evolve from connecting tens of billions of people to connecting hundreds of billions of things by 2030. The increasing network scale and data volume will lead to faults occurring more frequently. Passive, open-loop O&M cannot guarantee network stability. Meanwhile, intense market competition increases the cost of attracting more customers and the user churn, resulting in more economic losses. CSPs must take action to change the situation and avoid a vicious circle.

At the Mobile World Congress held in Shanghai in 2021, Li Huidi, Vice President of China Mobile, said, "To operate the world's largest mobile network with the most complex structure and the largest number of device vendors, China Mobile has assigned 59,000 network O&M engineers and invested about CNY 140 billion in network O&M every year. To improve network quality and reduce OPEX, China Mobile will further accelerate the digital intelligent transformation of network O&M, use automation and intelligence technologies to provide end-to-end (E2E) O&M capabilities to optimize customer experience, achieve agile service provisioning, and boost network O&M efficiency."

Network SLA guarantee remains a challenge. Freezing, intermittent disconnection, and poor-QoE problems caused by network congestion frequently occur and are difficult to accurately locate and quickly rectify even if user complaints are reported. Under the current complaint-driven user experience management mechanism, 75% of network faults are detected by users or cannot be quickly and accurately located. Likewise, it is difficult to identify network bottlenecks and predict risks. Sixty percent of CSPs adopts a "black box" O&M mechanism without E2E visualization. When a network fault or bottleneck occurs, services cannot be quickly restored or network resources cannot be quickly optimized. No E2E closed-loop measures are available to quickly resolve problems [3]. Faults cannot be detected in advance or prevented, and customer experience and satisfaction cannot be guaranteed.

Proactive network O&M is the future. CSPs must use cutting-edge automation and intelligence technologies to enable networks to complete more simple, repetitive tasks, provide proactive customer care, and take the initiative in developing services.

Last but not least, O&M experience is difficult to accumulate, inherit, and evolve because O&M tasks mainly rely on humans or entail high costs. O&M experience needs to be digitalized and integrated into the system for inheritance.

CSPs' O&M experience is often scenario-specific and includes a large number of manual operations. Adapting this experience to new scenarios is either impossible or expensive and cannot be done automatically. Repetitive tasks cannot be automatically or quickly completed in batches.

As the network scale increases, there is a shortage of telecom experts. According to its first A-share prospectus released in 2021, China Telecom launched an innovative talent project to train 1000 leading IT cloud experts who have industry knowledge, understand customer requirements and the ecosystem, specialize in technologies, and are good at communicating. This project also selected 2,000 leading industry experts.

However, the problem cannot be solved by simply training more experts.

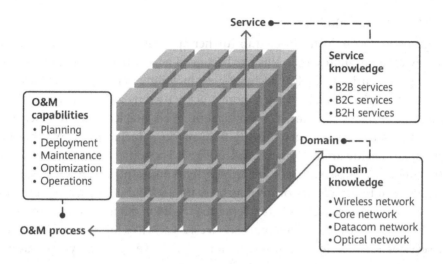

FIGURE 1.4   Telecom network O&M expert capability model.

First of all, it takes a lot of time and effort to train a telecom expert, and the training process cannot be replicated at scale. The telecom network O&M expert capability model has high requirements, as shown in Figure 1.4. Different network domains require different O&M knowledge. In addition to learning basic O&M knowledge, experts need a lot of practical experience. It takes a few years to train a telecom expert, and once trained, they are assigned to different work environments, making the training difficult to replicate at scale.

Second, experts are mostly engaged in handling network emergencies (the handling process is often accident-specific), with little time to spend on researching proactive O&M or prediction and prevention technologies.

Finally, experts cannot be quickly trained to meet network O&M labor requirements. The increasing network scale and complexity have exceeded human management capabilities. Training experts becomes more difficult and takes longer, and younger generations are reluctant to do repetitive O&M work.

To bridge the widening gap between the number of available experts and the increasing network O&M requirements, the idea of digitalizing O&M expertise in a knowledge base was proposed in the industry. This knowledge base can permanently store the expertise and quickly replicate the expertise at scale in different scenarios. Experts can learn and use the expertise in the knowledge base to summarize more advanced expertise, which will be injected into AN to achieve continuous knowledge evolution.

Digitalizing network knowledge and expertise is the task for higher-level intelligent networks. Further research is required on this booming technology to address the key challenges. For details, see Section 5.5.

In summary, current network O&M efficiency cannot meet the requirements of rapid network development. Advanced automation and intelligence technologies must be used to boost efficiency, meet unlimited service requirements with limited labor, and improve user experience.

1.2.2 New Scenarios and Services

The fast-growing ICT industry has led to further application of innovative technologies across many different industries – this has become a new pattern of development for the global economy. Cutting-edge ICT technologies, including 5G, AI, big data, cloud, edge computing, and digital twin, have been more quickly used by global enterprises to implement digital transformation. The technological progress enabled CSPs to discover many new business-to-business-to-everything (B2B2X) markets (including 5GtoB, smart manufacturing, smart healthcare, and smart education) with potential revenue growth of at least USD 700 billion [3]. These vertical industries will become a major growth engine. In the future, CSPs need to develop innovative business models and network services to explore the new B2B2X market as well as better serve the traditional business-to-customer (B2C) market. There are three types of emerging services: 2B services for vertical industries, convergent services for individual consumers, and innovative emergency communications assurance services.

According to a Keystone Strategy report, the size of the global 5GtoB market for CSPs will reach USD 602 billion by 2025 [4]. The 2B market encompasses various vertical industries (such as smart city, smart factory, and smart healthcare), demonstrating huge potential. This market has differentiated requirements on network performance, such as connection density, rate, latency, reliability, mobility, and positioning accuracy. For example, drones require mobility of 500–1000 km/h, self-driving cars require an E2E latency of no more than 5 ms and submeter-level positioning, and the industrial Internet requires reliability of 99.999%. More flexible and reliable network SLA assurance is needed to fulfill these requirements. With the increasing network scale, 2B services also require more advanced network O&M capabilities, including highly differentiated and customizable connection services for millions of application scenarios in various industries; online one-stop on-demand, real-time, and flexible service subscription, provisioning, and change; and committed and guaranteed E2E deterministic SLAs. In addition, network knowledge about 2B services needs to be accumulated in order to support network self-evolution and self-optimization.

Today, 2H and 2C services are converging with 2B services. More mobile phones and home networks are using enterprise applications. And work from home, anywhere operations, and online-offline education have become common scenarios and require different forms of interaction, for example, real-time video call, many-to-many online education, and immersive experience of extended reality (XR). These scenarios require network infrastructures that deliver better performance. CSPs must detect the performance of applications for various home terminals to provide SLA assurance and large uplink bandwidth and ensure that networks are controllable and secure. CSPs must also increase their investment in O&M to improve user experience, which cannot be guaranteed simply by offering basic mobile or home network service packages. Network service customization and user self-service are the starting points for achieving automation. Real-time SLA assurance, proactive fault prediction and prevention, and intelligent poor-QoE optimization are key to improving user loyalty.

Satellite private broadband communications networks will be mainly used to provide innovative emergency communications assurance services in disasters or other major incidents. Such networks involve many satellite terminals, private network communications terminals, and related systems. The rapid development of technologies such as 5G, satellite, and drone requires more comprehensive emergency communications capabilities, including multi-technology converged communications, flexible terminal/base station mobility, and wider signal coverage. These capabilities can be combined with intelligent search and rescue and 24/7 service capabilities to offer faster and more efficient emergency assurance. Multi-technology intelligent collaboration, uninterrupted and reliable services, and simplified, fast planning and deployment are the essential requirements for emergency communications networks.

Fundamentally, CSPs need to discover more application scenarios and extend the boundaries of networks beyond the dimensions of land, sea, air, and space to serve all industries. They also need to capture new opportunities in order to further improve user experience and achieve more business success.

1.2.3 Social Responsibility and Sustainable Development

Major incidents, such as the COVID-19 pandemic, can profoundly change the way we live, work, and study. The pandemic has created tremendous social and economic impacts on all industries, as well as individuals and households, and numerous social operations and economic activities have shifted from offline to online. Business models are undergoing substantial changes, with various contactless businesses and services emerging rapidly. ICT infrastructure has become a strategic cornerstone for overcoming the pandemic, providing powerful support for an increasing number of economic and social activities. In this section, we will take a look at how the pandemic has profoundly changed the education and network O&M modes.

The education mode has shifted from face-to-face teaching at schools to remote teaching at home, allowing students to study without going to a physical school. Online education is a testament to network coverage and large bandwidth. Large-scale remote teaching keeps the network load high and often causes many problems, such as frame freezing, audio asynchronization, and long buffering. Live streaming for online courses also has high network requirements. A high-quality, stable, and exclusive bandwidth of 20–50 Mbit/s is required for each course to ensure a satisfactory video interaction experience. Delivering an uninterrupted online education experience requires a more intelligent and automated network.

- Automation capabilities need to be provided for schools, households, and students in order to implement minute-level self-service provisioning.

- The quality of online education videos needs to be detected in real time to identify deterioration within seconds and optimize user experience, bandwidth and routes need to be automatically adjusted; acceleration technologies need to be provided for education applications.

- E2E automatic and intelligent network assurance needs to be provided for the cloud, pipes, and households. The assurance includes integrated fault detection, seconds-level fault locating, and minutes-level fault rectification.

- Future-oriented education experience and scenarios require immersive, holographic digital classes based on virtual reality/augmented reality (AR/VR).

Network O&M has changed from onsite maintenance to online remote processing. ICT networks are widely deployed as the digital infrastructure that underpins the society, playing a key role in overcoming the pandemic. Stability is the top priority for networks. In addition to providing support for home office, online education, and household entertainment, network O&M engineers also need to help enterprises perform capacity expansion in order to meet service requirements and ensure stable DC operations. Press conferences and video conferences for pandemic prevention and control also require O&M engineers. Manual O&M can no longer tackle the uncertainties caused by the pandemic or minimize the risks of the virus spreading.

- Network O&M has shifted from human-centered to machine-centered.

- O&M for network faults has changed from long-process ticket forwarding and processing to quasi-real-time "zero-touch" processing.

- Predictive prevention based on machine learning is added to periodic rule-based inspection, quickly identifying network risks.

- O&M knowledge is injected into machines to train and supervise machines, continuously improving intelligence and automation capabilities.

As digital transformation is accelerating across various industries, they need better ICT infrastructure. The impact of the pandemic on networks offers a brand new perspective for CSPs to rethink and plan network evolution. Future telecom networks must be able to efficiently coordinate and flexibly schedule social resources across different regions, facilitate large-scale mobilization of labor, and further apply AI and other technologies to achieve automation and intelligence, providing better support for major incidents, such as the pandemic.

Meanwhile, many serious issues regarding energy, resources, population, and global warming are threatening the sustainable development of humankind. A global consensus has been reached on tackling climate changes and achieving green and low-carbon development. On December 12, 2015, 197 countries signed the Paris Agreement, which was the first universal and legally binding global climate change agreement in history. It set the goal of limiting global warming to well below 2°C in the 21st century and, if possible, pursuing efforts to cap warming at 1.5°C. According to the roadmap released by different countries and regions, such as China, Japan, the USA, and the European Union, green development has become another major goal and global consensus alongside developing the digital economy. The need for low-carbon development in various industries creates new challenges for ICT networks and requires higher energy efficiency. It is estimated that the ICT industry accounts for 5%–9% of the world's total electricity consumption and over 2% of the world's total carbon emissions [5]. To meet the energy-saving requirements within and outside the ICT industry, the industry is accelerating the pace of energy conservation and emission reduction in its pursuit of green development.

DCs are also facing many energy-saving issues. With the maturity of computing-intensive services such as AI and the continuous development of various types of computing power, the power density of DCs keeps increasing. However, a large number of device types and parameters are obstacles to manual analysis to quickly find an optimization solution. Take a cooling system in a large DC as an example. It consists of 64 types of devices, and the air conditioning system alone has more than 1000 parameter combinations. Sensors are used to intelligently collect various types of data (including temperature, electricity volume, pump speed, power consumption, and preset values) for comprehensive AI analysis to adjust the running mode and control thresholds for the DC. Based on AI decision-making, an innovative, collaborative energy-saving policy can be defined for power supply, servers, and loads to improve power densities and continuously reduce power usage effectiveness (PUE).

With the large-scale deployment of 5G, the energy consumption per bit on 5G communications networks is lower than that of 4G. However, the overall energy consumption increases due to the large throughput improvement achieved in 5G, resulting in high OPEX. Striking an optimal balance between energy consumption and network performance is one of the top priorities of CSPs. Take a typical wireless network as an example. Wireless sites consume more than 70% of the energy on the entire network. However, improving energy efficiency at such wireless sites faces many challenges. There are a large number of wireless sites providing many different services. Coverage scenarios are complex and diversified, including residential areas, universities, main roads, and commercial districts with different population density and peak hours. And interoperability has a huge impact on adjacent base stations. Traditional optimization methods based on expertise cannot be used to overcome these challenges. More intelligent and automated methods are required to adjust devices based on service requirements. For example, a base station can shut down uplink carriers when the mobile traffic demand is low, so as to reduce radio frequency (RF) and baseband power consumption. With intelligent network management, the network can dynamically adapt to changing requirements and minimize energy consumption. In this way, energy can be saved without compromising network performance or user experience. Network operations need to use adaptive control technologies – including automation, AI platforms, and robot process automation – to proactively predict network energy consumption, automatically adjust energy-saving policies, and enable energy-saving models to evolve. Automated data collection and analysis, and automated policy delivery and maintenance need to be implemented in order to maximize energy-saving gains and achieve an optimal balance between energy consumption and KPIs.

In addition to intelligence, communications networks can use optical-electrical hybrid power technologies and a simplified architecture to save energy and reduce carbon emissions. Such technologies are key to fundamentally improving the energy efficiency of communications devices at the network, device, and chip levels. The simplified architecture can streamline all network domains to reduce the demand for computing power and O&M costs, achieving green and low-carbon networks.

1.3 TWO APPROACHES TO NETWORK AUTOMATION AND INTELLIGENCE

Based on the discussions on the driving forces of network automation and intelligence, we can see that large-scale application of automation and intelligence technologies can be used to simplify networks, improve network performance, enhance customer experience, and minimize OPEX. AI and machine learning are common automation and intelligence technologies that can be used to manage and orchestrate networks, simplifying networks and reducing OPEX. Two approaches have been proposed by industry players to implement network automation and intelligence.

Approach 1: Implement full-stack AI based on network endogenous intelligence and numerous intelligent OSS applications to deploy a next-generation network. The core idea of this approach is implementing "single-domain autonomy and cross-domain collaboration" based on autonomous domains (ADs)[2] to promote digital transformation. Network automation and intelligence capabilities can be developed from the bottom up to achieve business, service, and resource operations closed loops for digital services, delivering an optimal user experience, maximizing resource efficiency, and achieving full-lifecycle automation and intelligence.

In 2019, TM Forum initiated an AN program to develop industry-leading, E2E network automation and intelligence methods, helping CSPs simplify service deployment, improve Self-X capabilities (self-serving, self-fulfilling, and self-assuring), and deliver a Zero-X (zero-wait, zero-touch, and zero-trouble) experience for vertical industries and consumers. Then, in November 2021, TM Forum jointly released the *Autonomous Networks - Empowering Digital Transformation* whitepaper with 35 industry partners, including China Communications Standards Association (CCSA), China Academy of Information and Communications Technology (CAICT), CSPs, and vendors, announcing that AN has entered the phase of large-scale pilot verification and systematic deployment on live networks. Huawei responded quickly and released its own ADN solution.

AN achieves automation and intelligence through three layers and four closed loops, as shown in Figure 1.5.

- The three layers are resource operations, service operations, and business operations. Each layer offers common operations capabilities and introduces AI to provide

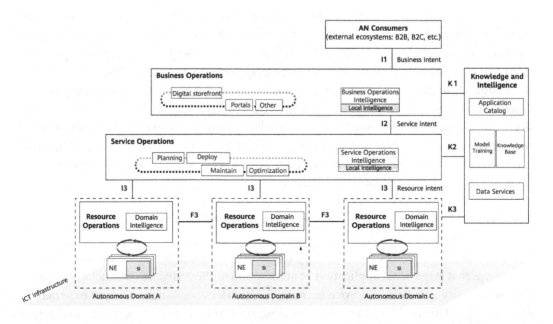

FIGURE 1.5   AN reference architecture.

automation and intelligence capabilities for different purposes in order to meet service requirements in all scenarios.

- The four closed loops (resource, service, business, and user) fulfill intra- or inter-layer interaction throughout the entire lifecycle. The resource operations layer implements a real-time or quasi-real-time resource closed loop through the collaboration within and among ADs, masking network complexity. The three layers interact with each other through simplified intent APIs to mask interaction complexity.

Approach 2: Deploy software-based network functions, develop intelligent capabilities at the OSS layer, and define the overall architecture for communications networks from the top down based on OSSs. A typical solution for this approach is software-based network functions+Open Network Automation Platform (ONAP). At the network layer, network functions are virtualized, and hardware and software are separated. At the OSS layer, the ONAP-based open-source solution is used to build an automation platform that provides common platform functions, including lifecycle management, AI/machine learning training and execution, security assurance, data management, policy making, analysis, services, and resource orchestration, as shown in Figure 1.6. These functions can be used to

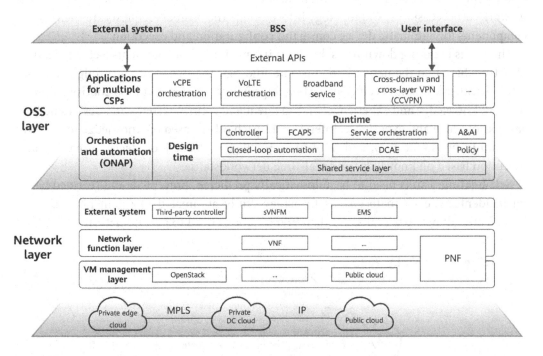

FIGURE 1.6   Software-based network function architecture.

Note: VNF is short for virtual network function. PNF is short for physical network function. ONAP is short for Open Networking Automation Platform. vCPE is short for virtual customer premises equipment. VoLTE is short for voice over long term evolution. CCVPN is short for cross-domain and cross-layer virtual private network. FCAPS is short for fault, configuration, accounting, performance, security. DCAE is short for Data Collection, Analytics and Events. sVNFM is short for specialized virtualized network function manager.

develop automated and intelligent applications at the OSS layer, and CSPs integrate these applications horizontally or vertically to define and manage networks from the top down.

It has become an industry consensus that network automation and intelligence will greatly improve CSPs' efficiency and enable new digital services that will change society and all industries. The rest of this book will focus on the first approach to discuss Huawei ADN.

1.4 VISION OF ADN

With the rapid development of network automation and intelligence technologies, Huawei proposed the vision of ADN to better fulfill customer requirements. The vision is to use an intelligent, simplified network architecture driven by data and knowledge in order to deploy a self-fulfilling, self-healing, and self-optimizing autonomous network. This network can provide new services, deliver a superior customer experience, implement automated O&M, and maximize resource and energy efficiency (Figure 1.7).

The vision includes four key aspects.

Self-fulfilling: Services need to be automatically deployed based on user intents. The ultimate goal is to achieve fully automated service deployment. Specifically, users' business intents need to be automatically translated into business requests based on current network resource, status, and topology information. The business requests are then sent to components for automatic device command configuration and execution.

The key is breaking down users' business intents into network intents, setting detailed objectives based on the network intents, and finding a feasible solution through trial and error. Another key point is efficient and intelligent automatic closed-loop control based on network knowledge and experience. Management and control systems and devices need to share knowledge and experience, interact with each other based on knowledge to improve communications efficiency, and implement intelligent closed-loop decision-making and execution based on knowledge and real-time network status.

Self-healing: Faults need to be automatically predicted, prevented, and rectified based on incidents. The ultimate goal is to achieve fully automated O&M in all scenarios. Specifically, all network faults and their combinations need to be automatically identified

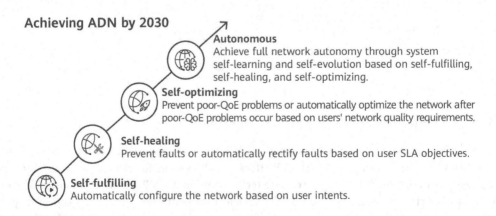

Achieving ADN by 2030

Autonomous
Achieve full network autonomy through system self-learning and self-evolution based on self-fulfilling, self-healing, and self-optimizing.

Self-optimizing
Prevent poor-QoE problems or automatically optimize the network after poor-QoE problems occur based on users' network quality requirements.

Self-healing
Prevent faults or automatically rectify faults based on user SLA objectives.

Self-fulfilling
Automatically configure the network based on user intents.

FIGURE 1.7   Vision of ADN.

and predicted, network resources and maintenance labor need to be automatically scheduled, and remedial actions need to be automatically implemented in order to recover services and minimize service loss. Network troubleshooting has transformed from passive to proactive, from "networks commanded by humans" to "humans commanded by networks." Hardware faults can be manually rectified based on machine instructions, and software faults can be automatically rectified even without manual intervention.

Self-healing requires network survivability simulation and high-availability network topology design, as well as real-time adjustment based on the network status and customers' SLA objectives. Faults need to be predicted, prevented in advance, and automatically rectified. Tickets need to be quickly and accurately dispatched for faults that cannot be automatically rectified. After faults are rectified, follow-up measures need to be taken with manual assistance to achieve fully automated O&M and eliminate user complaints.

Self-optimizing: Adaptive adjustment and optimization need to be performed to improve user experience. The ultimate goal is to achieve fully automated optimization. Specifically, network parameters and resource configurations need to be quickly adjusted at each layer based on user-specified goals, network environment/resource/status changes, network knowledge, and built-in learning and optimization algorithms in order to achieve an optimal network running status.

E2E self-optimization is needed to deliver an optimal user experience. Centralized and distributed network resources need to be efficiently used to reduce network maintenance costs. Communications network and environmental changes need to be fully detected to improve energy efficiency and reduce carbon emissions.

Autonomous: A self-fulfilling, self-healing, and self-optimizing network also needs to evolve by itself. An autonomous network is like a human being. It can understand itself by learning to perceive internal and external environments, accumulate network knowledge, and perform inference based on knowledge. It can make decisions independently, cope with complex uncertainties, and manage itself.

This network requires an intelligent foundation as a platform and framework to support closed-loop control, independent adaptive decision-making, and self-fulfilling, self-healing, and self-optimizing functions. Such a network can provide new services, deliver a superior customer experience, achieve fully automated O&M, and maximize resource and energy efficiency. A cognitive closed loop needs to be established in order to inject and generate knowledge, facilitating continuous self-learning and self-evolution of the system. This will allow the system to iteratively improve its self-fulfilling, self-healing, and self-optimizing capabilities and finally achieve a full autonomous network.

Based on the joint research and exploration with TM Forum, GSMA, and leading CSPs, Huawei has released several ADN whitepapers and case reports. An industry consensus has been reached on the objectives, architecture, and levels (L1 to L5) of ADN, shaping the landscape of the AN industry.

Meanwhile, TM Forum officially proposed the vision of AN in related standards. AN aims to provide vertical industries and consumers with a zero-wait, zero-touch, and zero-trouble experience based on fully automated networks, intelligent ICT infrastructures, agile operations, and all-scenario services, leveraging cutting-edge technologies to "leave the complexity

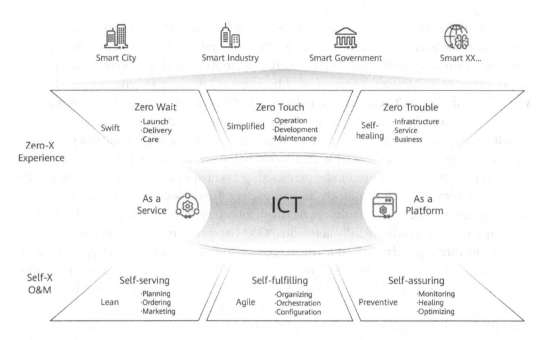

FIGURE 1.8   Vision of AN.

with the providers and deliver simplicity to the users." AN needs to provide a self-serving, self-fulfilling, and self-assuring telecom network infrastructure for the planning, marketing, operations, and management departments of CSPs. Figure 1.8 shows the vision of AN [6].

Zero-Wait

Zero-wait means that CSPs must efficiently handle customer requirements during service consultation, provisioning, and use.

Service consultation: In this stage, the customer tells the CSP their service requirements and expects the CSP to provide a feasible solution as quickly as possible. However, the TTM of new network services is long. This is because network design and construction for new services involve many network domains and departments, resulting in complex processes, slow responses, and a higher customer churn rate. CSPs must identify the demands for capacity expansion in advance based on the service development trend, proactively improve network coverage, and provide flexible cross-domain orchestration capabilities in order to quickly roll out new services and reduce TTM.

Service provisioning: In this stage, the customer wants services to be delivered as quickly as possible after the purchase. However, network service delivery involves different locations, network domains, and processes, significantly increasing the delivery time. Automated closed-loop control capabilities must be introduced to accelerate service provisioning and acceptance based on the customer's business intents (or even achieve real-time provisioning in the case of good network precoverage), and make real-time network changes after service provisioning.

Service use: In this stage, the customer wants stable and high-quality network services and quick, automatic rectification (or even no impact) of network faults and quality issues. However, most faults still need to be identified by user complaints. Fault handling involves collaborative diagnosis, analysis, and rectification across multiple network domains, resulting in a long process and slow responses. Quick self-healing capabilities are needed to overcome this challenge. When physical device problems occur, backup devices can be used to ensure service continuity until O&M engineers rectify the problems as quickly as possible.

A zero-wait network aims to deliver services within a short time after the customer clarifies their service requirements or even support seconds-level out-of-the-box (OOTB) provisioning for mature services, greatly improving customer experience. Such a zero-wait network can also rectify faults within minutes or even seconds (for mature services).

Zero-Touch

Zero-touch means that AN can offer services and assurance in a convenient e-commerce mode during service consultation, provisioning, and use, eliminating the need for customers to go to customer service centers, talk to customer service personnel, or wait for onsite visits by O&M engineers.

Service consultation: In this stage, the customer wants a more convenient method to tell the CSP their service requirements and to get clearer, more intuitive network service information. However, the customer has to visit the service center in person to get the information (sometimes multiple times due to the limited business hours and scope of the service center). E-commerce self-service capabilities are required to accurately and efficiently collect customers' service requirements, recommend services or products, pre-evaluate service quality, provide committed service assurance, and facilitate service provisioning.

Service provisioning: In this stage, the customer requires services to be delivered all in one go. However, service provisioning involves onsite visits by different CSP engineers. The customer has to talk to them repeatedly about resource survey, network installation and interconnection, and commissioning and acceptance, confirm the progress, urge them to speed things up, or handle their inconvenient visits multiple times. Network pre-coverage planning needs to be performed based on the service development trend to facilitate zero-wait service provisioning and acceptance all in one go.

Service use: In this stage, the customer expects that network faults and quality issues can be automatically rectified so that there is no need to repeatedly talk to O&M engineers or handle their visits. However, fault handling involves onsite check, confirmation, and rectification by O&M engineers. Repetitive visits compromise customer experience. Self-service maintenance, remote diagnosis, and automatic rectification are needed. Physical device problems must be rectified all together in only one visit.

A zero-touch network aims to deliver both enterprise and individual users with a self-service e-commerce experience for subscription, change, maintenance, and optimization to meet their service requirements at all times. There can be various self-service modes, including mobile phone/tablet apps, PC apps, web sites, or even customer terminals (such as optical modems). With the continuous evolution of AN, end users will be able to obtain network services in full self-service mode.

Zero-Trouble

Zero-trouble means that AN can effectively improve service assurance, prevent faults or performance deterioration, significantly reduce or even eliminate the impact of faults and quality issues, and ensure high service reliability before, during, and after faults occur.

The customer expects that services can run continuously and stably, and faults or quality issues can be quickly and automatically rectified without affecting any services.

- Before faults occur, AN can detect performance deterioration, accurately predict faults and the impact on customer services, and automatically implement contingency plans or analyze feasible solutions to eliminate risks. Performance deterioration risks can be automatically analyzed to optimize network quality. If risks persist after the preventive measures are taken, the customer will be quickly notified.

- When faults occur, AN can quickly detect, diagnose, and rectify them and use quick rectification methods (such as switchover) to ensure that customer services are not affected. If the faults cannot be quickly rectified through software configuration (e.g., due to hardware faults occurring on multiple networks at the same time), the system will quickly inform the customer of the impact, handling plan, and workaround suggestions and start the troubleshooting process to rectify the faults.

- After the faults are rectified, AN will quickly notify the customer and take follow-up measures.

This so-called proactive O&M mode can ensure that service commitments are fulfilled, provide customer care, and deliver a user experience beyond expectation.

A zero-trouble network aims to boost network reliability by 10–100 times and offer 99.9999% service availability, improving user satisfaction and reducing user complaints.

According to TM Forum's third AN whitepaper, Self-X operations capabilities are the prerequisites for delivering a Zero-X experience. Table 1.1 describes these capabilities.

Some of these capabilities (such as self-marketing and capability delivery) are closely related to the business and delivery processes of CSPs and enterprises. Self-monitoring/reporting is a mature capability. This book will only focus on self-governing, self-healing, and self-optimizing (hereinafter referred to as Self-X).

TABLE 1.1   Self-X Operations Capabilities of AN

Self-serving	**Self-planning/capability delivery:** provides the customization (DIY) capabilities of network/ICT service planning, design and deployment
	Self-ordering: provides the online, digitalized, and/or one-click ordering capabilities of network/ICT services
	Self-marketing: provides the automated marketing activities for general and/or personalized campaign/promotion
Self-fulfilling	**Self-organizing:** provides the collaboration of business/service/resource intent delivery on demand
	Self-managing: provides the orchestration of business/service/resource intent delivery on demand
	Self-governing: provides the governance of business/service/resource intent delivery on demand
Self-assuring	**Self-monitoring/reporting:** provides the automatic, continuous monitoring and alerting in real time
	Self-healing: provides the recovery of SLA (e.g., performance, availability and security) in real time
	Self-optimizing: provides the optimization of SLA (e.g., performance, availability and security) in real time

Self-governing

Self-governing means that AN can provide automated E2E service deployment, change, and upgrade to reduce manual configurations. In addition, it can automatically translate service intents into network configurations to reduce the configuration workload and difficulty, as well as faults caused by human errors, while also improving the efficiency of service provisioning and adjustment. Self-governing can significantly reduce the workload of O&M engineers during routine maintenance and eliminate the need for them to apply for service deployment and implementation.

During routine network maintenance (such as system upgrade and capacity expansion), the system can check the network status in advance based on the maintenance requirements specified by O&M engineers and simulate maintenance tasks to ensure that the processes are correct. Then, the system can automatically and quickly implement the tasks, reducing the impact of maintenance on network services. Real-time detection can be performed to evaluate the task result. No manual intervention is required throughout the entire process. Service provisioning and changes will no longer rely on customer service personnel or O&M engineers. AN can automatically perform service provisioning and changes based on the service applications initiated by customers.

A self-governing network aims to automatically handle all service applications without any intervention from O&M engineers, improve the self-service provisioning rate to almost 100%, and run automatic maintenance tasks as planned to complete all routine O&M activities.

Self-healing

Self-healing means that AN can automatically predict, prevent, and quickly rectify faults, ensuring high service reliability. Faults can be classified as either software or hardware faults, which require different capabilities to rectify. AN can automatically rectify software faults by adjusting software parameters, resetting parameters, or performing a switchover. AN can also rectify hardware faults with onsite manual assistance. Self-healing can significantly reduce the troubleshooting workload of O&M engineers.

A self-healing network eliminates the need for constant manual fault monitoring. O&M engineers only need to define fault principles and policies. AN can then automatically detect, prevent, and rectify faults based on these principles and policies. Complex faults can also be automatically predicted, prevented, and rectified after their patterns and root causes are identified.

A self-healing network aims to extract prediction, prevention, and rectification knowledge from the fault patterns of new services. The knowledge can be used to automatically rectify almost all software faults and help O&M engineers rectify hardware faults, significantly reducing the manual troubleshooting workload.

Self-optimizing

Self-optimizing is a continuous, automated process that involves O&M engineers. In this process, the service quality of the entire network is monitored, and network parameters are adjusted to optimize service quality and maximize network efficiency.

Traditionally, systems cannot detect service quality deterioration in real time, meaning that O&M engineers have to spend a long time to rectify faults. AN can liberate O&M engineers from constant network quality monitoring. All they need to do is set strategic objectives for automatic optimization of network services and quality. AN can be used to monitor network KPIs in real time, analyze KPI trends, predict the risks of network quality deterioration based on the patterns of network quality problems and O&M knowledge, formulate feasible optimization solutions through simulation, and automatically start optimization tasks, ensuring that the network is always in an optimal state.

A self-optimizing network aims to use awareness, intelligent prediction, and automatic optimization capabilities to implement fully automated optimization without any intervention from O&M engineers and improve the capabilities of predicting and preventing service deterioration, thereby boosting the automated optimization rate to almost 100%.

1.5 LEVELS OF ADN

To fulfill the ADN vision of deploying a "self-fulfilling, self-healing, and self-optimizing autonomous network" and achieve Zero-X and Self-X AN, industry partners need to continuously collaborate on making key technology breakthroughs, including integrated network sensing, intelligent human-machine collaboration and decision-making, and intent-driven closed loop. The long-term, sustainable evolution of the AN industry needs to be supported by the division and definitions of ADN levels, as well as an industry consensus, unified standards, and consistent objectives regarding the levels of AN.

ADN is essentially a complex automation system. To put it simply, an automation system evolves by replacing manual operations with automation capabilities. For ADN, automation means meeting CSPs' O&M requirements (including troubleshooting, quality optimization, and service provisioning) with minimum manual intervention.

Early in 2000, Raja Parasuraman, Professor of Psychology at George Mason University in the US, proposed a basic theory on the types and levels of automation [7]. The theory includes three core ideas.

The first one is that automation can be applied to four broad classes of functions: (1) **information acquisition**; (2) **information analysis**; (3) **decision and action selection**; and (4) **action implementation**.

The second one is that within each of these types, automation can be applied across **a continuum of levels from low to high**, that is, from **fully manual** to **fully automatic**. This implies that automation is not all or none.

The third one is that a particular system can involve **automation of all four types at different levels**. The levels of automation for different types of tasks may be different during the evolution of the automation system. For example, the information acquisition task has been automated, but decision and action selection is still a manual or semi-automatic task.

Professor Raja Parasuraman proposed ten detailed levels of automation (from "human must take all decisions and actions" to "the computer decides everything") for the decision and action selection task, as shown in Figure 1.9.

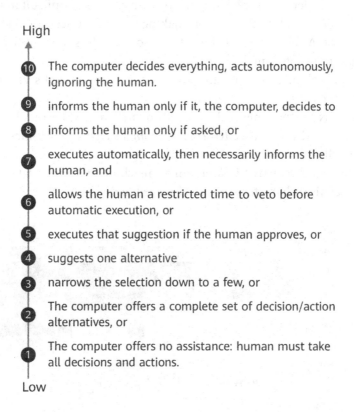

High

10 The computer decides everything, acts autonomously, ignoring the human.

9 informs the human only if it, the computer, decides to

8 informs the human only if asked, or

7 executes automatically, then necessarily informs the human, and

6 allows the human a restricted time to veto before automatic execution, or

5 executes that suggestion if the human approves, or

4 suggests one alternative

3 narrows the selection down to a few, or

2 The computer offers a complete set of decision/action alternatives, or

1 The computer offers no assistance: human must take all decisions and actions.

Low

FIGURE 1.9   Detailed levels of automation for decision and action selection.

Different levels of automation and level standards are defined for automation systems in different industries. For example, the International Electrotechnical Commission (IEC) defined the IEC 62290-1 for Automatic Train Operation (ATO), and SAE International defined the SAE J3016@2021 for driving automation.

All these levels are defined by breaking down an automation system into general tasks (e.g., the general tasks for ATO include starting or stopping the train and opening or closing the train doors; the general tasks for driving automation include acceleration, deceleration, direction change, environment monitoring, emergency decision-making, and handling) and by analyzing the labor division of human (e.g., driver) and system. The level of automation of different tasks at different levels is also considered. These levels are highly consistent with the levels of automation proposed by Professor Raja Parasuraman.

Based on these theories about levels of automation and mainstream level practices in the industry, industry partners jointly defined the levels of AN (TM Forum *IG1218 Autonomous Networks Business Requirements and Architecture* [8]), as shown in Figure 1.10.

There are six levels (L0 to L5) and five types of cognitive closed-loop activities: intent/experience, awareness, analysis, decision-making, and execution (I-AADE). Each type of activity is classified into P (manual), P/S (semi-autonomous), and S (autonomous) based on human-machine division of labor.

The levels of automation vary according to different cognitive activities. For example, execution is generally deterministic and more objective. It is less difficult in terms of technology and fully automated at L2. Decision-making is usually uncertain and more subjective and depends on AI and other intelligent technologies. It is more difficult in terms of technology and is fully automated at L4.

In terms of applicability, L1 to L4 are only applicable to selected scenarios, and L5 is applicable to all scenarios.

The levels of ADN are the same as those of AN defined by TM Forum. For details about L0 to L5 defined by TM Forum, see *IG1218 Autonomous Networks Business Requirements and Architecture* [8].

In addition to cognitive activities and human-machine division of labor, effectiveness indicators and technical characteristics are also used to divide ADN levels.

Autonomous Levels	L0: Manual Operation & Maintenance	L1: Assisted Operation & Maintenance	L2: Partial Autonomous Networks	L3: Conditional Autonomous Networks	L4: High Autonomous Networks	L5: Full Autonomous Networks
Execution	P	P/S	S	S	S	S
Awareness	P	P/S	P/S	S	S	S
Analysis	P	P	P/S	P/S	S	S
Decision	P	P	P	P/S	S	S
Intent/Experience	P	P	P	P	P/S	S
Applicability	N/A	Select scenarios				All scenarios
	P People (manual)		S System (autonomous)			

FIGURE 1.10 Levels of AN.

- Effectiveness indicators
  Indicator values are used to define the levels (e.g., if an indicator decreases by 50%, L3 is reached). This method is not driven by any specific technology, and it has no clear evolution path. It cannot be used to identify weaknesses or improve automation capabilities. For example, we can shorten the mean time to repair (MTTR) by assigning more O&M engineers, but this clearly goes against the essential idea of ADN. The selection, calculation, and target values of effectiveness indicators depend heavily on products, services, and scenarios. Defining unified ADN levels based on effectiveness indicators at a company level is difficult. Effectiveness indicators should be the standards for defining goals based on the expected ADN effect and for evaluating the automation effect after ADN level improvements, instead of the basis for defining ADN levels.

- Technical characteristics
  Key technologies (such as digital twin, network simulation, and AI knowledge reasoning) are used to divide the levels from the perspective of how to implement ADN. This method requires extensive knowledge about the implementation and technologies of ADN, making evaluation and verification difficult. Because specific automation technologies must be used to reach a specific level, this method is not conducive to technological innovation and breakthroughs in different product domains. Some ADN scenarios require complex technologies, whereas others can achieve full automation with simple technologies. If ADN levels are defined based on technical characteristics, the scenarios that do not need complex technologies can never reach higher levels. Human-machine division of labor, which can be easily observed, is a more suitable basis for defining ADN levels. Technologies and implementation schemes are the means of improving the ADN level, not the purpose. Technical characteristics should be the systematic guidelines to ADN implementation, helping different Huawei product domains to systematically develop automation and intelligence capabilities.

This section summarizes ADN levels. These levels can facilitate the implementation of a self-fulfilling, self-healing, and self-optimizing autonomous network. Each Huawei product domain needs to define more specific level standards and evaluation methods based on the generic levels. For details, see Chapter 7 Level Evaluation of ADN.

1.6 DEVELOPMENT OF THE AN INDUSTRY

The concept of AN was first proposed by TM Forum in 2019, and the 3 years since then have seen the AN industry develop rapidly. An industry consensus was reached on the core idea and vision of AN. CSPs responded quickly by setting AN goals for different stages, formulating long-term strategies, and launching AN practices. Industry players have been jointly exploring L3 and L4 standards in an effort to achieve a more mature standards system.

In terms of exploration and practices, AN levels, and technological prospects, the history of the AN industry can be divided into four stages: industry incubation, L3 development, L4 development, and L5 development, as shown in Figure 1.11.

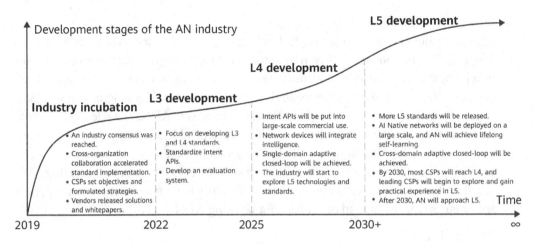

FIGURE 1.11   History of the AN industry.

Stage 1: Industry incubation

An industry consensus was reached. Leading CSPs and vendors focused on the four elements key to AN implementation, namely, target architecture, level standards, evaluation system, and operation practices. Nine standards development organizations (SDOs) – including TM Forum, CCSA, 3rd Generation Partnership Project (3GPP), and European Telecommunications Standards Institute (ETSI) – initiated AN standards or research projects and set up a multi-SDO AN collaboration platform (called Autonomous Networks Multi-SDO) to accelerate the implementation of AN standards. In September 2022, TM Forum and 54 industry partners (a significant increase since 2019, when the number was only 6) jointly released the fourth edition of the AN whitepaper. CCSA, CAICT, and TM Forum proposed the idea of using automation and intelligence technologies to deliver innovative network services and deploy convergent, intelligent, and green networks.

Huawei actively worked with industry partners to promote the implementation of AN standards. The Self-X and Zero-X vision, target architecture, level standards (L0 to L5), and core concepts (e.g., single-domain autonomy, cross-domain collaboration, and intent-based interaction) proposed by TM Forum quickly gained recognition across the industry. Since then, SDOs – such as 3GPP, ETSI, IETF, and CCSA – initiated AN standards projects for various network domains and set up an initial AN standards system through Autonomous Networks Multi-SDO. This system includes generic ANL and domain-specific ANL, and provides use cases, reference architecture, level standards, and technical specifications for AN, laying a solid foundation for efficient industry collaboration and a thriving ecosystem. In particular, Huawei assumed 14 senior roles in TM Forum, 3GPP, ETSI, and IETF, and contributed to the initiation of more than 30 standards, helping accelerate standards formulation and industry development.

Leading CSPs set goals for different stages and define long-term strategies. According to *Autonomous Networks: Business and Operational Drivers* released by

TM Forum in 2021, 88% of respondents said they would definitely or most likely deploy AN on a large scale over the next decade. The main drivers for this were improving customer experience, delivering new services, efficiency gains/lowering costs, faster TTM, and zero-touch partnering.

- At the beginning of 2021, China Mobile announced the strategic goal of achieving L4 in all network domains by 2025. To achieve this goal, it proposed a 2–3–4 AN system with 2 objectives (support customer development and cement quality advantages), 3 closed loops (closed-loop management of single-domain resources, cross-domain services, and customer requirements), and 4 layers (NE, network, service, and business).

- As AN became an essential component in its cloudification and digital transformation strategy, China Telecom set the goal of implementing L4 cloud-network O&M by 2025.

- China Unicom set the goal of reaching L3 by 2023 and L4 in major scenarios by 2025, using a top-level target plan and multiple innovative technologies to speed up digital intelligent transformation.

- Vodafone defined zero-touch operation (ZTO) as one of its strategic goals for the Tech 2025 strategy and set the goal of reaching L4 for automated fault handling, automated configuration, and predictive maintenance by 2025.

- To fulfill the Ambition 2025 strategy, MTN Group announced the goal of achieving L4 by 2025, with the intention to develop an AN architecture. This architecture includes an AN blueprint, an agile development & operations (DevOps) environment, a high-performance network, and innovative high-value use cases.

- AIS set the goal of achieving L4 for wireless customer complaint handling and event management based on TM Forum's AN architecture by 2025.

Vendors released various innovative AN solutions or whitepapers. A number of vendors started to work on the basic research, technical architecture, products, and solutions of AN and released the latest findings in the industry, helping CSPs explore and gain practical experience in AN. In October 2019, Huawei released its ADN solution, becoming the world's first vendor to release an AN solution. In November 2020, Ericsson released *Cognitive processes for adaptive intent-based networking*. Then in December 2021, five companies, including Intel, China Mobile, and China Telecom, jointly released *Communication Artificial Intelligence Empowers Autonomous Networks*, announcing that AI and network digital twin would become key technologies for AN evolution.

Through the ongoing efforts of Huawei and industry partners, the AN industry began to take shape. To facilitate level-by-level AN evolution from concept to reality, more extensive collaboration is needed. According to *Autonomous Networks: Business and Operational Drivers*, most CSPs want to reach L3 within 3 years. The period from 2022 to 2025 will witness vigorous development of L3 AN.

Stage 2: L3 Development

This is a key stage for improving the AN standards system, whereby all SDOs will focus on formulating and improving L3 and L4 standards. 2025 will be a key milestone for reaching L4, which means that all ADs can implement intent-based closed-loop autonomy. Intent APIs are a key capability at L4 and have become a focus for AN standards from 2022 to 2024. Other areas of focus are intent-driven closed-loop autonomy technologies and distributed AI.

Focus on developing L3 and L4 standards, following the principle of "improving generic ANL first and then defining domain-specific ANL." This stage is a critical juncture for standards development. It is key to improving L3 standards, as well as laying a solid foundation for the evolution toward L4. During stage 1, SDOs developed a system of "generic ANL+domain-specific ANL" from the perspectives of ANL, evaluation systems, architectures, interfaces, and key technologies. Generic ANL was defined by TM Forum, covering the general architecture and level standards. Based on this definition, other SDOs need to define domain-specific ANL. Some of them made tremendous progress in 2022. For example, CCSA jointly established a collaboration mechanism with several international SDOs, including TM Forum and ETSI. Members of Autonomous Networks Multi-SDO started to discuss technological details for the collaboration intention formed in 2021.

Intent APIs are a key capability at L4 and have become a focus of AN standards. As it evolves toward higher levels, AN will adopt more new intelligent automation and intelligence technologies and improve its interaction efficiency between new APIs, helping CSPs not only enhance quality and efficiency but also achieve agile innovation. Intent APIs are developed to realize these goals and have become a focus of AN standards in this stage. In 2022, Huawei and 15 industry partners (including MTN, AIS, Vodafone, VNPT, Telenor, TIM, Orange, CAICT, Ericsson, Intraway, and CloudBlue) initiated the *Intent-driven autonomous networks Catalyst* at TM Forum to discuss and define the intent API framework and also define scenario-specific APIs based on the high-value use cases in each domain, facilitating the standardization of intent APIs. To ensure interoperability between intent APIs developed by different SDOs, relevant testing will be conducted.

Develop an AN evaluation system for robust industry development. AN faces many challenges during the evolution toward L4, including inadequate industry collaboration, inconsistent progress of level improvements, and lack of business value. CAICT launched the *Autonomous Network Pilot Program* in the first half of 2022 to jointly overcome these challenges with industry partners. The objectives of the program are to better explore user requirements, promote industry standards, and help vertical industries and individual users select the most suitable businesses and services based on production and operations scenarios. The program also enables industry partners to jointly research and deploy high-level AN based on unified level standards and helps CSPs and software and hardware vendors improve service, NE, and product/solution capabilities, accelerating industry development. This program includes both a Partner Program and Certification Program. The Partner Program is designed to recruit lab partners in order to build an industry ecosystem and a multi-scenario E2E test and verification environment, while the Certification Program is launched to evaluate network solutions and service capabilities. Specifically, the AN capabilities of vendor solutions will be evaluated to help CSPs make procurement decisions, and the service capabilities of CSPs will be evaluated to help users select CSPs.

Stage 3: L4 Development

As the global digital economy continues to grow, new technologies may evolve beyond the horizon by 2025, bringing about exponential growth in the number of connected devices. By that time, the digital transformation of enterprises and social changes may reach a level beyond the current expectations and predictions. According to GSMA, the total number of global IoT connections will reach 24.6 billion by 2025, among which 8.57 billion will be mobile connections and 1.8 billion will be 5G connections. The potential 5GtoB market for CSPs keeps growing and driven by the demand for agile innovation of 2B services, they are more eager to deploy AN. During this stage, AN construction will reach a period of maturity on a global scale. Furthermore, the AN industry will witness tremendous changes:

- Scenario-specific intent APIs will be put into large-scale commercial use.

- Network devices will integrate endogenous intelligence. AN will reach L4 and achieve a single-domain adaptive closed loop.

- Human-machine collaboration will enable machines to dynamically generate processes and instruct humans to perform O&M tasks.

- Industry partners will start to explore the evolution toward L5 and release initial L5 standards.

Stage 4: L5 Development

By 2030 or so, communications networks will evolve toward L4 and witness groundbreaking development of automation and intelligence capabilities, unlocking the journey to L5. Sixth-generation mobile communications technology (6G) and F6G are expected to be put into large-scale commercial use at this stage. The number of connections, bandwidth, and security capabilities will significantly improve, and latency will be greatly reduced, facilitating service innovation. CSPs will shift their focus toward 2B services while still maintaining steady development of 2C and 2H services. The rapid growth of 2B services in many industries will raise diversified and differentiated requirements in terms of automation and intelligence capabilities, and the demand by CSPs for implementing AN will grow at an unprecedented rate. The AN industry will undergo the following trends in this stage:

- Tremendous breakthroughs will be made in endogenous intelligence technologies, and AN will be capable of lifelong self-learning. Network functions and O&M based on endogenous intelligence will be fully deployed and put into commercial use. Communications networks will achieve cross-domain adaptive closed loops.

- Human-machine interaction will completely change from "human-dominated" to "machine-dominated + human-assisted." Humans and machines will collaborate, finally achieving human-machine symbiosis and mutual learning.

- L5 standards will reach maturity.

- AN will evolve toward L5.

In the future, communications networks will become a basic productive force of CSPs. AN and hyper-automation have become inevitable choices for CSPs to seize opportunities in an era where everything is intelligently connected. Implementing AN will be a long journey and a grand vision that requires collective efforts from the entire telecom industry. Huawei hopes to work with all industry partners to build an open ecosystem and deploy a self-fulfilling, self-healing, and self-optimizing autonomous network, aiming to accelerate the development of cubic broadband, AI Native, and green communications networks featuring a deterministic experience.

NOTES

1 TM Forum is a non-profit international industry association in the field of digital economy. With over 900 members from over 180 countries, including leading CSPs, device vendors, system integrators, and consulting firms, TM Forum is dedicated to helping CSPs and industry partners achieve digital transformation and business success. It provides members with various services, including architectures and standards, best practices, tools, research reports, conferences, and training and certification.
2 According to TM Forum IG1251, an AD is a basic unit for implementing an automatic closed loop for specific network operations, eliminating the need for manual intervention.

REFERENCES

1. TM Forum, "Autonomous Networks: business and operational drivers," [R/OL], (2021-4) [2022-09-15].
2. GSMA, "The mobile economy 2022," [R/OL], (2020-2-28) [2022-7-14].
3. Ericsson, "Our latest 5G business potential report: set your compass now," [R/OL], (2019-10-15) [2022-09-15].
4. Chen Xiaosheng, "Yunyingshang 5G to B Shichang Chao Liuqianyi Meijin Chongfenghao Yijing Chuixiang" [The 5GtoB market for CSPs will exceed USD 6 billions], [N/OL], thepaper. cn, (2020-10-30) [2022-09-15].
5. European Commission, "Shaping Europe's digital future," [R/OL], (2020-2-19) [2022-09-15].
6. TM Forum, "Autonomous Networks: empowering digital transformation," [R/OL], (2021-9-20) [2022-09-15].
7. R. Parasuraman, T. B. Sheridan, "A model for types and levels of human interaction with automation," *IEEE Transactions on Systems, Man, and Cybemetrics-Part A: Systems and Humans*, 2000, 30, 286–297.
8. TM Forum, "IG1218 Autonomous Networks business requirements and framework," [R/OL], (2021-11-22) [2022-09-15].

Application Scenarios of ADN

O VER THE PAST THREE decades, the communications network has developed from telegraph, voice, and SMS to the Internet that connects 4.6 billion people and 20 billion terminals around the world. Video chat, online shopping, and electronic payment have undergone tremendous changes as well as the way people queue in restaurants. The emergence of network applications has completely changed the way people live and work. Today's world is far beyond what could have been imagined in the past – people then would think they were in a work of fiction seeing the world today.

Standing at the beginning of a new decade, people can take a glimpse of the future intelligent world. The number of network connections and bandwidth will significantly increase, facilitating the move from connectivity of everything to intelligent connectivity of everything. The number of global connections is expected to exceed 200 billion, and the monthly cellular network traffic per capita will increase by 40 times to 600 GB. The penetration rate of Gigabit or higher home broadband services is expected to grow 50 times, meaning that more than 55% of home broadband users will enjoy such services. The average monthly network traffic will increase by eight times, reaching 1.3 TB. Enterprise network, home broadband, and personal wireless access will enter the 10-Gigabit era. People's passion and aspiration for a better life require us to make breakthroughs in key technologies such as cubic broadband network, deterministic experience, native AI, security and trustworthiness, harmonized communication and sensing (HCS), and green and low-carbon technologies. In particular, AI has made a number of breakthroughs over the past 10 years, benefiting all aspects of people's everyday lives. In the coming decade, AI will advance from the consumer field to industrial production, reshaping the way of using, operating, and maintaining networks.

In this chapter, we provide some prospective use cases of the network in the future. By discussing how our work, life, entertainment, and healthcare can benefit from high-quality networks, we attempt to define the corresponding automation and intelligence requirements for ADN. Faced with the rapid technological and industrial development, we invite everyone in the industry to explore new use cases and build the capabilities of ADN, in the hope of opening up the infinite possibilities of ADN.

DOI: 10.1201/9781032662879-3

2.1 MOBILE ADN

The mobile network overcomes the limitations of its wired counterpart by enabling wireless information transmission and free access to the network. In terms of speed, capacity, latency, and reliability, it has improved significantly as mobile technologies, such as 4G/5G/6G and Wi-Fi 6/7, continue to evolve. These technologies will play an important role in 2C/2B/2H and more use cases. This section describes two challenging use cases of future mobile ADN, namely, emergency assurance of integrated terrestrial and non-terrestrial communications and all-wireless enterprise LAN. In addition, the requirements for ADN will be discussed based on the insight into user requirements.

2.1.1 Emergency Assurance of Integrated Terrestrial and Non-terrestrial Communications

In the past 10 years, a Chinese CSP has completed 41,523 emergency communications assurance activities, involving more than 4.16 million person-times. On average, ten emergency assurance activities were performed every day, requiring 1000 person-times. The costs for emergency assurance (including assurance for large events and emergencies) are huge.

In the Henan floods in July 2021, more than 30,300 emergency assurance personnel, 8237 emergency communications vehicles (ECVs), 8018 power generators, and 148 satellite phones were involved. The communications sector deployed over 11,700 people, 4607 ECVs, and 6302 power generators to restore the base station communications in urban areas in 4 days.

The complexity and huge investment involved in emergency assurance has given risk to discussions among communications experts. Their opinions can be summarized into the following three aspects: First, wireless infrastructure. Compared with fixed network infrastructure, wireless network infrastructure is less vulnerable to disasters and easier to be deployed in emergencies, meaning that wireless networks (including terrestrial- and satellite-based networks) are more effective in such cases. Second, hierarchical assurance. Assurance solutions should be customized for different people, and the application scenarios of networks and devices should be determined based on the network and device types. Third, routine service. Emergency networks and devices can be used in non-emergency situations. For instance, the 1400 MHz emergency communications network can serve as the urban IoT, the emergency broadcast system can be used for radio and television coverage in rural areas, and non-terrestrial base stations can be used as general-purpose UAVs after related modules are replaced.

In recent years, the civilian use of satellite communications has accelerated. Although emergency SMS messages can be sent through the BeiDou navigation satellite system, using it to carry large-scale voice and video services is currently not feasible because the cost is too high. Due to insufficient network resources in emergency scenarios and other cost issues, the development of emergency assurance should focus on the combination of ground base stations, temporary base stations (such as UAVs and ECVs), and non-terrestrial base stations. In this way, it will be possible to provide differentiated services for different users and scenarios to preferentially meet the requirements of users with higher priority.

Wireless communications networks should serve both public and emergency communications, and the efficiency of emergency communications should be further improved. We can improve the automation and intelligence of these networks so that they can respond more flexibly to various planned and emergent events. We can also improve their utilization rate and energy efficiency in order to reduce the network OPEX and emergency communications assurance costs. When ADN achieves L5, the personnel required for emergency communications and large event assurance are expected to be reduced by 90%.

2.1.1.1 Use Case Description

Major scenarios of emergency communication and large event assurance can be categorized into planned large gatherings and unexpected emergencies or natural disasters. Large gatherings include sports events, international conferences, scenic spots, and concerts. Unexpected emergencies or natural disasters include severe traffic accidents, earthquakes, fires, and terrorist attacks. However, regardless of category, the core of emergency communication assurance is to quickly solve the insufficiency of network resources.

Currently, satellites, ECVs, and UAVs are most commonly used in communications assurance.

Satellites generally operate on the Ka/Ku band, functioning as relay nodes for multiple terrestrial base stations or terminals to communicate with each other. However, satellite communications and related terminals are too expensive to make them available to everyone in major disasters or emergencies. As a result, satellite communications terminals are limited to specific applications such as on long-voyage ships.

ECVs are among the most commonly seen emergency equipment. An ECV is like a mobile base station and is used to expand the communications capacity in large activities. Though widely used around the world, ECVs have a small coverage area and are easily restricted by road conditions.

The UAVs used in emergency communications include large medium- and high-altitude long-endurance (MALE and HALE) UAVs (also known as backhaul UAVs), medium- and low-altitude rotor UAVs, and small tethered UAVs. MALE and HALE UAVs are flexible and adaptable and can provide coverage over a wide area. They can handle unfavorable conditions in terms of terrain, climate, and natural disasters and can further improve the response speed of emergency communications assurance. An example of such UAVs is the Wing Loong UAV, which uses 4G/5G and satellite communications technologies and can operate at an altitude of 4300 m to provide communication signals covering over 50 km^2 for up to 8 hours. Most medium- and low-altitude rotor UAVs are powered by batteries, so they have a short endurance (generally shorter than 1 hour with a payload of about 1 kg). Even if multiple UAVs can work in turn, the continuity of assurance will be greatly reduced. Small tethered UAVs are usually used as emergency base stations. They are light and flexible and can be quickly deployed. In addition to less stringent requirements for takeoff and landing, these UAVs can provide fast, reliable, and affordable broadband communications covering dozens of square kilometers. However, their application is restricted by the mobility of ground assurance vehicles, and they are less flexible than large MALE and HALE UAVs.

An integrated terrestrial and non-terrestrial communications system is a natural solution for emergency communications with strict timeliness requirements. Currently, several challenges remain to be addressed. China is planning to build an integrated network by enhancing the terrestrial network and extending the non-terrestrial network. The construction is divided into three phases:

First, break down the connectivity barriers between the satellite network and the terrestrial core network in order to implement comprehensive coverage and develop satellite Internet services.

Second, integrate the access system, build a secure and reliable integrated network, and provide users with a multi-mode network that can be accessed at any time. Inter-RAT mobility and dual-mode operations enable the integration of terrestrial and non-terrestrial communications on terminals. In this way, users can preferentially use the terrestrial network when it is available and switch to the non-terrestrial network when the terrestrial network is unavailable. This phase is expected to be completed around 2025.

Third, complete the construction of the integrated terrestrial and non-terrestrial network by unifying the networking system. Once completed, continuous global communications, reliable and secure communications, and large-capacity regional communications will become a reality. This will be achieved around 2030 – the same time as when the integrated terrestrial and non-terrestrial network of 6G will be established. In the meantime, systematic planning is required for applications, terminals, and chips. The integrated terrestrial and non-terrestrial network is impossible without efforts from the entire industry.

2.1.1.2 Examples

Currently, an application for emergency assurance needs to be submitted 1 week in advance. Once an application for emergency assurance is received, experts prepare network configurations. The assurance requirements of most planned activities can be satisfied. However, this process fails to meet the assurance requirements of unexpected emergencies. The development of connectivity results in higher requirements on emergency assurance. The automated and intelligent scheduling capability of ADN can provide the optimal solution to ensure network availability in emergency assurance.

Example 1: Traffic burst in an unknown small area. Shanghai Pudong International Airport, a large-capacity transport hub, adaptively saves energy based on traffic changes. If an unexpected security incident occurs at the security entrance, crowds gather and the security check requirements are enhanced. Onsite unattended communications vehicles can respond in only a few seconds and automatically expand the communications capacity to ensure the optimal network experience of users at the airport. In this way, people have access to the latest notifications and accurate information, ensuring they remain well-informed at the airport. In addition, the overall network energy efficiency remains optimal.

Example 2: Assurance for a planned large event. A large concert is planned at the National Stadium in Beijing. Engineers input assurance requirements (concert locations and crowd prediction) into the ADN management and control unit 1 day before the concert takes place. The management system recommends a capacity expansion solution based on the geographic information. Before the concert begins, ECVs and UAVs are deployed, and related deployment and optimization operations are completed automatically. During the concert, the network capacity can be expanded to meet traffic demands while also achieving the optimal energy efficiency. Tens of thousands of people in the stadium can share the experience of the live concert with their family and friends through phone calls, SMS messages, and video calls. VIP ticket holders can even use the HD XR service and other value-added network services (flat-rate ticket holders can purchase such services on demand) to experience being on stage and interact with the performers in different places.

Example 3: Traffic burst in an unknown large area. Due to a major accident on a busy highway, tailbacks begin to form, causing a burst of communications traffic. Based on the network traffic change detection, surrounding base stations complete adaptive RF coordinated adjustment in real time to improve the network capacity on the highway. In addition, UAVs are deployed to the congested sections of the highway to implement adaptive networking capacity expansion. This meets people's basic communication requirements, enabling them to call the police or their family. On-site police officers, medical personnel, and ambulance workers have the highest connectivity priority and can make phone calls or video calls without delay, ensuring unimpeded rescue and efficient command.

Example 4: Large-scale network exceptions. Traffic and communication are interrupted after a major earthquake. In addition, people are congested in some areas (such as emergency command centers, disaster shelters, highways, and railways). In a few seconds, the network fault is automatically isolated, emergency assurance and other high-priority services are automatically switched to the standby site (through air-ground collaboration and space- and satellite-based base station allocation), and automatic network compensation is implemented, ensuring uninterrupted core services. The ADN management and control unit automatically plans for communications recovery, and basic voice, SMS, and location services are automatically recovered with hardware deployed for capacity expansion (ECV and collaborative deployment and automatic service provisioning of space- and satellite-based base stations). In this manner, the network is optimized based on dynamic requirements, and the experience is restored to the level before the earthquake.

2.1.1.3 Technical Requirements for ADN

1. Network Architecture

   Emergency assurance requires co-management of non-terrestrial and terrestrial networks. When the terrestrial network is unavailable, its services must be seamlessly switched to a non-terrestrial network in real time. This poses three challenges to the network architecture:

   First, real-time autonomy and collaboration of heterogeneous networks. In emergencies, satellite networks, wireless networks, core networks, and fixed networks need to evaluate their status in real time and preferentially implement autonomy in the respective domain. If the requirements cannot be met, these networks need to collaborate with heterogeneous dynamic networks in real time. This requires not only ADN capabilities in a single domain but also efficient cooperation and timely collaboration between ADNs in different domains.

Second, intelligent layered software and hardware capabilities. Timeliness is one of the top priorities in emergency assurance. Both software and hardware (including chips) must have intelligent awareness, analysis, decision-making, and execution capabilities to implement self-configuration, self-healing, and self-optimizing and thereby realize timeliness of emergency assurance.

Third, a framework for providing differentiated services on demand. The requirements on network capabilities in emergencies vary with users. When resources are limited, the communications requirements concerning life and social responsibilities must be satisfied first. Applications, services, devices, chips, and protocols of the heterogeneous network need to be considered when resources are allocated based on the user priority.

2. Hardware

The low millimeter-wave band is expected to become the core frequency band of the future network that integrates satellite and 5G/6G technologies. Technical challenges such as high site density and high attenuation must be addressed.

Wireless terminals can access the network almost anywhere. As such, wireless devices need to detect and respond to traffic changes and adjust the network capacity accordingly within milliseconds to seconds.

The significant increase in the number of terminals, the commercial use of the millimeter-wave band, and the increasing density of wireless devices raise a question of energy efficiency. To achieve a balance between the optimal energy efficiency and terminal user experience, wireless devices in the future must be able to dynamically adjust the power.

3. Software

Self-configuration: Non-terrestrial base stations need to be remotely deployed. This brings challenges of dynamic non-terrestrial networking and integrated terrestrial and non-terrestrial networking. In addition, network unit checks, configuration generation, and wireless transmission link provisioning need to be automatically performed.

Self-healing: After a fault occurs, the system must simulate the self-healing solution in order to ensure it is reliable. However, the simulation of mobile networks involves complex geographical environment factors and heavy computational electromagnetics workload. Online and real-time simulation requires technical breakthroughs. At present, if a severe fault that affects services availability occurs, large-scale switchovers need to be performed through manual operations. However, insufficient information makes it difficult to determine such operations. Moreover, manual operations are complex and the process information is scattered. Automatic disaster recovery capabilities should address these problems in order to implement fast fault determination and automatic switchover and simulation. In this way, the disaster recovery governance is automatically implemented in a regular and systematic manner.

Self-optimizing: It should be possible to optimize the energy efficiency and experience of the integrated terrestrial and non-terrestrial system within minutes or even seconds. Effective status awareness (subsecond-level interaction delay), multidimensional data analysis (second-level computing architecture), and optimization of autonomous decision-making policies are technical difficulties we need to address.

2.1.2 All-Wireless Enterprise LAN

4G and 5G high-speed networks and high-performance smartphones are changing our lives and work. In enterprises, there are still desktop phones, workstations, and printers that are connected to the Ethernet through twisted pairs, maintaining the presence of wired communications. Working on laptops, tablets, and mobile phones allows for collaboration anytime and anywhere among different parties inside and outside the campus. In this manner, employees can get closer to customers and can work from home in emergencies. Mobile office will become a culture that people accept. This trend will lead to a revolution in which wireless technologies will ultimately replace wired technologies in enterprise networks.

We expect the future enterprise LAN to be an intangible all-wireless network. All enterprise users and anyone who connect to the network can enjoy intangible protection and wireless connectivity. At that time, employees will no longer be limited in certain physical spaces (offices, meeting rooms, buildings, and campus networks). Moreover, enterprises can monitor and manage infrastructure and processes on the network, and services can be automatically customized based on the application and device requirements.

2.1.2.1 Use Case Description

The revolution of all-wireless LAN relies on breakthroughs in wireless communications technologies. Different technologies (Wi-Fi hotspots and cellular 3G/4G/5G) and spectrums (license-free, cellular, and shared spectrums) need to be combined so that access technologies are abstracted to allow terminals to access each other through enterprise wireless networks instead of a single hotspot or cellular network. The all-wireless LAN is highly flexible because it can provide services for users based on the technologies supported by their terminals and application requirements. To this extent, resources are balanced and fairly allocated to users. Compatible terminals can connect to distributed or combined access nodes through different access technologies at any time. Data flows of these terminals may be sent through parallel paths, meaning that the uplink and downlink paths of the data flows are not necessarily the same. For mobility purposes, the network controller dynamically increases or decreases available connections and updates routing instructions. In this way, the IP address of a terminal does not change when it moves to a new IP network, ensuring uninterrupted sessions and service connections between wireless LANs. Connections are no longer established using a single access technology, and the quality of service (QoS) is measured based on the aggregated link instead of the connection of a certain access technology. This provides us with a virtual private wireless network (VPWN) that is cellular-free and not bounded by specific wireless access technologies.

Currently, when a terminal connects to an enterprise network, interactive configuration actions involve access technology selection, access point selection, and enterprise security authentication. In addition, if the connection is interrupted or the terminal needs to switch to another network, all these actions need to be repeated, which is inefficient. For security purposes, when the terminal leaves the enterprise network and connects to the external network, the traffic cannot be directly routed from the external network to the enterprise. In addition, the public network that the traffic passes through cannot provide QoS services. In the future, these configuration actions will no longer be required. The entire access process is completed automatically and transparently, saving time and improving production efficiency. Secure and QoS-guaranteed network connections across LANs and WANs will be automatically established so that terminals can securely access enterprise applications anytime and anywhere, improving work efficiency.

This technological transformation will foster a new kind of CSPs, in-building operators (IBOs). IBOs can provide enterprise services as WLAN vendors and manage and operate wireless resources in the campus such as Wi-Fi hotspots and cellular networks in a unified manner. They work with WAN CSPs to share the right to use spectrums. In this way, users inside and outside the enterprise can seamlessly connect to the enterprise network. Mobile access will soon become part of the integrated LAN and WAN services. WAN CSPs can charge users for in-building network access without paying for the network construction, but they need to allow users to use their spectrum in the building. WAN CSPs can also choose to become IBOs [1].

2.1.2.2 Examples

The future all-wireless LANs will provide ultra-large network capacity, with convenient, secure, and uninterrupted connection across the LAN and WAN. This will deliver the ultimate experience to users of mobile office on enterprise networks.

Example 1: Occasional heavy traffic load in campus. During a forum in the campus, many participants are using the campus Wi-Fi to live stream on social media, leading to heavy traffic load on the campus network. The fluctuation of network quality is detected in real time. As such, the traffic of important customer conferences is switched to the cellular network in milliseconds to prevent SLA deterioration. Users are unaware of the switchover because it does not interrupt services. This millisecond-level allocation and scheduling of network-wide traffic paths achieves large throughput and ensures service quality.

Example 2: Exit from the campus network during a video conference. An employee is holding an important customer conference that overruns but needs to travel to the customer's office. On the way to the customer's office, the employee continues the conference via mobile phone. The campus network detects that the employee may leave the campus based on the access locations of the mobile phone, so it establishes another connection path on the cellular network in real time. In this way, data can be sent and received concurrently through Wi-Fi and the cellular network. When the employee's Wi-Fi signal in the campus is weak, the primary connection is switched from the campus LAN to the external cellular network in milliseconds, ensuring that the video conference is uninterrupted without the employee being aware of the switchover.

Example 3: Access to confidential enterprise assets outside the enterprise campus. While driving to the office, an employee wants to check confidential information such as customer quotations in the company's configuration library. When accessing the company's network via mobile phone, the employee does not need to select access technologies or access points. Network authentication is automatically completed without verification. An encrypted channel is automatically established with data packets routed to the enterprise gateway and then to the enterprise configuration management application. Even if the cellular connection is occasionally interrupted, the employee does not need to perform the configuration or authentication again. When the employee arrives at the office, the encrypted connection is seamlessly and automatically switched to the enterprise WLAN. Services are not affected, and the employee is unaware of the switchover.

2.1.2.3 Technical Requirements for ADN

In the future, all-wireless LANs require automatic and intelligent management and operations that integrate multiple wireless technologies and spectrum resources and will replace LANs of single wired technologies.

Self-healing and self-optimizing: Large LAN throughput and high service quality are achieved through real-time awareness of LAN-wide network status, objective-oriented optimization, and online scheduling of network resources.

Internal wireless resources of an enterprise must be dynamically organized. The network should be aware of network status and user locations in real time and continuously monitor and evaluate the network quality. To achieve this, it is necessary to consider distribution models of users and buildings in the campus, and the distribution and quality of the cellular network connected to the campus. When the network quality fluctuates or deterioration is predicted, an optimization plan is generated based on the live network throughput and SLA optimization objective. The service traffic paths are reallocated and scheduled within milliseconds, with users being unaware of any of these changes on the network. At the same time, the optimization model keeps evolving by tracking the effect of the optimization plan execution in order to further improve the throughput and service quality.

Self-configuration: Secure connections are automatically established across the LAN and WAN through a "zero-operation" security service with no configuration or authentication.

In the future, users can access the enterprise's network applications and services from inside and outside the enterprise without any interaction ("zero-touch"). The installation and connection setup of virtual private networks (VPNs) are automatic. In addition, users do not need to manually enter security codes or select the access technology or access point. All of these operations are automatically completed.

The network controller implements a software-defined VPN through extension. A simple switching element (PE-F) managed by the network controller on the mobile terminal will be enough to allow for connections to the VPN from the mobile phone. In this way, we do not need to install and manage an IPsec client on each mobile terminal. (IPsec involves complex operations and is not supported by most IoT devices.) In the example shown in Figure 2.1, the network controller automatically configures flow tables and establishes

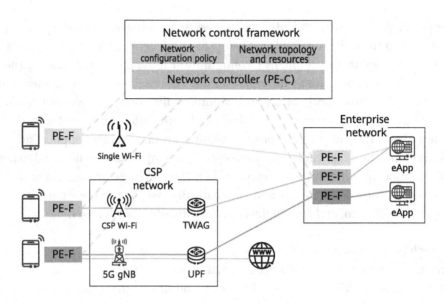

FIGURE 2.1 Network control of the VPN service. TWAG, trusted WLAN access gateway; UPF, user plan function.

tunnels to ensure that IP packets can be directly and securely routed to application servers in the enterprise data center. Because the same policy can be applied to all application data flows destined for the same data center, we do not need to establish a separate tunnel [1] for each application.

Integrated operations: Wireless networks integrate different wireless technologies and spectrums and are operated by IBOs in a unified manner to improve internal operations efficiency of enterprises.

IBOs are the hub for enterprise connections. They manage network access within enterprises, provide value-added applications, and manage multiple enterprise networks. Compared with the current multi-vendor mode that involves enterprises, IT vendors, and multiple WAN CSPs, the IBO mode not only simplifies the relationship between organizations by eliminating roaming negotiation across different parties but also provides public network access services for enterprises while supporting their own devices. Dedicated nodes deployed by mobile CSPs will be eliminated, so that the WLAN will be greatly simplified.

2.2 FIXED ADN

After decades of infrastructure construction, the world is interconnected by cable-based fixed networks. Thanks to the reliability of cable transmission, the fixed network can provide a high bandwidth and reliable network quality and is key to cloud, private line, private network, and home broadband services. This section describes two challenging use cases of future fixed ADN: secure, reliable, and immersive remote office and remote control of deterministic WAN. In addition, this section identifies requirements for ADN through insight into user requirements.

2.2.1 Secure, Reliable, and Immersive Remote Office

In the near future, some companies and employees will choose remote office out of epidemic, transport, or lifestyle concerns. At present, tech giants like Amazon, Microsoft, Google, and Apple have provided their employees with a hybrid working model, allowing them to work from home on a regular basis. This trend was accelerated by the outbreak of the COVID-19 pandemic in 2019. According to its Seventh National Population Census, China had more than 494 million households in 2021. Even if one-tenth of the households have remote office requirements, it is still a huge market of nearly 50 million households. Home office users are sensitive to the latency, reliability, and security of the network, and they are more willing to pay for better services. Therefore, CSPs should seize the opportunities to increase revenue by selling services (connections+immersive terminals+experience assurance) instead of connections alone.

2.2.1.1 Use Case Description

The development of blockchain, network communications, display, and interaction technologies paves the way for metaverse applications. In the future, technologies such as 360-degree immersive VR/AR/holographic experience, ultra-high resolution, and video frame rates approaching human perception will bring various aspects of our lives (such as gaming, shopping, working, and education) to the metaverse, where immersive working will become the mainstream. In this sense, there is an attractive prospect ahead for immersive remote office applications. Because of the security and reliability requirements of remote office, features such as low latency, physical isolation, and large bandwidth give all-optical networks unparalleled advantages in remote office.

All-optical networks utilize optical technologies in the signal transmission and exchange between users – every bit from the source to the target is transmitted in the optical domain. Adopting all-optical throughout the communications network makes it more manageable, flexible, and transparent. Compared with traditional networks and the current optical system, the all-optical network has the following advantages:

- Ultra-large bandwidth. The all-optical network exchanges signals in the optical domain, maximizing the transmission capacity of optical fibers.

- Transmission transparency. Because optical path switching is used to select routes based on wavelengths, the transmission bit rate, data format, and modulation mode are transparent. In other words, there is no restriction on the signal format, and different rates and protocols are allowed.

- The all-optical network is compatible with the existing communications network and will reform the broadband integrated service digital network (BISDN) to enable it to provide higher processing speed and lower BER compared with the copper- and wireless-based networks.

- Scalability. In the all-optical network, the addition of a node does not affect the network structure or devices on each node.

- Reconfigurability. The structure of an all-optical network can be dynamically adjusted based on the communications capacity requirements by restoring, establishing, and removing optical connections.

- Convenient maintenance, fast switching, and reliability. The all-optical network mainly uses passive components, eliminating many electrical/optical conversion devices and thereby simplifying the network structure.

2.2.1.2 Examples

Tom is employed by company A. According to his contract, he needs to access the company's virtual office in the metaverse via home broadband connection during working hours. He attends meetings in virtual meeting rooms, works in virtual offices, and talks face to face with his colleagues. Everything is the same as in the real world. Immersive experience is the key in this case. People want to see each other's facial expression and body language, just as they do in real-life communications. Tom's deliverables in the metaverse (such as documents and code) are directly transmitted to company A's server in the metaverse. The company's information security requirements are met, the same as if Tom was working in a physical office.

In this use case, the immersive remote office people use is implemented through 360-degree immersive VR/AR technologies. Its performance depends heavily on the communications network. Optical networks have significant advantages in terms of low latency and large bandwidth. However, to meet the requirements listed in Table 2.1, all-optical virtual private lines must be dynamically created, and autonomous capabilities of intelligent bandwidth assurance and fast fault detection and recovery are required.

2.2.1.3 Technical Requirements for ADN

Immersive remote office services are sensitive to network latency, reliability, and throughput. In order to guarantee E2E SLAs, ADN needs to continuously monitor and predict the network quality and schedule network resources based on multiple objectives. As such, ADN needs to be capable of real-time modeling and awareness. We propose three research directions:

First, self-configuration and self-optimizing. Based on the user model and real-time network status, ADN dynamically predicts and optimizes network resources and adjusts the network.

Users active in different time periods and with different traffic characteristics can be grouped into one optical line terminal (OLT) in order to optimize network resource utilization. For example, home office users and commuters can be put into one group, so that different access policies can be applied to differentiate residential areas and business

TABLE 2.1   Latency and Bandwidth Requirements of XR

Typical Scenario	Latency (ms)	Bandwidth
XR (video and audio)	10	About 1 Gbit/s
XR (location sensing)	5	About 1 Mbit/s
XR (haptics)	5	About 2 Mbit/s

districts. In this way, network resources can be utilized more efficiently while service continuity is ensured. The following features are the core of such a network:

- **Network-level service modeling:** Modeling of optical distribution networks (ODNs) and application traffic.

- **Dynamic prediction:** Prediction based on the overall spatiotemporal traffic and microsecond-level application traffic.

- **Optimization decision-making:** Global resource optimization implemented by integer programming and multi-objective reinforcement learning.

- **Dynamic adjustment:** Dynamic adjustment of network resources based on optimization policies.

Second, self-configuration and self-healing. To achieve low latency and high reliability of the network, fluctuations of slice network quality can be predicted so that the slice can be adjusted based on multi-objective optimization.

- **Pooling network architecture:** Multi-level pooling, elastic, and flexible network architecture.

- **Real-time sampling of slice resource usage:** Millisecond-level sampling of entities such as passive optical networks (PONs), Wi-Fi media access control (MAC) addresses, and network processors (NPs)+terminal multiplexers (TMs).

- **Dynamic slice resource adjustment:** Predicting slice network quality fluctuations enables the multi-level resource pool to be scheduled based on multiple objectives (such as latency and usage) to ensure low latency and high reliability of the network and improve the slice capacity to maximize resource utilization.

Third, self-healing and self-optimizing. SLA commitment is achieved through real-time visualization of Wi-Fi SLA and intelligent multi-objective optimization of NEs.

- **SLA visualization:** Millisecond-level collection and awareness of indicators such as latency, packet loss rate, and rate

- **Wi-Fi quality visualization:** Millisecond-level collection and awareness of indicators such as Wi-Fi latency, roaming, and rate

- **Embedded service modeling:** Millisecond-level static timing analysis (STA), air interface data (duty cycle, channel, frequency bandwidth, and power), and interference matrix are sampled for real-time Wi-Fi simulation.

- **Embedded intelligence:** Intelligent NE models are self-adaptive, self-learning, and self-evolving. SLA fluctuations can be predicted for real-time multi-objective SLA optimization.

2.2.2 Remote Control of Deterministic WAN

IP networks of traditional CSPs mainly provide statistical multiplexing-based services. Although quality can be guaranteed for packets and differentiated services, flow-based and comprehensive service quality assurance is still challenging. Future WANs must be deterministic in terms of time, resources, and paths to better meet user requirements.

2.2.2.1 Use Case Description

5G ultra-reliable low latency communications (URLLC) services oriented to vertical industries demand deterministic E2E low latency. In addition, digital transformation of industries – represented by the industrial Internet – drives enterprises to migrate their services to the cloud. This poses strict requirements on latency, jitter, and reliability, which traditional IP networks based on statistical multiplexing and best-effort services cannot meet. WANs should evolve to be deterministic in terms of the following aspects:

- **Time:** Ensure deterministic latency, jitter, and packet loss rate on communications nodes through innovations in the forwarding architecture and scheduling algorithms.

- **Resource:** Ensure deterministic bandwidth required by services through innovations in bandwidth multiplexing and isolation technologies.

- **Path:** Ensure E2E deterministic experience through path computation and orchestration based on deterministic requirements.

2.2.2.2 Examples

Example 1: Remote driving. A company provides remote driving services based on the WAN and edge wireless network. These services include remote designated driver after drinking, automatic parking and pickup, remote driving escort, and emergency rescue.

After drinking, a car owner wants to use the automated driving function. He applies for a remote designated driver to supervise automated driving as required by law. Based on the car owner's geographical location and destination, the company's system finds the branch with the lowest latency and assigns a driver. The driver monitors the driving status of the car in real time through VR. If the driver identifies complex road conditions that automated driving cannot deal with, the company's system will immediately take over remote control of the car.

Benjamin Wolfe, a postdoctoral researcher at Computer Science and Artificial Intelligence Laboratory (CSAIL) of the Massachusetts Institute of Technology (MIT), has recently published a new study on *Journal of Experimental Psychology: General*. In this study, he proposes that young drivers are quicker in detecting and avoiding hazards through videos. For drivers aged 55–69 years old, they take 403 ms to detect hazards in videos, and 605 ms to correctly respond to the hazards. In contrast, drivers aged 20–25 years old take only 220 ms to detect the hazards and 388 ms to respond to the hazards. At a speed of 100 km/h, a car moves 27.8 m/s. Considering the driver's age and the car's performance, an instruction must be delivered within 5 ms through the network, and the reliability must be at least 99.9999% to ensure the safety of remote driving.

TABLE 2.2   QoS Requirements of Five Typical Scenarios of Deterministic Networks

Scenario	E2E Latency (ms)	Jitter (ms)	Bandwidth (Mbit/s)	Reliability (%)
Remote control	5	-	10	99.9999
Discrete automatic motion control	1	1	1	99.9999
Discrete automation	10	1	10	99.99
Process automation remote control	50	20	1–100	99.9999
Process automation monitoring	50	20	1	99.999999

With a high-quality deterministic network, HD videos and instructions are transmitted within milliseconds, so that the remote driver can properly respond to emergencies and escort people to their destinations.

Example 2: Telemedicine. A patient's condition suddenly deteriorates. After consultation, surgery must be performed immediately. However, the attending doctor who is most familiar with the patient's condition is 500 km away. After comprehensive evaluation, the hospital decides that the attending doctor should remotely perform the surgery through the virtual operating table. The network assures instruction response within 5 ms, allowing the remote surgery to be completed smoothly and safely. The operation time, bleeding, and surgical complication rate of the remote surgery are almost the same as on-site surgery.

2.2.2.3 Technical Requirements for ADN

We use five typical scenarios of deterministic networks as examples to define the QoS requirements, including E2E latency, jitter, bandwidth, and reliability, as shown in Table 2.2.

Because random conditions are common in the preceding scenarios, networks should be dynamically created and managed based on service requirements. In addition, the networks must be autonomous in order to create routes that meet the quality requirements of latency and bandwidth.

In terms of self-configuration, wireless and core networks must collaborate with each other within minutes and provide ultra-low latency and high-quality private lines to ensure reliable remote control. The network status should also be monitored in real time for remotely controlled services so that backup routes can be prepared before risks occur.

For self-healing and self-optimizing, the network status should be evaluated in real time, and possible faults need to be predicted and automatically rectified.

2.3 NETWORK TECHNOLOGY INNOVATION

Optical, wireless, and IP technologies for telecommunications are still developing. Virtualized, containerized, and web-based software technologies have made considerable progress in O&M management and user experience. These technological advances are fundamental to the development and evolution of ADN. AI-empowered telecommunications hardware and software are the features that distinguish ADN from its predecessors. AI capabilities not only enable the telecom network to provide services with millisecond-level latency, Gbit/s bandwidth, and 99.9999% reliability but also make the network intelligent so that it can adapt to changes.

The innovations of ADN can be summarized from aspects of single domain, cross domain, and global security.

Single-domain innovations focus on the adaptive capabilities of hardware and software introduced by AI and are represented by the Self-X capabilities:

- **Self-configuration:** Supports automatic creation and changes of network connections. Faced with rapid changes in industrial interconnection, emergency assurance, remote emergency, and network-computing collaboration scenarios, we expect that the network can be configured automatically based on service requirements.

- **Self-healing:** Allows the network to automatically recover from faults. In the future, networks will play a more important role in improving production efficiency and ensuring personal safety – uninterrupted services will become a fundamental requirement for these networks. In this sense, the networks should recover from faults without delay.

- **Self-optimizing:** Enables the network to optimize and update itself based on analysis of historical O&M data so that it can prepare for possible faults and deterioration. In contrast with self-healing, self-optimizing focuses on the prediction of faults and automatic parameter optimization before faults occur. In an unlikely case that the network fails to optimize itself, it can notify O&M personnel of the predicted faults so that they can take preventive measures.

Cross-domain innovations call for collaboration between different technologies and convergence of different industries. The integrated management of non-terrestrial and terrestrial networks entails data sharing and automation collaboration across wireless, cloud core, datacom, and optical domains. The automatic collaboration between networks and computing is expected to optimize resource utilization.

Global security will be the most basic requirement in terms of industrial production, remote office, and personal healthcare. In the future, networks will be highly automated and intelligent, and security must be automatically and intelligently implemented. Building a scientific multi-layer autonomous protection system is the first priority.

To summarize, manual operations cannot keep pace with the increasing efficiency requirements and O&M complexity of future networks. As such, the software and hardware must be equipped with AI capabilities in order to implement full automation and intelligence of networks. And because the existing network architecture and technical capabilities cannot meet requirements, the commercial applications discussed earlier can be realized only through major breakthroughs in basic theories, system architecture, and key technologies.

REFERENCE

1. M. K. Weldon, *The Future X Network*, Boca Raton, FL: CRC Press, 2016.

CHAPTER 3

Fundamental Theories of ADN

To realize the "self-fulfilling, self-healing, self-optimizing, and autonomous" vision of ADN, communications networks must gradually evolve toward automation and intelligence and be able to cope with the tremendous challenges presented by the rapid growth of network users and devices as well as the uncertainty and unpredictability of network environments. In addition, such networks – as an infrastructure beneficial to national interest and people's livelihood – have high requirements on security and reliability.

As a core requirement of ADN, autonomy aims to maximize the intelligence of communications network systems and minimize manual intervention. This vision challenges our capability to build complex open trustworthy autonomous systems. We lack a rigorous common semantic framework for autonomous systems. It is remarkable that the debate about autonomous vehicles focuses almost exclusively on AI and learning techniques while ignoring many other equally important autonomous system design issues. Another core requirement of ADN is to leverage and generate knowledge, dynamically adapt to environmental changes, and possess the self-learning and self-evolution capabilities [1].

To enable new services on communications networks and achieve the ultimate user experience, we need to understand the attributes of individual or group users as well as their intents in specific situations and tasks. In this way, we can then provide services through various hardware and software, including devices, pipes, edges, and clouds. When various devices, multiple terminals, different networks, and massive applications serve one user or one group, a natural need is to form user agents and make the information and trust boundaries sufficiently clear. Based on these user agents, we will model users, situations, tasks, and intents, and establish a collaboration mechanism between user agents and other agents. The data and computing power of the communications networks are distributed to all four corners of the world, potentially leading to a high number of devices and high density of information in the environment. This entails the need to establish environment agents and offer public capabilities to different users and devices. The entire environment needs to be split into hierarchical discrete spaces with static, quasi-dynamic, and dynamic attributes, enabling environment agents to share and collaborate with other agents.

DOI: 10.1201/9781032662879-4

We conclude that autonomy is a kind of broad intelligence. Building trustworthy and optimal autonomous systems goes far beyond the AI challenge. To build the autonomous, self-learning, self-evolution, and human- and environment-oriented capabilities in the ADN system, we still lack a 'must-have' element – a solid theoretical foundation. We must therefore focus our efforts on establishing a complete theoretical system to guide the exploration of ADN system architecture and key technologies. This theoretical system spans multiple disciplines, including control theory, cognitive intelligence theory, user environment theory, and engineering technologies such as system engineering, automation, AI, software/hardware engineering, computing simulation, and algorithms. After 180 years, systematic research on ADN-related theories in both academia and industry has accumulated fruitful results, as shown in Figure 3.1.

Currently, basic ADN theories are not perfect. Looking ahead, we must make theoretical breakthroughs in the following aspects to ultimately make communications networks autonomous:

- **Network adaptive control theory:** copes with environment uncertainties and unpredictable problems via reliable, automatic, and closed-loop control and adaptive decision-making capabilities.

- **Network cognition theory:** enables networks to perform reasoning and decision-making like humans, and support self-learning and self-evolution.

- **User and environment agent model theory:** establishes agent models for the internal and external environments and users of network systems in order to better address user experience and service issues.

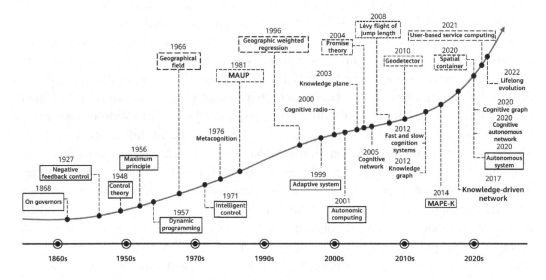

FIGURE 3.1 Development history of ADN-related theories.

Note: User and environment agent model theories are shown in dotted boxes, network adaptive control theories are shown in solid boxes, and network cognition theories are shown without boxes.

3.1 NETWORK ADAPTIVE CONTROL THEORY

Network adaptive control means that network or device management systems automatically adapt to and correctly handle network changes, environment changes, and uncertainties. This involves scientific issues and theoretical development in the fields of control theory, software engineering, autonomous systems, etc.

3.1.1 Driving Forces behind Network Adaptive Control

Driving force 1: As network functions and service scenarios continue to increase, networks must be more intelligent and require less manual intervention.

Conventional network management systems (NMSs) are oriented to NEs, and each NE is manually configured. Upon network environment or requirement changes, O&M personnel have to modify NE configurations accordingly. This is the main motivation behind the proposal of reducing the manual workload involved in network maintenance by using rules that are composed of three elements: event, condition, and action. The rule mechanism defines when to trigger a rule. Once a rule is triggered, the condition is evaluated. If true, the action is triggered. However, as network service processes become increasingly complex, simple rules cannot meet network O&M requirements.

It is in this context that a new network management technology emerges – policy-based network management technology. By centrally creating, storing, and distributing policies, this technology extracts and shields NE configuration details in conventional NMSs and shifts the focus of network management from NE functions to network services. When O&M is narrowed down to network services, network O&M becomes much more efficient. However, the policy-based network management technology relies on policies to automatically manage networks. If any new changes beyond the scope of the configured policies are made to the network environment or user requirements, the technology cannot automatically manage networks based on real-time network running status.

As such, a key goal in ADN is to reduce the amount of manual intervention. In policy-based network management technology, though the discussed policy-driven operations allow most standard and repetitive execution tasks to be done by automated systems, network expert supervision is always needed to capture special situations where the automated systems expect direct intervention from network experts. In ADN, user inputs are regarded as intents, which serve as a content element to convey user expectations. With intents, autonomous systems know what requirements, goals, and constraints they should act on. As the basis for making decisions and optimizing action priorities, intents determine customer needs and service providers' contractual obligations. They help systems continuously explore potential solutions and evaluate intent-driven policies until they find one that can produce the best achievable business results. Intents do not give the configuration or information of a particular node but may give information about nodes with a particular role (e.g., edge switch) or a particular function. In addition, intents do not reflect the internal implementation technology of networks.

Therefore, given a communications network running environment, autonomous systems must go through a series of processes such as system analysis, mapping, collaboration, and execution based on the external intents input to them or the internal goals set within themselves.

Driving force 2: Network running environments are becoming increasingly complex, requiring the networks to automatically adapt to uncertainties.

Uncertainty refers to any situation that deviates from the deterministic knowledge of the network system and therefore cannot be implemented. In real-world communications network environments, the system faces a variety of uncertainties at runtime – for instance, functions may not be properly executed due to software and hardware exceptions, or the system may go beyond the preset capability range due to external environment changes. Complex environment changes and uncertainties are issues that autonomous systems must face and solve. In a CSP's live network, fiber link jitter once caused bit errors, resulting in the receiving ends of network switches being intermittently disconnected and customers' video services being negatively affected. Many O&M experts conducted extensive analysis but were unable to identify the root cause of the problem. Eventually, someone noticed that many of the CSP's fibers hung on trees and monkeys often swung on the fibers. This caused fiber link jitter and then bit errors, triggering frequent switchovers, keeping the system in a busy state, and deteriorating the quality of customer services. In normal cases, fibers will not sway because they are buried underground, at fixed positions. If they hang on trees, they will sway frequently. This case shows that, due to the complexity of the network system, it is impossible to predict all problem scenarios in advance.

Therefore, information received and perceived by the autonomous systems – including status changes within the autonomous systems themselves, intents input from external systems, and the surrounding environment – is subject to various unknown changes and unknown factors. As such, the ADN system must control its own behavior based on the internal and external network environments and system running status, by means of adaptive control. In this way, it will be possible to continuously fulfill system goals (external or internal) and finally achieve system autonomy.

3.1.2 Fundamental Theories of Network Adaptive Control

Network adaptive control theory is developed from control theory, adaptive systems, and Joseph Sifakis' autonomous system theory, while also combining the principles and applications of communications networks. During the running of a communications network, the adaptive control of the network will be implemented by adapting to the network changes, environment changes, as well as some uncertain changes.

3.1.2.1 Development of Control Theory

From the 1930s to the 1950s, the classical control theory formed a relatively complete theoretical system. Based on the transfer function, this theory usually controlled single-input single-output (SISO) linear time-invariant systems, with the following analytical methods: time domain analysis method, frequency domain analysis method, and root locus method. Its mathematical tools mainly included differential equation, Laplace transform, and function of complex variable, and control policies were feedback control, proportional-integral-derivative (PID) control, etc.

From the 1960s to the 1970s, modern control theory adopted an analytical method based on state spaces. It leveraged modern mathematical methods and computers to analyze comprehensive complex control systems. In this period, the theory could control multi-input multi-output (MIMO) time-varying or nonlinear systems. The control system could be a continuous control system or a discrete or digital one. The time domain method was its main analytical method. Based on state spaces, there was no need to use the transfer function; instead, the state vector equation was used to simplify mathematical expressions. Matrix theory of linear algebra was the mathematical tool it used most often, and control policies included pole placement, state feedback, output feedback, and more.

Since the 1970s, intelligent control theory has emerged as a non-traditional control method that can better imitate human intelligence. The theoretical methods it adopts mainly come from scientific disciplines like automatic control theory, AI, and operational research, so that the design of control systems no longer depends entirely on the mathematical models of the controlled objects. Nonlinear, time-varying, and uncertain complex control systems are now well within reach. Its mathematical tools are fuzzy mathematics, operational research, etc.

3.1.2.2 Applications of Adaptive Systems in Control Theory

During the development of adaptive systems, "Architecture-based Adaptation" was proposed in 2004, laying the foundation for adaptive system engineering. To address uncertainties, "Guarantees Under Uncertainty" was introduced in 2010, but solutions developed to ensure that a system met its adaptability goals often proved to be very complex. "Architecture-based Adaptation" and "Guarantees Under Uncertainty" became the driving forces behind the development of adaptive systems based on application control theory in 2014. Adaptive systems focus on using the mathematical basis of the control theory to implement adaptive systems and both implement and analyze software systems running under uncertainties.

More than a decade ago, different control solutions based on control theory were widely used to address the complexities in computing systems, including network protocol, DC, and cloud issues. However, the focus of these solutions is to control the underlying resources of the computing system, such as CPUs, storage, and bandwidth. At a higher level of the computing technology stack, applying control theory to adaptive software is an even more complex problem. Here are a few reasons: the diversity of software quality requirements, the interplay between complex software, and the fact that software often has some nonlinear behavior. These all make it difficult to model software accurately, obtain measurements from sensors, and control the system through actuators.

To address these issues, the adaptive system based on control theory offers such a solution: automatically constructing the dynamic model of the software system – with the system's quality requirements managed by a controller – and retaining the control theory's capability of guiding system control. This automatically constructed control-based adaptive software solution adopts a basic control policy, feedback control, which measures system outputs and adjusts the system until it can output the required response. There are three approaches to applying the control-based adaptive software: (1) Use the proportional-integral (PI) control policy to process a single setpoint goal, which lays the foundation for automatic building of adaptive control system software. (2) Extend the first approach by processing multiple goals, including optimization goals. (3) Apply model predictive control to make the optimal control decision within the forward-looking scope of multiple goals.

3.1.2.3 Joseph Sifakis' Autonomous System Theory

1. Limitations of the Prior Art

   With respect to the key requirements of future autonomous systems, the established technical conditions are rather limited in a few aspects [1]. First, the trustworthiness of infrastructure and systems does not meet requirements, for example, communications security cannot be guaranteed. Second, in communications, it is impossible to guarantee the response time and thus the timeliness, which is essential for autonomous reactive systems. Last, critical systems and best-effort systems follow completely different design paradigms, making it extremely difficult to integrate hybrid critical systems. At the same time, new methods and practices are emerging one after another [1]. The widely used learning-enabled components, such as AI-based E2E solutions, break the traditional critical system engineering practices. Critical software is now customized through updates. A good example is some automobile software that is updated once a month.

2. Challenges

   Systems engineering has reached a turning point where non-evolvable automated systems are replaced by future-proof evolvable autonomous systems [1], but there are still some challenges. First, we need a general-purpose reference semantic model, which can be used as the basis for evaluating system autonomy, not just a list of fancy "self-" terms (e.g., self-healing, self-optimizing, self-protection, self-awareness, and self-organizing). Second, what technical solutions do we have to enhance system autonomy? And what technical difficulties and risks does each technical enhancement bring? Last, we are in urgent need of a common engineering foundation for next-generation autonomous systems, and this foundation must solve some fundamental problems. For example, it must integrate model-based and data-driven technologies with the "hybrid" design process to determine the trade-off between trustworthiness and performance; model and simulate systems in a real physical environment; and combine experience verification with evidence verification to evaluate trustworthiness and performance.

3. Autonomous System Reference Model

   In [2], Joseph Sifakis defined an autonomous system reference model (see Figure 3.2), which combines five key features of an autonomous system [3,4]: perception, reflection, goal management, planning, and self-learning. The following explains the exact meaning of each feature.

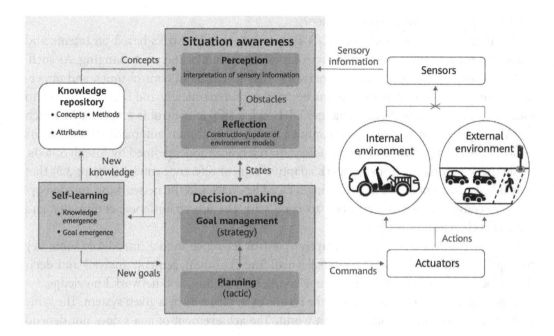

FIGURE 3.2 Autonomous system reference model.

- *Perception* is a feature required to input stimulation, explain its basic meaning, eliminate ambiguity and vagueness in complex inputs, and generate relevant information. In addition to data from other systems, perception often receives and combines multimodal inputs, such as video, audio, heat, touch, and radar.

- *Reflection*, upon receiving the combined information from the perception feature, starts to work by creating and continuously updating the model that represents the system environment and system state.

- *Goal management* is to select goals that match the current situation from the goal set.

- *Planning* is the act of computing a plan that satisfies the system state constraints and the goal set generated to meet goal management requirements. The computing of this plan determines the action that the system will take to respond to the current environment state.

- *Self-learning* has two facets: knowledge emergence and goal emergence. Over time, it dynamically adjusts the goals of the system and the planning process of the goals, by means of learning and reasoning, based on the evolving state of the system and its environment.

In all these features, perception combines with reflection to represent the internal and external environment states of the system, and goal management and planning constitute the adaptive decision-making process of the system. Decision-making needs to consider potentially conflicting goals and the current environment state.

3.1.2.4 Network Adaptive Control Theory

As discussed in Section 3.1.1, the ADN system manages networks based on intents and goals, and the network system and environment are complex and ever changing. As such, the ADN system requires that NEs, network management and control units, and upper-layer management and control systems be capable of dynamically and flexibly reacting to such complexity and uncertain changes. Network adaptive control is a process in which the ADN system perceives the environment and itself and then automatically adjusts its behavior. Drawing on the autonomous system reference model defined by Joseph Sifakis, we define a communications network adaptive control reference model (Figure 3.3) that fully takes into account the key challenges faced by ADN and the networking and deployment of communications networks, to cope with the aforementioned complexity and uncertain changes.

The communications network adaptive control reference model introduces some key concepts pertaining to adaptive control, including goal management, analysis and decision-making, planning, network and environment modeling, and network knowledge.

In goal management, *goal* refers to the results to be achieved by a given system. The same goes for the communications network world. The achievement of goals does not depend

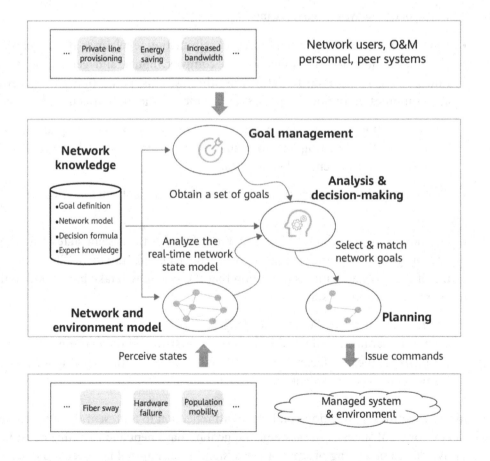

FIGURE 3.3   Communications network adaptive control reference model.

on the current state of the system or environment; rather, the system should orient itself to the goals and make continuous attempts until the goals are met. In real-world network applications, goals are classified into two levels: global goals and sub-goals. *Global goals* are those that the whole network system must achieve. By breaking down a global goal or specific goal, we will obtain *sub-goals*. Multiple sub-goals collaboratively support the achievement of system goals. *Goal management* is the practice of processing different goals and collaboration between goals in a unified manner.

As the name suggests, *analysis and decision-making* includes two processes: analysis and decision-making. *Analysis* is the process of comprehensively analyzing the state data of the current network and environment, including historical data that records the network and environment states, with the goal of finding feasible solutions to given system goals. The analysis may produce none, one, multiple, or many feasible solutions. The complexity of the analyze-to-solve process depends on factors like goal definition, network topology, service scale, and network size. *Decision-making* refers to the selection of an optimal result that best matches the given goals. To this end, it verifies and evaluates all the results given by the analyze-to-solve process. The decision-making process is constrained by goals, especially when there are multiple goals or goals conflict with each other.

Planning is the computation of executable commands that meet the given goals with regard to the system and environment state constraints.

Network and environment modeling is a way to build data models based on the network features, physical network components, and peripheral environment. It obtains data online by collecting the network and environment status of managed objects.

Network knowledge is a collection of data that is effectively used and executed by computer technologies in the communications network. Network knowledge includes the knowledge of the communications network itself and the knowledge of experts who use the network.

The communications network adaptive reference model includes the key processes of goal-based analysis and decision-making, goal-based automatic execution, and self-verification to cope with uncertainties. The following describes these processes:

1. Goal-based analysis and decision-making

    To cope with complex network changes and uncertain factors, analysis and decision-making must be aligned with goals. *Decision-making* is the process of selecting an actionable solution from a set of candidates based on preferences, uncertainties, and other "optimal" or "rational" choices. The decision-making process can be divided into six steps: define a problem, determine the goal criteria, weigh the goal criteria, generate candidate solutions, evaluate the candidate solutions, and select an optimal solution.

    Problem definition, as the first step in the decision-making process, must be done with a full understanding of the current state and correct ring-fencing of factors in relation to the problem. By doing so, we can gain a clearer understanding of what needs to be decided and choose the right solution from all the candidates.

During step 2 (determine the goal criteria), we obtain the factors associated with decision-making. The preferences and weights of these factors may affect the final criteria (in areas like functionality, security, and reliability).

Given the fact that influential factors are usually of different importance, the decision-making system needs to weigh each factor (i.e., assign a correct priority or weight to them during decision-making). This is known as "weighing the goal criteria." In some cases, we use the weigh method; in others, security and reliability become top concerns in addition to some other less important factors.

"Generate candidate solutions" is a key step in the decision-making process. In essence, decision-making is to make a choice from multiple candidates – we seldom have just one option. Therefore, on the one hand, the decision-making system generates as many candidate solutions as possible for the same problem. On the other hand, it analyzes and narrows down the scope based on resource or time restrictions. In terms of generating candidate solutions, common methods are decision matrix, decision tree, etc.

With candidate solutions on hand, evaluation is a natural thing to do. After the problem is clearly defined and candidate solutions are generated, the decision-making system can now make a comprehensive analysis and evaluation of these candidates based on quantitative data such as various time, cost, and network indicators.

Following the evaluation, the decision-making system has to make a careful choice. The choice must be clear enough, without any confusion or uncertainty. It may be one of these exact candidates initially listed, an improvement of one of these candidates, or a combination of multiple candidates from different aspects.

In goal-based analysis and decision-making, determining and weighing goal criteria are the basis, whereas generating, evaluating, and selecting feasible solutions are the key points.

2. Goal-based automatic execution

Figure 3.3 illustrates how a system runs automatically with given goals and environments, regardless of the technical implementation details. For example, we need to establish an enterprise private line with 99.99% availability (the goal). Private line availability can be further broken down into device availability, fiber availability, protection availability, etc., along the private line's path. Device availability refers to the availability of each component, such as optical modules, input/output boards, and cross-connect boards. Fiber availability is not just determined by fibers themselves but also by the physical environment. In terms of protection, we have 1+1/1:1 protection for service channels, 1+1/1:1 protection between ports, 1+1/1:N protection between boards, and 1+1 protection for fiber links. After obtaining the private line availability goal from the network knowledge repository, goal management breaks it down to device availability, fiber availability, protection availability, etc., and sends the results to the analysis and decision-making system. This system obtains device, fiber, and protection data via the network and environment models, calculates device, fiber, and protection availability, and ultimately calculates the E2E private line availability based on the private line's path. Based on the existing network resources and topology relationships, private line paths with 99.99% availability are generated. After several iterations of evaluation and verification, one path that best meets the availability goal will be selected, and an executable plan will be generated based on managed objects to automatically execute the goal.

In network applications, the system may have multiple goals that conflict with each other, explicitly or implicitly. For explicit conflicts, the system should prompt users to make adjustment. On the contrary, implicit conflicts can only be detected during the analysis, decision-making, and planning processes. If such conflicts are found, the system needs to switch to other candidates iteratively. If none of these candidates meets the goal, the goal is displayed as unsatisfied. Even so, the system will continue to make more attempts to find a feasible solution for the goal.

In network applications, the goal of a system may cover multiple managed objects. In this situation, the goal needs to be decomposed among the managed objects. One method is linear assignment, that is, decompose the goal simply based on the number of managed objects. However, linear assignment cannot work for some goals (e.g., optical signal-to-noise ratio) or some objects (e.g., optical NEs in optical networks). In these cases, network knowledge will be of help in finding an executable solution based on the state data of the network and environment. This relies on rounds of iterations between managed objects to find the right fit for the goal.

In automatic goal execution, goal breakdown, goal conflict and collaboration, and decision-making on executable solutions are the key points.

3. Self-verification to cope with uncertainties

The complexity of network adaptability is directly related to the uncertainty of the network environment. There are diverse sources of uncertainty, including time-varying network traffic, mobility-triggered dynamic changes, emergencies, and key events like failures and network attacks. Once uncertain events occur, goal management needs to generate a new goal based on the state data of the network and environment to cope with situations like incomplete knowledge or lack of predictability. Based on the new goal, the system automatically executes related processes with the established network knowledge to address uncertain issues.

During the adaptive control process, the online data of the network and environment models must be fully utilized, and iterative evaluation and verification must be performed to meet the new goal. If a goal is found unsatisfied during evaluation or verification, the system will dynamically generate a new goal and repeat this process until executable solutions are found for uncertain events, that is, the system goal is met.

Section 3.1.1 mentioned a case wherein the fibers at a CSP's site were distributed over trees. This led to fiber link jitter and frequent bit errors, triggering service path switching and rerouting. To address this issue, the adaptive control model collects and perceives the quality status of network-wide fiber links online, and analyzes the regularity of bit errors in fiber links as well as the distribution and topology of fibers.

It then concludes that these fibers are not fixed or buried underground. Based on the deployment scope of fibers, it generates a new service rerouting policy to automatically extend the confirmation time of bit errors before rerouting services. Such an undesirable situation is thus avoided: A service is rerouted to one of these swaying fibers, and because of bit errors in that fiber, another rerouting request is triggered, which greatly affects service quality. The extended confirmation time prevents repeated rerouting caused by fibers swaying irregularly, thereby improving the stability of service quality and reliability of the network system.

In self-verification, to cope with uncertainties, the key points lie in network knowledge, goal emergence, and online evaluation and verification.

To sum up, in the face of dynamic network requests from users and O&M personnel as well as unknown or uncertain events in the network environment, future ADN development and research must focus on dynamically adapting to and iteratively verifying system goals, with the aim of continuously satisfying and maintaining system goals.

3.2 NETWORK COGNITION THEORY

Network cognition is an effective approach to solving the mismatch between network static rules and deterministic constraints and between network complexity and dynamics during the evolution of communications networks. This theory covers some fundamental scientific problems and theoretical basis in fields like network cognition systems and AI.

3.2.1 Network Cognition is the Basis of ADN

The global outbreak of COVID-19 made people more dependent on communications networks than ever in both work and life scenarios. Networks must meet the application requirements of larger capacity, higher rate, wider coverage, more diversified services, faster response, and more reasonable resource allocation. These application requirements fueled CSPs' demands for fast and simple network operations, leading to the vision of *zero-touch network management and operations* being proposed. Continuous network development and evolution also face the following problems and challenges:

High dynamics of the internal and external network environments: To better meet end users' requirements, networks must be fully aware of the changes in internal and external environments so as to dynamically improve network configurations, rather than just relying on static automation rules and deterministic factors.

High O&M complexity: To deal with the O&M complexity compounded by heterogeneous networks, devices from different generations and layers, multi-region collaboration, and diversified stringent network service requirements, network O&M management has to continuously strengthen process collaboration, information identification, and automatic execution.

Accumulation of O&M knowledge and experience: Currently, network O&M still requires a large amount of labor and relies heavily on expert experience. Unfortunately, expert experience is not digitalized yet and therefore cannot be stably or regularly input into machines. Machines cannot use the established experience or knowledge to make trustworthy decisions.

Inherent challenges facing trustworthy AI: Even though AI technologies have embraced numerous applications in subordinate fields of communications networks, AI is not a one-size-fits-all approach. Building a manageable, controllable, and trustworthy technical support system for data security governance still faces challenges in many aspects.

To overcome these challenges, networks must evolve from the static working to dynamic adaptive working mode, and from monolithic closed networks to heterogeneous convergent ones. In the future, the ADN system must have the cognition capability, that is, be able to sufficiently perceive the network environment, user intents, and system itself, and take a step further by introducing certain measurement criteria for autonomous decision-making control and achieve adaptability by means of network and system reconstruction.

Cognition, which is one of the most important capabilities in the ADN system and devices, will be distributed to ADN's management and control units and AI-native NEs, forming a distributed cognitive architecture. Thanks to the ability to self-learn from interaction and experience with the environment, the management and control units and AI-native NEs can adapt to and understand complexity, deal with uncertainties, generate assumptions and reasonable arguments, and propose suggestions and actions.

3.2.2 ADN Cognition System and Its Features

Daniel Kahneman, 2002 Nobel Prize laureate in Economics, elaborated on thinking and decision-making in his book *Thinking, Fast and Slow* [5]. He used a two-system metaphor to explain the two mechanisms that work when human brains make decisions. System 1 is fast and unconscious, with no sense of voluntary control. One of the most noticeable characteristics of System 1 is the change of thinking in a very short period. The operations of System 2 are often associated with the subjective experience of agency, choice, and concentration – all of its activities require concentration and complex logical reasoning.

Likewise, communications networks, including software-defined networking (SDN), and network function virtualization (NFV), resolve the problem of network automation and intelligence. Such networks operate under well-defined parameters or predefined constraints. When confronted with a specific problem or a group of problems, they introduce AI technologies such as deep learning and knowledge graph. In scenarios such as fault discovery and diagnosis, various machine learning technologies have been proven to be effective in automatically solving network problems. However, when unforeseen changes occur, the communications network cannot perform further logical analysis or reasoning; instead, it expects humans to intervene. Therefore, from the perspective of intelligence, this is more like fast thinking according to Daniel Kahneman's definition, that is, within the scope of System 1.

In pursuit of autonomy, ADN will go beyond clearly defined parameters or constraints and make systems/networks run independently, with little or no manual intervention – this is the design goal of ADN. Telecom networks are constantly changing environments full of new technologies, new services, and complex traffic patterns. In the future, being automated is not enough. Instead, networks must be autonomous so that they can adapt to unknown challenges. They are expected to learn new knowledge and technologies without being explicitly informed of purposes, apply whatever they have to deal with the ever-changing problem areas, and effectively manage knowledge – all these will be done independently. In this sense, ADN is a more complete cognition process as it resembles both fast thinking and slow thinking, that is, System 1 + System 2.

The concept of cognitive networks has existed for many years, but no uniform definition has so far been reached upon in the industry. In the early stage, Joseph Mitola proposed cognitive radio [6] for dynamically adjusting physical layer (PHY) configurations in real time. In 2003, Professor David D. Clark from Massachusetts Institute of Technology (MIT) became the first to introduce a knowledge plane into communications networks [7], and this plane provides services and suggestions for other units in the networks. In 2005, Ryan W. Thomas from Virginia Polytechnic Institute and State University (Virginia Tech) gave a broader definition of cognitive networks in his doctoral dissertation [8], emphasizing the overall and E2E goals of networks. Dr. Thomas believed that, via a proper learning mechanism, network configurations could be dynamically adjusted in real time based on the perceived network and environment information, thus intelligently adapting to environment changes and guiding autonomous decision-making. Even so, Thomas' definition is not complete enough because it is silent on knowledge and the knowledge construction process. The fact is that autonomous construction of knowledge is an integral part of cognitive ADN.

Network cognition is an application and extension of cognitive science and cognitive computing in communications networks. In ADN, network cognition can play a role without human intervention or coordination and take a quantum leap forward, from reactive, imperative, and adaptive intelligence to what are called *complex cognition capabilities*, that is, autonomous and cognitive intelligence. Put differently, through online self-learning and self-evolution, networks themselves have the ability to discover and generate new knowledge. At the core of network cognition is the learning capability, which involves interacting with and perceiving the internal and external complex, dynamic environments to support local decision-making, cross-domain collaborative decision-making, and proactive prediction and reasoning.

In ADN, the network cognition capability is realized through a *network cognition system*. This system interacts with humans to fully understand their high-level goals. Based on the perceived network state and real-time network environment information, this system uses intelligent judgment methods such as learning and reasoning to make trustworthy and explainable decisions in accordance with users' high-level goals and networks' E2E goals. In this way, the networks can be managed independently in terms of resource configuration, quality of service (QoS), security, etc.

According to the preceding definition, we can see that designing and implementing such a network cognition system in ADN is a complex and colossal project. The system must have the following features:

Multi-domain perception: Reasoning is a core capability of network cognition systems. It requires the network cognition systems to perceive their own behavior and surrounding environments, including users, O&M personnel, network domains, and network environments, and reflect the perceived content in their behavior.

Human-machine interaction: Network cognition systems can express themselves and effortlessly understand human instructions that are somewhat ambiguous, achieving collaboration between humans and machines while also facilitating decision-making by humans.

Self-learning: The learning capability makes it possible for network cognition systems to advance. By learning from previous experience, network cognition systems improve their own adaptability.

Reasoning and decision-making: They are the basic capabilities of cognitive networks. By using proper knowledge representations to perform reasoning on what the networks encounter, cognitive networks are able to predict what losses will occur due to abnormal behavior in the future and provide reliable suggestions on further adjustments.

Self-evolution: This process, in which software systems must continuously adapt to environment and requirement changes, focuses on the coexistence of old and new systems, adaptability to changes, and continuous growth. It is a basic capability of a network cognition system.

Network digital expert: Network cognition systems can reason and decide like humans, and more importantly, do so in a trustworthy way. They can even substitute for human experts to make regular and adaptive decisions and better adapt to complex network environments, especially those fraught with uncertainties. This is considered one of the fundamental features of networks.

3.2.3 Key Elements in ADN Cognition

As evident in Figure 3.4, the ADN cognition system interacts with humans through the network digital expert system with the ultimate goal of attaining human-machine symbiosis. The ADN cognition system ("fast system") quickly responds to external state changes and performs complex computing and decision-making based on the "slow system." Knowledge representation and reasoning constitute the foundation of the cognition system. Through lifelong self-learning, this system copes with internal and external complex, dynamic network environments independently. The autonomous system itself needs to evolve continuously to meet all the dynamic requirements – this is where the self-evolution capability comes into play. Put simply, network digital expert, fast and slow cognition systems, knowledge representation and reasoning, network lifelong self-learning, and adaptive evolution constitute the key elements of the future ADN cognition system. The following describes each of these elements.

Network digital expert: It is a high-level agent that learns from both internal and external network environments and interaction with humans to form human-like high-level cognition. In this way, it gains the ability to independently process tasks. In ADN, network digital expert is mainly responsible for high-level network goal management and task monitoring.

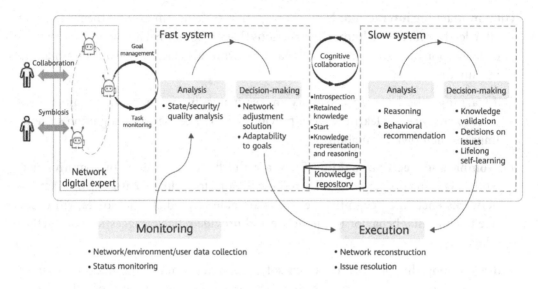

FIGURE 3.4   Basic working principles of the ADN cognition system.

Fast and slow cognition systems: In closed-loop control of network cognition, the closed-loop fast system builds the network autonomy capability, and the closed-loop slow system implements the network's logical reasoning capability.

Knowledge representation and reasoning: This is the basis of network cognition and system evolution. In ADN, knowledge includes both network knowledge and system knowledge.

Network lifelong self-learning: It is through this process that original knowledge is updated and new knowledge is generated in order to deal with uncertainties in internal and external network environments.

Adaptive evolution: It refers to the process of adapting to the ever-changing environments and requirements.

Each of the preceding elements is confronted with some critical scientific and technical issues. We cannot sidestep these issues when attempting to design and implement the ADN cognition system. The only thing we can do is to seek support from fundamental theories.

3.2.3.1 Network Digital Expert

AI development has three phases: computational intelligence, perceptual intelligence, and cognitive intelligence. In the fields of computational intelligence and perceptual intelligence, current AI technologies have the capability to surpass humans. Network digital expert will be oriented to the cognitive intelligence field in the future ADN. It has human-like advanced cognition capabilities and can perform non-specific tasks in complex network environments. Network digital expert is developed based on cognitive computing theories. It adopts human thinking theories and models to imitate human thinking in computer systems, so as to create cognition and assumptions that resemble human thinking and generate high-level agents that can "understand" things.

Network digital expert emphasizes understanding of and interaction with networks, environments, and network operators. Through cognition and learning, network digital expert can learn, think, decide, and act like human brains. Compared with traditional machine learning technologies, cognitive learning attaches more attention to simulating the perception and behavior of human brains, hands, eyes, and bodies. This gives network digital expert similar high-level cognition capabilities to humans. Through interaction with humans, networks, and environments, digital network expert can understand and adapt to complex network environments, fully understand humans' high-level goals, and make real-time adjustments according to the network running status. In this way, it not only fulfills human goals but also completes complex network O&M tasks, such as automatic fault rectification and automatic state optimization. To this end, network digital expert must be able to proactively perceive, learn, and reason the network world, interact with humans and environments, and dynamically react to changes in the network environments. In network digital expert, cognitive learning is a closed-loop process that spans from perception to behavior and vice versa. Dynamic, adaptive, robust, and interactive are regarded as the most important features expected of the learning process.

Cognitive models are the basis of network digital expert, and cognitive architecture is the core. The cognitive architecture is used to create cognitive models to implement network digital expert. In the early stage of cognitive science, academia has been debating whether the essence of human cognition is symbolic or distributed. This leads to three categories of cognitive architectures (including cognitive computing architecture): cognitivism, connectionism, and hybrid.

Cognitivism is symbolism wherein knowledge representation is deemed the core of cognition. In this category, cognition is to process symbols, and reasoning – which can be described in some formal languages – is to solve problems by using heuristic knowledge or heuristic search.

Architectures in the *connectionism* category are similar to neurons and synapses in brains – they consist of a large number of homogenous units and weighted connections between the units. A main task of connectionism is to adjust the weights of connections between neurons until optimality is achieved through techniques such as gradient descent. A significant difference between symbolism and connectionism is that connectionism uses a distributed method to represent knowledge (i.e., knowledge is distributed all over the network), so it is more robust to data noise, damage, and information overload.

The cognition processes of symbolism and connectionism have their unique advantages, disadvantages, and limitations. It is impossible to have a cognitive method that is applicable to any problem in any field. The cognition process of human beings usually combines deduction and induction, which also implies that both deductive reasoning (symbolism) and inductive reasoning (connectionism) are acceptable cognition patterns. Given this, there should be no strict distinction between them. Next-generation cognitive computing or AI should also be studied and evolved toward this direction. For instance, for third-generation AI, Fellow Bo Zhang proposed a three-space model [9], which fuses dual-space and single-space models. The single-space model, based on deep learning, places all the processing work into a sub-symbol (vector) space, and the dual-space model mimics the working mechanism of brains.

To network digital expert, knowledge learning and accumulation are also essential. Knowledge learning is an online process for learning new knowledge and experience during interaction with internal and external network environments and humans. Knowledge accumulation requires a human-like long short-term memory (LSTM) structure and conversion from short-term memory to long-term memory.

In order to build network digital expert in the future ADN, there are still many theoretical challenges standing before us: self-learning of cognitive models (especially in open self-learning scenarios), general multimodal cognitive models, self-correction mechanism with feedback capabilities to avoid the spread of wrong knowledge, and theory and implementation technology oriented to high-performance computing of large-scale data.

In the AI field, natural language processing (NLP) and embodied AI are also key to realizing network digital expert. NLP is extremely important because network digital expert needs to interact with different environments and people. The complexity, diversity, and ambiguity of natural languages all make NLP rather challenging. The ultimate goal of NLP is to enable cognitive virtual employees to accurately understand human languages, and naturally interact with humans. Embodied AI has an artificial agent and learns by interacting with the surrounding environment, including multimodal interaction, to take intelligence to the next level. A prominent example is that in the decision-making process, by learning human bodies, actions, facial expressions, etc., it judges human preferences, which further improves decision-making efficiency.

To conclude, the cognitive attribute presented by human beings is set to be the direction of network digital expert in the future ADN.

3.2.3.2 Knowledge Representation and Reasoning

The goal of ADN cognition is to equip networks with cognitive intelligence so that they can think like humans. Knowledge representation and reasoning provide an indispensable foundation to this journey.

Knowledge representation is a description of knowledge, or rather a convention of knowledge. It provides a data structure recognizable to computers to describe knowledge.

J. Friedenberg and G. Silverman summarized four approaches to presenting human knowledge [10]: concept, proposition, rule, and analogy. *Concept* represents objects of interest in a field, such as people, places, and events. Words in natural languages are good examples of concepts. *Proposition* is a statement about the field. For example, the sentence "Cognitive computing is an emerging field of computer science" is a proposition. *Rule* specifies the relationship between propositions and can explore new information from original information. *Analogy* is a comparison of two things, typically based on their structures.

Research on knowledge representation can be dated back to the very beginning of cognitive science. Traditional knowledge representation methods include semantic network, production rule, framework system, and logical representation. Proposed in the 1960s, *semantic network* abstracts the real world to some extent. It is a kind of network graph that represents knowledge with concepts and semantic relations, that is, directed graph with identifiers. *Production rule* is used to represent knowledge with the help of rules and is also known as *IF-THEN representation*. Expert library and fuzzy logic both belong in this category. *Framework system* is similar to a template. It believes that people's understanding of things in the real world is stored in memory in a framework structure. When facing a new situation, people search for similar frameworks from memory in order to form an understanding of current things. *Logical representation* is a first-order predicate method, which represents the subject and object of an action through a predicate. It is more like a narrative representation of knowledge.

Ontology was originally a branch of philosophy that studied the essence of objective things and expressed semantics in an explicit and formal way. Since the 1990s, ontology has been widely used in the field of knowledge representation, giving rise to formal specifications of terms, concepts, and their relationships in this field. Ontology promotes the reuse of domain knowledge and can analyze this knowledge.

At the end of the 20th century, *Semantic Web* emerged, which is a general framework proposed to make data on the network readable to machines. *Semantic* is a way to express the meaning behind data in a richer manner so that machines can understand the data. Semantic Web links different pieces of data to each other, thereby forming a gigantic information network. At the heart of Semantic Web are a resource description framework (RDF), resource description framework schema (RDFS)/Web Ontology Language (OWL), ontology, trustworthiness, etc.

In 2012, Google first proposed the concept of *knowledge graph* and successfully applied it to search engines. A knowledge graph describes the concepts, entities, and their relationships in the objective world in a structured form, expresses web information in a form closer to that of human cognition, and provides better means to organize, manage, and understand massive web information. A knowledge graph is essentially a large-scale semantic network, which represents knowledge in the form of a directed graph.

The knowledge representation methods described above are basically categorized as traditional *symbolic representation methods*. With the development of representation learning, signified by deep learning, significant progress has been made in representation learning oriented to entities and relationships in knowledge graphs, giving birth to another category of knowledge representation method – *distributed representation*. Figure 3.5 demonstrates the differences between the two categories of knowledge representation methods.

Based on the idea of distributed representation, knowledge representation learning maps entities and relationships to dense low-dimensional vectors, thereby implementing distributed representation of entities and relationships. This method can efficiently compute entities and relationships, alleviate knowledge sparsity, and improve computational accuracy, and is therefore beneficial to knowledge fusion. Knowledge representation learning mainly includes: (1) translation-based representation learning, which embeds entities and relationships into a low-dimensional vector space to obtain the representations of entity and relationship semantics – Trans series models are good examples; (2) information fusion-based representation learning, which fuses multi-source heterogeneous information to

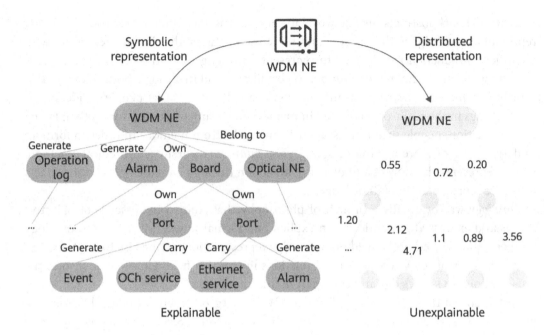

FIGURE 3.5   Knowledge representation methods.

Note: **WDM stands for wavelength division multiplexing.**

represent knowledge – for example, description-embodied knowledge representation learning (DKRL); and (3) relational path-based representation learning, which reflects semantic relationships between entities by factoring in multi-step relational paths – a typical example is path-based TransE (PTransE). Distributed representation can significantly improve computational efficiency and alleviate the data sparsity problem, but it also adds to difficulties in explanation.

Knowledge reasoning is a process of deriving new knowledge from existing knowledge. It is mainly used for knowledge supplementation, error correction, and question answering. In terms of methods, knowledge reasoning is classified into traditional knowledge reasoning and knowledge graph reasoning.

Traditional knowledge reasoning includes deductive reasoning, inductive reasoning, and default reasoning. *Deductive reasoning* is a general-to-individual reasoning process, *inductive reasoning* is a process that summarizes general conclusions from a sufficient number of cases, and *default reasoning* assumes that some conditions are met even though knowledge is incomplete.

Knowledge graph reasoning is divided into logical rule-based knowledge graph reasoning, embedded representation-based knowledge graph reasoning, and neural network-based knowledge graph reasoning. *Logical rule-based knowledge graph reasoning* refers to deriving new knowledge by applying simple rules and features to knowledge graphs, and this class can be further classified into logic-based reasoning, statistics-based reasoning, and graph structure-based reasoning. *Embedded representation-based knowledge graph reasoning* is the reasoning of knowledge vector representations, and this class can be further divided into tensor decomposition, distance model, and semantic matching model. *Neural network-based knowledge graph reasoning* leverages the neural networks' capability of modeling nonlinear complex relationships to deeply learn graph structure features and semantic features and effectively predict the missing relationships in graphs.

In the future, the knowledge system in cognitive computing will require agents to continuously interact with the outside world for iterative knowledge emergence and reasoning. This is an embodied interactive cognition process that is expected to support multimodal knowledge representation and reasoning. More in-depth theoretical exploration and research need to be invested in these aspects.

3.2.3.3 Fast and Slow Cognition Systems

A main goal of cognitive science is to understand and explain the basic process of cognition (usually human cognition), and the motivation behind related research efforts is to establish a cognitive model that can be replicated in AI.

Although advances in AI theories and technologies have boosted many successful applications, these successes are typically focused on a very limited set of capabilities and goals, coupled with an independent and identically distributed (IID) assumption, and tightly linked to the availability of immense data and computing power. Compared with humans, current AI theories and technologies still lack some capabilities, such as adaptability, generalizability, common sense, causal reasoning, and explainability.

In the thinking and decision-making psychology field, the different logical cognitive processing mechanisms of human beings in different situations are always the focus of researchers. According to Daniel Kahneman's two-system theory, described in Section 3.2.2, humans' decisions are produced by two interactive processes: one is an intuitive, imprecise, fast, and often unconscious decision-making process (System 1, Fast Thinking), while the other handles more complex situations where logical and rational thinking is needed to reach a complex decision (System 2, Slow Thinking). System 1 is guided mainly by intuition rather than deliberation. It gives fast answers to very simple questions. Such answers are sometimes wrong and usually do not have an explanation. When a problem is too complex or new to System 1, System 2 will take charge of it. System 2 does not usually work by itself; instead, it is supported by System 1. With this complex internal machinery, humans can reason at various levels of abstraction, adapt to new environments, and generalize from specific experiences to reuse their skills in other problems.

System 1 can quickly control and close the preset models, constraints, and logic of the network. Functions of the network adaptive control system are implemented through a perception-analysis-decision-execution loop. Because this loop is a cognition process in its own right, System 1 is essentially the adaptive control system mentioned in Section 3.1.

Inspired by the two-system theory, the AI field is currently focusing on this cutting-edge topic: how to build higher-level machine intelligence via System 2. System 2 should take charge of problems that are out-of-distribution (OOD) because they seldom occur. Many experts, including Turing Award winner Y. Bengio, have been discussing the implementation mechanism of System 2 [11]. Deep learning may be a solution as it further develops symbolic reasoning capabilities by combining meta learning, knowledge representation learning, and consciousness priori-improved deep neural networks (DNN). As such, deep learning exhibits higher generalizability for OOD problems, which have long been a source of frustration for traditional machine learning.

Another key difficulty in introducing the two-system theory into the network cognition system is interaction between System 1 and System 2, that is, how System 1 and System 2 cooperate to perform logical reasoning in the face of complex problems. The academia believes that metacognition may play an important role in it.

Metacognition is the cognition of cognition. This concept, originally proposed in 1976 by J. Flavell, an American development psychologist [12], refers to individuals' mental process of understanding (monitoring) and regulating (controlling) their personal cognition activities. It is a human ability to adapt to new environments and tasks. Metacognition is of great significance to agents. It connects two systems by regulating the intuitive fast response of System 1 and the supervisory prudent response of System 2. In the learning phase, it helps agents better understand their pros and cons and flexibly arrange more targeted learning or training. During decision-making, metacognition evaluates the states of the current agent and other agents and then decides on the next step in order to avoid major losses caused by wrong decisions: whether to allocate more computing resources or seek help from a higher-level agent if the current agent outputs a low-confidence solution. Some scientists from IBM and academia have introduced metacognition to solve the problem of collaborative interaction between System 1 and System 2 [13], but it is still in its infancy.

The structure of ADN cognition based on the two-system theory is still an open challenge. Many theoretical questions remain unanswered, including [14]: (1) whether there are other machine intelligence systems besides System 1 and System 2; (2) metrics to evaluate the quality of a hybrid System 1/System 2; (3) definition of machines' consciousness and level of capabilities; (4) governance of System 1 and System 2, including mechanisms like collaboration and evoking; (5) abstraction and generalization of knowledge; (6) methodologies for ethical reasoning in machine intelligence; (7) mutual learning and reasoning between multiple agents, etc.

Guided by the two-system cognition theory, the future ADN cognition system will make network cognition more adaptable, robust, and explainable, have human-like cognition capabilities, and truly realize the vision advocated by ADN. Though the prospect is promising, the journey is fraught with challenges.

3.2.3.4 Lifelong Self-Learning

Humans have the ability to continuously acquire, fine-tune, and transfer knowledge and skills throughout their lives. This is a continuous self-learning capability that contributes to the development of human perception and the consolidation and recovery of long-term memory.

In ADN, such a capability is critical to information exchange and processing by intelligent agents during network operations. At present, this capability is still a long-term challenge in the network cognition field. Despite machine learning having made impressive progress and even surpassed humans in some specific fields, its algorithms still cannot define goals by themselves or adapt to task changes – or simply put, they are not autonomous. Once a model is learned, it remains unchanged in actual use and therefore cannot fit into dynamic networking environments. Although models can be updated incrementally, doing so involves continuously acquiring available knowledge from non-stationary data distributions, which often leads to catastrophic forgetting or interference in learned tasks.

To cope with these challenges, ADN – which is devoted to dynamic, open network environments – must be capable of lifelong self-learning, that is, continuously learn new things for stable operations.

Network lifelong self-learning is a machine learning solution that can store learned task knowledge and use the knowledge learned from old tasks for fast transfer learning of new tasks. In this way, the network cognition system will not only accumulate more and more knowledge but also continuously strengthen its learning capability.

Setting it apart from traditional machine learning, network lifelong learning has the following characteristics: autonomy, adaptability, and self-evaluation and self-decision-making.

Autonomy: It is an important trait of truly powerful self-learning algorithms. Humans have a memory system wherein one memory can compensate or train another if needed. The ADN cognition system should also be able to decide when to start learning and how to leverage existing knowledge rather than simply learning the same knowledge repeatedly. Autonomy also emphasizes the continuity of self-learning. Continuous self-learning will transform the mainstream deep learning paradigm into a dynamic multi-task process with no need to retrain afresh, that is, forgetting is mitigated and knowledge is quickly and effectively transferred.

Adaptability: Humans are able to learn and master the rules for interacting with themselves and the external environment, but that does not mean these rules are unchangeable. Uncertainties lie in the fact that predictions based on these rules will lead to uncertain results and a non-stationary prediction process (due to the changeable rules). The ADN cognition system addresses the former by using a standard probability model, but there is still a great deal of room for improvement in terms of non-stationarity in dynamic environments. To detect and adapt to uncertainties, autonomous systems need to explain whether uncertainties are caused by data noise or rule changes. In the latter case, they need to modify the attributes of existing rules through self-learning, or even learn and master a new rule.

Self-evaluation and self-decision-making: Humans are able to define their own goals according to internal and external environments and adapt to their learning behavior through self-evaluation. Self-learning is a continuous process. The knowledge learned earlier may be found incorrect later, and this incorrect knowledge is spread and consequently affects the new knowledge learned, hence more and more errors. To prevent this vicious circle, the self-learning mechanism must have the capability of self-evaluating the learned knowledge. In ADN, different agents not only need the perception capability to implement intelligent collaboration but also need the knowledge evaluation and decision-making capabilities, including evaluating new knowledge and judging whether a piece of knowledge or rule is applicable to the current task, given uncertainties in the internal and external network environments.

Figure 3.6 illustrates how lifelong self-learning works.

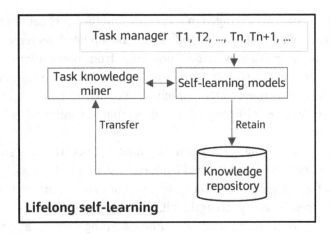

FIGURE 3.6   Working principles of lifelong self-learning.

In this diagram, *task manager* receives and manages tasks, arranges the learning sequence of these tasks based on the learning performance and efficiency, and sends new learning tasks to self-learning models. *Task knowledge miner* mines useful knowledge from the knowledge repository and transfers the knowledge to assist self-learning models in learning new knowledge. *Self-learning models* are responsible for quickly learning new tasks, based on the knowledge transferred from task knowledge mining. By retaining the learned knowledge, working memory is converted into long-term memory and incorporated into the knowledge repository. This explains how knowledge in the knowledge repository is continuously updated. To ensure that the knowledge is correct, the knowledge retaining process employs knowledge evaluation and verification.

In the future, networks will continuously learn at scale from the experience and observations of themselves and environments, and from interactions with humans. This will form the cognition capability of the networks so that they can adapt to the uncertainties presented by the dynamic environments inside and outside the networks. However, building the cognition capability by means of self-learning is a long-term process hindered by numerous theoretical challenges.

The first challenge is the evaluation of knowledge, that is, how to guarantee the correctness and applicability of knowledge. Just like the self-learning mechanism of human beings, self-learning in the ADN cognition system is an iterative process based on the existing knowledge. Being able to determine whether the existing knowledge is correct remains critical to the correct construction of the cognition system. Incorrect knowledge is harmful and may disrupt networks. In humans' cognition system, backtracking and repair will be performed upon errors. The same is expected from the self-learning mechanism of the ADN cognition system. In addition, when new uncertainties arise in the network, it is also critical to judge whether the existing knowledge or rules remain applicable. Indeed, the academia has made a few attempts in this regard, but they remain in their infancy. We still have a long way to go.

Another challenge is self-learning based on meta-knowledge. Humans can comprehend by analogy. However, state-of-the-art machine learning, including supervised learning, unsupervised learning, and reinforcement learning, is mainly designed for specific types of tasks (e.g., root cause analysis); therefore, to machine learning, it is easier to use past knowledge. In the future ADN cognition system, self-learning may be performed between different tasks, entailing the need to establish connections between tasks of similar types so as to transfer existing knowledge from one task type to another. In this way, the system is able to comprehend by analogy as humans do. To accomplish this, the system needs a self-learning capability similar to meta-knowledge learning, that is, to learn based on the knowledge of knowledge. When self-learning tasks from different domains are involved, how to express, construct, and reason meta-knowledge remains a major theoretical challenge.

Another fundamental aspect in network cognition system self-learning is interactive self-learning. It is far from enough to rely solely on network cognition system developers to inject knowledge into the system. The ADN cognition system must be able to perceive, observe, and understand the operation capabilities of network O&M personnel. By learning their successful or failed operations, the ADN cognition system forms its own knowledge or rules. Natural language understanding and knowledge representation and reasoning are the foundation of this interactive self-learning pattern, but there are still many theoretical challenges in this regard.

Despite the past efforts and attempts made by the industry – for example, the Lifelong Learning Machines (L2M) program of Defense Advanced Research Projects Agency (DARPA) – the self-learning mechanism of cognition systems remains a broad field open to research. Introducing these features into ADN still requires more theoretical research and breakthroughs.

3.2.3.5 Adaptive Evolution

Why does the ADN system need the adaptive evolution capability? The reason is threefold.

1. **Super-complex system:** The scale of the ADN system will keep growing, as too will system complexity. More internal modules mean more internal conflicts, hence the inability to interact precisely as expected. These factors eventually cause qualitative changes in system complexity.

2. **Continuously iterating system:** It is a continuous process to develop, deploy, update, and tune the ADN system – it is one that will take several years or even decades. Throughout the long lifecycle of the system, new modules will be launched, old modules will be updated, and new interconnection relationships will be established between different modules. This constant evolution is often done at runtime.

3. **Continuous changes in the internal and external environments and network requirements:** Such changes expose the ADN system to a wide array of uncertainties from sources like scenario uncertainty, dynamic changes of the environments and system, and effect uncertainty. To cope with these uncertainties, adaptive evolution becomes a must-have capability for the ADN system.

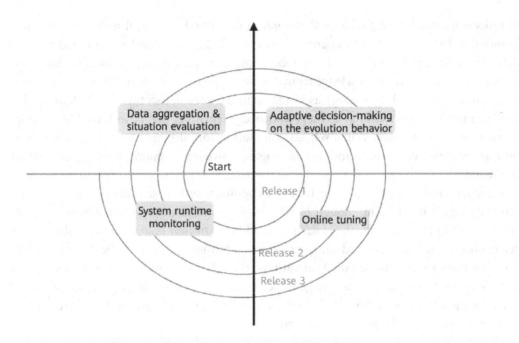

FIGURE 3.7   Adaptive evolution.

To date, no uniform definition has been reached upon for adaptive evolution. In our opinion, adaptive system evolution is both a capability attribute of the ADN cognition system and a process. More specifically, the adaptive evolution of software systems is typically dynamic and purposeful. Even when disturbed by environment changes, requirement changes, or other uncertainties, the systems can still tune themselves to dynamically approach their adaptive goals.

In ADN, adaptive evolution is centered on system knowledge and consists of four phases: system runtime monitoring, data aggregation and situation evaluation, adaptive decision-making on the evolution behavior, and online tuning. Generally, it is a spiral evolution pattern (see Figure 3.7). System knowledge includes system uncertainty measurements, rules, and reasoning, as well as domain knowledge such as uncertainty classification and characteristics. All the knowledge is indispensable to each phase in the closed-loop of evolution.

The ADN cognition system can realize adaptive evolution in three modes: tuning system parameters, tuning system behaviors, and tuning system structures. The **parameter tuning mode** influences software performance by manipulating and altering the internal state variables of software systems, or by replacing the original model with a new one without changing the model interface. Adhering to the principle of "use it or lose it" – in this case, the objects are software modules – this mode is relatively simple in terms of construction and implementation. The **behavior tuning mode** influences the runtime behavior of software by changing or replacing the internal methods called within software systems. Figure 3.8 demonstrates how software system evolution is implemented by reorganizing different software modules. Compared with the parameter tuning mode, this mode produces a larger impact (measured by both granularity and strength) on autonomous systems.

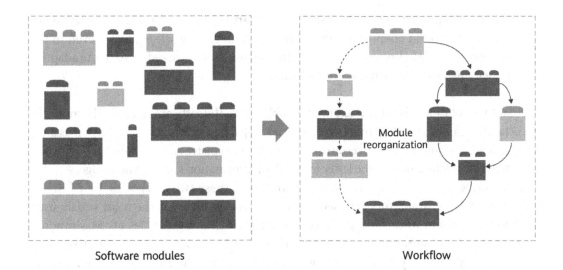

Software modules   Workflow

FIGURE 3.8   Adaptive evolution through software module reorganization.

The **structure tuning mode** is the most complex one in that it requires systems to be component-based. The configurations of the target system are generated by means of reasoning and then verified prior to reorganizing the system structure. This mode involves the evolution of elements such as software architecture constraints, which needs to be further studied.

The core of adaptive evolution lies in adaptive policies, which can be constructed in three ways:

First, predefined rule policy. Following rules like event-condition-action (ECA), we can construct a policy that implements an action under a certain condition. This is the simplest policy.

Second, adaptive policy based on control theories, including modern control theory and intelligent control theory. Modern control theory describes the adaptive logic and controlled software with a state space equation and can determine all the internal running states of systems at the same time. The model built by this theory reflects changes to all the independent variables of systems. The biggest challenge lies in computational complexity and the difficulty in establishing a state space equation. In comparison, intelligent control theory can mimic human thinking, eliminating the need to establish accurate mathematical models for the controlled software systems. The complexity of software systems is therefore shielded to a large extent.

Third, AI-based policy, which has recently become an area of intense research. AI methods (represented by machine learning) are used to construct adaptive policies for software systems. The principle behind the construction is to convert the adaptive behaviors of software systems into classification, regression, clustering, and decision-making problems that machine learning is good at tackling. In this field, reinforcement learning and Bayesian network are typical machine learning technologies used to build adaptive policies. Their advantages are self-evident – even in the absence of domain knowledge, uncertainty analysis can proceed to learn the adaptive policies meeting performance requirements.

Adaptive evolution solves the uncertainty problem faced by software systems. Theoretically, uncertainties can be classified into two categories [15]: data uncertainty (also known as aleatoric uncertainty) and model uncertainty (also known as epistemic uncertainty). The former is caused by randomness, and the latter by a lack of information such as knowledge.

To describe, measure, and reason uncertainties in these two categories, we often use probability theory, ambiguity set theory, etc. *Probability theory* is the most widely used method to represent uncertainties. Based on the statistical regularities of mass random phenomena of the same type, probability theory makes scientific and objective judgments on the probability of results in these random phenomena, and gives a quantitative description of the probability to perform reasoning and decision-making on uncertainties. *Ambiguity set theory* falls into the scope of intelligent control theory. It depicts the ambiguity and uncertainties of things, and yields clear and highly actionable computation results. It achieves remarkable results in systems with a lot of ambiguity and uncertainty features.

In the future, the adaptive evolution system in ADN will possess AI capabilities such as adaptive online learning. Experience and knowledge will be accumulated and learned in order to form an uncertainty knowledge repository, enabling the system to cope with complex, variable network environments and requirements more independently and flexibly for the purpose of achieving network autonomy and system autonomy.

3.3 USER AND ENVIRONMENT AGENT MODEL THEORY

As networks are deeply integrated with users and environments, the entire composition has the typical features of a complex system. Users and environments are regarded as agents formed by natural cohesion, and they enable a simplified, flexible architecture. Recurrence of requirements and problems are regarded as low-cost improvement goals. Focusing on users and their environments is conducive to guaranteeing service quality and experience, and seizing every opportunity to provide continuous services for users. These all constitute the appealing advantages of ADN: simplified architecture, ultra-low cost, ultra-high quality, and extreme experience. This section will delve into user and environment agents.

3.3.1 Driving Forces behind User and Environment Agents

3.3.1.1 Why Do We Introduce the Concept of Agents?

Based on digital twins, *agents* describe and provide solutions to recurring requirements and problems. Such solutions, which are adaptive to environment changes, free users from doing the same work again and again. We define an autonomous system as a group of agents, and the interactions or dependencies of these agents form a whole that not only has clear boundaries but also exhibits typical characteristics such as self-organizing, emergence, nonlinearity, adaptability, and feedback cycle. Autonomous systems are not controlled by external instructions; instead, they are opened up in order to continuously exchange personnel, materials, energy, and information with the outside world. Despite their relatively stable state, state transition may occur in these systems. In many cases, network models are employed to represent autonomous systems, with nodes representing entities – entities take on the form of agents more often – and connections representing interactions. Each agent is located in a specific environment and reacts with the environment. By perceiving the environment at any time, an agent takes appropriate actions and gradually establishes its own activity plan to cope with the potential environment changes that might be perceived in the future. Agent interaction is a knowledge-based social process because agents can determine the interaction contexts and start interactions that are not foreseen in the design phase. Through certain organizational relationships and structures, multiple agents comprise an autonomous system wherein the relationships between agents and agent interaction contexts are determined by the autonomous system. ADN is such an autonomous system, consisting of not only network devices but also served users and environments.

3.3.1.2 Why Do We Build User and Environment Agents?

Human activities in hierarchical spatial containers as well as activities and data processing volumes in different space containers are unbalanced. Oftentimes, immense data volumes occur in just a few small-scale spaces, meaning that a specific small-scale space may experience explosive growth of diverse real-time data. We can therefore conclude that, depending on hierarchical and focused human activities, data processing volumes are regularly distributed and unbalanced. Given that more than 93% of human activities are predictable [16] – with only 17 patterns [17] – and that high-frequency stay points are relatively fixed or extremely regular, we can drive the centralized architecture toward a user-centric, device-first, cloud-native, and connection-intelligent architecture based on the spatiotemporal distributions of data processing volumes.

The spatial hierarchy of human activities is predictable and highly concentrated in some spaces. Driven by business value, high-value spaces can be discretely identified in the form of containers by frequency, time, information volume, and controllable variables. The use of globally unique, three-dimensional, cross-scale, binary spatiotemporal benchmarks will facilitate space identification, indexing, and computation. High-frequency activity points of people, reference points for device information processing, and dense information distribution points can serve as key spatial anchors that associate global and local coordinate systems. With clear global locations, these spatial anchors form the spatial association points of multiple pieces of information and enable the information to be shared between multiple devices and subjects. Spatial anchors also allow the information to persist in different time periods.

In the ADN setting, the subjects become network device agents with the autonomous attribute. The agents need to continuously perceive external environment information and user feature information. When the density of users, services, and devices in a specific space exceeds a critical value, each network device acquires external environment information through its own sensors and obtains user features through user profiling.

However, this is an inefficient method. To improve the overall system efficiency and final business effect, we build user and environment agents that will function as common sources of environment information and user information for all devices and service systems. As such, devices no longer perceive environments or users; instead, they will get whatever they need simply by interacting with the agents.

Bearing the ADN goals (i.e., self-fulfilling, self-healing, self-optimizing, and autonomous) in mind, we introduce user and environment agents to open and integrate network capabilities into the following areas: (1) ubiquitous data processing for every person, home, and organization; (2) hierarchical physical environments, including cities, campuses, buildings, floors, and rooms, all the way to high-frequency stay points; and (3) service-oriented architecture across devices, pipes, edges, and clouds. As a result of these efforts, networks, users and environments constitute an autonomous system, thereby implementing the self-learning and adaptive evolution capabilities.

3.3.2 Fundamental Theories of User and Environment Agents

3.3.2.1 Progress of the Agent Theory

In the 1980s, Christopher Alexander described the fundamental properties of life structures in his four-volume *The Nature of Order*: levels of scale, strong centers, thick boundaries, alternating repetition, positive space, good shape, local symmetries, deep interlock and ambiguity, contrast, gradients, roughness, echoes, void, simplicity and inner calm, and non-separateness. These properties not only apply in architectural contexts but can also be used as criteria for object-oriented system modeling and as a reference during agent design.

Alexander created an architectural pattern language, whereby each pattern describes not only a problem that repeatedly occurs in our environment but also the solution to this problem. The solution can be used again and again, eliminating the need for us to rebuild the same pattern. Alexander's architectural pattern language consists of the following elements: pattern name (title), internal priority, picture, context, problem, force, solution, and contextual result. A summary of representations of pattern languages in different fields by Helmut Leitner is shown in Figure 3.9. Leitner encouraged people to use the patterns appropriate to the needs of their respective fields.

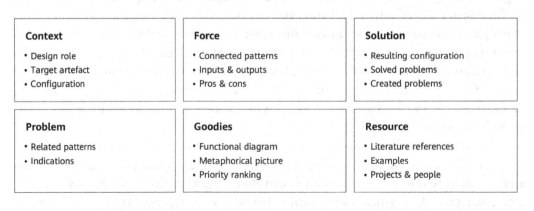

FIGURE 3.9 Representations of pattern languages [18].

Building on this, some scholars [19,20] went a step further by summarizing the features of digital twin-based agents, as listed in Table 3.1.

In 2004, Mark Burgess proposed *promise theory*, which he used to prove that an autonomous system consists of agents. As objects with the autonomous attribute, agents make promises based on their own capabilities and do their best to keep these promises. After the other party accepts the promises, their fulfillment is evaluated to maintain mutual trust. Through interactions in this promise-evaluate pattern, agents finally collaborate with each other. Collaborative agents form a larger agent to deliver new capabilities – a larger agent is also autonomous and able to make promises. In this way, an entire autonomous system is created. Promise theory has a notation system called *promise algebra*, which makes it possible to apply promise theory to rigorous system design.

Agents – including humans, machines, and environments – are relatively independent and autonomous entities that can be uniquely identified or grouped. They can make and accept promises, complete functions within the promised scope, and learn and grow. While they exhibit autonomy at certain scales, they cannot do so at all spatiotemporal scales. Together, agents and promises constitute an autonomous system. Implemented through a pattern language, the top-level design of agents describes the agents included in the autonomous system and provides brief information about them.

Based on the top-level design described in this pattern language, we can leverage the digital twin language to decompose the agent into more detailed representations of attributes or relationships. In the past, environments were used as contexts, and users as served objects. In the digital twin setting, they both appear as digital agents that interact with each other through promises, thus forming an autonomous system.

3.3.2.2 User Agent

A *user agent* is a digital entity of an individual or group user with the autonomous attribute. With a unique identifier and digital twin capabilities, it carries user attributes, perceives user situations in a specific context, identifies tasks, sends intents on the user's behalf, and

TABLE 3.1   Features of Digital Twin-Based Agents

Feature	Description
Identity	A problem-solving entity that can be clearly identified and has definite boundaries and interfaces.
Reaction - Perception and Action	In specific environments, sensors receive inputs related to the environment state, and actuators act on the environment.
Goal-oriented	A specific problem-solving role that is essential to achieve explicit or implicit design goals.
Autonomy	An agent's ability to control its own internal state and behavior.
Continuity in time	An agent's ability to continuously run on a platform/system.
Learning and adaptability	The ability to flexibly solve problems in order to achieve design goals. The principal manifestations of this ability are the responsiveness to environment changes and the initiative to select new goals and implement them independently.
Knowledge evolution	The ability to iteratively update knowledge based on interactive feedback from the environment or other agents, thereby achieving knowledge evolution and self-improvement.

perceives service experience. Through self-learning, a user agent is able to understand the user attributes, situations, tasks, intents, and experience and proactively provide better services for the user.

Figure 3.10 shows the various studies conducted by the industry on user agents. Two scholars in particular provide research results that directly guide the modeling of user agents in ADN. One is Endsley, who divided situation awareness into three levels: level 1 – perception of elements in the current situation (this is the most fundamental part in situation awareness); level 2 – comprehension of the current situation, that is, integrating different information and making goal-related decisions (people at level 2 can obtain important operation information, subjective or objective, from the clues given by level 1); and level 3 – projection of future status, specifically, the ability to project future situational events, which is the highest level of situation awareness. Building on Endsley's situation awareness, Professor Liezhong Ge proposed a psychological theory termed *situation-task-user (STU) theory*, which creatively introduces task analysis and clearly divides Endsley's *situation* into *situation* (describing the environment) and *user*. This move not only enriches the connotation of the situation theory but also makes the original theory easier to understand and apply.

All user-related information is represented and computed using a user-situation-task (UST) model. Based on this model, the ICT industry designs user agents in ADN. The *user* part in the UST model includes the user identifier, user activity pattern, user behavior entropy, and user-container model. The *situation* part includes situation-based perception, comprehension, and projection (of time/hierarchical spaces/environments). The final part, *task*, is to establish an association with ICT and to represent and compute user intents, as shown in Figure 3.11.

Individual user identifier: Referencing Erikson's *8 Stages of Psychosocial Development*, the *user* adds a profession dimension to identify users. In essence, this dimension determines the user activity pattern, user behavior entropy, and user-container model in

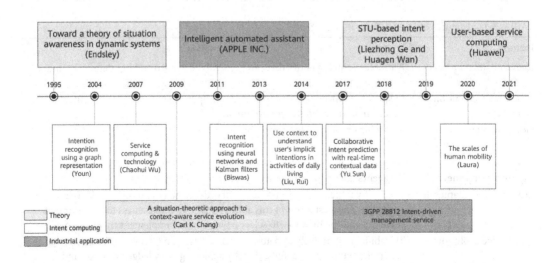

FIGURE 3.10 Studies on user agents.

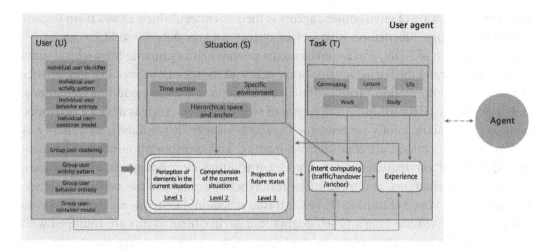

FIGURE 3.11   UST model.

a large-granularity period. For example, an adult worker typically goes back and forth between office and home.

Individual/group user activity pattern: The activity patterns of individual users are relatively regular. For both individual and group users, all of their activities can be classified into 17 patterns, making it possible to accurately describe and compute users' activity patterns in specific periods.

Individual/group user behavior entropy: More than 90% of user behaviors are regular (because these behaviors are periodically repetitive). The use of entropy helps us compute user behaviors in specific situations.

Individual/group user-container model: Based on the user behavior entropy, a user is associated with environment agents at different levels. The resulting spatiotemporal distribution is not a simple mixture of the user's activities in each space; instead, it is transitioned between environment agents at different levels. This differs completely from the traditional user analysis of trajectory patterns.

Group user clustering: Although user activities exhibit some personalized characteristics, users in the same group share a lot in common. Based on the radius of users' daily activities, frequently visited places, travel mode, and mobile traffic usage, users can be grouped from two dimensions: user mobility and mobile traffic usage. In this way, users with consistent mobility ranges, travel modes, and mobile traffic usage can be clustered into the same group.

3.3.2.3 Environment Agent

An *environment agent* is a relatively independent spatiotemporal object with the autonomous attribute (at certain spatiotemporal scales), a clear boundary, and a unique identifier. Inside the agent, which can be constructed hierarchically, is a cognitive structure that carries the agent's stable static attributes, learns the quasi-dynamic spatiotemporal regularities of services, and enables dynamic real-time processing based on service goals.

A noteworthy feature of environment agents is their openness, which allows them to continuously exchange information with service systems and the outside world.

In the research of ADN, environment agents provide self-organizing hierarchical units for us to understand the business value of services and the service behavior characteristics of users. Static information includes the location hierarchy, spatial grid representations, and device-space relationships. A full lineup of sensing devices, such as devices, networks, cameras, and radars, jointly perceive the regularity of user distribution and mobility as well as communications, air conditioning, heating, and transportation needs, and measure QoS based on spatiotemporal supplies (including electromagnetic distributions, spatial heat distributions, and traffic). The results will be output to the network, heating, ventilation, and air conditioning (HVAC), traffic scheduling systems, etc. In addition to being capable of self-learning and self-adaptation, environment agents are equipped with a knowledge module – this results in good convergence in semantic representation, pattern extraction, and paradigm induction. On the one hand, environment agents learn and augment the static, quasi-dynamic, and dynamic information of established models. On the other hand, they adaptively reduce the data measurement intensity of proficiently mastered knowledge and modules. In this way, optimal resource and energy utilization can be achieved based on user experience during system planning, construction, maintenance, optimization, and scheduling. In addition to typical network operations (e.g., policy formulation, indoor/outdoor network planning, spatial coverage simulation, indoor/outdoor network interoperability, user experience measurement, and network handover parameter adjustment), environment agents play a supportive role in scenarios like closed-loop optimization of IoT devices based on population intents. A good example of this is air conditioners, which can be dynamically adjusted based on the spatial user distribution and spatial heat distribution. Table 3.2 describes the information carried by hierarchical environment agents and the corresponding usage scenarios.

Environments, as independent agents, play an increasingly important role in environment modeling, such as hierarchical information refining and pattern induction. Given that the service distributions and service traffic representations in the hierarchical spaces of environments are highly convergent, modeling approaches are generally model-based or data-driven. The data-driven approach has been widely applied in numerous industries. As such, we will focus on the model-based approach (see Figure 3.12).

In analyzing spatiotemporal data, we can apply machine learning approaches (e.g., random forest, particle swarm, and LSTM) in each time section, and then connect the spatial statistical results of each time section to observe how data changes with time. Dimension reduction approaches like self-organizing feature map (SOFM) and empirical orthogonal function are also of help in extracting condensed information from spatiotemporal data. Other approaches specialized in spatiotemporal computing and analysis include: Bayesian maximum entropy (BME) model for spatiotemporal interpolation, and Bayesian hierarchical model for spatiotemporal trend and factor analysis. Compared with general data approaches, the spatial whole or spatial data exhibits three distinctive attributes: spatial autocorrelation, spatial heterogeneity, and modifiable areal unit problem (MAUP). Spatial autocorrelation means that the sample data is non-independent; spatial heterogeneity

TABLE 3.2 Information Carried by Hierarchical Environment Agents and Corresponding Usage Scenarios

Environment Agent	Information			Usage Scenarios
	Static	Quasi-Dynamic	Dynamic	
TAZ/BAZ[a]	TAZ/BAZ scope TAZ/BAZ type	Regularity of population distribution/ migration between TAZs/BAZs Regularity of TAZ/BAZ-level network traffic distribution	Real-time population distribution/ migration between TAZs/BAZs Real-time distribution of TAZ/BAZ-level network traffic	Discover high-value areas to support network development strategy formulation and network planning.
Building	Building shape Building structure Building material Building ID/grid code Building ontology Building type	Regularity of population distribution/ migration between buildings Regularity of building-level network traffic distribution	Real-time population distribution/ migration between buildings Real-time distribution of building-level network traffic	Optimize indoor/outdoor network interoperability (neighboring cell optimization). Plan wireless network indoor distribution. Design wireless networks and simulate coverage.
Indoor space	Indoor space structure Indoor aisle Floor/room ID Floor/room grid code Indoor space ontology Functional layout in the indoor space	Regularity of indoor population distribution/ migration Indoor 5G and Wi-Fi electromagnetic coverage and distribution Regularity of indoor network traffic distribution	Real-time indoor population distribution/ migration Real-time indoor network traffic distribution Real-time indoor network experience	Design and optimize wireless network indoor distribution (cell splitting and capacity expansion, coverage and interference optimization). Optimize IoT devices based on population intents in a closed-loop manner. Analyze the utilization of indoor space (cubicles).
Anchor	Anchor ID/grid code Equipment/facility/ cubicle/etc. Equipment/facility/ cubicle ontology Distribution of anchors such as equipment, facilities, and cubicles	Individual behavior/ distribution/ migration pattern 5G and Wi-Fi electromagnetic signal strength of anchors Regularity of network traffic distribution between anchors	Individual location/ activity Real-time network traffic distribution/ network experience of anchors Working conditions of anchors such as equipment, facilities, and cubicles	Optimize user communications experience based on individual intents. Optimize campus IoT devices based on individual intents in a closed-loop manner. Optimize the energy consumption of base stations.

[a] TAZ is short for traffic autonomous zone, and BAZ is short for business autonomous zone.

means that the sample data is non-homogeneous; and MAUP means that attribute values vary with the division of spaces. From these attributes, methods such as Kriging and spatiotemporal weighted regression are derived. Traditional research on heterogeneity mainly focuses on the spatial dimension, including global and local indicators of spatial association. Global indicators of spatial association measure spatial heterogeneity by comparing the similarity of observations from adjacent spatial positions. Studies on local indicators of

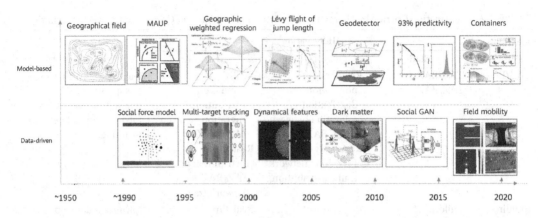

FIGURE 3.12   History of environment modeling theory.

spatial association aim to search for the possible phenomenon of local spatial autocorrelation being concealed in the absence of global spatial autocorrelation, or analyze spatial heterogeneity and determine the heterogeneity value and locations of influential observations in the presence of global spatial autocorrelation. Traditional heterogeneity evaluation indicators are mainly based on single-variate analysis. With the development of spatiotemporal big data, there is growing attention being paid to how the heterogeneity of multivariate data that intersects with time and space dimensions is considered. In this context, spatiotemporal heterogeneity – represented by spatiotemporal weighted regression models – has recently become a trending research topic in academia.

In addition to being two defining characteristics of spatial data, spatial autocorrelation and spatial stratified heterogeneity are also two major information resources of spatial data. We can dig deeper to peer into the mechanism behind them. While modern spatial statistics is developed around spatial autocorrelation, the concept of spatial stratified heterogeneity is related to the ratio between the variance within the strata and the pooled variance of an entire study area. Geodetector is a new tool for measuring, mining, and utilizing spatial heterogeneity. Its theoretical core is to harness the power of spatial heterogeneity in order to detect whether spatial distributions are consistent between dependent and independent variables, and subsequently measure the explainability of independent variables on dependent variables.

Independent environment agents are widely used in modeling how to influence human behavior. However, systematic research can be carried out only after location information is widely perceived. One of the important foundations for this was laid by González et al. who modeled individual behavior, with the accomplishments first published in *Nature* in 2008. Two years later, Barabási and Chaoming Song published an article in *Science*, stating that 93% of movements are predictable. This heralded the beginning of environment-based mobility modeling research. In recent years, research has shown that many features of environments play an increasingly important role in human mobility and behavior modeling. For instance, Alessandretti pointed out that human activities were restricted by and converged in hierarchical spatial containers, as evident in Figure 3.13.

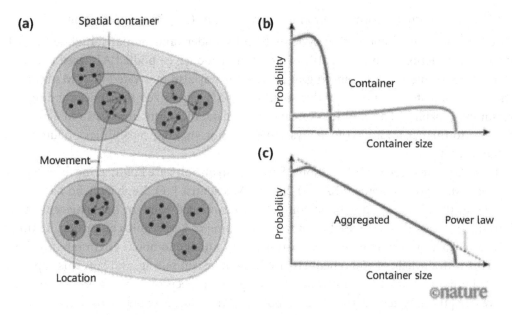

FIGURE 3.13 Hierarchical spatial containers and their characteristics. Source: *The scales of human mobility* (Alessandretti et al., Nature, 2020) [21].

3.4 PRACTICAL APPLICATION OF THEORIES

The fundamental theories of ADN come to fruition only when sufficient explorations and practices have been made in the communications field and relevant industries. We are delighted to see that the academia and industry have made significant progress in different fields.

3.4.1 Practices of Adaptive Control in Aerospace

Deflection in the control surfaces of flying objects will generate torque, which is viewed as the function of speed, altitude, and angle of attack. Because of this, the transfer function of flying objects is changing constantly and substantially. Consequently, linear control systems cannot obtain satisfactory results. The rise of aircraft performance, especially the emergence of spacecrafts, leads to deeper and deeper research on adaptive control in the aerospace field.

After extensive study, Pramod Gupta et al. from NASA concluded that the performance of neural network-based adaptive controllers must be properly monitored and evaluated so that these controllers can be safely and reliably used for controlling modern cruise missiles. They also discussed how they used the Bayesian approach to verify and confirm this conclusion, and shared the simulation results they obtained in NASA's intelligent flight control system.

Gary L. Slater from University of Cincinnati proved that by using an adaptive approach, we can better predict aircrafts' ascent performance during take-off. Based on the tested and computed energy ratio, this approach adaptively adjusts aircrafts' dependence on thrust, helping aircrafts merge with other aircrafts in the air while ascending.

3.4.2 IBM's Practices from Autonomic Computing to Cognitive Computing

To enable autonomic computing systems to fully understand humans' high-level goals through interaction with people, IBM started to introduce embodied AI-based cognitive computing to autonomic computing in 2015 – this was also motivated by IBM's business strategy of transforming to cognitive solutions. IBM emphasized the understanding and reasoning capabilities of machines on large-scale data, including unstructured data, with the aim to further improve the analysis and decision-making capabilities of autonomic computing systems.

In his keynote speech at International Symposium on Software Engineering for Adaptive and Self-Managing Systems (SEAMS) 2021, IBM scientist J. O. Kephart, who had led an article on the vision of autonomic computing, introduced some of the achievements in introducing embodied AI-based cognitive computing to autonomic computing. Taking a DC scenario as an example, he demonstrated how an autonomous system interacts with humans with the help of embodied AI-based cognitive computing, and how this approach assists humans in making optimization decisions. In the decision-making process, the cognitive computing system learned human bodies, actions, facial expressions, etc. in order to judge human preferences, thereby further improving the decision-making efficiency.

IBM's autonomic computing+embodied AI-based cognitive computing approach provides a solution and direction to represent the high-level goals of users. However, there is still a long way to go before the solution reaches maturity. How to apply it in communications networks remains an open question to be studied further.

Following IBM, the industry also tried to introduce the concept of autonomic computing to ICT networks that feature more complex management and a much larger scale. For example, Motorola, with joint efforts from academia, launched the "Foundation, Observation, Comparison, Action, and Learning Environment" (FOCALE) architecture in 2006. Then in 2013, ETSI launched the "Generic Autonomic Network Architecture" (GANA). Both architectures aimed to introduce IBM's "Monitor-Analyze-Plan-Execute over a shared Knowledge" (MAPE-K) architecture to communications networks. At that time, however, the idea of doing so was ahead of its time. Despite a great deal of research being conducted by academia, the industry did not follow up.

At present, the ICT field is throwing its full weight behind ADN, with the vision of implementing goal-based single-domain autonomy and cross-domain collaboration through the cognitive closed loop and control closed loop, and realizing the autonomous characteristics of self-learning and self-evolution in networks. All the past explorations into autonomy and cognition by the industry, including IBM, will serve as good references for ADN.

3.4.3 Practices of User and Environment Agents

The pattern language used extensively in the architecture field by Alexander and his successors has not only inspired the design of user agents and environment agents but has also been extended and applied to game scenario modeling in the gaming software field by Kent Beck. In the computer application field, Erich Gamma, also inspired by Alexander, applied the pattern language idea to object-oriented programming design.

The promise theory that formally represents agents and autonomous systems has been widely used in the ICT field. Burgess, proposer of the promise theory and founder of the configuration system CFEngine, was the first to apply the promise theory to the configuration management of computer networks. The promise theory also plays a role in the design of Kubernetes – container orchestration system.

Huawei has extensive practices in the application of environment agents, including in the telecom field (e.g., TAZs for telecom infrastructure network grid division, hotspot identification, and mobile network energy saving based on spatiotemporal features) and outside the telecom field (e.g., TAZs for store site selection and key event assurance). Meanwhile, the hierarchical space theory is used for wireless network coverage analysis and prediction in the telecom industry. Originated from the geographical statistics field, this theory has been widely spread to statistical analysis of socio-economic factors (e.g., population, vegetation, and crops), land use and urban structure analysis, transportation analysis, air pollution administration, key event assurance, and more.

Sitting at the core of user agent theories, the intent perception theory has been applied to a broad range of scenarios, such as financial business, robotics, sports health and rehabilitation, transportation, dialogue and search, human-machine interaction, network, military, big data, and industrial applications. Here is a typical example: With externally perceptible traffic data, some self-driving vehicles are able to identify drivers' intents and predict their behaviors such as highway lane changes.

REFERENCES

1. D. Harel, A. Marron, and J. Sifakis, "Creating a foundation for next-generation autonomous systems," *IEEE Design & Test*, 2022, 39(1): 49–56.
2. J. Sifakis, *Understanding and Changing the World: From Information to Knowledge and Intelligence*, Singapore: Springer Nature Singapore, 2022.
3. M. Boreale, F. Corradini, M. Loreti, et al., *Models, Languages, and Tools for Concurrent and Distributed Programming*, Aarau: Springer Cham, 2019.
4. D. Harel, A. Marron, and J. Sifakis, "Autonomics: In search of a foundation for next generation autonomous systems," *Proceedings of the National Academy of Sciences*, 2020, 117(30): 17491–17498.
5. D. Kahneman, *Thinking, Fast and Slow*, New York: Macmillan, 2012.
6. J. Mitola III, et al., "Making software radios more personal," *IEEE Personal Communications*, 1999, 6(4): 13–18.
7. D.D. Clark, C. Partridge, J.C. Ramming, et al., "A knowledge plane for the internet," *Proceedings of the 2003 Conference on Applications, Technologies, Architectures, and Protocols for Computer Communications*. 2003: 3–10.
8. W. Thomas, *Cognitive Networks*, Virginia: Virginia Polytechnic Institute and State University, 2007.
9. B. Zhang, J. Zhu, and H. Su, "Toward the third generation of artificial intelligence," *Science China*, 2020: 50(9): 1281.
10. J. Friedenberg and G. Silverman, *Cognitive Science: An Introduction to the Study of Mind*, 3rd ed., Thousand Oaks, CA: SAGE Publications, 2015.
11. Y. Bengio, "From system 1 deep learning to system 2 deep learning," *Neural Information Processing Systems*, 2019.

12. J. Flavell, "Metacognitive aspects of problem solving," In Resnick L. B. (ed.), *The Nature of Intelligence*. Hoboken, NJ: Wiley, 1976, pp. 231–235.

13. M. B. Ganapini, et al., "Thinking fast and slow in AI: the role of metacognition," arXiv preprint arXiv: 2110.01834, 2021.

14. G. Booch, F. Fabiano, L. Horesh, et al., "Thinking fast and slow in AI," *Proceedings of the AAAI Conference on Artificial Intelligence*, 2021, 35(17): 15042–15046.

15. J. M. Aughenbaugh, *Managing Uncertainty in Engineering Design using Imprecise Probabilities and Principles of Information Economics*, Georgia: Georgia Institute of Technology, 2006.

16. C. Song, Z. Qu, N. Blumm, et al., "Limits of predictability in human mobility," *Science*, 2010, 327(5968):1018–1021.

17. C. M. Schneider, V. Belik, T. Couronne, et al., "Unravelling daily human mobility motifs," *IEEE/ACM International Conference on Advances in Social Networks Analysis & Mining*, IEEE, 2013.

18. J. Zhang, *Agent juese moxing yu duo Agent xitong gouzao fangfa yanjiu* [Research on agent role model and multi-agent system construction method], Shandong University, 2012.

19. S. Franklin, A. Graesser, J. Jörg, et al., "Is it an agent, or just a program?: A taxonomy for autonomous agents," In: Müller, J.P., Wooldridge, M.J., Jennings, N.R. (eds.) *International Workshop on Agent Theories, Architectures, and Languages*, 1996. Lecture Notes in Computer Science, vol. 1193, Berlin: Springer.

20. C. Alexander, S. Ishikawa, and M. Silverstein, *A Pattern Language: Towns, Buildings, Construction*, Oxford: Oxford University Press, 1977.

21. L. Alessandretti1, U. Aslak, and S. Lehmann, "The scales of human mobility," *Nature*, 2020, 587: 402–407.

CHAPTER 4

Reference Architecture of ADN

T ELECOM STANDARDS ORGANIZATIONS HAVE defined some reference architectures for AN or network intelligence and automation, such as TM Forum in its *IG1251 Autonomous Networks – Reference Architecture v1.0.0* [1] and ETSI in its *Zero-touch network and Service Management (ZSM); Reference Architecture.*

The ADN reference architectures described in this chapter can help CSPs to build ADN and vendors to design ADN components.

These architectures cover CSPs' communications networks as well as the software systems and cloud services related to network O&M.

4.1 TOP-LEVEL ARCHITECTURE

At the heart of ADN is the vision of using an intelligent, simplified network architecture driven by data and knowledge in order to deploy a self-fulfilling, self-healing, self-optimizing, autonomous network. Such a network will be able to support new services, deliver a superior user experience, implement fully automated O&M, and maximize resource and energy efficiency. This vision can be divided into the following architecture objectives:

- **Self-fulfilling:** Services can be automatically deployed based on user intents. The ultimate goal is to achieve fully automated service fulfillment.

- **Self-healing:** Faults can be automatically predicted, prevented, and rectified based on incidents. The ultimate goal is to achieve fully automated O&M.

- **Self-optimizing:** Adaptive adjustment and optimization can be performed based on user experience. The ultimate goal is to achieve fully automated optimization.

- **Autonomous:** A self-fulfilling, self-healing, and self-optimizing network also needs to adapt, learn, and evolve by itself.

The architecture design principles of ADN can be divided into six general principles and five special principles.

DOI: 10.1201/9781032662879-5

4.1.1 General Design Principles

1. Layered Closed Loop

Organizations such as TM Forum and ETSI ZSM have reached a consensus on the macro layering principle from the industry and customer perspectives. ADN consists of the resource operations layer, service operations layer, and business operations layer.

In the future, ICT infrastructure is expected to process over 1000 times more intelligent data. The network status awareness is more granular (from pipelines to sessions), the sampling frequency is higher (from hours or minutes to seconds or even milliseconds), and the processing latency varies according to service types (from milliseconds to days). This requires a layered closed loop.

2. Continual Learning and Evolution

Intelligent ICT infrastructure should be able to continuously learn and evolve at all of its layers (including the business, service, and resource operations layers) so that it can make appropriate decisions and control complex situations without relying on predetermined procedures.

Such learning and evolution should start as soon as the infrastructure is deployed and put into use and continue for the life of the infrastructure. This is referred to as lifelong learning and evolution.

The system needs to learn knowledge from experts' network operations in terms of decision-making, learn environment models from environment status changes and adapt to the environment, and improve network operations based on end user experience.

This requires the system to be capable of fast local learning and optimization, abstract learning, and self-evolution to achieve radical innovation.

3. Hybrid Architecture Based on Data and Models

"Trustworthy" autonomous decision-making is the prerequisite and architecture design basis for comprehensive intelligence of ICT infrastructure. In the communications and industrial fields, ICT computing, storage, and networks are critical infrastructure and intelligence must be both interpretable and predictable. However, traditional intelligent methods and processes can only be used to improve awareness and analysis efficiency locally due to black box problems – they are not suitable for autonomous decision-making or control. For key services, a trustworthy and autonomous decision-making approach must be adopted.

With a model-based architecture, guaranteed and trustworthy models can be established based on mathematical formulas or computable functions in the R&D phase, infrastructure design phase, or both. The logical process is reasonable, and the decision-making result is predictable.

The hybrid adaptive architecture based on data and models uses efficient data-based methods in awareness and analysis to improve awareness and problem identification efficiency. The decision-making and execution processes are performed using model-based methods to ensure rational reasoning and predictable results. In the case of unpredictable and uncertain problems such as changes in complex environments and end users, objective-based adaptive closed-loop methods are used to find the optimal or near-optimal solution.

4. Task Collaboration Based on Human-Machine Symbiosis

Human-machine symbiosis is an ideal human-machine collaboration mode for intelligent ICT infrastructure. In this mode, humans are responsible for creative and intellectual activities, such as defining new services, establishing goals, setting assumptions, determining standards, and performing evaluation. ICT infrastructure is responsible for routine work, such as task breakdown and execution, and facilitates human activities and decision-making. The human-machine collaboration mode adopts a "people outside the loop" approach rather than a "people inside the loop" one.

Human-machine interactive learning is required. Machines should learn expert tasks and results to obtain expertise and improve machine intelligence, and in turn provide simulation and twin environments for humans to perform quasi-onsite learning in simulated environments.

5. Distributed Intelligent Load Sharing Between Machines

Machine–machine swarm intelligence, like the ant colony and honey bee colony in nature, enables multiple ADs or intelligent network devices to interact with each other and with their environments in order to complete global intelligent behavior. Intelligent collaboration is characterized by: (1) Decentralization and strong robustness; (2) High scalability, making it easy to add new agents; (3) Simple capabilities or behavior rules of each agent; (4) Self-organization: Intelligence emerges through simple machine interactions and takes effect under the guidance of appropriate evolutionary mechanisms.

Layered swarm intelligence in ADN can be achieved between NEs or ADs.

6. Manual Takeover Anytime

Humans can proactively intervene and take over ICT infrastructure at any time and have absolute priority in order to act as an emergency channel to handle disasters, faults, and scenarios not supported by the system.

When an unexpected incident occurs, the system can send a takeover request to humans, who then perform the takeover activity.

4.1.2 Special Design Principles

Special design principles are grouped by purpose to guide the design of some user requirements.

1. Service Agility Improvement

This group of design principles is used to make network service operations more agile and efficient.

- Continuously evaluate the fulfillment of each service objective online. Evaluate service objective fulfillment to trigger real-time fault remediation. Evaluate network risks and provide optimization suggestions. Quantitatively evaluate key services with low objective fulfillment and identify new service opportunities.

- Proactively predict service and capacity requirements. Conduct planning and deployment in advance to achieve a reasonable balance between customer requirements and network resources and service provisioning capabilities.

- Periodically check and modify the resource usage of services. Ensure that data is consistent with that in the physical system. Provide methods for checking and modifying data about the usage of various types of resources, including physical pipes, fibers/cables, ports, logical IP addresses, domain names, number segments, and ports.

- Periodically optimize and evolve services. Identify important services that are popular with customers. Eliminate services that customers are not interested in. Optimize and improve services with low service fulfillment. Define and launch new services to meet new requirements.

2. O&M Efficiency Improvement

This group of design principles is used to guide the improvement of network resource O&M efficiency.

- Continuously analyze the performance and status of resources and services. Predict deterioration events instead of passively waiting for event reports.

- Proactively check and correct human-induced operation errors. In activities such as complex network expansion and reconstruction, emergency service recovery, and fault remediation, manual operations are inevitable. As such, it is vital to minimize the volume of network accidents caused by human errors.

- Periodically simulate production and fault events. Proactively check and confirm the gap between the network capability and the design expectation, and detect and rectify problems and risks caused by network design restrictions and improper use in advance to avoid production faults. Simulation, check, risk identification, response, and correction activities should be automated and intelligently repeated, and real network status and environment data should be used as much as possible.

- Learn from all resource and service faults. ICT networks must be able to: (1) Continuously learn and evolve from faults in addition to quickly detecting resource and service faults and recovering services. (2) Intelligently summarize the rules from historical faults periodically, and enhance the prediction methods, detection, and troubleshooting. (3) Periodically analyze and identify known but unpredictable/non-deterministic network traffic congestion and environment faults, learn cross-node comprehensive fault analysis and handling knowledge from experts' analysis and handling experience, and improve the proportion of self-handled faults. (4) Periodically analyze and identify unknown network faults, and provide intelligent onsite information collection and analysis methods to assist experts in analyzing and solving problems.

- Share O&M experience and knowledge. Formulate O&M rules to improve the overall O&M capability and lower the possibility of system faults caused by misoperations.

- Periodically evaluate the resource and service TCO. From the perspective of the overall top-level network design, use automation and intelligence to control the TCO, especially the OPEX.

3. System Reliability

This group of design principles are used to ensure the system reliability of the network.

- Design ADs to control the impact scope of faults.

- Intelligently and automatically recover from faults. Continuously monitor KPIs and the status of resources and services automatically, and trigger automatic service recovery when the specified threshold is exceeded.

- Predict or proactively identify faults. Compared with post-event remediation, this mode can effectively control risks because proper measures can be taken in advance, improving system reliability.

- Simulate and verify the effectiveness of the fault handling solution. During network planning and service definition, provide solutions to possible faults, and simulate and verify the effectiveness of the solutions.

- Periodically test the troubleshooting process. Test or simulate any possible fault in advance to observe the network response, determine the reliability and fault tolerance capability of the network, and verify the effectiveness of various policies. In addition, identify unexpected weaknesses on the network to improve system reliability. Fault tests must comply with the principles of regularization (periodic), standardization (minimum scenarios and countermeasures), and intelligence (based on architecture and service recommendation).

- Reserve redundant resources to cope with multi-point failures. Redundancy is the core principle for improving network reliability. There are many ICT network devices, and their operating environments are complex. It is likely that multiple points of failure occur. Therefore, redundancy design is required in terms of topology networking, service routes, links between devices, and device hardware to improve system robustness and reliability.

4. Sustainability and Energy Saving

This group of design principles provides guidance for achieving green, energy-efficient, and sustainable development of ADN.

- Continuously evaluate and analyze resource consumption and emissions. Establish emission calculation models for different resources and services on a per-scenario basis, continuously collect and analyze emission data, and establish KPIs. In addition, forecast emission data and change trends, and evaluate the measures that improve network efficiency while having little environmental impact. Analyze and evaluate emission data throughout the network lifecycle, including the impact of equipment purchase, use, disuse, and scrapping.

- Formulate the overall sustainable development goals. Establish sustainable development and energy-saving goals for the entire network, and continuously plan and provide necessary resources to ensure the goals are achieved.

- Dynamically update resource consumption and emission strategies and methods. Intelligently and dynamically adjust energy-saving policies for network devices and services based on service load differences in aspects including regions, time, and users. Ensure that emissions of network devices are reduced without affecting user experience or services. During new network planning and construction, the design should be flexible so that new and more efficient devices and software products can be quickly adopted.

- Reduce the cost and resource consumption of upgrades and switchovers on the customer side.

- Fully utilize redundant resources. Redundant resources can be used to carry non-critical services with low priorities, maximizing the utilization of such resources.

5. Systematic Learning and Evolution

This group of design principles provides guidance for achieving continual learning and evolution of ADN.

- Use a layered continual learning architecture. Different data needs to be collected and processed at the business layer, service layer, and resource operations layer of an ICT network depending on their capabilities. The requirements on the frequency and real-time ability of learning and evolution are also different. Therefore, different learning architectures are required.

- Learn from the operational history of experts. Extract digitalized expert experience and knowledge to further assist decision-making or make decisions on behalf of people.

- Adopt a fast adaptive evolutionary architecture with finite boundaries. By setting a finite boundary, the solving space of knowledge calculation and extraction is controlled within the finite range. This makes it possible to implement continual learning and knowledge verification feasible. Local learning and evolution through self-optimization are preferred to quickly respond to environmental changes.

- Use a transformative evolution architecture that functions like gene mutation. Based on the agent swarm, innovative learning and evolution can be achieved through natural selection and survival of the fittest. The theory and architecture of this method are still in the early research phase and need to be tracked continuously.

- Support correction and rollback of incorrect or inefficient evolutions.

- Regularly evaluate the effects of learning and evolution to determine whether the results can be switched from the twin verification environment to the product environment for application.

4.1.3 Logical View of the Top-Level Architecture

The existing AN reference architecture in the industry is *TM Forum IG1251 Autonomous Networks Reference Architecture v1.0.0* released in 2021.

We provide the ADN system with the new contexts and top-level reference architecture and the definition of the AD, as shown in Figure 4.1. Differing slightly from TM Forum's AN, Huawei's ADN solution focuses more on the OSS layer and lower layers.

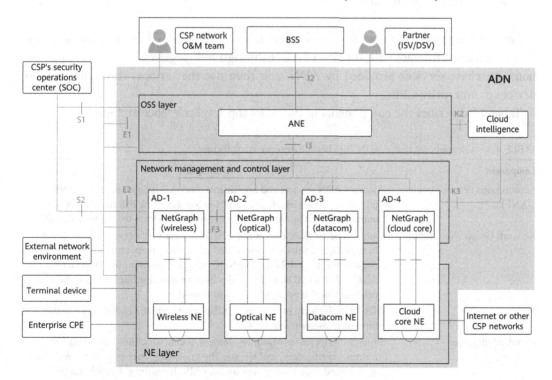

FIGURE 4.1   Context and top-level architecture of the ADN system.

The contexts of a CSP's ADN include:

- Network O&M teams, such as O&M personnel, network planning and design personnel, and outsourced maintenance personnel, can access the ADN through the UI.

- Business support system (BSS), which provides network customers with charging, settlement, accounting, customer service, and business support for network services. The BSS interacts with the ADN through machine-machine interfaces.

- Partners, including integration service vendors (ISVs) and delivery service vendors (DSVs), are responsible for system integration and delivery deployment.

- Customer devices that are directly connected to the communications network, for example, mobile terminals or enterprise customer-premises equipment (CPEs).

- Internet or other CSP networks, which are interconnected with the current CSP's network.

- External environment of the network, such as equipment rooms, towers, power supply units, heat dissipation systems, buildings, vegetation, and weather within the coverage scope of wireless channels.

- Other software systems that interconnect with ADN, such as the CSP's security operation center (SOC) that provides functions such as centralized user authorization, authentication, and audit, and system security vulnerability management. These software systems are optional.

End customers of CSPs, such as enterprise users, individual users, and home users. These customers interact with the BSS of ADN through web pages or third-party applications, purchase services provided by ADN, and then use the services through terminal devices or enterprise CPEs.

Table 4.1 describes the components in the ADN top-level reference architecture.

TABLE 4.1   Components in the ADN Top-Level Reference Architecture

Component	Description
Autonomous network engine (ANE)	Manages ADN services and implements cross-AD collaboration. The ANE provides a unified interface for ADN to connect to the BSS and provides human-machine interfaces for the network O&M team to interact with ADN.
Network Graph (NetGraph)	Controls network resources in an AD, manages services or service segments in the AD, and provides centralized AD management and cross-AD collaboration capabilities. The NetGraph provides a unified interface for the ANE and other ADs, and provides human-machine interfaces for the network O&M team to interact with the AD.
NE	May be in the form of intelligent NEs with AI native capabilities or in the form of non-intelligent NEs.
Cloud intelligence	Provides ADN knowledge management, including offline knowledge training, verification, and release. The knowledge may come from network device vendors, software vendors, or CSPs themselves. As such, multiple cloud-based intelligent systems may exist.

This book considers an AD to be an ADN subnet and software system (such as NetGraph) that can achieve the closed loop of specific network operations. ADN can be classified into multiple ADs (which can be nested) based on factors such as the technical domain, vendor, and administrative area. The ADN managed by the ANE can be considered as a large AD.

Table 4.2 describes the interfaces in the ADN top-level reference architecture.

4.1.4 Architecture Characteristics

The ADN top-level architecture has the following characteristics:

1. Layered closed loop

   Autonomous closed-loop management is performed according to objectives.

   Process and characteristics of the autonomous closed-loop method: (1) Long-, medium-, and short-term monitoring and analysis of status, such as service traffic status, energy saving status, service SLA target, and energy saving target; (2) Machine decision-making (e.g., deciding to enable the night energy saving mode for base stations in an area); (3) Target breakdown and execution (e.g., determining whether to enable energy saving for a specific base station and which energy saving mode to use); (4) Target achievement result and impact evaluation (energy saving effect and impact on different services, for example, changes in SLA indicators such as average bandwidth of 2C services and E2E delay of key 2B services in each cell); (5) Impact on customers (acceptable and unacceptable); (6) Continuous iterative optimization

   The architecture consists of the following layers:

   Resource operations layer: This layer, where NEs and single-domain NetGraph form an AD, is responsible for allocating infrastructure resources in real time or near-real time.

   Service operations layer: This layer is responsible for enabling services and assuring experience for users.

TABLE 4.2   Interfaces in the ADN Top-Level Reference Architecture

Interface Type	Description
I interfaces	Interfaces between upper- and lower-layer ADN agents, including the interfaces between customers' ADN applications and the BSS, between the BSS and the ANE (I2 in the figure), between the ANE and the NetGraph (I3 in the figure), and between the NetGraph and NEs. Intent APIs or traditional APIs can be used between ADN agents.
F interfaces	Interfaces provided by a NetGraph to another NetGraph between ADs of the same level (F3 in the figure). F interfaces can reuse I interfaces.
K interfaces	Knowledge interfaces, which are located between the cloud intelligence and ADN agents such as ANE, NetGraph, and intelligent NEs (K2 and K3 in the figure). These interfaces provide knowledge training and update for ADN agents.
S interfaces	Security interfaces, which are located between the SOC, ANE, and NetGraph (S1 and S2 in the figure). These interfaces are optional and provide functions such as centralized user authorization, authentication, and audit, and system security vulnerability management for the ADN.
E interfaces	Human-machine interaction interfaces (E1 and E2 in the figure) provided by the ANE and NetGraph for O&M experts.

Business operations layer: This layer, oriented to business enablement, is responsible for offering management, subscription, charging, and help desk management.

Nearby closed-loop control is required on the service processing latency:

Data processing in NEs (with latency at the millisecond or subsecond level for services such as high-reliability switchover of services and devices and user mobility)

Data processing in a single AD (with latency at the second or minute level for services such as rerouting, service migration, and network-level association analysis)

Network-wide processing (with latency at the hour or day level for services such as capacity planning and site migration)

2. Distributed digital twins

Layered digital twins are one of the foundations for ICT infrastructure to become intelligent. The resource, service, and business operations layers establish their own digital twins based on the layered closed-loop principles to maintain consistency with the physical world.

The digital twins technology has the following characteristics:

- Provides basic, normalized, and atomic data and status services for various ICT infrastructure applications (including R&D design environment applications and onsite service design applications) of the same layer and provides data and status replay capabilities.

- Digitally records the physical world and supports repeated replay. Historical resource, service, and business data carrying time tags and their status change data can be replayed repeatedly. In this way, the training and verification results in the simulation and decision-making processes are closer to the real world.

- In the digital world, training data is manually or intelligently created. Edge scenario data that is difficult or almost impossible to capture in the physical world is manually created to improve the comprehensiveness of simulation and training.

- Data is decoupled from functions. Various ICT infrastructure applications are constructed based on abstract digital twins in order to reduce the complexity of adaptation to differentiated physical worlds. Digital twins and application change points are divided to reduce system complexity. The coupling points between applications are reduced.

- By accessing and operating digital twins in the virtual space, users can indirectly access and operate the ICT infrastructure and services in the physical space, thus hiding the differences between vendors and between software and hardware versions.

Digital twins provide various types of data, including basic data (environment, resource, service, and commercial product data), running data (resource and service status data; fault, performance, and log data; analysis and prediction results; planning, construction, and maintenance data), and business data (charging, subscription, etc.).

3. Distributed knowledge, training, and inference

In the reference architecture, cloud intelligence, cloud-premise synergy, and federated learning cooperate with each other to implement knowledge release, sharing, reasoning, and training.

Cloud intelligence: It provides the release and sharing capabilities of AI models, knowledge, and datasets. Cloud intelligence consists of AI application management, data services, AI training services, knowledge services, and AI collaboration services. ADN cloud intelligence functions as the cross-domain sharing center of knowledge and AI models and the knowledge center of the BSS, OSS, and ADs. It provides distributed AI for cross-domain collaboration and single-domain autonomy.

Cloud-premise synergy: Knowledge and model transfer and collaborated AI capability control solve the problems of computing power, data volume balance, and data silos. AI models are applicable at different network layers and are executed in different heterogeneous environments. AI adapts to different device environments in order to meet requirements in scenarios that have limited resources. AI real-time response is supported to meet low-latency requirements.

Federated learning: Data of all parties is stored locally with network isolation, protecting against privacy disclosure and legal/regulatory violation. In a federated learning system, each participant has the same identity and status (equivalent in the network structure). The modeling effect of federated learning is the same as or similar to that of placing the entire dataset in one place. (Each participant interacts only with a single model, as if it were their own private model.) The participants combine the data to establish a virtual common model that is a system of shared benefits.

4. Lifelong learning and self-evolution

The layered knowledge plane makes ICT infrastructure increasingly intelligent. Given that such infrastructure cannot achieve intelligence all at once, continuous self-learning, self-optimization, and self-evolution are required during the use of this infrastructure to obtain knowledge and cognitive capabilities that are increasingly aligned with the real physical environment and business scenarios. After being screened and confirmed, the new knowledge will be applied to the next step of autonomous closed-loop control, thereby enhancing the intelligence level of the infrastructure, autonomous closed-loop efficiency, and even learning capabilities.

Lifelong learning and evolution: Machines continuously perform self-learning on the environment, status, robot behavior, and results in order to continuously optimize their knowledge and models so that they can quickly adapt to the environment. This learning and evolution should start as soon as the machines are deployed and put into use and continue for the entire lifecycle.

Evolutionary method: Machines perform fast parameter optimization, combinatorial evolution based on functional blocks, and evolution-oriented natural selection for the entire lifecycle.

The ultimate goal of self-learning and self-evolution is to achieve human-like cognition, including: (1) Reliable, causal-based logical reasoning, logical induction, and deduction; (2) Basic cognition capabilities (common sense and value assessment); (3) (Mid- and long-term goal) Advanced cognition, such as feelings, demands, self-awareness, association, and network knowledge refinement (knowledge abstraction).

5. Human-machine collaboration and symbiosis

In 1998, Garry Kasparov held the world's first "Centaur Chess" game, in which the human players collaborated with AI, pairing their decision-making and gameplay skills with the AI's deduction and computing advantages to surpass the capabilities of solo human and solo computer players. This proves that human-machine collaboration can outperform solo humans and solo computers. As an advanced form of human-machine cooperation, human-machine collaboration has the following characteristics:

- The collaboration mode has shifted from human-in-the-loop to human-out-of-the-loop. Machines undertake simple and repeated tasks that were originally undertaken by humans, and humans are responsible for key creative tasks, such as defining system objectives, formulating strategies, planning, designing, and defining and developing new services. With the shift from human operation to human directions, machines become the main body of task execution, and humans affect infrastructure operation through objectives, policies, and takeover. They take over and intervene in machine running only when necessary. Machines must be able to initiate dynamic tasks on demand in order to handle uncertain and unpredictable tasks, such as network congestion and frequent faults. In the future, it is expected that people will be responsible for specifying the intent of the target and strategy, whereas machines will be responsible for breaking down the target and guiding the onsite personnel and machines to perform tasks in collaboration.

- In case of emergency, people can take over and control machines and intervene in critical tasks.

- Humans and machines can interact with and learn from each other.

6. Machine-machine swarm collaboration

Swarm intelligence originates from studying the group behavior of social insects represented by ants and bees and was first used in the description of cellular robotic systems. Swarm intelligence is characterized by distributed control instead of centralized control and can be self-organized. It has the following features:

Improving performance through parallelization: Swarm intelligence systems are ideal for parallelization because group members run based on their own rules and can perform different operations at different locations at the same time.

Task enablement: An agent group can complete some tasks that are difficult or even impossible for a single agent (e.g., mass transport of heavy objects, dynamic objective tracking, collaborative environment monitoring, and large-scale autonomous monitoring).

Scalability: New agents can be incorporated into a group without the need to reprogram the entire group.

Distributed awareness and action: A group of simply interconnected mobile agents deployed in a large search space has greater exploration capabilities and wider awareness scope than a single complex agent.

Stability and fault tolerance: Due to the decentralized and self-organizing attributes of swarm intelligence, the failure of a single agent does not hinder the completion of a given task. If one or more agents fail or exit a task, the group can adapt to changes in population size through implicit task reallocation without any external operation.

Typical swarm intelligence applications in ADN include intelligent collaboration between NEs and between ADs.

Intelligent collaboration between NEs features real-time or near-real-time data processing capabilities and provides intelligent protocols, semantic interfaces, or intent collaboration interfaces to transfer status, semantics, or knowledge between NEs. It also performs multi-system and multi-domain collaboration to complete tasks, such as service provisioning, traffic control, service protection, and disaster recovery collaboration for MBB E2E networking.

Intelligent collaboration between ADs is used for multi-domain and multi-vendor service provisioning, and network-level quality awareness and assurance. After a task is initiated by an AD, the ADs at the same layer collaborate to complete the task. For example, after an E2E XR service provisioning task is initiated from a terminal side, the RAN, bearer network, core network, and cloud cooperate to establish the E2E channel, enabling service provisioning to be completed within 1 second.

7. Intrinsic security

Self-defense: ADN adopts the concept of endogenous security and builds its own defense capabilities. The security technologies involved in this include system security protection, identity authentication and access control, security isolation, data security protection, and AI security technologies.

Self-detection: To ensure system security, NEs and NetGraph have necessary security protection capabilities and can provide a secure running environment. However, because they cannot completely defend against the wide range of attacks they might encounter, security detection technologies must be used to detect attacks in real time, thereby enabling security risks to be identified promptly.

Self-recovery: The goal of autonomous cyber security is self-response and self-closed-loop management of cyber security incidents – this requires the Security Orchestration, Automation and Response (SOAR) system to integrate the security capabilities of different systems or components in a system based on certain logical relationships in order to implement automatic closed-loop handling of a threat event or a type of threat events.

Dynamic trust: Networks are evolving from having borders to being borderless. The outdated border-based defense concept is gradually being replaced by the zero-trust-based network security protection concept, which is gaining industry recognition. The core idea of zero-trust is "continuous verification and never trust," meaning that the peer end, regardless of whether it is a natural person, device, or system, is not trusted by default. Continuous risk assessment must be performed on the peer end, and dynamic policy control must be executed based on the assessment result to ensure the security of the entire network.

4.2 ANE

Similar to self-driving in the automotive industry, which aims to create a third space for humans outside of daily life and work, ADN also strives to continuously improve network automation capabilities. Through such efforts, ADN aims to quickly adapt to various innovative services in the context of connectivity of everything and provide support for CSPs' innovative business scenarios. The network serves as the core and underlying architecture of ADN, whose automation involves considerable challenges but also brings significant value.

The ANE is used to achieve business interconnection of the network and directly monetize the network value for customers. It aims to improve the network operations efficiency and streamline the underlying algorithms from the network to the business impact analysis using the underlying unified language of the business, service, and network. It also aims to build multiple twins of the environment, network, and knowledge to form a bidirectional, real-time, and quantitative mapping model from services to networks. In this way, the ANE transforms resources into capabilities and then into value, and it transforms the support system into a transaction system to quickly meet business and service requirements.

4.2.1 Concepts

A CSP network is classified into the following four layers, listed from top to bottom: user & environment layer, service quality layer, network status layer, and NE & environment layer.

1. **User & environment layer:** refers to the end users of the telecom network and their environment where the users are located, such as residential areas, shopping areas, medical facilities, and industrial campuses. User requirements vary depending on user types, environments, time periods, and locations. This layer aims to resolve the problems of how to divide user environments and areas in a standardized manner, how to accurately identify users and their environments, and how to accurately match user requirements with environments and time periods.

2. **Service quality layer:** reflects network capabilities, which are indicated by network service indicators, such as bandwidth, rate, and latency. These indicators are directly related to video user experience and SLA clauses involving bandwidth, rate, delay, and more. This layer aims to provide deterministic service assurance and high-quality experience for users.

3. **Network status layer:** provides the network status, configuration, management, and control capabilities for the NE & environment layer. This layer aims to handle massive quantities of network alarms in real time, quickly locate root causes, and rectify network faults in real time.

4. **NE & environment layer:** consists of physical and virtual network devices and the environment where the devices are located. This layer is an essential part of the network.

The four layers are connected by three closed loops: user requirement/experience closed loop, service quality closed loop, and network fault closed loop. This makes it possible to manage user requirements in an E2E closed-loop manner. The user requirement/experience closed loop is responsible for mapping user requirements with the network capability of business grids, achieving automatic closed-loop management of user intents. The service quality closed loop is responsible for assuring service quality, such as latency, jitter, and bandwidth, based on deterministic SLAs. The network fault closed loop is responsible for assuring network status, including predicting and rectifying potential risks, automatically detecting and rectifying faults, predicting network performance, and intelligently optimizing network performance. The goal of ANE is to achieve the three closed loops efficiently, as shown in Figure 4.2.

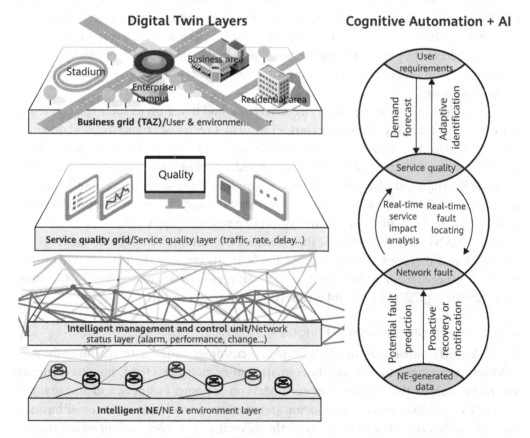

FIGURE 4.2   ADN layers and service closed loops.

To realize the four layers and three closed loops, a series of concepts, including business autonomous zone (BAZ), simulated reality communication networks (SRCON), expected demand not satisfied (EDNS), and hyper-automation, are introduced.

The BAZ is a refined grid of geographical locations in compliance with global standards and can be as small as 1.5 cm. In preparing the BAZ, the CSP carefully considers the running characteristics of network services, such as traffic characteristics, user characteristics, and spatiotemporal characteristics as well as their geographical locations, administrative areas, cities, and communication big data. The ANE can automatically identify residential, shopping, medical, and campus areas and divides them into grids. It then designs and promotes businesses and services for different grids, improving the business value of each area. For example, shopping malls, supermarkets, and residential areas in a central business district (CBD) have different traffic characteristics, and these areas have a compensation relationship. Dividing grids appropriately can improve the resource efficiency and encourage service development. It is an optimal choice in terms of value and feasibility to reasonably and automatically divide BAZs and implement L5 ADN in high-value BAZs.

SRCON simulates network structure and policy optimization based on network-layer mathematical models to solve problems such as difficult awareness of the environment and modeling of complex networks.

EDNS evaluates network reliability for the entire system based on user requirements and defines and evaluates user dissatisfaction about network services based on the service capabilities of the communications network. Based on the average energy not supplied (AENS) model of the power system, it is possible to build system and user service dissatisfaction models in order to model and measure the user network service dissatisfaction in a unified manner.

Hyper-automation, a standard service-driven method that aims to automate everything in an organization, was proposed by Gartner in 2020. Enterprises typically build organization digital twins to evolve from automation to hyper-automation. It is not a new technology but rather a collection of technologies, including robotic process automation (RPA), low-code development platform, and process mining. Hyper-automation can be used to quickly identify, review, and automate as many services and IT processes as possible based on the organization digital twin, achieving service autonomy for CSPs.

With the ANE, CSPs will reshape their business from administrative area- or geographical grid-based divisions to standardized BAZs and transform the network O&M from extensive, generalized, and best-effort to refined, personalized, and deterministic assurance, supporting CSPs' digital and business transformation.

4.2.2 Core Architecture Design Principles

The ANE aims to streamline network O&M and customer business. In designing the ANE architecture, we need to consider how to streamline network O&M, how to accurately match and evaluate the impact of network O&M on customer business, and how to implement E2E closed-loop process automation and continuous evolution of customer business. The ANE architecture must comply with the following principles, each of which requires a series of key technologies.

Principle 1: The relationship between business value and user experience in the network O&M domain must be measurable, and all links from business to network must be streamlined.

Construct E2E standardized TAZs from business to network. Define and evaluate the EDNS to establish an O&M workbench based on the service capability provided by the communication network for users and shift from efficiency-oriented O&M to business value-oriented O&M.

TAZ is a grid-based urban space zoning system oriented to the entire process of telecom services such as wireless network planning, construction, maintenance, optimization, and operations. By analyzing the requirements for the full lifecycle and full spatiotemporal scale of network activities, we can construct the digital grid technology for unified network management based on atomized and multi-level TAZ generation with a unified model (based on layered people flow rules) and zone profile capabilities.

Similar to AENS in the power industry, the EDNS model is constructed based on the distributed system service reliability model to quantify the final impact of network quality on users.

Principle 2: Driven by knowledge and data, the network status, services, and users must be quantitatively associated.

Build a cross-layer cross-domain network status model, construct a projection from network status to service quality, establish a quantitative association model among networks, services, and users, and associate networks with businesses to achieve transformation from network efficiency optimization to user-oriented value creation.

To establish a quantitative association between network status, services, and users, a holographic model regarding networks and services needs to be constructed first. This is necessary to statistically simulate complex network systems, thereby ensuring that the statistical features are the same as those of the real network, the network status can be simulated, and user experience can be predicted. In order to learn the impact of network status on service quality, a cross-layer cross-domain network status model needs to be constructed to build a Bayesian deep learning network based on communications protocols. Furthermore, a continuous knowledge accumulation and optimization model in the telecom domain needs to be constructed to inject complex problem handling knowledge into the knowledge graph foundation model, thus forming telecom knowledge twins.

Principle 3: O&M automation must have self-iteration and self-evolution capabilities.

Build a digital twin organization (DTO) model for telecom network O&M organizations to represent the construction, operations, and development of the organizations, streamline people, services, and processes, and implement self-discovery, self-evaluation, and self-optimizing of automation capabilities. This will enable CSPs' O&M automation to evolve through continuous iteration. As a prerequisite for CSPs' digital transformation and hyper-automation, the DTO model technology builds dynamic software models for organizations, integrates organization operations service models based on operations and context data, and connects to the current status in order to respond to changes, deploy resources, and provide expected customer value. The service simulation verification technology is used to perform service simulation and verification, process mining, and task mining based on the DTO technology.

4.2.3 Target Reference Architecture

4.2.3.1 Overall Architecture

The target reference architecture of the ANE consists of seven parts: business autonomy center, domain knowledge center, digital twin center, network collaboration center, human-machine collaboration center, application development center, and security management center, as shown in Figure 4.3. The seven centers form the business network autonomy closed loop, knowledge management closed loop, and network collaboration closed loop.

1. Business autonomy center

    The business autonomy center undertakes the service intent, such as user experience, of the upper layer, adaptively identifies user experience requirements based on the business grid, and establishes business autonomy objectives in line with cost and efficiency targets.

    Based on the unified business grid analysis from multiple dimensions, such as traffic (including data and voice), user, terminal, revenue, complaint, and coverage, the typical application scenarios are as follows:

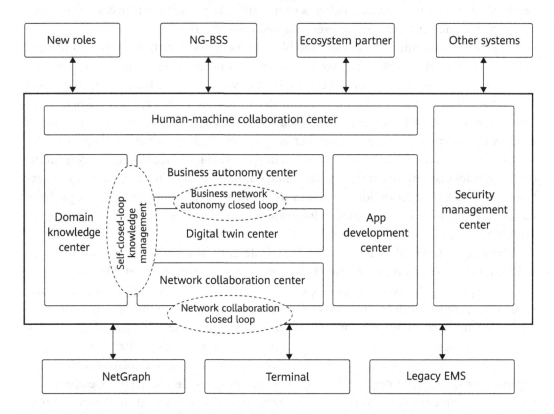

FIGURE 4.3   Target reference architecture of the ANE.

Network health evaluation and optimization: Using information such as site topology locations and Assisted GPS (AGPS) information reported by terminals in massive measurement reports on the network, the ANE can perform high-precision geographic positioning to accurately identify call initiation or problem locations, quickly and accurately evaluate the network performance of each location through grid aggregation, and display network coverage, voice and data traffic, abnormal events, users, and service KQIs in grids. In this way, the network health is comprehensively analyzed, facilitating refined network optimization.

Network coverage optimization: The ANE can quickly identify weak coverage, coverage holes, and overshoot coverage problems in different cells, different frequency bands, and frequencies on the network, further identify in-depth problems, and provide guidance for engineers to perform RF optimization in a timely manner. It can also periodically evaluate network coverage, such as identifying coverage changes after optimization, to avoid incorrect optimization.

User experience optimization: The ANE can accurately identify the specific locations of traffic hotspots and areas where the network rate is low through traffic gridization so that special measures can be taken to ensure customer satisfaction. The ANE can identify any signal quality problems and exceptions during the call and simulate drive tests based on the geographic recording of mobile locations during a call, resolving problems and user complaints in a timely manner.

Fault self-healing: The ANE can quickly perform fault locating based on grid-based management of abnormal events, problem occurrence locations, data drilling from the time dimension, cell access and release information, signaling procedures, and MRs.

Service quality optimization and assurance: The ANE can perform geographical grid representation for the KQIs of different services, such as call latency and buffer times, to identify the location where service quality problems occur. It then analyzes and demarcates the fault based on network coverage and geographic information of abnormal events.

The business autonomy center mainly provides two capabilities. One is to divide the network spatiotemporal environment into grids and assign different business attributes to them (e.g., whether a grid belongs to a business district or a residential area). In this way, business grids are formed. The second capability is to manage business objectives. The business autonomy center works with the traffic autonomy center to set user experience objectives, compare the objectives with the network experience, and set the experience satisfaction indicator as the basis of objective management based on human, machine, and environment factors.

2. Domain knowledge center

Knowledge in the O&M domain can be classified into two types: traditional knowledge for human use, such as cases, rules, and policies, and knowledge for machines, such as models, labels, and features. Knowledge can be O&M experience of various people or the experience learned by machines during machine-based delivery.

The domain knowledge center provides a hybrid knowledge management architecture for single-domain and cross-domain scenarios to build all-domain knowledge repositories such as graphs, AI models, rules, policies, and O&M experience. In this way, the knowledge center can automatically learn knowledge from autonomous decision-making and process operations, perform knowledge collaboration between multi-agent systems, external centralized knowledge centers, and NetGraph, and provide knowledge services for machines and people.

The domain knowledge center provides capabilities such as all-domain knowledge repository, knowledge recycling, knowledge collaboration management, and knowledge service. The all-domain knowledge repository provides various knowledge asset libraries in the domain and uses different storage modes (e.g., graph databases and files) based on knowledge categories. The knowledge recycling function automatically learns knowledge from autonomous decision-making and process operations to implement closed-loop knowledge management. Knowledge collaboration management implements knowledge collaboration between NetGraph and NEs. Knowledge services provide machine-oriented and human-oriented knowledge services.

3. Digital twin center

The ANE aims to streamline the dynamic changes between businesses, services, and networks so that the system can control dynamic network changes and quickly trace network performance. In the ANE, the three major digital twins provided by the digital twin center (e.g., business objective twins, business service twins, and network basic information twins) form a system-level network digital image to help achieve this goal.

The business objective twins divide time and space into grids, identify the business attributes, environment features, and human activity rules of the grids, and aggregate the time and space grids with similar attributes to form the minimum business objective control unit. Through the business objective twins, customers' business intents can be separated into different business objective twin instances based on the characteristics of the objective twins, forming differentiated business requirements.

The quality of services provided by the network can be evaluated subjectively and measured objectively. In addition to these subjective and objective results, L5 ADN also needs to know the network causes of the service results and build a clear relationship between the two. This is necessary for ADN to achieve the closed-loop management of service requirements and network requirements. The business service twins aim to describe and evaluate models based on different business services, network status, and service quality provided by the network, and identify the relationship between them, as shown in Figure 4.4.

The basic network information twins, which consist of single-domain NE information and cross-domain connection information, need to describe devices on the entire network and topological connections between them to form a virtual image of

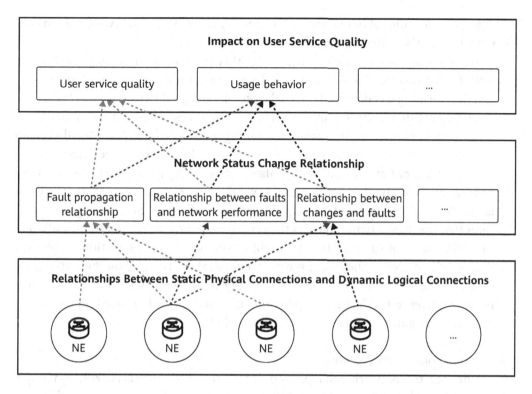

FIGURE 4.4   Mapping between services, network status, and service quality.

the physical network. Based on the image, wireless coverage and network configurations can be simulated to identify the impact of network adjustments.

A twin can be logically divided into three parts: physical entity, twin, and planning twin. A physical entity represents the physical world. A twin mirrors the physical entity in the digital world and unidirectionally maps a physical entity to a twin in real time. The planning twin is a replica of the twin in the digital world. The ANE adjusts the network on the planning twin rather than directly on the twin. By simulating network changes on the planning twin, the ANE allows people to check whether the impact of network changes meets expectations before the changes are delivered to the network without affecting the twin.

The digital twin center performs centralized internal closed-loop management through network and service simulation and iterative optimization before network changes are delivered. By collaborating with NetGraph, the digital twin center applies, provides feedback on, and optimizes network services or configurations to achieve distributed external closed-loop management.

The digital twin center is mainly responsible for all-domain digital twin imaging, digital twin simulation, and digital twin services.

All-domain digital twin imaging involves digital twin modeling for devices, sites, networks, network services, network users, user experience, service quality, network traffic, network energy consumption, and BAZs. Through on-demand and real-time data collection, digital twin imaging ensures physical entities, and twins remain consistent while also reducing the amount of collected data.

Based on all-domain digital twins, digital twin simulation is performed in the ANE for network/service simulation and iterative optimization before change delivery, thus forming a centralized internal closed-loop digital twin network (DTN).

The digital twin service provides services such as system cognition, system diagnosis, system prediction, and decision-making assistance based on the all-domain digital twin. System cognition enables the digital twin not only to describe and display the status of physical entities but also to provide higher-level capabilities: independent analysis and decision-making beyond awareness and computing. The latter is also the goal and trend of intelligent system development. System diagnosis indicates that the digital twin monitors the system in real time and determines whether instability is about to occur (i.e., foresight capability). Status prediction enables the digital twin to predict the future status of a physical entity based on the system running data (i.e., predictability). Decision-making assistance enables the digital twin to provide reference for decision-making during system running based on the results presented, diagnosed, and predicted by the digital twin.

4. Network collaboration center

Through the network collaboration center, the ANE interacts with NetGraph, terminals, and the legacy EMS to collaborate on cross-domain intents and single-domain autonomy.

Internally, the network collaboration center transfers network impact events and network changes to systems such as the digital twin center and business autonomy center. Externally, it exchanges service intents with NetGraph through intent APIs and provides simplified control command interfaces for emergency use. The center also provides the hyper-automation framework capability.

5. Human-machine collaboration center

In essence, ADN is a process in which an intelligent agent (machine) gradually undertakes routine O&M work. As machine capabilities gradually improve, the role of a machine gradually changes from an assistant to an independent manager. Eventually, human-machine collaboration will be common in ADN. How to effectively collaborate, how to help machines gradually become independent and controllable, and how to convert knowledge mainly used by humans into machine-perceivable knowledge are key issues that need to be resolved by the human-machine collaboration center. This center provides a human-machine collaboration interaction interface for process personnel, builds O&M-oriented DTOs, and continuously evaluates and optimizes the human-machine automation level to achieve hyper-automation.

The primary concern of human-machine collaboration is the relationship between humans and computers, from the initial interaction between humans and physical systems, to the interaction between humans and digital systems, and finally to the collaboration between humans and intelligent systems, as shown in Figure 4.5.

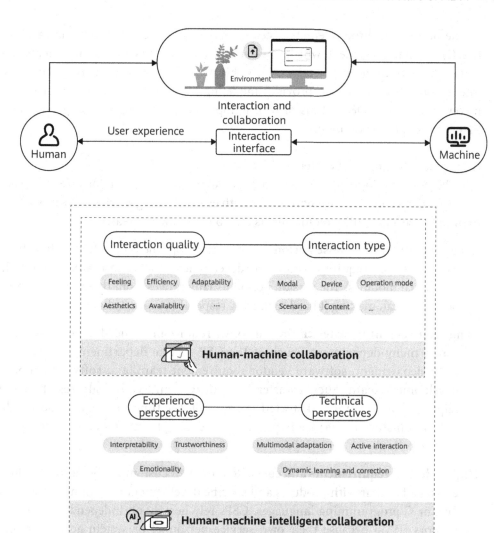

FIGURE 4.5   Collaboration between humans and intelligent systems.

Closed-loop human-machine collaboration promotes the transformation from the traditional automatic closed-loop mode to the hyper-automation closed-loop mode and from the traditional automatic closed-loop optimization mode driven by experts/projects (such as processes and interactions) to the organization-level automatic efficiency evaluation and optimization mode based on organization twins (model-driven). Instead of automatic optimization being limited to process and interaction efficiency evaluation, automation capabilities can be directly associated with service objectives. The capabilities involve automatic implementation based on service intents/objectives (decomposable and evaluable, from traditional coding-based implementation to low-code implementation and finally to codeless implementation) and systematic self-evaluation (automatic efficiency evaluation model) and self-optimizing (objective-driven based on organizational KPI breakdown).

The human-machine interaction center mainly provides the following capabilities: (1) Intent management, which translates business intents into service intents and service-layer translation objectives. (2) O&M ChatOps based on natural language interaction. (3) DTO, which provides modeling of human behavior and processes involved in service O&M, thus providing input for predicting problems and areas that require special attention.

6. Application development center

CSPs used to adopt the suite + customized development mode for OSS construction. In today's competitive environment with ever-changing services, this mode fails to meet the service agility requirements due to the following reasons:

Long requirement response period: Most suites adopt the monolithic architecture. New functions require coordinated development and release among multiple functional modules. The version period usually ranges from three to six months or even a year, making it hard to quickly respond to market changes.

Long requirement transfer chain: Customer requirements need to be transferred across many departments, such as the CSP service department, IT management department, software vendor requirement team, and software supplier development team. Such transfer is inefficient and can easily result in the requirements becoming distorted. As a result, the functions that go online do not fully match the service requirements, leading to rework and affecting the service rollout.

High technical requirements and costs: Requirement customization needs developers to be familiar with products and specific development environments such as Java or C programming languages. CSPs rely heavily on independent software vendors (ISVs) because their own service personnel or system administrators cannot directly develop and optimize services.

As networks become more autonomous and platforms evolve, the role of network O&M personnel will change from traditional network maintenance experts to new roles such as automation experts, data analysts, and AI experts. To meet the requirements of service agility, the service delivery mode will be changed from customized delivery to low-code platform development, and a new service delivery mode of "agile team + asset library + platform" will be built.

The application development center provides low-code development capabilities. It can quickly construct application service capabilities such as processes, GUIs, data, and AI through drag-and-drop and natural language-like operations. Assets in multiple domains can be quickly reused. Based on the customized extension capability of the platform, the application development center can easily cope with complex service characteristics on the live network and quickly customize services. The running state is separated from the development state.

7. Security management center

The security management center provides centralized security policy management for the ANE, including network security, platform security, application security, and data security. Network security management includes security domain division, firewall isolation, remote maintenance security management, and intrusion detection. It also uses secure networking technologies to protect the O&M network. It uses platform security management, including system hardening, security patching, and antivirus protection, to improve the security levels of operating systems (OSs) and databases to provide a secure and reliable platform for service applications. It also offers application security management, including transmission security management, user management, session management, log management, security alarm management, and security monitoring. These security policies apply to specific service applications. And data security management includes providing a privacy protection lifecycle management solution and using technologies and management methods such as minimum collection, anonymization, encryption, and authorization to explore the maximum value of user data while strictly protecting user privacy. Sensitive data protection capabilities are integrated into the security management center, including data isolation, data permission control, encryption and decryption, and key management.

The security management center also provides security protection for network devices, OSs, databases, middleware containers, services, interfaces, and data used by communications and applications throughout the lifecycle. In addition, the center monitors and ensures system maintenance and operation activities through management methods to ensure system security continuity.

4.2.4 Modules and Components

The ANE architecture can be further decomposed into the following modules and components, as shown in Figure 4.6.

1. Human-Machine Collaboration Center

The human-machine collaboration center consists of the intent management and interaction module and the ChatOps module. It provides the following functions:

- **Intent recognition:** This center provides natural language-based interaction and API-based structured description through multiple external interaction channels, such as human-machine interfaces and machine-machine interfaces. Through intent recognition, the system converts the expectations of intent creators of different interfaces into intent models that can be recognized by the system.

- **Intent evaluation:** This center can estimate intent achievements, detect intent conflicts, and evaluate risks. If the intent evaluation function predicts that the intent cannot be achieved, conflicts with the activated intent exist, or the execution of the

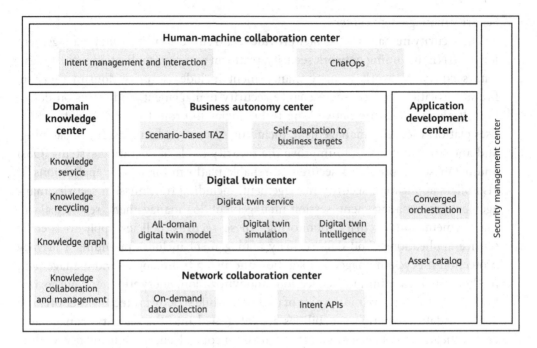

FIGURE 4.6   Modules and components of the ANE.

intent brings major system risks, it reports the failure to the intent creator. Intent evaluation is performed when an intent is created or activated.

- **Intent execution:** Intent execution is a process of continuously monitoring intent fulfillment during the intent lifecycle, including awareness, analysis, decision-making, and execution. Awareness is a process of obtaining the current system data. The data can be obtained through the all-domain digital twin of the system. Analysis is a process of evaluating the current system data based on intent models. System analysis tasks include identifying whether the current system data meets the intent objective, whether the data that does not meet the intent objective meets the intent execution prerequisites, and possible policies after intent decomposition under the current conditions. Decision-making is a process of simulating and evaluating possible execution policies decomposed from intents and selecting the optimal policy. Execution is a process of converting the selected intent execution policy into system configuration changes or network intents.

- **Chat room:** O&M interaction of the ChatOps module is performed in chat rooms, in which users interact with the system using commands or natural language. The system matches commands or performs word segmentation and recognition on natural languages to identify users' intents and then distributes the intents to the corresponding robots for processing. The processing results of the robots are displayed in chat rooms in the form of messages.

- **Robot:** A robot connects various services provided by the system and is presented as a chat object in a chat room. Users interact with robots to invoke system functions and complete system O&M.

2. Business Autonomy Center

The business autonomy center consists of the scenario-based TAZ management module and the adaptive service objective management module. It provides the following functions:

- **TAZ generation service:** The system identifies and divides geographical space based on data such as municipal road network data, combines areas with similar functions to form different types of TAZs (such as residential areas and commercial areas), and encodes TAZs based on the Geographical Coordinates Subdividing Grid with One Dimension Integral Coding on 2n-Tree (GeoSOT) technology. The system identifies the traffic characteristics of these areas, such as the number of users and mobility rules.

- **Scenario-based TAZ:** The TAZ generation service generates basic TAZs, which can be aggregated in different service scenarios to form areas with distinct service features. Service objectives are broken down based on these areas. Scenario-based TAZs provide management functions such as aggregation for these areas.

- **Business objective adaptation:** The system provides a closed-loop control process of breaking down business objectives into scenario TAZs and analyzing, evaluating, executing, and verifying TAZ objectives.

3. Digital Twin Center

The digital twin center consists of the all-domain digital twin model, twin instance simulation module, and digital twin service module. It provides the following functions:

- **All-domain digital twin management:** Digital twin modeling is performed for devices, sites, networks, traffic, users, user experience, network quality, and energy consumption based on the unified digital twin modeling language to form images of people, machines, and environments. Then, the system identifies the relationship between network quality and user experience based on these twins.

- **Digital twin simulation:** Based on the simulation model provided by the service, service policies and solutions are simulated and verified on the all-domain digital twin. Before the policies and solutions are delivered to the network, the effect of the service solution is verified to find the optimal service solution without affecting the running of devices on the live network.

- **Twin system collaboration:** The system provides collaboration with intelligent agents in other systems, for example, twin cities.

- **Twin service:** The system provides services such as system cognition, system diagnosis, system prediction, and decision-making assistance based on the all-domain digital twin. System cognition enables the digital twin to not only describe and display the status of physical entities, but also provide independent analysis and decision-making beyond awareness and computing. System diagnosis indicates that the digital twin monitors the system in real time and determines whether instability is about to occur. Status prediction enables the digital twin to predict the future status of a physical entity based on the system running data. Decision-making assistance enables the digital twin to provide reference for decision-making during system running based on the results presented, diagnosed, and predicted by the digital twin.

4. Domain Knowledge Center

The domain knowledge center consists of the knowledge graph, knowledge recycling, knowledge collaboration, and knowledge service modules. It provides the following functions:

- **Knowledge graph:** provides graph expressions for domain-specific knowledge.

- **Knowledge recycling:** automatically recycles knowledge from autonomous decision-making and process operations to implement closed-loop knowledge management.

- **Knowledge collaboration:** implements knowledge collaboration between NetGraph and NEs.

- **Knowledge service:** provides machine-oriented and human-oriented knowledge services.

5. Network Collaboration Center

The network collaboration center consists of the on-demand data collection module and the network intent API module. It provides the following functions:

- **On-demand data collection:** provides on-demand and real-time data collection capabilities to ensure that twins can be consistent with physical entities at the minimum cost.

- **Network intent API:** interacts with NetGraph and reports network changes to the ANE in a timely manner.

6. Application Development Center

The application development center consists of the converged orchestration module and the asset catalog module. It provides the following functions:

- **Asset catalog:** manages twins and knowledge provided by the system as assets based on unified specifications.

- **Converged orchestration:** provides different orchestration capabilities such as data orchestration, process orchestration, and job orchestration based on assets to support the new operation mode after CSP personnel transformation.

7. Security Management Center

The security management center provides the following functions:

- **Network security:** includes security solutions such as security zone division, firewall isolation, remote maintenance, and intrusion detection. Security networking technologies are used to protect O&M networks.

- **Platform security:** includes system hardening, security patching, and antivirus protection. OS and database security levels are improved to provide a secure and reliable platform for service applications.

- **Application security:** includes policies such as transmission security, user management, session management, log management, security alarm management, and security monitoring. These security policies are applicable to specific services and applications.

- **Data security:** includes providing a privacy protection lifecycle management solution and using technologies and management methods such as minimum collection, anonymization, encryption, and authorization to explore the maximum value of user data while strictly protecting user privacy. The security management center provides sensitive data protection capabilities, including data isolation, data permission control, encryption and decryption, and key management.

4.2.5 Key Characteristics of the Architecture

In this section, we summarize the key architecture characteristics into seven "reshapings," defining the principles of the architecture and deducing the target reference architecture based on those principles.

System reshaping: The O&M system is reshaped based on 3Ps (people, process, and platform) + 2Ts (theory and technology), driving the transformation of organizations, processes, and personnel.

Business reshaping: Network O&M shifts from network-centric to business value-centric. The improvement of network efficiency and performance drives the improvement of service quality and user experience, which in turn helps customers achieve business success.

Process reshaping: Processes and organizations are optimized through modeling and hyper-automation technologies to reduce manual intervention and process waiting time, enabling intelligent process automation.

Theory reshaping: The network reliability evaluation method (reliability theory EDNS), which aims to meet user experience requirements, accurately measures the reliability of the O&M system, objectively reflects various network faults, and performance problems, and user experience of network services, effectively locates problems in each network domain, and significantly improves user experience after problems are resolved.

Knowledge reshaping: In the future, knowledge services should be provided to both humans and machines. Knowledge can be human knowledge (such as expert O&M experience, rules, and policies) and knowledge learned by the system from autonomous decision-making and process operations. Knowledge collaboration can be performed between different twins to improve decision-making intelligence.

Simulation technology reshaping: TAZ modeling refers to the refined grid division of geographical locations based on the running characteristics (traffic, user characteristics, and spatiotemporal characteristics) of network services, geographical locations, administrative areas, and big data of cities and communications. TAZ modeling enables residential, shopping, medical, and campus areas to be automatically identified and divided into grids. SRCON simulation uses anonymized base station channel measurement data and optional digital twin or over-the-top (OTT) services to design models (even complex network ones that are based on machine learning models) and simulates random wireless behaviors of 4G/5G networks to effectively optimize network performance.

The precise TAZ modeling and SRCON technologies automatically identify service characteristics of TAZs and integrate elements such as the environment and users into the simulation process. In this way, the service quality and user experience of the communications network can be accurately simulated, providing decision-making support for automatic network adjustment.

Personnel skill reshaping: The business delivery modes, roles, and skills are changed. The traditional delivery mode in which vendors provide customized functions cannot ensure services are delivered fast enough. A new service delivery mode of "agile team + asset library + platform" is designed to address this issue. In the new delivery mode, vendors provide a service platform that supports low-code development and integrates the network delivery and O&M capabilities and experience accumulated by the vendors as assets. This mode enables network O&M personnel to shift from traditional network maintenance roles to new roles such as automation experts, data analysts, and AI experts.

4.3 NETGRAPH

As the next-generation operation and maintenance center (OMC), NetGraph forms an AD with NEs. Internally, it collaborates with all NEs to manage its AD, and externally, it opens autonomous capabilities on behalf of the AD, reducing the complexity of NEs and networking.

4.3.1 Concepts

NetGraph is a core component that undertakes and presents AD-level autonomous capabilities in an AD. The following describes the concepts involved in the architecture and capabilities of NetGraph.

4.3.1.1 AD

AD is a method of dividing subnets on a telecommunications network. The core feature of an AD is to provide automatic closed-loop management, self-adaptation, and self-learning capabilities for scenarios such as service provisioning, fault rectification, and network optimization in the subnet. The capabilities are presented by subnet and carried by NetGraph on behalf of the subnets. An AD can contain multiple NEs, but each AD has only one NetGraph.

On live networks, ADs are divided based on CSPs' management and control requirements. For example, a telecom network oriented to individual users in a province can be divided into a RAN AD, core network AD, transport AD, and datacom AD, whereas a telecom network oriented to enterprise users can be divided into enterprise-level ADs by enterprise user. Each enterprise-level AD can contain multiple domain-specific services such as RAN, core network, and datacom services.

4.3.1.2 Self-Adaptation

Self-adaptation is classified into the self-adaptation of the network environment and of autonomous targets.

Network environment self-adaptation: In a new network environment, NetGraph can formulate a network adjustment plan based on environment characteristics to meet service requirements for ADs.

For example, in the future, UAVs may become a major means of cross-regional communications and therefore need to provide high-definition and uninterrupted video acquisition and transmission capabilities at any time. To ensure high-bandwidth and low-latency transmission for UAVs that fly across wireless coverage areas, NetGraph needs to cooperate with NEs in order to automatically adjust network resource configurations in wireless, transport, and core networks based on network conditions. As illustrated in this example, self-adaptation is a capability by which the system can automatically allocate and use optimal network resources based on service requirements, without requiring manual planning.

In the future, there might be huge numbers of widely distributed wireless access points, leading to extremely high energy consumption. If an AD could accurately adjust the signal transmission direction and signal strength of wireless access points based on users' precise locations and service requirements, and if they could even start or shut down wireless access devices automatically based on users' entry into and exit from coverage areas, a significant amount of energy could be saved. This is also a self-adaptation capability of the AD.

Autonomy target self-adaptation: When a new requirement is added to an objective that can be met, the network can formulate a network adjustment plan based on the characteristics of the objective, existing knowledge, and knowledge reasoning in order to meet the requirements of the new objective for the AD. For example, in the preset autonomy target of the wireless network, the downlink bandwidth objective or energy consumption objective of the 5G user is met. If both the downlink bandwidth objective and the energy consumption objective must be met, both objectives can be achieved only by upgrading the NE or NetGraph under the existing technical conditions. With objective self-adaptation, the network can automatically formulate a network adjustment plan based on the existing knowledge and data through knowledge reasoning in order to achieve the objectives of uplink and downlink bandwidth guarantee and energy saving.

4.3.1.3 Self-Learning

Self-learning enables NetGraph to automatically perform knowledge mining and reasoning and to obtain a new network adjustment plan in order to meet service requirements in the AD when new network requirements emerge.

For example, for a RAN AD, the original capability objective is to ensure high bandwidth. If the new requirement for low latency needs to be added to the objective of high bandwidth, but there is no knowledge ready in the system to meet this requirement, knowledge mining must be performed to find a new network adjustment plan that can meet both the new and old objectives and store the verified new plan for future use. The process of knowledge mining, verification, and application forms the self-learning mechanism.

4.3.1.4 Quasi-Real-Time Processing

In the management and control field, management and control capabilities are classified into real-time, quasi-real-time, and non-real-time processing based on the processing duration (less than 100 ms for real-time processing, greater than 30s for non-real-time processing, and between these two durations for non-real-time processing). In an AD, NetGraph's management and control processing latency needs to be shortened from minutes to seconds or even subseconds in order to achieve quasi-real-time processing. The specific processing latency is subject to specific AD services. NetGraph's processing duration must meet the requirements for both non-real-time and quasi-real-time processing.

4.3.2 Core Architecture Design Principles

In the traditional network management process, personnel who are responsible for making decisions and performing operations play a critical role. In addition, the architecture involved in this process is designed based on the human-centered closed-loop process. In conventional O&M mode, after a network fault occurs, O&M personnel analyze network data to determine the cause and impact scope of the fault, then plan service recovery schemes based on their knowledge and experience, and finally perform O&M operations and determine whether services recover based on network data. If services do not recover, the O&M personnel repeat this process until services do recover. This is a typical human-centered closed-loop control workflow: data collection > analysis > decision-making > execution > data collection > analysis. The closed-loop control process is triggered by data acquisition.

The conventional network management process also has high requirements for the continual learning capabilities of personnel. When encountering a new problem, humans typically have a human-centered closed-loop learning process: new problem > knowledge learning > knowledge application > knowledge assessment > knowledge optimization > another new problem. The human-centered learning process is triggered by knowledge aging.

As the core component of AD network management and control, NetGraph is designed to replace humans in implementing the preceding closed-loop control and learning processes. The overall architecture design of NetGraph involves achieving data-driven automatic closed-loop control and knowledge-driven automatic closed-loop learning. To ensure that the two closed-loop control capabilities are scalable while also meeting increasing service requirements, they need to be separated from a lightweight framework or platform.

Based on the preceding principles, the NetGraph design principles are as follows:

1. Self-closed-loop control

   Self-closed-loop control means that each phase (data collection, analysis, decision-making, verification, and execution) in the closed-loop control flow can be automatically executed after being orchestrated to achieve the expected objective.

   Self-closed-loop control requires the following key capabilities:

(1) Process self-orchestration

Closed-loop processes are designed to meet the expected objectives. These processes may vary with the objective type and user requirements. For example, simulation and verification are optional in the self-healing process depending on fault types, and the sequence of data collection/analysis and decision-making for the service provisioning process is different from that for the network optimization process.

The self-orchestration capability requires that the data collection, analysis, decision-making, verification, and execution processes and the process interruption conditions be customized. Examples of the interruption conditions include achieving the expected target, requesting manual intervention if the target is not achieved for a long time, and performing manual interruption proactively.

(2) Process self-execution

In addition to manual triggering (e.g., service provisioning), the closed-loop process also needs to support multiple automatic triggering modes, for example, automatic triggering by network status changes (e.g., fault alarms) or network performance deterioration (e.g., service overload).

After being triggered, the closed-loop process is automatically executed based on the orchestrated logic, and the data collection, analysis, decision-making, verification, and execution capabilities are invoked in sequence until the interruption conditions are met.

The self-execution capability requires that multiple closed-loop processes be executed concurrently.

2. Network digital twin

When NetGraph manages and controls the network through self-closed-loop control, it must be able to describe and understand the network in a digital manner. Therefore, network digital twin [2] is required. Network digital twin is a basic principle of the NetGraph architecture.

The network digital twin must have the following key capabilities:

(1) Network information modeling

The network digital twin requires precise modeling of device and service information on the network, such as geometric shapes, physical features, service attributes, service status, and connections of devices. This is necessary for mapping physical networks to virtual digital networks. All NetGraph services perceive network behavior based on network digital twin information models.

(2) Network behavior modeling

The network digital twin also requires precise behavior modeling for device behaviors on the network (e.g., output of devices for different data inputs, feedbacks or status changes for different device operations). This is necessary for mapping physical network behaviors to virtual digital network behaviors. All NetGraph services perceive network behavior based on network digital twin behavior models.

A virtual digital network consists of network multiple levels and types of digital twins, including device-level, network-level, service-level, and connection-level digital twins.

In the initial phase, NetGraph directly operates the physical network. Changes on the physical network need to be synchronized to the virtual digital network in real time or quasi-real time. In the target architecture, NetGraph only needs to operate the virtual digital network, which takes over the physical network control capability and synchronously operates the physical network in real time or quasi-real time.

In self-closed-loop control, data acquisition and analysis are performed based on virtual digital network information, and network operations are performed based on virtual digital network behaviors.

3. Knowledge-driven design

Knowledge-driven design means that NetGraph software reads and analyzes knowledge from documents, human knowledge, and code to implement original service capabilities. In NetGraph, knowledge is presented in a digital form.

In the knowledge-driven system architecture, new knowledge is injected into NetGraph to improve/change the business logic of data collection, analysis, decision-making, simulation, and execution in software.

New knowledge can be injected by experienced O&M experts or obtained through machine learning [3]. Knowledge-driven design is an inevitable way to realize self-adaptation and self-learning of NetGraph.

4. Self-closed-loop knowledge management

In the knowledge-driven system architecture, the processing capability can be improved by adding or optimizing knowledge. In addition to adding/optimizing knowledge through humans, our goal is to enable the NetGraph system to automatically add/optimize knowledge, achieving self-closed-loop knowledge management.

There are several ways to achieve this goal.

First, each service must evaluate the effect of using the knowledge [4]. For example, NetGraph can dynamically evaluate the quality of knowledge. When a service uses knowledge for a second time, NetGraph allows the service to select the best knowledge in order to form a closed loop of knowledge usage, evaluation, reuse, and re-evaluation.

Second, if the quality of knowledge in a new environment is low, or if no knowledge is available for the new target [5], a closed loop of knowledge mining, knowledge verification, knowledge use, evaluation, and re-mining is formed.

The knowledge injected manually determines the lower limit of the knowledge-driven capability. The knowledge optimized/newly generated through self-closed-loop knowledge management determines the upper limit of the knowledge-driven capability.

5. Quasi-real-time processing

In certain scenarios where autonomous services are deployed, automatic closed-loop management needs to be completed quickly. For example, the key video conference service or the XR service requires fault analysis, recovery policy decision-making, and policy execution to be completed within seconds in an E2E manner when a fault occurs. Therefore, the following capabilities need to be considered in the overall architecture design:

- **Subsecond-level collection:** High-frequency data collection can be started as required, and data precision and collection costs are balanced [6].

- **Subsecond-level awareness:** The network status can be perceived based on the requirements on service objectives and results, and the subsecond-level analysis and second-level prediction capabilities are available.

- **Subsecond-level decision-making:** High-performance knowledge retrieval, knowledge pre-discovery, pre-reasoning, and preparation can be used to improve decision-making efficiency.

- **Subsecond-level execution:** The interfaces between the network and NEs are simplified, and the number of interactions can be reduced through intent APIs.

6. Flexible cross-domain assembly

In the future, ADs can be used in 2C or 2B scenarios. In 2C scenarios, ADs can be constructed based on service types, such as wireless ADs and optical transmission ADs. In 2B scenarios, cross-domain ADs can be constructed based on users, such as enterprise-level ADs across the wireless network, datacom, optical transmission, and core network.

The network must therefore be able to flexibly combine different service domains on demand. Based on the basic platform/framework, new service capabilities must be provided by adding applications and plug-ins.

7. Self-closed-loop trustworthiness

After people are separated from closed-loop control and closed-loop knowledge management, the trust in people will become a requirement for machine trustworthiness. For machine trustworthiness, the closed-loop process must be trustworthy. Specifically, the closed-loop control process and the closed-loop knowledge process must be explainable and traceable and knowledge verification and evaluation capabilities must be provided.

8. Continuous online simulation

After machines take over responsibility for decision-making, a key capability requirement is determining how to achieve the target after the decision-making plan is executed without introducing new problems. For this, we introduce continuous online simulation capabilities into the architecture.

Continuous online simulation can isolate the verification environment from the virtual digital network to verify the new plans. Only the plan that passes the verification can be implemented on the physical network. Continuous online simulation is a capability that cannot be provided by the solution on the live network. It is verified in an isolated virtual digital environment, and simulation and innovation verification are performed based on the most current data on the live network. It supports pre-evaluation of objective achievement, verification of newly mined knowledge, commissioning before being released, and creation of new upgrade/evolution modes.

4.3.3 Target Reference Architecture

4.3.3.1 Overall Architecture

Based on the preceding architecture design principles, the NetGraph target reference architecture is divided into the system level and module level. The system consists of multiple modules, between which capability invoking and information transfer are performed, as shown in Figure 4.7. In this figure, arrows between modules indicate capability-invoking relationships.

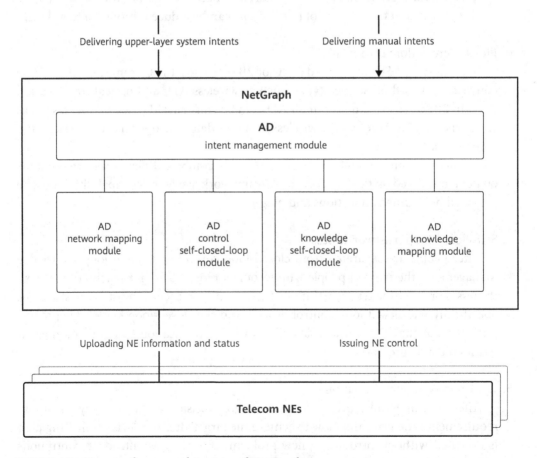

FIGURE 4.7 Target reference architecture of NetGraph.

NetGraph can be divided into the following logical modules: AD intent management module, AD network mapping module, AD self-closed-loop control module, AD self-closed-loop knowledge management module, and AD knowledge mapping module.

1. AD intent management module

   As an important component that provides NetGraph's autonomous capabilities externally, the AD intent management module converts external service intent requests into objectives and closed-loop processing flows [7] that can be identified and processed by machines, based on network information and knowledge. The module then delivers the objectives and processing flows to the self-closed-loop control module, which completes data collection, awareness, decision-making, simulation, and execution based on the closed-loop processing flows. The self-closed-loop control module also provides the final objective achievement results to the intent management module, which then converts these results into the intent achievement results.

2. AD network mapping module

   The AD network mapping module represents the physical network and functions as its proxy. Other NetGraph function modules access this module to obtain required network information or operate the network without the need to directly interact with the physical network.

   The AD network mapping module uses the digital twin technology to describe network status information and behavior. It performs digital twin modeling for multi-layer and multi-type network objects and constructs a virtual digital network in the NetGraph system based on the network digital twin [8]. The virtual digital network enables functions in NetGraph to perceive the physical network. The virtual digital network changes synchronously with the physical network – when each function operates the virtual digital network, the real physical network is also operated. The network mapping module based on the digital twin technology enables NetGraph to understand the physical network [9] and provides a prerequisite for implementing telecom network autonomy.

3. AD self-closed-loop control module

   The AD self-closed-loop control module receives the objectives and closed-loop processes delivered by the AD intent management module and automatically performs closed-loop actions. In this process, in addition to using network information and knowledge, the control module provides feedback on the knowledge usage result to the self-closed-loop knowledge management module.

   The AD self-closed-loop control module requires the closed-loop process running capability that complies with the MAPE-K model so that NetGraph can run continuously based on the objectives until they are reached. In this way, iterative self-healing and self-optimizing are achieved.

   The AD self-closed-loop control module is different from the conventional autonomy capability. In the conventional automation capability, after a policy or plan is triggered at a time, humans need to manually determine whether the execution result meets the objective. If the objective is not achieved, humans then need to manually adjust the policy or plan before executing it. After being triggered by the intent management module in one-off mode, the self-closed-loop control module automatically checks and determines whether the objective is achieved. If the objective is not achieved, the control module automatically searches for a new execution plan based on the network information and knowledge and then executes the plan again. In this way, multiple iterations are performed until the objective is achieved. By default, no manual intervention is required in the automatic control process, unless the steps and conditions that require human intervention are defined when the intent management function orchestrates the closed-loop control process.

4. AD self-closed-loop knowledge management module

The AD self-closed-loop knowledge management module evaluates the confidence and aging of knowledge based on the knowledge usage feedback provided by the self-closed-loop control module and initiates knowledge mining, reasoning, verification, and clearance. After receiving the knowledge usage feedback delivered by the self-closed-loop control module, the self-closed-loop knowledge management module modifies and adjusts the knowledge quality or explores new knowledge based on the feedback. This enables the self-closed-loop control module to filter more valuable knowledge retrieved from the knowledge mapping module for business processing next time. The collaboration between the self-closed-loop control module and the self-closed-loop knowledge management module enables ASs to become more and more intelligent [10].

The AD self-closed-loop knowledge management module represents NetGraph's self-adaptation and self-learning capabilities. Whether the self-closed-loop knowledge management module is provided and whether collaboration is formed between it and the self-closed-loop control module are critical criteria for determining whether NetGraph has self-adaptation and self-learning capabilities.

5. AD knowledge mapping module

In the future architecture, continuous knowledge growth and optimization must be considered. However, in the existing knowledge governance system, knowledge is statical (such as some models or manuals) or directly carried in code. The existing architecture cannot meet the requirements of online automatic growth and optimization of knowledge. Therefore, it is inevitable to separate knowledge from code, models, and manuals to form digital knowledge.

In the NetGraph architecture, a dedicated knowledge mapping module is required to digitally store and retrieve knowledge required for AD management and control. Knowledge required by other functions (intent management, network mapping, self-closed-loop control, and self-closed-loop knowledge management) in NetGraph is obtained from the knowledge mapping module.

4.3.3.2 Key Functions

This section describes the architecture functions: self-provisioning, fault self-healing, network self-optimizing, and autonomous evolution.

1. Self-provisioning

   Service provisioning involves two phases: network construction and service provisioning.

   Through plug-and-play, automatic provisioning enables network services to be immediately available during network construction. After receiving network construction requirements, NetGraph automatically plans operations required for network construction (e.g., network resource and NE configuration operations) based on network construction objectives. After detecting that the hardware is powered on, NetGraph automatically allocates resources, loads software, configures data, and checks basic network capabilities based on the planned resource operations and NE configuration operations. In this process, the network construction intent needs to be manually input, and the hardware installation personnel need to install and power on the hardware, thereby implementing plug-and-play.

   The automatic service provisioning mode also changes considerably, breaking the barrier between service domains and CSPs. Service provisioning requests can come from the OSS/BSS or be initiated by a neighboring AD, forming a new agile service provisioning mode across service domains and between CSPs. The mode achieves E2E automatic service provisioning without being impeded by the complex cross-domain and cross-CSP collaboration process required in the traditional process.

   The automatic service provisioning process has the following changes after NetGraph receives the service provisioning requirements:

   - The manual planning process is eliminated. The network automatically plans operations (i.e., network resource and NE configuration operations) required for service provisioning based on service objectives.

   - Manual verification on the test bed is eliminated. NetGraph automatically performs simulation and verification on the results of network resource and NE configuration operations based on digital network information.

   - Manual dialing tests are eliminated. After network resource operations and NE configuration operations are automatically performed, the network automatically monitors and detects service provisioning results to ensure that service provisioning objectives are achieved.

   Due to the preceding changes, no manual operation is required during service provisioning, and the provisioning efficiency of various services can be improved to seconds. User requirements for on-demand service provisioning can be met, ensuring that telecom services can be obtained at any time.

2. Fault self-healing

Fault self-healing enables the network to continuously detect and predict faults based on network information in order to meet specified network/service SLA requirements. When predicting that a fault is about to occur, the network adjusts network resources or NE configurations for fault avoidance, preventing service loss. When detecting that a fault has occurred, the network adjusts network resources or NE configurations to restore services as soon as possible.

In future XR services, long-lasting SLA quality deterioration is unacceptable for users. In experience-oriented scenarios such as holographic communication, video conferencing, and gaming, service recovery within seconds is expected to be a rigid demand.

To continuously meet the preceding SLA assurance requirements, O&M personnel will act as observers and be responsible for emergency handling during routine assurance.

The automatic assurance process will have the following changes:

(1) The SLA assurance process of a service is automatically triggered after the service is provisioned, the need to manually specify the SLA assurance objectives.

(2) The trouble ticket handling process driven by manual alarm handling is eliminated. For service SLAs that require recovery within seconds, the data collection frequency will evolve from the minute or second level to the subsecond level, the exception identification capability will evolve from the minute level to the second level, and the efficiency will be improved from the minute level to the second level.

(3) The manual fault demarcation and locating process are eliminated. NetGraph automatically simulates the root cause of a fault based on digital network information.

(4) Manual planning of restoration operations is eliminated. NetGraph automatically plans operations (i.e., network resource and NE configuration operations) required for service restoration based on the objective SLA and current exceptions.

(5) Manual verification on the test bed is eliminated. NetGraph automatically performs simulation and verification on the results of network resource and NE configuration operations.

(6) Manual dialing tests are eliminated. After network resource operations and NE configuration operations are automatically performed, NetGraph automatically monitors and detects service provisioning results to ensure that service recovery objectives are achieved.

(7) Attendance of O&M personnel is eliminated. NetGraph automatically restores services until the services are successfully restored.

The preceding changes eliminate the need for any manual operation during service restoration and improve the SLA restoration efficiency to within seconds. This ensures that the quality of telecom services can be committed in the real sense.

3. Network self-optimizing

Network self-optimizing enables NetGraph to continuously adjust network resources or NE configurations based on specified network or service SLA optimization requirements. Self-optimizing is a continuous iteration process in which, even if the optimization objective is achieved, SLA monitoring needs to be continuously performed to prevent the performance from deteriorating. If the performance deviates from the objective, optimization is automatically performed again.

In the complex network and service environment in the future, the network must meet the SLA requirements, security, and energy consumption requirements. Continuing to use the existing manual optimization mode will involve a huge workload. In addition, the human-controlled optimization process takes too long, and the optimization result cannot match the ever-changing network and service conditions.

To efficiently and continuously meet network optimization requirements, network optimization personnel will act as observers and take ultimate responsibility for emergency handling during routine network optimization.

The automatic optimization process will have the following changes:

- The data preparation process is eliminated. Analysis and planning activities are directly carried out based on digital network information, shortening the data preparation duration from days to seconds.

- The manual planning process is eliminated. Network optimization personnel only need to specify optimization objectives, and NetGraph can automatically plan operations (i.e., network resource and NE configuration operations) required for service optimization.

- Manual verification is eliminated. NetGraph automatically performs simulation and verification on the results of network resource and NE configuration operations.

- The manual configuration process is eliminated. NetGraph automatically performs network resource operations and NE configuration operations.

- Manual attendance is eliminated. NetGraph automatically optimizes services until the services are successfully optimized.

    Given the preceding changes, only optimization objectives need to be manually specified during network optimization. No manual operation is required to achieve objectives. Network optimization changes from weekly manual tasks to continuous monitoring and optimization tasks that can be performed at any time.

4. Network autonomy

In the complex network and service environment in the future, different types of networks will gradually have different preferences for network and service management and control due to fast services evolution and network changes. Therefore, vendors' delivery capabilities must quickly adapt to the changes and preferences in order to accommodate networks and services. At present, some CSPs want to provide

DevOps capabilities for software in order to improve the requirement response efficiency. However, limitations in the inherent device development, network entry test, and rollout processes make it difficult to release telecom network services in agile mode.

To solve this problem, automatic knowledge update is required. In essence, the software converts knowledge into system capabilities. The improvement of software capabilities involves converting new knowledge into new software code. Therefore, as long as volatile knowledge is separated from software code, software capabilities can be improved by updating knowledge.

Network autonomy enables knowledge related to AD management and control to be preset into NetGraph. As NetGraph performs self-fulfilling, self-healing, and self-optimizing, it continuously uses knowledge and evaluates the effect of such usage. According to the evaluation result, if the priority of knowledge needs to be adjusted, NetGraph can automatically adjust the priority of knowledge in order to achieve knowledge update. If knowledge needs to be supplemented, NetGraph can automatically mine new knowledge based on knowledge and information.

The network autonomy process has the following changes:

- Knowledge is digitally described and stored as a key asset, and it is delivered with NetGraph.

- The priority of knowledge delivered with NetGraph can be changed dynamically and continuously adjusted based on the results.

- New knowledge is automatically added to NetGraph.

Thanks to the preceding changes, NetGraph capability improvement evolves from a human-dependent software upgrade process to a continuous automatic knowledge update process.

4.3.4 Modules and Components

1. AD Intent Management Module

The AD intent management module provides the following capabilities:

- **Objective conversion capability:** Based on network information and knowledge, the AD intent management module converts external intents into one or more objectives that need to be achieved by the self-closed-loop control module, for example, awareness, decision-making, and simulation objectives. The conversion process also ensures the integrity and accuracy of objective description specifications and constraints.

- **Intent conflict detection capability:** NetGraph needs to accept and maintain multiple intents, but conflicts may exist between them. For example, the energy-saving intent usually conflicts with the SLA in the case of heavy traffic. The intent subsystem needs to perform preliminary intent conflict judgment and conflict pre-mitigation based on knowledge and network information.

- **Closed-loop process orchestration capability:** The closed-loop process may vary according to service intents. For example, in a self-optimizing intent, NetGraph needs to collect and sense the completed network analysis and then makes decisions based on the discovered problems. However, in an automatic service provisioning intent, NetGraph needs to make decision on service provisioning and then schedules the collection and awareness capabilities to check whether the service provisioning is successful. In the self-healing process, for example, some intents need to be automatically executed, and some intents need to be manually confirmed. These processes need to be orchestrated by the intent subsystem based on different knowledge and actual network status.

In most cases, the preceding objective conversion, conflict detection, and process orchestration capabilities are implemented based on network information and knowledge. In actual implementation, the technical requirements of the preceding capabilities may vary significantly according to services and domains. Therefore, the AD intent management module allows flexible installation and uninstallation of domain intent applications for various services and domains.

2. AD Network Mapping Module

The AD network mapping module provides the following capabilities:

(1) Digital information presentation capability

The digital information presentation capability enables various types of information in telecom networks [11] – including device information, device status, connection information, connection status, session information, and session status – to be digitally presented. This capability has the following requirements: (1) Information models need to be constructed for various information on the telecom network. Then, the AD network mapping module collects data from the physical network based on the description of information models, extracts, filters, aggregates, and converts the data to form digital network information, and stores the digital network information. (2) When an information model has different requirements on the scope and timeliness of data to be collected, the AD network mapping module can control the data collection scope and period as required to display digital network information in real time or quasi-real time. Compared with the existing network management system, the NetGraph architecture has cross-domain requirements on data collection efficiency and reliability due to quasi-real-time requirements. A large amount of data needs to be collected within seconds or even subseconds.

To avoid the heavy consumption of resources due to the unlimited large-scale data collection, the scope and frequency of data collection are closely related to the objective of NetGraph. Cost-efficient and reliable collection of valuable data is required.

To achieve cost-efficient and reliable collection, optimization and improvement can be performed from the perspectives of protocol layers, including the low-layer transmission protocol, application-layer protocol, data encoding, data model, and collection mechanism. Overall, the data collection efficiency can be effectively improved in terms of protocols, encoding, and collection mechanisms.

It is recommended that knowledge be used to describe collection policies so that collection capabilities can be updated through knowledge updates in the future. For the collection policies that cannot be described by knowledge, the collection can be implemented by using the code developed by domain.

(2) Digital behavior simulation capability

The digital behavior simulation capability presents the relationships between the behaviors and results of devices, services, and sessions on telecom networks. This capability requires that behavior models be constructed based on network behaviors and corresponding response results. It makes it possible for the AD network mapping module to simulate the entire network results that may be caused by behavior changes at any point on the network based on behavior models.

The simulation capability can be used in various scenarios. For example, it can be used in the service provisioning scenario after decision-making is completed to perform service dialing tests in order to ensure service connectivity. It can also be used in the fault analysis scenario to review the fault injection results in order to locate the root cause of the fault as soon as possible. In the network optimization scenario, optimization objectives can be gradually approached through iteration between decision-making and simulation.

The preceding simulation scenarios require online real-time simulation, which necessitates various behavior characteristics (such as discrete event simulation and continuity simulation), service characteristics (such as traffic simulation and signaling simulation), and user characteristics (such as single-user connection and multi-user concurrency). Simulation also involves a variety of NE types and networking modes. Therefore, the core of the simulation capability is to build a powerful simulation running environment and a rich simulation model library.

(3) Physical network agent execution capability

The physical network agent execution capability refers to real-time interaction with the physical network through the southbound interface. This capability requires NetGraph to manage various connections between itself and NEs and deliver control commands.

The AD network mapping module needs to open the information presentation capability and behavior simulation capability to other functional modules so that other functional modules can carry out service activities such as service prediction, fault analysis, and optimization verification based on digital information and behavior.

The AD network mapping module provides the basis of all automation and intelligent capabilities of NetGraph. The module ensures the integrity, consistency, and timeliness of digital information and enables NetGraph to provide accurate and effective awareness and analysis capabilities for ADs. In addition, it ensures the integrity and accuracy of network behavior and corresponding result information, and helps NetGraph accurately and effectively perform automatic decision-making and evolution for ADs.

3. AD Self-Closed-Loop Control Module

After referring to and extending the MAPE-K model, NetGraph divides the entire AD self-closed-loop control process into four steps: awareness, decision-making, execution, and backtracking.

(1) Awareness

This step is responsible for automatically detecting the status of the objective based on the objective requirements so that exceptions can be predicted or promptly detected. Exception awareness is used to quickly and accurately detect existing exceptions and their causes, and trend prediction is used to discover exceptions and identify their causes in advance.

The requirement for awareness in the self-closed-loop control process has evolved beyond the traditional network management capability. First, the exception determination principles are changed. For example, the current network management system relies heavily on NE alarms or log analysis to detect faults, whereas the awareness capability enables NetGraph to determine whether an exception occurs based on whether it affects or may affect the achievement of objectives. In this process, traditional data such as alarms, indicators, logs, and CDRs cannot meet the requirements. Therefore, the preceding data needs to be integrated based on the objective. Second, the timeliness of exception determination is changed. In some strict scenarios, exception determination based on the preceding data must be completed within seconds or even subseconds, meaning that some awareness capabilities may need to be reconstructed on NEs.

It is recommended that knowledge be used to describe the logic and algorithm of awareness so that the awareness capability can be updated through knowledge updates in the future. Awareness logic that is temporarily difficult to describe through knowledge can be implemented through domain control applications.

After an exception is detected or predicted, it needs to be converted into a decision-making objective and submitted to the decision-making step, which determines the actions to be taken based on the objective.

(2) Decision-making

The decision-making step is responsible for translating the objective into executable network operations based on the network situation and using knowledge. This step is a key function that embodies the core autonomous capability in NetGraph and is one of the most complex steps.

The decision-making step can be further split into two phases: solution and simulation. As shown in Figure 4.8, in the decision-making step, the behavior plan to be executed on the network is obtained based on the objective, and then the behavior simulation capability of the network mapping module is invoked to inject the behavior plan into the network mapping function.

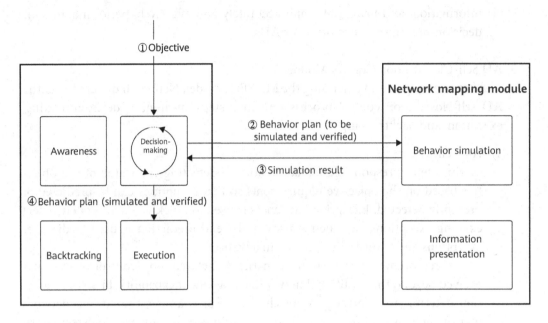

FIGURE 4.8   Iterative decision-making.

The network mapping function responds based on the behavior-result mappings defined in the behavior model and then sends the response result to the decision-making module. After obtaining the response result, this module determines whether the decision-making plan can achieve the decision-making objective. If the decision-making objective cannot be achieved, the decision-making module makes decisions again. Repeated iterations involving decision-making, simulation, and new decision-making form a small closed loop of automatic decision-making and simulation verification. This helps the decision-making module gradually approach the optimal decision-making plan without affecting the network.

Based on the objective type, the decision-making module can be divided into decision-making under deterministic objectives and decision-making under non-deterministic objectives.

Deterministic objectives generally refer to those that can be directly covered by existing knowledge in the system. The decision-making process under deterministic objectives directly translates the objectives into executable NE operations based on knowledge and network information. In such cases, the operation results will achieve the objectives.

Non-deterministic objectives generally refer to those that cannot be directly covered by existing knowledge in the system. In addition to using existing knowledge and network information, this type of decision-making process needs to collaborate with the knowledge mapping module and self-closed-loop knowledge management module in order to mine and verify knowledge, and then use new knowledge to translate objective requirements into executable NE operations. In this case, the translated NE operations may not achieve the objectives, meaning that the process of data mining, verification, and execution may need to be repeated. This process takes significantly longer than the decision-making process under deterministic objectives.

The decision-making module can perform single-objective decision-making and multi-objective decision-making.

Single-objective decision-making generally has a decision-making result that contains optimal achievements of one objective. Such decision-making may cause other objective results to deteriorate. Single-objective decision-making is typically applicable in scenarios where the objective is unique or the objective with the highest priority needs to be preferentially guaranteed. For example, in the case of a major disaster, if the only objective is to deliver the optimal call completion rate, any decision-making related to the call completion rate belongs to single-objective decision-making.

Multi-objective decision-making generally refers to the decision-making process in which the requirements of multiple objectives need to be met at the same time and the overall optimal result needs to be achieved. For example, in a business district, multi-objective decision-making is required to achieve a balance between the call completion rate and energy-saving requirements. Because multiple objectives are involved in decision-making at the same time, objective conflict detection and resolution are important during decision-making to avoid mutual impact.

The decision-making module should use knowledge to describe the decision-making logic so that such logic can be updated through knowledge updates in the future.

(3) Execution

The execution step is responsible for executing the plan prepared after decision-making. The execution actions are performed through interaction with the network mapping module. Interconnection with NEs is not required, and there is no need for the execution subsystem to provide sophisticated intelligent capabilities. It is mainly responsible for the automatic execution of a single command or commands in batches.

The execution function needs to allow humans to take over the execution process in emergencies and authorize key commands during the execution.

(4) Backtracking

The self-closed-loop control backtracking capability is important for the AD self-closed-loop control module. If self-closed-loop control fails, manual backtracking on the closed-loop control process is required. By reviewing self-closed-loop control step by step, humans can check the failure point and identify the failure cause. Due to security and trustworthiness reasons, humans need to audit the self-closed loop control process. The audit process also needs to demonstrate the information required in self-closed-loop control through backtracking.

4. AD Self-Closed-Loop Knowledge Management Module

Similar to the closed-loop process of the MAPE-K model, the self-closed-loop knowledge management process consists of the evaluation, mining, verification, consolidation, and backtracking steps.

(1) Evaluation

In this step, the self-closed-loop knowledge management module evaluates knowledge quality based on the knowledge usage feedback of the self-closed-loop control module [12] and then injects the evaluation results into the knowledge mapping module. Knowledge evaluation is performed to proactively detect knowledge quality so that new knowledge can be promptly reasoned and mined. In addition, knowledge in the knowledge mapping module can be updated in a timely manner so that other modules can effectively select knowledge based on its quality when retrieving it through the knowledge mapping module.

Self-closed-loop knowledge management requires knowledge evaluation steps to be accurate and complete. Knowledge evaluation can be performed based on the number of use times, number of valid use times, time period, user, and use objective. In this process, continuous and effective modeling is required.

(2) Mining

In the mining step, knowledge mining is proactively initiated based on the knowledge evaluation result, or knowledge control is proactively detected based on the self-closed-loop control request. In essence, knowledge mining involves generating new knowledge using AI technologies. It can be classified into three modes: data > knowledge, knowledge > knowledge, and data+knowledge > knowledge.

- Data > knowledge mode

    In this mode, machine learning is used to identify data rules based on network information and related data so that possible knowledge can be identified. For example, assume that machine learning results indicate a large probability that two types of alarms are reported in associated mode. In this case, the association between the two types of alarms is regarded as a new knowledge item.

- Knowledge > knowledge mode

    In this mode, the hidden association between two pieces of knowledge is identified through knowledge reasoning based on the existing knowledge in NetGraph. For example, if a multi-hop relationship chain is found between a hardware fault and a feature service fault through knowledge reasoning, the relationship chain associates the two faults, producing a new knowledge item.

- Data+knowledge > knowledge mode

    This mode combines the advantages of the preceding two modes and uses both statistics-based machine learning and knowledge graph-based knowledge reasoning to discover more obscure and valuable new knowledge.

(3) Verification

In this step, the mined knowledge is automatically verified. Because new knowledge can be used only after it is properly verified, verification is an indispensable step in closed-loop knowledge management.

There are a variety of verification methods. In terms of verification objectives, there are verification methods and falsification methods, and in terms of verification methods, there are verification methods based on knowledge, or on the simulation function of the network mapping function, or manual judgment.

(4) Consolidation

In this step, the new verified knowledge is injected into the knowledge mapping module. This allows the new knowledge to enter the self-closed-loop control process, thereby achieving the knowledge output from the self-closed-loop knowledge management to self-closed-loop control.

(5) Backtracking

Similar to the self-closed-loop control process, the self-closed-loop knowledge management process also requires self-closed-loop backtracking. If self-closed-loop knowledge management fails, manual backtracking on the self-closed-loop knowledge management process is required. By reviewing self-closed-loop knowledge management step by step, humans can check the failure point and identify the failure cause. Due to security and trustworthiness reasons, humans need to audit the self-closed-loop knowledge management process. The audit process also needs to be backtracked in order to demonstrate the information required in self-closed-loop knowledge management.

5. AD Knowledge Mapping Module

In the knowledge mapping module, knowledge can be preset during system installation, injected from external systems during system running, or mined through machine learning and machine reasoning during system running. The knowledge rights must be strictly controlled. Except for the knowledge mapping module and self-closed-loop knowledge management module, other modules should have only the read permission on knowledge.

The complexity of the knowledge mapping module depends on the complexity of knowledge, which is subject to its expression characteristics. For example, knowledge can be classified into: (1) structured knowledge and unstructured knowledge from the perspective of structural features; (2) procedural knowledge and declarative knowledge from the perspective of logical features; (3) explicit knowledge and tacit knowledge from the perspective of knowledge availability; (4) telecom network knowledge and human and environment knowledge from the perspective of knowledge scope; (5) mathematically explainable knowledge and difficult-to-explain knowledge accumulated based on statistics and expert experience from the perspective of explainability; and (6) scientific knowledge and knowledge created by humans in different scenarios and environments from the perspective of the effective scope of knowledge. The relationship between knowledge varies depending on scenarios and environments.

Considering the breadth and depth of knowledge, it is continuously built by people with different roles, backgrounds, and capabilities. Therefore, during knowledge construction and update, we must consider how to ensure the accuracy and consistency of knowledge in the knowledge mapping module through technical means.

The knowledge mapping module should support multiple technical means to construct knowledge representation, convergence, storage, retrieval, reasoning, and mining capabilities based on different knowledge classification features.

4.3.5 Key Characteristics of the Architecture

To summary, we define the principles of the architecture and then deduce the target reference architecture based on those principles. The key architecture characteristics of NetGraph include humans outside the loop, self-adaptation, self-learning, and machine trustworthiness.

4.3.5.1 Humans Outside the Loop: Self-Closed-Loop Control Based on Intent Collaboration

In the NetGraph architecture, the AD intent management function and AD self-closed-loop control function are mandatory. AD intent management simplifies the input requirements for O&M personnel and orchestrates the closed-loop control process, whereas AD self-closed-loop control eliminates the need for O&M personnel to participate in the control process. The combination of the two functions enables O&M personnel to become requirement proposers without participating in the closed-loop process. In this way, O&M personnel become supervisors rather than executors of closed-loop control.

In our proposed architecture, an AD intent management function and an AD self-closed-loop control function are separately defined. The AD intent management function orchestrates a process that can be automatically executed by the AD self-closed-loop control function, receives the execution status and result from the AD self-closed-loop control function, and integrates the execution status and result into the intent achievement result. In this way, it is possible to achieve structural coupling between service input/presentation and service implementation.

4.3.5.2 Humans Outside the Loop: Knowledge-Driven Self-Closed-Loop Control

In the NetGraph architecture, the AD self-closed-loop control function needs to update its own services and processing logic based on knowledge. This makes it possible for the AD self-closed-loop control function to find the most appropriate network control method based on knowledge when encountering new environments and objectives and eliminates the need for O&M personnel to make extra preparations or interventions for different environments and objectives.

According to this concept, knowledge is first and externally placed in the human brain and software code. The knowledge can be understood by machines, which then control their behavior based on it. As such, knowledge-driven management includes at least the following typical characteristics:

- **Knowledge digitalization:** All knowledge is digitally expressed, stored, and retrieved for machine understanding.

- **External knowledge management:** Various pieces of software code need to be reconstructed so that software behavior can be controlled based on knowledge. This is a major innovation and challenge in contrast with the traditional architecture. External knowledge management is a key path for enabling software to improve and for improving behavioral capabilities through self-learning.

- **Centralized knowledge management:** Knowledge is centrally managed to maximize the potential of knowledge analysis and mining. Centralized knowledge management does not exclude the use of distributed processing capabilities in actual implementation; instead, it emphasizes the centralized management of relationships between knowledge.

Therefore, the AD knowledge digitization capability and the knowledge-based software processing capability are the key features of humans outside the loop.

4.3.5.3 Self-Adaptation: Real-Time Online Simulation

In the NetGraph architecture, high-quality self-closed-loop control relies on real-time online simulation to ensure the objective achievement success rate. Real-time online simulation depends on real-time and accurate mapping to the physical network. Therefore, self-adaptation can be determined based on whether there is a network mapping module that provides real-time mapping and real-time online simulation.

In our architecture, we define both mapping capabilities and online simulation capabilities in the AD network mapping module to provide real-time online simulation capabilities.

4.3.5.4 Self-Learning: Two-Way Collaborative Self-Closed-Loop Knowledge and Self-Closed-Loop Control

In the NetGraph architecture, the only way to provide the capability of continuously optimizing and mining knowledge is through the mechanism involving knowledge application, knowledge feedback, knowledge optimization/control, and knowledge re-application. In this way, we can build autonomous capability and form an evolving mechanism. Self-learning can therefore be determined based on whether there is an AD self-closed-loop knowledge management module and whether it collaborates with the self-closed-loop control module.

In our architecture, we define a separate AD self-closed-loop knowledge management function and form a closed loop between self-closed-loop control and self-closed-loop knowledge management.

4.3.5.5 Machine Trustworthiness: Closed-Loop Backtracking

In the NetGraph architecture, self-closed-loop control cannot be like a black box – humans must supervise machine self-closed-loop control and self-closed-loop knowledge management. Such supervision enables humans to understand the running logic of machines and to adjust knowledge and software in order to ensure that machine-made decisions comply with human laws, morals, customs, and industry conventions.

In our architecture, we define the closed-loop process and decision-making information backtracking capability in the AD self-closed-loop control function and AD self-closed-loop knowledge management function. This makes it possible for O&M personnel to monitor, review, and control the self-closed-loop process at any time.

4.4 AI NATIVE NES

From the perspective of industry evolution, telecom NEs evolve from IP native, to cloud native and then to AI native in the future. From the perspective of service challenges, AI technologies will be widely used in 6G networks to optimize services, improve experience, and promote innovation.

4.4.1 Concepts

To facilitate the future evolution of communications networks, the industry proposes six features: cubic broadband network, deterministic experience, Harmonized Communications Sensing (HCS), security and trustworthiness, AI native, and green and low-carbon. At the network device layer, the delay needs to be further reduced and energy efficiency, deterministic service, intrinsic security, and AI native need to be continuously improved. Over the next decade, AI – a fundamental technology – will be embedded into the network device architecture to promote the evolution of network devices toward intelligent autonomy. For example, as wireless networks evolve toward 6G, network coverage will extend from the ground to the air, dramatically improving the experience of existing applications and creating many new applications. Intelligent and awareness capabilities will be introduced into mobile network facilities. AI will be a key enabling technology for 6G and will be applied in key 6G functions, including new radio interface, coding, multiple access, and ultra-large-scale MIMO [13].

From the perspective of industry practices, AI technologies have been used in service optimization, system security, and O&M optimization of the telecom field for a long time. For example, DNN, convolutional neural network (CNN), and reinforcement learning are used to optimize signal analysis and encoding/decoding algorithms for the physical layer and data link layer on base stations. In the 5G era, the network data analytics function (NWDAF) is used on the core network to improve services such as mobility management using AI [14]. Current research in the telecom industry indicates that various AI algorithms are used, but that there is a lack of standardized and systematic practices.

In addition, as a form of embedded devices, NEs also comply with the evolution rules of the embedded field. The evolution of embedded devices can be divided into three generations: digitalization (in the 1970s, when microchips and computer technologies entered the embedded field to describe physical systems in digital mode), network-based (represented by IoT applications and Industry 4.0 applications such as cyber-physical system (CPS) in the mobile Internet era, significantly expanding the depth of information integration), and intelligence (data-driven, system self-learning, and efficient swarm collaboration). The latter generation is developed based on the former one and continues to evolve. In the current phase, typical intelligent fields include smartphones, IoT, robots, and self-driving cars. Our architecture aims to realize autonomous system (AS) and swarm intelligent collaboration. In the hardware represented by smartphones, vendors have launched dedicated chips and software ecosystems. For example, Huawei released Kirin series systems on a chip (SoCs) integrated with AI acceleration and the HiAI solution to enable AI native devices. In this way, intelligence is achieved in application scenarios such as photography, media decoding, character recognition, and human-machine interaction. Devices such as UAVs and robots use various sensors to observe the environment, and the device behaviors are autonomously determined through awareness and decision-making. This makes it possible to gradually realize equipment autonomy and swarm intelligence collaboration.

To sum up, the future evolution of network devices meets the six features proposed by the industry. The existing architecture requires AI native, intrinsic security, heterogeneous computation, real-time system awareness, decision-making, and cognition to implement local intelligence and system autonomy of NEs. Through swarm collaboration with NetGraph and NEs, the network will evolve in a more intelligent direction. We believe that the combination of telecom networks and AI will create huge innovation space in the future.

4.4.2 Core Architecture Design Principles

In designing the future NE device architecture, we should consider the basic AI capabilities such as data, knowledge, computing power, and algorithms required by AI native. We should also consider systematic capabilities such as awareness, decision-making, and planning required for AI-based evolution toward system autonomy, and swarm collaboration-based single-AS expansion capabilities as well as intrinsic system security and trustworthiness native capabilities.

Principle 1: Based on the data- and knowledge-driven architecture, continual learning and evolution are required to achieve real-time local intelligence of NEs.

Data: Introducing AI to NEs poses requirements for quantity, quality, and timeliness of data samples. However, this conflicts with the limited computing and storage resources of NEs and therefore poses a challenge for NEs to apply AI. In addition, data of different NEs and NetGraph is directly or indirectly shared to promote data-driven applications and AI model optimization. Therefore, data security and privacy, governance, collaboration, and application processes and specifications need to be considered.

Knowledge: In addition to data, knowledge is another key element for AI-based evolution toward cognition [15]. NE knowledge includes basic theories on which the communications field depends, industry standards and specifications, engineering experience, and service modeling or data-driven models. In engineering practices, it is difficult to obtain knowledge due to limited NE resources and many closed and separated application scenarios. We therefore need to consider how to identify valid knowledge, process and store it efficiently, apply it to closed-loop services in real time, and continuously learn and update it. Similarly, knowledge security, collaboration, and application processes and specifications must be considered for knowledge collaboration and application between NEs and NetGraph to promote local knowledge refining and application optimization.

Algorithm: Algorithms are key to applying AI on NEs, especially in the case of resolving high-dimensional and complex problems. Algorithm deployment and application mainly involve the running of algorithm models and engines required for intra-device inference. Due to the limited resources of NEs and real-time service inference requirements, we need lightweight model technologies, lightweight real-time inference engines, acceleration mathematical libraries, and operators. There is also an increasing number of valuable AI applications that require online training and deployment and distributed AI technologies – such as federated learning – to adapt to data changes, model generalization, and online optimization. Furthermore, computing power needs to be flexibly scaled in order to adapt to service changes.

Computing power: To accommodate various markets, application scenarios, and device forms, NEs need to support several forms of AI computing power, including independent acceleration cards/accelerators and AI SoCs. In addition, common CPU scenarios involving a small number of light-load algorithms and applications on existing hardware also need to be considered. We need to take cost, power consumption, and other challenges into account when integrating computing power solutions on NEs

Principle 2: Based on the layered autonomy principle of the top-level architecture, NEs gradually achieve self-fulfilling, self-healing, and self-optimizing, and evolve toward device autonomy and multi-device collaboration.

According to the AS reference paradigm [16] and industry standards exploration [17], the key components of AI native include the knowledge repository, awareness, decision-making, execution, and self-learning modules – these form a closed loop and can evolve continuously.

Knowledge repository: As the "brain" of the AS, the knowledge repository provides services for other modules, and includes different types of knowledge such as awareness information association and interpretation, rules and principles involved in objective resolution and planning during decision-making, and models and rules involved in environment simulation and evaluation after decision-making.

Awareness: Based on environment, status, and configuration data, telecom NEs use data analysis technologies and system/behavior modeling to perceive environment and scenario information in real time and predict network/service status. When the awareness result is applied to service control, continuous model update, low data processing overhead, and real-time data processing must be implemented with limited resources on the device side to meet the requirements of real-time service scenarios and convergence of model-driven and original services.

Decision-making: Logically, decision-making can be divided into objective management and planning. Objective management aims to resolve optimization problems using operations such as converting objectives into utility function strategies. During the conversion, objectives are described as a desired set of feasible states, and objective functions are optimized under a set of constraints.

For the selected objective, the planning twin formulates a plan based on the perceived system status. To overcome the complexity of the planning process, various heuristic methods and pre-computed patterns based on the knowledge repository can be used. The decision-making function on the NE side needs to support the existing service control logic and takes into account the challenges of computing complexity, confidence, and certainty brought by the objective solution.

Execution: AI native NEs perform operations according to the decision-making result, which they report to the awareness phase for closed-loop control. We need to consider the convergence and collaboration of tasks planned based on objectives and traditional service logics as well as multi-task collaboration in complex scenarios.

Self-learning: The NE architecture manages and updates knowledge such as service logic, experience, and standards/protocols. The architecture also accumulates knowledge through data modeling learning and updates configuration rules that adapt to system changes and sends the knowledge to the knowledge repository.

For complex service scenarios such as emergency communication during a disaster, collaboration between aerial and ground networks and dynamic optimization [18] may involve single-device autonomy and multi-device swarm collaboration. According to industry research [19], it is necessary to consider theories such as collaboration mechanisms and models, methods (e.g., system modeling, quantitative analysis, and multi-dimensional evaluation), and practices (e.g., group management, collaboration, and O&M).

4.4.3 Target Reference Architecture

4.4.3.1 Overall Architecture

Figure 4.9 shows the current reference architecture of an NE system, which consists of a hardware system and software system. The hardware system is related to services in different domains and may use various chips and take different product forms. Based on service types, the hardware system consists of main control boards, service boards, and interface boards. In some domains, the hardware system may also use switch boards. The software system can be divided into the system software layer (also called the platform layer) and the service software layer. The system software layer provides the environment for software development, management, and running, including the board support package (BSP), driver-related bottom-layer software, basic software related to the real-time operating system (RTOS), software management/running framework, and distribution-related middleware. The service software layer provides management, control, and data (or forwarding) services for various domains.

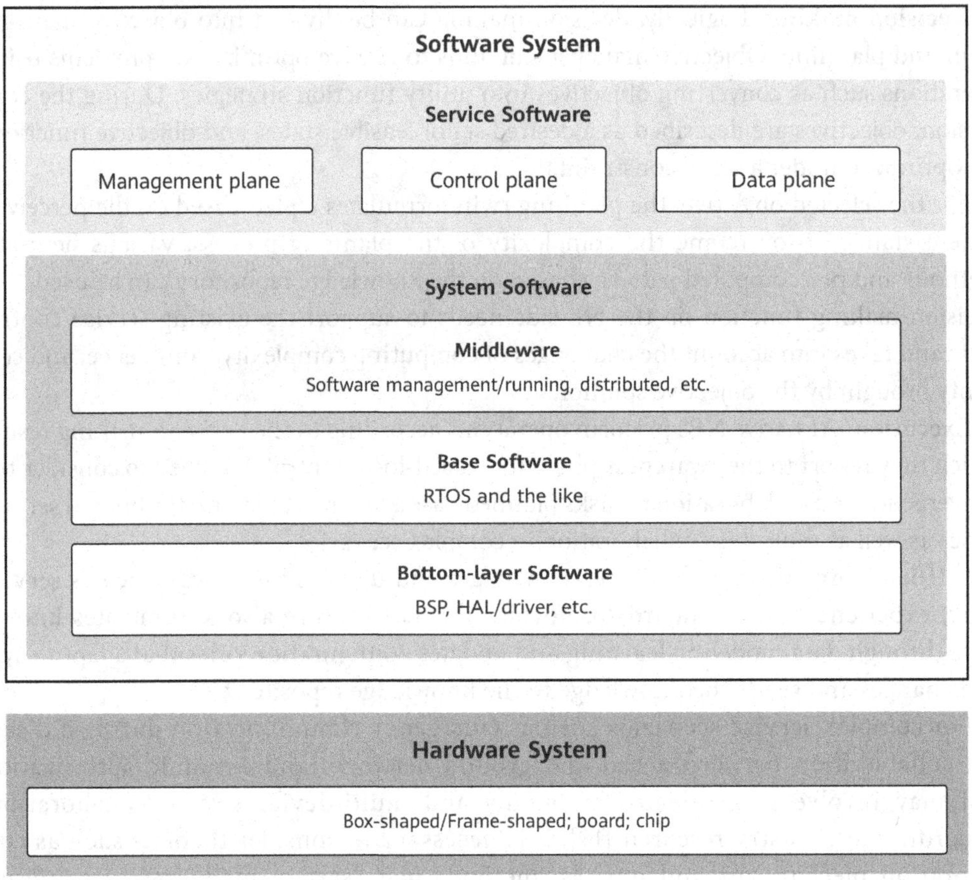

FIGURE 4.9   Reference architecture of legacy NE systems.

To meet strict quality requirements on reliability, performance, and security, the embedded system of telecom NEs adopts software-hardware collaboration and dedicated hardware acceleration. For example, even if cloud-based evolution is adopted for the core network, dedicated computing methods are used in AI and forwarding fields.

The future NE architecture focuses on AI native and device autonomy. The following items need to be added on the system software layer: AI engine, data/knowledge engine, derived data-based embedded real-time awareness layer, and derived knowledge-based "brain" knowledge subsystem, adaptive control layer, and algorithm (based on awareness/analysis/decision-making/execution) required by the AS, and security and collaboration subsystems for intrinsic security and service coordination of management-, control-, and data-plane services.

Figure 4.10 shows the vision of the overall architecture. Based on the existing architecture, AI-related hardware and software capabilities, embedded real-time awareness, adaptive control layer, knowledge, security, and collaboration subsystems are added. The architecture performs data/knowledge collaboration and model/control interaction with NetGraph in the northbound direction.

Table 4.3 describes the elements in the next-generation NE system architecture.

TABLE 4.3   Elements in the Next-Generation NE Reference Architecture

Architecture Element		Function Positioning
Hardware system		Provides general computing and dedicated computing acceleration required by legacy services, data processing, knowledge processing, and AI models/algorithms. Embedded SoCs or independent acceleration cards are used for acceleration as required.
Software system	System software layer	Hides the differences between lower-layer devices and provides the development framework and runtime capabilities for the upper layer, including the framework, engine, and algorithm operators required by AI.
	Embedded real-time awareness layer	Provides full-lifecycle governance capabilities such as data collection, preprocessing, storage, analysis, and distribution, and data warehouses to implement real-time system awareness based on data modeling and service simulation.
	Adaptive control layer	Supports adaptive control loops (such as service flow combination and execution control) and self-fulfilling, self-healing, and self-optimizing of service functions through awareness, analysis, decision-making, and execution.
	Knowledge subsystem	Provides lifecycle governance based on knowledge extraction, convergence, processing, storage, and reasoning. It builds knowledge such as service rules and experience to achieve autonomous closed loop of management, control, and data plane services.
	Security subsystem	Provides common security components based on security isolation, such as security management and security policies, to ensure security and reliability of management-, control-, and data-plane services.
	Collaboration subsystem	Provides frameworks and algorithms required for task awareness, deployment, and collaboration between device agents, and performs service collaboration with the management, control, and data planes.
	Management plane application	Provides management functions such as configuration management, fault management, and performance management. The future architecture involves AI-based reconstruction and autonomy of some services.
	Control plane application	Provides control services for the corresponding domains. The future architecture involves AI-based reconstruction and autonomy of some services.
	Data plane application	Uses the traditional CU-separated architecture to process real-time services, such as packet forwarding and signal processing. The future architecture involves AI-based reconstruction of some services.

4.4.3.2 Key Functions

Based on NE autonomy and AI native, intelligent management, control, and forwarding services pose the following requirements:

- Deterministic and trustworthy services need to be provided by using the intelligent online evolution logic of huge and complex systems.

- Service self-fulfilling, self-healing, and self-optimizing need to be supported.

- Specifications, energy efficiency, and experience need to be improved and higher quality needs to be ensured in IoE scenarios.

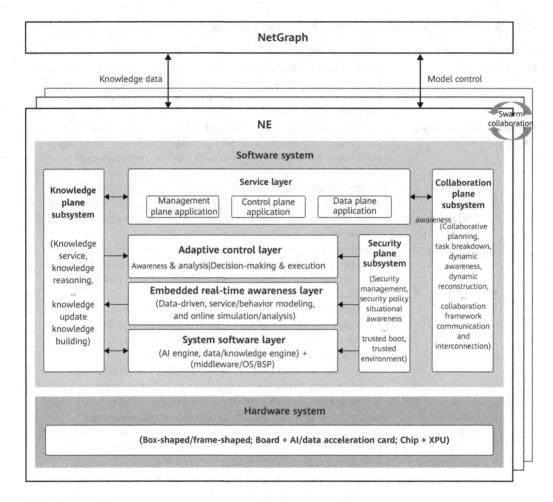

FIGURE 4.10   Vision of the next-generation NE reference architecture.

1. NE service self-fulfilling

    The NE system evolves toward full-scenario self-configuration and self-detection to gradually implement automatic network deployment, network design, commissioning, and acceptance and achieve device plug-and-play.

2. NE service self-healing

    The NE system ensures that services are always online based on prediction, diagnosis, and recovery. The O&M system gradually evolves from passive manual O&M to proactive O&M based on prediction and prevention.

3. NE service self-optimizing

    Data- and knowledge-driven AI enables services to adapt to various scenarios online and achieve continuous closed-loop optimization.

4.4.4 Modules and Components

1. Hardware System

The hardware system of an NE consists of boards, power supply units, fans, and subracks with different functions. Such a system can be divided into three levels: chip level, board level, and entire system level. The specific solution and product form are closely related to the product. This section focuses on the capabilities related to AI native. In the future, NEs will provide AI/data computing required by the system through the built-in AI core, data compression, and transmission acceleration capabilities of the embedded SoC, or independent AI/data acceleration card. The following factors should be taken into account:

Cost: Implementing AI computing in an embedded field is heavily dependent on the costs involved. In scenarios with low computing overhead, embedded SoCs can be adopted to reuse mature AI-accelerated IP solutions. In scenarios with high computing overhead, independent acceleration cards can be used as required. The specific selection depends on a series of factors such as the business pace and strategy.

Performance and power consumption: The AI-oriented design aims to achieve higher performance under the given power consumption and chip area. The hardware design and coordination with I/O system and software (such as OS kernel and network stacks) need to be considered.

Dedicated computing unit: Computing units need to be designed for various computing scenarios and modes, such as scalar computing unit, vector computing unit, tensor computing unit, and large-capacity on-chip cache. Neural network morphology computing is optimized to support hybrid precisions such as INT16, INT8, and FP16.

High-speed on-chip interconnection: The on-chip ultra-high-bandwidth mesh network is required to support high-speed interconnection between different computing units.

From the perspective of the evolution of the AI-dedicated computing architecture, the industry has explored and practiced in the following directions:

Data-centric computing: The memory-centric architecture or storage-compute integrated architecture is used to ease the computing pressure posed by data-driven loads.

Brain-like computing: Memristors and the like are used to implement brain-like computing by referring to the structure and information processing of a biological neural network. This is also referred to as neuromorphic computing [20].

2. Software System

(1) System software layer

The system software layer hides lower-layer hardware differences and enables hardware configurations. It provides the running environment and framework required for service software running, management, and maintenance for the upper layer, including the BSP, hardware abstraction layer (HAL), and driver. It also provides basic software related to OS, database, and compiler and system software such as the software management and running framework and distributed middleware. The AI native architecture introduces framework capabilities related to AI inference, data, and knowledge. The following items need to be considered:

Hardware enablement: Because embedded SoCs integrate multiple forms of products such as dedicated accelerators and acceleration cards, the dedicated acceleration hardware needs to be abstracted and runtime frameworks and development tools need to be provided. The frameworks and development tools include the running management frame, task scheduling frame, acceleration framework, AI model and operator development tools, and compilers.

Basic framework: The framework provides runtime, algorithms, and operators required for intra-device inference and online learning, as well as AI trustworthiness capabilities. It also provides engines and frameworks related to data collection, preprocessing, storage, and computing of data and knowledge.

Application enablement: Communication AI models, algorithms, and matching tool sets oriented for the telecom field need to support secondary development.

(2) Embedded real-time awareness layer

Based on local service configurations, system status, and traffic statistics, NEs collect, cleanse, process, and locally store data, and subscribe to applications in real time. Based on data modeling, service behavior modeling, and real-time data-driven online simulation, embedded real-time service awareness is implemented to support online optimization and evaluation of service functions, online learning and evaluation based on AI models, and virtual data sample generation and application to data-driven services. The following factors need to be considered:

Data engine: provides capabilities such as data collection, preprocessing, storage, analysis, and release, as well as full-lifecycle governance, trustworthiness, and quality evaluation.

Online real-time simulation engine: provides lightweight online optimization, running, simulation, and analysis capabilities for models.

Collaboration framework: manages NE collaboration activities with NetGraph, including model collaboration, data collaboration, and simulation collaboration.

Design and engineering: provide modeling languages, engineering methods, and tools. For embedded systems, related lightweight implementation technologies also need to be considered.

If adaptive system control is introduced, online simulation based on the real-time awareness layer can reduce the uncertainty of control. It is also necessary to consider introducing knowledge-to-data analysis and model optimization to optimize data-based computing efficiency and system confidence.

(3) Adaptive control layer

The adaptive control layer supports adaptive control loops (such as service flow combination and execution control) and self-fulfilling, self-healing, and self-optimizing of service functions through awareness, analysis, decision-making, and execution. In addition to service control of ontologies, it also performs swarm collaboration control.

Awareness: Based on data analysis and model prediction, the adaptive control layer recognizes the service system, status, and interaction objectives. It is challenging to achieve real-time system information acquisition and processing, consistency of multi-dimensional information, and accuracy of scenario understanding.

Analysis: The adaptive control layer understands requirements and objectives based on the analysis of management objectives and intents as well as system behavior and status.

Decision-making: The adaptive control layer performs service decision-making and task breakdown based on objective resolution, converting requirements and objectives into executable tasks. Dynamic adaptation is required for incomplete predictability and uncontrollability in real-world scenarios.

Execution support service: The adaptive control layer combines and orchestrates tasks based on service flows to implement requirements and objective execution. In addition, a closed loop is formed based on the execution status and negative result feedback for continuous iterative optimization.

The theory of adaptive control comes from the traditional cybernetics field. However, applying it to the real-time control closed-loop of the NE system involves various engineering challenges.

(4) Knowledge subsystem

The NE knowledge subsystem is positioned as the local "brain." It provides the knowledge, logic, and reasoning capabilities required for the real-time running of the intelligent system. Considering the entire lifecycle, including knowledge repository construction, knowledge reasoning, update, service, and introduction, the knowledge plane subsystem needs to provide capabilities including local knowledge repository construction and management, and knowledge application and update. It is used for the autonomous closed loop of management, control, and data plane services.

Knowledge repository construction: The knowledge plane subsystem establishes, manages, and protects local knowledge repositories based on knowledge extraction, convergence, processing (online and offline), and storage (most knowledge repositories are dense but some are sparse).

Knowledge reasoning: The knowledge plane subsystem performs lightweight knowledge representation based on dimension reduction and vectorization, and lightweight reasoning based on ontology, rule, and representation learning.

Knowledge update: The knowledge plane layer adaptively learns and integrates knowledge, and continuously updates it based on knowledge learning/reasoning generation in the service application process and rule/experience-based knowledge aging.

Knowledge service: The knowledge plane layer provides knowledge retrieval and reasoning.

Knowledge introduction: This function compensates for the shortcomings of the data-driven architecture and drives the evolution to cognitive intelligence.

(5) Security subsystem

The security subsystem abstracts common capabilities such as security management from the current service architecture, implements security isolation and threat-based dynamic awareness/response based on trustworthy computing technologies, and provides local, real-time, and endogenous security service capabilities for other functions and services. A complete technology stack includes key security assets (such as certificates and root keys) based on trustworthy environments and key security services. It also provides security analysis, security policies, and security management based on situational awareness to achieve intrinsic security.

Trustworthy computing environment: Based on TrustZone-based security isolation, the security plane subsystem provides the lightweight real-time TrustOS environment and security computing framework to achieve system trustworthiness and minimization. It provides secure storage and encryption and decryption services for key assets of service systems, including certificates and keys.

Security awareness and analysis: The security plane subsystem collects service and system information of the management, control, and forwarding planes, and implements dynamic security awareness of the system and services based on AI-based analysis and prediction.

Security management and policy: Different security policies, such as those related to access control and service access, are formed based on the security design models of the system and services on different planes.

Security service: The security plane subsystem provides security services, such as access control (e.g., authentication and audit), security configuration, and certificate services.

Data security: AI requires data privacy and data security to be further protected. Security and privacy protection need to be considered throughout the lifecycle of data sources, transmission, storage, and use.

Due to future service challenges and security technology evolution, system security needs to shift from passive defense to proactive defense. The application and implementation of technologies such as multi-party computing, homomorphic encryption, privacy computing, post-quantum security, and automatic system vulnerability mitigation need to be further explored.

(6) Collaboration subsystem

The NE collaboration subsystem provides the corresponding applications and framework for collaboration between devices based on a service scenario. From the perspective of service flows, scenario objectives need to be understood, planned, and dynamically reconstructed, and tasks and objectives of heterogeneous individuals need to be broken down and dynamically coordinated. In addition, individual execution and dynamic awareness and collaboration are required. From the perspective of technology stack:

Objective planning and reconstruction: The collaboration plane subsystem needs to provide scenario-based objective understanding and unified planning as well as dynamic reconstruction, adjustment, and optimization capabilities based on scenario changes.

Task breakdown and collaboration: The collaboration plane subsystem needs to provide capabilities such as complex task breakdown and management, task-driven device configuration and collaboration, algorithm mechanisms, group resource sharing, task matching, status measurement and evaluation, and control execution policies and incentives.

Individual awareness and execution: Individuals execute task breakdown, perceive surrounding objects and environments in real time, adaptively adjust operations, and provide feedback.

Distributed interconnection: The collaboration plane subsystem provides efficient communications and interconnection between groups.

(7) Management plane/control plane/data plane subsystems

The traditional management plane, control plane, and data plane correspond to the management, control, and forwarding functions. The planes are reconstructed based on AI and adaptive control, and the built-in native knowledge, security, and collaboration capabilities are added to implement intelligent and autonomous evolution of NE functions.

Based on data-driven service architecture evolution, AI technologies are used to reconstruct some services, such as high-dimensional space and complex task solving, and knowledge- and data-driven evolution.

The subsystem implements intrinsic security based on the security subsystem, implements layered isolation and defense for services on different planes, and dynamically detects and responds to threats.

Based on the knowledge subsystem and adaptive control, the subsystem provides service self-fulfilling, self-healing, and self-optimizing to achieve autonomy of the NE system.

Based on device swarm collaboration, intelligent collaboration between multiple devices is implemented in response to network changes and ensure SLAs in complex scenarios and tasks in the future.

4.4.5 Key Characteristics of the Architecture

The AI native NE architecture should have the following features in addition to those offered in conventional service systems:

1. Native computing acceleration

   Given the energy efficiency, wide application, and cost of computing, NE hardware must support dedicated accelerator (such as SoC integration or independent acceleration cards). In addition, the software frameworks and engines must hide hardware differences and maximize computing efficiency to support efficient and dedicated computing for services.

2. Driven by data and knowledge

   As the architecture evolves from a data-driven to a data- and knowledge-driven one, the NE subsystem continuously learns local knowledge and models to provide knowledge support for the control and cognition of service systems. In addition, the knowledge learned by the NE subsystem evolves together with knowledge in NetGraph toward cognitive intelligence, which more efficiently and extensively enables systems and applications.

3. System adaptation

   The service system introduces adaptive awareness, analysis, decision-making, and execution to implement system autonomy such as service self-configuration, self-optimizing, and self-healing. With intelligent enablement, the service system evolves toward device system autonomy and multi-device system collaboration. In addition, embedded real-time awareness and online simulation are required to implement adaptive and intelligent online solution and optimization, and to evaluate and eliminate uncertainties.

4. Intrinsic security

   In addition to the security and resilience of service systems, we need to focus on the security challenges brought by the introduction of AI and adaptation. From the perspective of system protection, dynamic awareness and prediction of system threats, dynamic response, and timely and effective mitigation must be considered.

4.5 DISTRIBUTED AI ARCHITECTURE

4.5.1 Concepts

Telecom networks are evolving toward the goal of "intelligent connectivity of everything." It has gradually become a consensus in the industry that AI-based ADN needs to be introduced. Currently, there are two AI architecture modes: centralized AI and distributed AI, as shown in Figure 4.11.

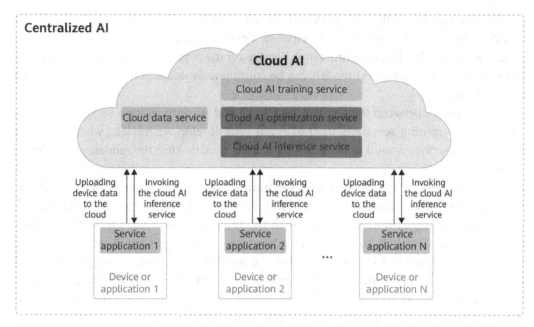

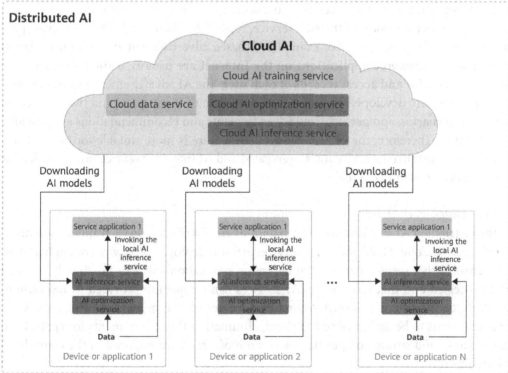

FIGURE 4.11   Centralized AI and distributed AI.

4.5.1.1 Centralized AI

In centralized AI, device or application data is uploaded to a centralized location (referred to as the cloud in this document, corresponding to the location where the device is) and AI models (referred to as the cloud AI training service in Figure 4.11) are trained based on the collected data. After being trained, the AI models are deployed through the cloud AI inference service to provide AI services for devices or applications. AI models can be optimized online by the AI optimization service on the cloud based on the continuously collected data. In this way, AI models can be continuously updated to better meet service requirements.

The differences between the AI training service and AI optimization service are as follows: The AI training service is used to create and develop AI models, whereas the AI optimization service is used to iteratively update AI models after the models are deployed and run.

The centralized AI architecture uses the unified computing power to provide AI services. By aggregating data of each device or application, a global AI model can be trained. The accuracy of the AI model increases with the amount of data used for training. While the centralized AI architecture has some advantages, it also has some disadvantages. For example, a large amount of data needs to be uploaded to the cloud, bringing potential data privacy risks and posing significant challenges to transmission bandwidth and service KPIs (such as latency). In addition, AI models trained or optimized in a centralized manner may be not optimal for all device or application scenarios.

In most cases, Internet services are processed in the background in a centralized manner. When a user accesses an Internet service, related data is uploaded to the service processing center for processing. For example, AI-based advertisement and recommendation models **for e-commerce applications on the Internet are usually trained based on the purchase behavior and access records of each user**. The AI advertisement and recommendation models are developed based on the access data of many users and the preferences of various scenarios, and personalized advertisements and recommendations are provided for each user. Therefore, the centralized AI architecture is more suitable for Internet services. With centralized AI, all data is aggregated and AI inference services are provided for consumers in a centralized manner.

4.5.1.2 Distributed AI

In the distributed AI architecture, AI capabilities are distributed on each application node. In addition to cloud AI, AI inference services are also deployed on devices or applications. This ensures that service data on the device or application side can be directly invoked and processed and that low-latency AI services can be quickly provided in response to service requests. The distributed AI architecture does not require data of many devices or applications to be uploaded to the cloud, eliminating the requirements for centralized large storage and strong computing power, both of which are required in the centralized AI architecture.

Because AI capabilities are distributed on each device and node, AI services can be invoked where AI is required, reducing the transmission latency and improving the service request response efficiency. In addition, there is no requirement to aggregate data of devices and nodes do not need to be aggregated, alleviating the high requirements for data storage and network bandwidth. The distributed AI architecture enables distributed computing power and data to be fully utilized in order to complete online AI optimization based on the local data of each device through the AI optimization service. In this way, the AI model can better adapt to the environment and data distribution characteristics of each device, improving the overall AI performance. In summary, this architecture better balances data processing efficiency, real-time inference, and computing power utilization, improving the efficiency of the entire network.

There are many latency-sensitive services on telecom networks. For example, in the industrial automation field, the latency involved in mechanical control must be at the millisecond level. Due to the physical latency of pipes (e.g., about 10 ms for 1000 km of optical fiber), centralized AI cannot meet the low-latency requirements of services. In this case, the distributed AI architecture is required so that AI services can be processed nearby to meet such requirements. The distributed AI architecture is therefore suitable for telecom networks so that AI capabilities can be deployed close to data and the distributed computing power at each network layer is used to implement intelligent telecom services.

4.5.1.3 Summary

Table 4.4 compares the centralized AI architecture and the distributed AI architecture.

The technology development trend indicates that a technological revolution driven by AI has come. AI – a common technology – will enable network devices and software to have endogenous AI capabilities. As telecom networks are evolving to ADN featuring single-domain autonomy and cross-domain collaboration, AI capabilities have become requirements of each domain and distributed AI has become an inevitable development direction of ADN. Through the distributed AI architecture, AI can be deployed on network devices or via software services in a distributed manner to promptly respond to service requests. In addition, AI can be continuously optimized online to quickly adapt to environment, service, and data changes, achieving AI self-learning and self-evolution. In this way, a self-fulfilling, self-healing, self-optimizing, and autonomous network can be achieved.

TABLE 4.4 Comparison between Centralized AI and Distributed AI

Architecture	Centralized AI	Distributed AI
AI inference service	Cloud-based inference	Available on both the cloud and local devices and distributed on each node.
AI optimization service	Cloud-based optimization	Available on both the cloud and local devices and distributed on each node.
AI real-time performance	Cloud-based inference, with a latency of hundreds of milliseconds	Local inference, with a millisecond-level latency.
Network bandwidth	Cloud-based inference, which requires high bandwidth to transmit data in real time.	Local inference, with services processed nearby and no need to transmit data to the cloud
Computing power	The cloud is responsible for computing in a centralized manner, and computing resources are sufficient.	Computing capabilities are distributed on the device side, and computing resources are limited.

4.5.2 Core Architecture Design Principles

4.5.2.1 *AI Has a Continual Learning Mechanism to Accommodate Scenario or Data Changes of Telecom Services*

The data of telecom network services varies significantly with CSPs, service scenarios, and sites. For example, the same AI model may deliver different performances at different sites – the accuracy of the KPI anomaly detection model may reach 95% or higher in the core network domain but only 70% or lower in the wireless domain. The feature distribution in AI data may change seasonally even for the same site, resulting in AI models producing different execution effects. For example, in DC energy saving, the data energy saving mode changes due to the change of cooling modes in winter and spring. If the AI energy-saving model in winter is directly used in spring, its performance will deteriorate. In this case, the AI model needs to be retrained based on new data features so that the AI model can adapt to model changes caused by service and data changes.

For each new service domain or site, algorithm developers need to adjust AI models based on site service and data distributions and train the models. With the increase of AI applications, it is impossible to adapt traditional manual solutions to rapid service changes. Therefore, AI models must be able to respond to the environment and automatically initiate the optimization mechanism in order to adapt to service changes in a way similar to biological evolution. This capability is called the AI continual learning mechanism. As shown in Figure 4.12, if there is no continual learning mechanism, the AI model in the AI inference service remains unchanged from the beginning of execution unless the AI model version is updated. If the continual learning mechanism is introduced, AI model retraining is started based on the model running monitoring status and service policies from the beginning of AI model running. The retrained model is verified and evaluated, and once it passes the evaluation, a comparison between the

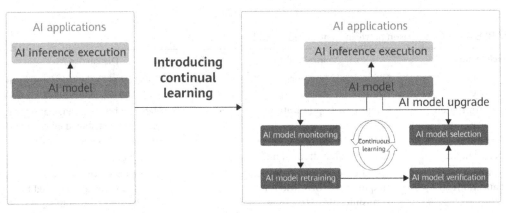

Without the continual learning mechanism

With the continual learning mechanism

FIGURE 4.12 Comparison between AI architectures with and without a continual learning mechanism.

old and new AI models is made, with the optimal model being selected for deployment and running. The optimization process forms an automatic closed loop, achieving continual learning.

The AI continual learning mechanism enables the distributed AI architecture to automatically accommodate various scenarios, optimize and evolve AI models based on environment and data changes, and adapt to service changes. In this way, the ADN objectives can be met.

4.5.2.2 AI Can Flow at Different Network Layers and Run in Different Heterogeneous Environments

Ensuring that AI models can be easily distributed to devices in order to support quick large-scale application of AI is a critical aspect of the distributed AI architecture. Therefore, distributed AI needs to support the mobility and distributed deployment of AI models on devices or nodes. AI models can be used immediately after they are automatically deployed. To support the mobility of AI models in different devices with different running environments, the architecture needs to support the AI model description specifications and define AI models in a unified manner so that AI models can be executed and continuously optimized in different environments, achieving the decoupling of service applications from AI models.

Figure 4.13 shows the AI model development process and running process. The AI model development process consists of AI algorithm development, AI model training, and AI model verification and release, and the process from AI model release to network deployment includes AI model deployment, AI inference service release, AI model running effect monitoring, AI model retraining, and AI model evaluation and selection. To reduce the amount of time and workload required for managing AI model running, the architecture needs to support automation of the entire model running process.

Through the collaboration mechanism, AI model development and running can be associated, shortening the AI model development and delivery period and improving the AI model distribution and deployment efficiency.

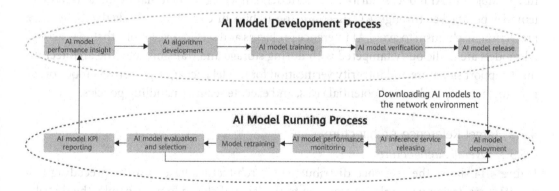

FIGURE 4.13 AI model lifecycle process.

4.5.2.3 AI Is Applicable to Different Device Environments Even When Resources Are Limited

In the distributed AI architecture, AI models are deployed on devices and edge nodes, significantly reducing data privacy, latency, and reliability issues caused by data processing on the cloud. The size of an AI model depends on the number of model parameters and is irrelevant to the input data. The number of model parameters affects the memory consumption and model package size. The time required for model running is subject to the input data.

Because the computing capabilities and memory resources on the device and edge sides are limited. Therefore, to meet the service requirements of AI applications distributed on each device, the architecture needs to support AI model adjustment based on the device environment and reach an optimal balance between the complexity and performance of AI models based on service scenarios. This is necessary to meet the service requirements of AI applications distributed on each device in resource-limited scenarios and will allow AI models to be used in various device environments.

4.5.2.4 AI Real-Time Response Is Supported to Meet the Requirements of Latency-Sensitive Scenarios

As the computing power of chips continues to improve according to Moore's Law, and the computing capability of devices also improves accordingly. For example, the processing capability of smartphones today is stronger than that of computers in the past. Therefore, the development of computing power provides a hardware basis for endogenous AI of devices. In most cases, telecom network devices are upgraded every three years and higher-quality network connections are provided, which propels the development of multiple fields such as urban transportation, healthcare, and smart manufacturing. These fields, in turn, require networks to be faster and more intelligent, especially for services with strong interaction capabilities. Therefore, devices must have endogenous AI capabilities to better provide real-time interactive services.

4.5.2.5 AI Security Is Ensured through the Proactive Detection and Response Mechanisms

Characterized by the distribution of AI models on different nodes, the distributed AI architecture is subject to AI model security issues. Model tampering or theft may occur, and the system may be attacked through AI. Therefore, the architecture needs to provide the AI security protection mechanism to avoid AI inference problems and service exceptions that may arise if AI models are maliciously tampered with during storage and transmission. The architecture must support signature and integrity verification for model packages, proactively monitor AI running, identify and record potential risks, and execute security handling policies.

4.5.3 Target Reference Architecture

4.5.3.1 Overall Architecture

Figure 4.14 shows the reference distributed AI architecture based on the preceding key architecture design principles. According to the layered closed loop principle, the distributed AI reference architecture consists of cloud intelligence, business domain intelligence,

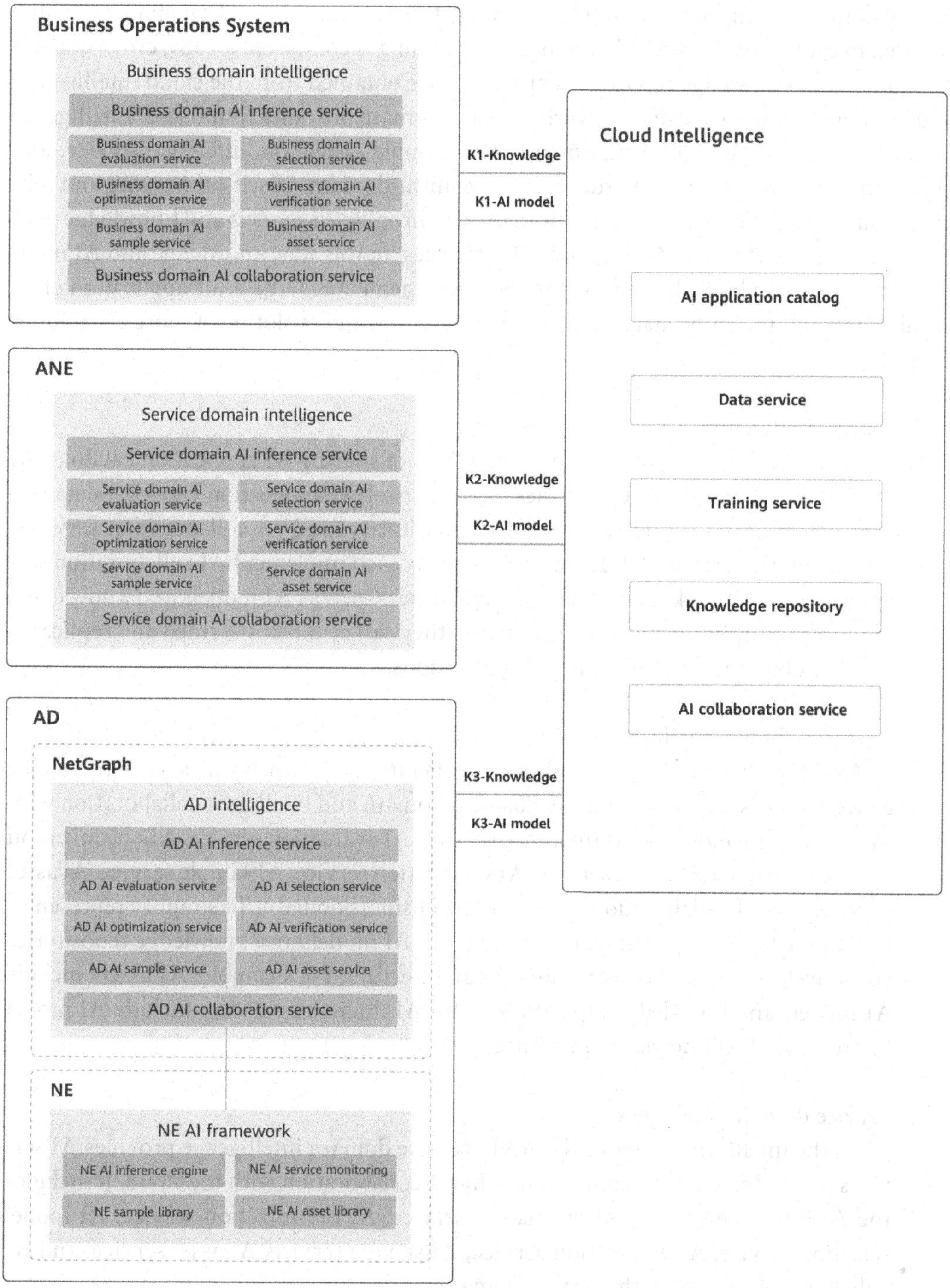

FIGURE 4.14 Distributed AI architecture.

service domain intelligence, AD intelligence, and NE AI framework. AI capabilities are distributed in each domain of ADN. Intelligent processing is completed locally, cross-domain AI models and knowledge repository experience are obtained from the cloud intelligence, and AI models or knowledge repositories of each domain are quickly updated. Intelligence in each domain focuses on intra-domain data sample collection, inference service, and continuous AI optimization in order to achieve intra-domain AI self-optimizing and self-evolution. Intelligent systems in each domain synchronize AI models and knowledge with cloud intelligence through K1, K2, and K3 interfaces. In this way, knowledge and AI models in a domain can be replicated to other domains, achieving large-scale application of AI capabilities and efficiently enabling continuous iteration and evolution of those capabilities in ADN.

1. Cloud intelligence

    Cloud intelligence provides the capabilities of sharing AI application catalogs, AI models, and knowledge repositories. It consists of AI application catalogs, data services, AI training services, knowledge repositories, and AI collaboration services. Cloud intelligence uses K1, K2, and K3 interfaces to implement AI collaboration services at each network layer. After AI capabilities (such as AI models and knowledge) are successfully implemented in a domain, they can be quickly formed and replicated in other domains for large-scale AI applications.

2. Business domain intelligence

    As the intelligent center of the business operations system, business domain intelligence provides AI services for the business domain and intelligent collaboration with the cloud. It includes the AI inference service, AI evaluation service, AI optimization service, AI model selection service, AI verification service, AI sample service, AI asset service, and AI collaboration service of the business domain. To simplify representation in the following descriptions, we refer to AI models and knowledge repositories collectively as AI in the distributed AI architecture. For example, AI assets include AI models and knowledge repositories, and AI inference services include AI model inference and AI knowledge inference.

3. Service domain intelligence

    As the intelligent center of the ANE, service domain intelligence provides AI services for the business domain and intelligent collaboration with the cloud. It includes the AI inference service, AI evaluation service, AI optimization service, AI model selection service, AI verification service, AI sample service, AI asset service, and AI collaboration service of the service domain.

4. AD intelligence

    As the intelligent system of an AD, AD intelligence provides the AI inference service, AI evaluation service, AI optimization service, AI selection service, AI verification service, AI sample service, AI asset service, and AI collaboration service for the AD.

5. NE AI framework

As a system enabling AI on NEs, the NE AI framework provides capabilities such as the NE inference engine, NE AI service monitoring, NE sample library, and AI asset library. The framework is integrated into NEs to provide AI models and knowledge-running environments for NE AI native. It provides common engineering capabilities for AI models and knowledge repositories, such as AI asset running, monitoring, deployment and upgrade, and download.

4.5.3.2 Key Functions

Based on the overall architecture, this section describes the main functions of the distributed AI architecture in terms of AI collaboration service, layered AI continual learning, and AI adaptive download.

1. AI collaboration service

The AI collaboration service is responsible for externally sharing AI capabilities and exchanging collaboration messages with other domains, such as interconnection configuration and authentication, message processing, and AI asset update.

2. AI continual learning

AI continual learning includes AI monitoring, AI optimization (the common optimization method is to retrain AI models based on new samples in order to generate a new AI version), AI evaluation, AI verification, and AI selection and upgrade. The five subfunctions form an iteration process to implement automatic AI update. Upon detecting AI performance deterioration, the system automatically starts optimizing the AI capability.

The following figure shows the AI continual learning function. (Figure 4.15)

3. Adaptive AI update

Because the distributed AI architecture may be used in various device environments, it must provide AI models that are applicable to the running environments of the business operations system, ANE, NetGraph, and NEs. The distributed AI

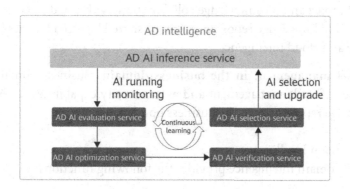

FIGURE 4.15   AI continual learning.

architecture must support the adaptive update capability so that an optimal model can be selected based on the environment information and AI models can be updated in various environments.

4.5.4 Modules and Components

1. Cloud Intelligence

   Cloud intelligence provides the following functions:

   - **AI application catalog:** contains the asset catalogs of AI models and knowledge. The catalogs provide entries for users to share and download AI models and knowledge.

   - **Training service:** develops and trains AI models.

   - **Data service:** provides capabilities such as data collection and generation, and provides samples for the training service.

   - **Knowledge repository:** develops knowledge on the cloud.

   - **AI collaboration service:** provides cross-domain AI collaboration capabilities. The service enables cloud intelligence to share AI models and knowledge repositories with business domain intelligence, service domain intelligence, and AD intelligence. In addition, the service provides security capabilities to ensure secure and reliable collaboration.

2. Business Domain Intelligence

   Business domain intelligence provides the following functions:

   - **AI continuous learning in the business domain:** The AI evaluation service, AI optimization service, AI asset verification service, and AI selection service in the business domain are used to continuously learn and optimize AI assets in the business operations system, thereby providing the AI asset self-optimizing capability.

   - **AI collaboration in the business domain:** The service performs AI collaboration (K1-AI model and K1-knowledge collaboration) with cloud intelligence so that AI models and knowledge repositories can be shared between business domain intelligence and cloud intelligence.

   - **AI asset management in the business domain:** Business domain intelligence provides lifecycle management and asset security capabilities for AI models and knowledge repositories in the business domain.

3. Service Domain Intelligence

   Service domain intelligence provides the following functions:

   - **AI continuous learning in the service domain:** The AI evaluation service, AI optimization service, AI asset verification service, and AI selection service in the service domain are used to continuously learn and optimize AI assets in the service system, thereby providing the AI asset self-optimizing capability.

- **AI collaboration in the service domain:** Service domain intelligence performs AI collaboration (K2-AI model and K2-knowledge collaboration) with cloud intelligence so that AI models and knowledge repositories can be shared between service domain intelligence and cloud intelligence.

- **AI asset management in the service domain:** Service domain intelligence provides lifecycle management and asset security capabilities for AI models and knowledge repositories in the service domain.

4. AD Intelligence

AD intelligence provides the following functions:

- **AI continuous learning in the AD:** The AI evaluation service, AI optimization service, AI asset verification service, and AI selection service in the AD are used to continuously learn and optimize AI assets in the AD, thereby providing the AI asset self-optimizing capability.

- **AI collaboration in the AD:** AD intelligence performs AI collaboration (K3-AI model and K3-knowledge collaboration) with cloud intelligence so that AI models and knowledge repositories can be shared between AD intelligence and cloud intelligence.

- **AI asset management in the AD:** AD intelligence provides lifecycle management and asset security capabilities for AI models and knowledge repositories in the AD.

- **AI inference service in the AD:** AD intelligence provides AI running services in the AD (including AI inference request processing, inference task scheduling, execution, and monitoring) and unified interfaces, collects O&M monitoring data during AI running, and queries the AI running effect.

5. NE AI Framework

The NE AI framework supports intelligent evolution of NEs and provides the following functions:

- **NE AI inference engine:** The framework provides lightweight and efficient AI running support services for NEs (including AI inference request processing, inference task scheduling, execution, and monitoring), unified interfaces, and the capabilities of AI deployment, upgrade, and uninstallation.

- **NE AI service monitoring:** The framework collects O&M monitoring data during NE AI running and provides query interfaces.

- **NE AI asset library:** The framework provides lifecycle management and security verification capabilities for NE AI models and knowledge.

- **NE AI sample library:** The framework provides lifecycle management and security verification capabilities for NE AI samples.

4.5.5 Key Characteristics of the Architecture

The distributed AI architecture has the following characteristics: layered AI closed loop, AI adaptive self-learning, data- and knowledge-driven, and flexible AI deployment.

4.5.5.1 Layered AI Closed Loop

According to the layered closed loop principle of ADN, an AI closed loop needs to be implemented at each layer. In addition, considering the explosive growth of intelligent data in the future, AI closed-loop processing needs to be performed at the nearest layer in order to reduce service response latency and meet service requirements.

4.5.5.2 AI Adaptive Self-Learning

Each layer of ADN must have the AI continual learning capability so that AI algorithms, models, and parameters can be continuously adjusted to meet requirements on user experience and other factors based on external environment changes and historical running data. In this way, the longer that ADN is used, the more intelligent it becomes.

4.5.5.3 Driven by Data and Knowledge

Continual learning enables ADN to obtain the knowledge and cognitive capabilities that better match service scenarios. In addition, the knowledge and models are continuously optimized to quickly adapt to the environment.

4.5.5.4 Flexible AI Deployment

Flexible deployment is critical to distributed AI. It promotes automatic deployment and running of AI at all network layers. For example, AI model deployment does not require a running environment for each service. Instead, the intra-domain intelligent AI inference service provides platform capabilities to support the flexible deployment of AI models and adapt to different running environments.

4.6 INTRINSIC SECURITY

Society has entered the digital economy era, and people's production and people's work and life habits are becoming more inseparable from software programs and information equipment. As key information infrastructure, the communications network provides vital support for government affairs management and important systems that are closely related to the economy and people's livelihood, for example, finance, energy, transportation, water supply, healthcare, and emergency services. It carries more and more high-value business and data related to the economy and people's livelihood. The security of communications networks is becoming increasingly important, and even affects the national security.

Therefore, many national regulatory agencies and public standards organizations are paying closer attention to the security of communications networks.

4.6.1 Concepts

Conventional networks adopt a security architecture in which security products, such as firewalls and Intrusion Prevention System (IPS)/Intrusion Detection System (IDS), are deployed at the edge of the network to detect and defend against attacks. But as attack methods continue to evolve and improve, the disadvantages of this architecture have become more apparent. Once attackers break through these security products, they can perform any operation on the internal network.

To address such security challenges, the industry proposes a new idea: intrinsic security. The core principle of this idea is that each device and system on the network must have security defense capabilities and the network can automatically detect security attacks, respond to security attacks, and recover from security attacks. In addition, the network must be able to adaptively defend against threats that may occur in the future.

4.6.2 Challenges

Compared with existing networks, ADN incorporates significant changes in the architecture and running environment, bringing greater security challenges. The main challenges are as follows:

1. NetGraph plays an increasingly important role on the network. Attacks on NetGraph have a large impact scope.

   More and more enterprises tend to manage their network devices via the cloud, and CSPs are also shifting their network device management from city-level distributed management to province/state-level centralized management. The result of this is a significant increase in the number of devices managed on NetGraph. The development of SDN and NFV helps enhance the network control scope of NetGraph. Once NetGraph is attacked, the impact is severe.

2. The security boundary of NetGraph has changed fundamentally, increasing the possibility of being attacked.

   NetGraph can be deployed on a public cloud to provide services. It also provides open programmability, considerably improving the openness. In addition, NetGraph uses the browser/server (B/S) architecture, instead of the traditional client/server (C/S) architecture, to provide access for users through ubiquitous browsers and for NEs through the Internet. The exposure surface of NetGraph is significantly increased, and the possibility of being attacked is also increased.

3. The possibility of attacking NetGraph from NEs increases significantly.

   NetGraph is more likely to be attacked from NEs because of the following reasons: (1) The architecture of virtualized NEs has been transformed from being a closed one to an open one due to the use of the NFV technology. (2) The development of edge computing technologies increases the openness of data centers, and an increasing number of applications will run on the Multi-Access Edge Compute (MEC) platform. (3) Many edge devices are deployed in an open environment, and NEs are more likely to be attacked. After an attack succeeds, NEs can be used as a springboard to attack NetGraph.

4. Security intrusion events need to be detected in real time and require quick response.

With the rapid development of IT technologies, more and more attack methods are emerging, bringing major challenges to network security defense. Security detection is a key technology. Because the detection time determines the loss caused by an attack, how to detect security intrusion events as soon as possible is an important challenge for ADN in the future. After an attack is detected, quick response is required. In many scenarios, the response is slow, and recovery measures are manually performed. Therefore, automatic response and recovery are required.

4.6.3 Core Architecture Design Principles

To cope with emerging cyber security events, the industry has proposed multiple cyber security theories and architectures, including Cyber Security Framework proposed by the National Institute of Standards and Technology (NIST) in 2018, Continuous Adaptive Risk and Trust Assessment (CARTA) proposed by Gartner in 2017, and the popular Zero Trust theory proposed by the chief architect of Forrester in 2010.

Cyber Security Framework consists of five core functions: Identify, Protect, Detect, Respond, and Recover (IDPRR) [21], as shown in Figure 4.16.

Identify: identifies the security assets of the entire network. This function serves as the basis of the entire framework and assists in developing an organizational understanding to manage the cyber security risks to systems, assets, data, and capabilities.

Protect: outlines appropriate safeguards to ensure delivery of security assets. This function supports the ability to limit or contain the impact of a potential cyber security event through, for example, identity management and access control, data security protection, and maintenance and protection technology.

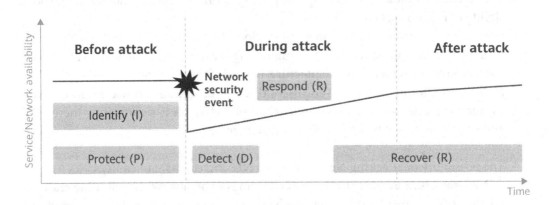

FIGURE 4.16 IPDRR theory.

Detect: performs cyber security checks and identifies the occurrence of cyber security events in a timely manner.

Respond: includes appropriate countermeasures to take action regarding a detected cyber security event. This function supports the ability to prevent the occurrence of a potential cyber security event and contain the impact of a detected cyber security event.

Recover: identifies appropriate activities to restore any services that were impaired due to a cyber security event. This function quickly restores operations to normal.

While all the preceding functions are important, Identify and Detect are particularly crucial. If some assets are not identified and therefore are not protected, they can be attacked easily. If threats cannot be detected or the detection takes a long time, the network will be subject to significant loss.

The CARTA security architecture is an advanced strategic method promoted by Gartner to cope with current and future security trends. It continuously evaluates network risks and the trust of various communication entities that access the network, and automatically responds to the evaluation results, as shown in Figure 4.17.

The Zero Trust theory [22] proposes that enterprises should not automatically trust any internal or external users, devices, or applications. Instead, they should verify any user, device, or application that attempts to access the enterprise system before authorization, that is, "never trust, always verify." The Zero Trust theory is established based on the following basic assumptions:

1. The network is always in a dangerous environment.

2. External and internal threats always exist.

3. The location of any user, device, or application is insufficient to determine their trustworthiness.

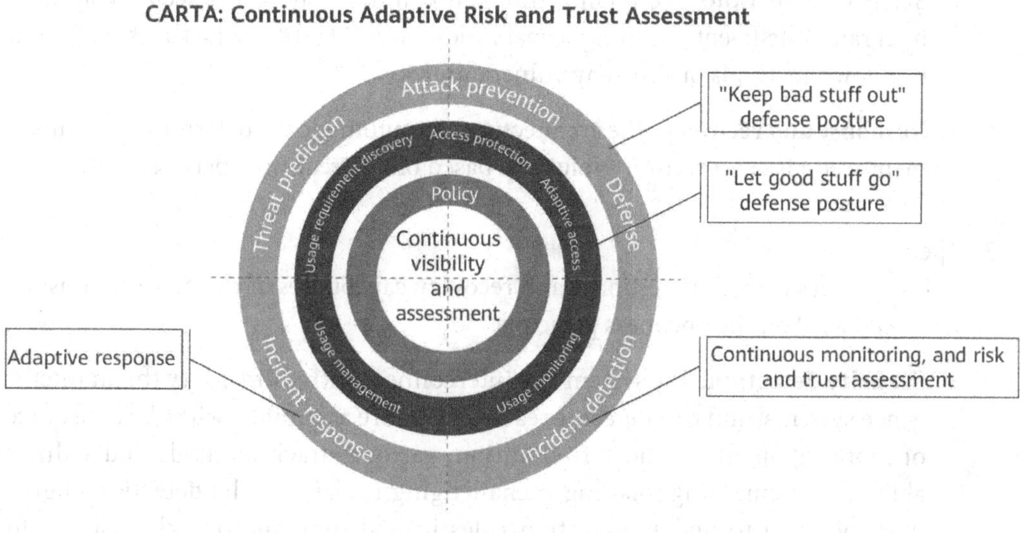

FIGURE 4.17 CARTA security architecture.

4. All devices, users, applications, and traffic must be authenticated and authorized.

5. Security policies must be dynamic and be prepared based on as many trust elements as possible.

This theory was first adopted by Google in its own network. Subsequently, vendors such as QI-ANXIN in China have proposed related solutions.

The Cyber Security Framework, CARTA security architecture, and Zero Trust theory provide ideas from different perspectives for designing a cyber security architecture. Based on related ideas and key challenges faced by ADN in the future, it is recommended that ADN adopt the following security architecture design principles:

1. Intrinsic

In compliance with the design principles of intrinsic security in the industry, NEs and NetGraph in ADN must have strong security capabilities. In addition, NetGraph must collaborate with NEs to automatically detect security risks, and automatically respond to such risks and recover services.

2. Adaptive

Network functions are evolving and increasing, security vulnerabilities are inevitable, and network attack methods are also evolving. As such, the security architecture of ADN must have the following adaptive capabilities:

- **Risk assessment:** The architecture can continuously assess the risks of users and systems that access the network, automatically learn normal behaviors, identify abnormal behaviors, and dynamically update access policies for access control.

- **Security detection:** The architecture can continuously detect security attacks, integrate intelligent learning capabilities, and identify attacks that exploit unknown methods or zero-day vulnerabilities.

- **Response and recovery:** The architecture can automatically determine and implement response and recovery solutions based on the real-time network status.

3. Open

The security detection, response and recovery capabilities of the network must be designed based on the openness principle.

- **Security detection:** The system can interconnect with third-party threat intelligence systems, and can detect threat events more accurately with the assistance of more input information. In addition, various attack methods and vulnerabilities are emerging, making it challenging to defend. The detection engine must be open to update detection rules in real time and quickly respond to security events.

- **Service recovery:** An open recovery mechanism is required when security events occur. Response policies and recovery measures should be edited in real time based on actual scenarios and environments to achieve real-time closed-loop management of security events.

4.6.4 Target Reference Architecture

4.6.4.1 Overall Architecture

ADN uses a three-layer collaborative architecture consisting of NEs, NetGraph, and security O&M center to ensure network-wide security. Figure 4.18 shows the intrinsic security architecture of ADN.

The security O&M center is responsible for security O&M across network domains. It provides the following functions:

Network-wide security asset management: The center collects security asset information of various network domains from NetGraph, such as virtual machines (VMs), containers, IP addresses, and ports, for unified management.

Network-wide security situational awareness: The center collects security event information of each domain reported by NetGraph, performs attack analysis and

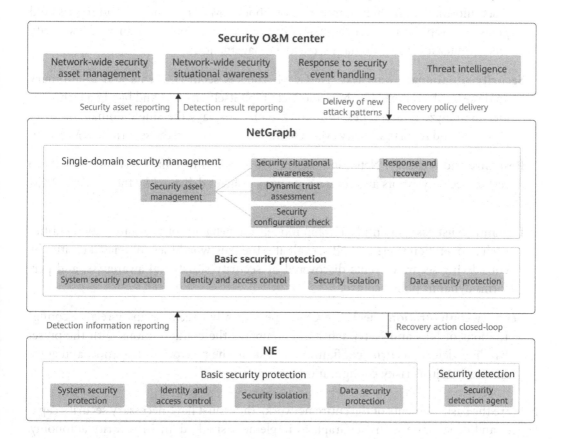

FIGURE 4.18 Intrinsic security architecture of ADN.

situational awareness across network domains, and displays the overall security situation.

Security event handling response: The center formulates recovery policies and actions based on security situational awareness information, and then delivers the policies and actions to NetGraph or other security devices for implementation, enabling quick attack prevention and service recovery.

Threat intelligence: The center is interconnected with mainstream intelligence centers in the industry to obtain the latest threat information, convert this information into new attack patterns, and send them to the security situational awareness module and NetGraph, helping them quickly detect attacks.

NetGraph is responsible for single-domain security management. It provides the following functions:

Basic security protection: NetGraph provides capabilities such as system security protection, identity and access control, security isolation, and data security protection.

Security asset management: NetGraph automatically collects single-domain security asset information, including information about VMs, containers, IP addresses, and ports, and reports the security assets in the local network domain to the security O&M center for single-domain security management.

Security situational awareness: NetGraph collects security events and preliminary analysis results reported by NEs and NetGraph itself, uses AI and big data technologies to analyze attack types and attack paths, displays the single-domain security situation, and reports security events of the local domain to the security O&M center.

Response and recovery: NetGraph uses preset or real-time edited recovery policies to restore security events and receives recovery policies delivered by the security O&M center.

Dynamic trust assessment: NetGraph models the behavior of communication entities such as operation users and NEs, evaluates the trustworthiness of related entities by considering security events discovered by security situational awareness, and performs dynamic policy control.

Security configuration check: NetGraph periodically checks security-related configurations of NEs and NetGraph itself, compares the configurations with the preset baseline, detects security configuration risks on the network in real time, and automatically adjusts risky configurations.

NEs are the basic elements of the entire network. They must have necessary security capabilities and collaborate with NetGraph to implement single-domain security autonomy. NEs provide the following functions:

Basic security protection: NEs provide capabilities such as system security protection, identity and access control, security isolation, and data security protection.

Security detection agent: NEs analyze their operation and run logs, detect possible intrusion and detection events or abnormal NE behaviors, and report the detection results to NetGraph.

4.6.4.2 Key Functions

1. Automatic single-domain configuration check and recovery

   Many network security risks are due to insecure network configurations, for example, the use of insecure communication protocols or algorithms, or the use of OS or open-source third-party software with insecure configurations. Because attackers may exploit these risky configurations to gain illicit access to the network, it is important to detect and repair such configurations quickly. The security configuration check function can be used to periodically collect security configurations on the network, compare them with the preset baseline, detect risks, and rectify them based on the preset policies.

2. Automatic detection of single-domain attacks and response and recovery

   Network attacks may occur at any time. To ensure network security, it is necessary to detect attacks and respond to them in real time in order to quickly identify attack sources, block attacks, and restore damaged services. In the intrinsic security architecture of ADN, NetGraph collaborates with NEs to quickly detect attacks on them and restore services based on preset policies.

4.6.5 Modules and Components

In the intrinsic security architecture of ADN, NetGraph plays an important role because it provides key functional modules, such as security situational awareness, response and recovery, dynamic trust assessment, and security configuration check.

4.6.5.1 Security Situational Awareness

The security situational awareness module provides the following capabilities:

1. OS attack detection. As the basis of the entire system, the OS is a major target for attackers, who can adopt various attack methods.

   - **OS user attack detection:** The module must be able to detect attacks such as brute-force cracking, unauthorized login, and user privilege escalation.

   - **Detection of malicious files and invalid processes:** The module must be able to detect attacks related to Trojan viruses as well as unexpected processes, ports, and files.

   - **Detection of tampering with key files:** The module must be able to check the integrity of files that are critical for the normal running of the system, such as key configurations and running programs.

2. User attack detection for NetGraph or NEs. Obtaining the authentication credentials of a system operator is a direct and effective attack method, one that is commonly used by hackers. Common attacks, such as brute-force cracking, login behavior analysis (e.g., login using blacklisted IP addresses or unauthorized accounts or at unauthorized time), and unauthorized access, must be detected. In addition, user behavior profiling must be supported to detect malicious users or spoofing attacks.

3. Attack detection for specific network protocols and services. Hackers may use different attack methods to attack different networks (e.g., wireless, optical, and IP networks), which have their own network protocols and services. For example, pseudo-base station attacks can be launched in the wireless field, and BGP route hijacking attacks can be launched in the IP field. Attack detection capabilities for these network protocols are required.

4.6.5.2 Response and Recovery
The response and recovery module provides the following capabilities:

1. Response and recovery policy management.
   Response and recovery policies can be preset for known types of attacks. After an attack is detected, the corresponding response action defined in the policy can be directly executed to quickly block the attack and restore services. For unknown types of attacks, response and recovery policies can be manually orchestrated online based on the obtained attack information and impact on services. In the future, the system must be able to automatically learn attack information and historical recovery policies so that response and recovery policies can be automatically generated when new attacks occur.

2. Evaluation of the impact of the response and recovery solution.
   The network status changes in real time. After an attack is detected, multiple response and recovery solutions may be available. Before implementing such a solution, the system must evaluate its impact on the network and select the optimal solution.

4.6.5.3 Dynamic Trust Assessment
Visitor authentication is a common security method adopted on conventional networks. A visitor who passes the authentication once is subsequently always trusted. However, this concept has been challenged because the visitor may be an attacker who obtains authentication credentials through illicit methods (such as phishing attacks) or an insider who uses a valid identity to perform illegal operations. The dynamic trust assessment module is used to assess the risks of network visitors and NEs with high attack risks in real time. It provides the following capabilities:

1. Risk assessment for NetGraph and NE operation users
   The security of NetGraph or NE operation users is critical. Attackers can perform any operations on the network after obtaining valid rights. Therefore, risks of specified users need to be evaluated in multiple dimensions, such as attacks (e.g., brute-force

cracking and privilege escalation), security status of user terminals (e.g., computers, mobile phones, and tablets), and abnormal behaviors of users. Based on the evaluation results, corresponding policies must be prepared for access control.

2. NE-specific risk assessment

In the future, the network environment will contain many NEs and become more and more open, meaning that attacks on NEs will be more common. Once access to an NE is gained through a successful attack, this NE can be used to launch other attacks against NetGraph or other NEs. Therefore, the trustworthiness of NEs needs to be evaluated in real time in terms of configuration risks, attack information, and abnormal service behaviors, and corresponding access control policies need to be prepared based on the assessment results.

4.6.5.4 Security Configuration Check
The security configuration check module provides the following capabilities:

1. Configuration risk check

The security configuration check module should periodically check the configurations of NetGraph, NE OSs, databases, network protocols, and services, compare the configurations with the preset baseline, and notify users of risks.

2. Configuration repair

For risky configuration items, the module should automatically generate recovery schemes, evaluate the impact on the network, and restore the configuration items if the result is acceptable.

4.6.6 Key Characteristics of the Architecture
The preceding architecture should provide the entire network with the capabilities of self-defense, self-detection, self-evaluation, and self-recovery.

4.6.6.1 Self-Defense
In this architecture, NEs and NetGraph have necessary security protection capabilities, including system security protection (such as secure/trusted boot and OS security hardening), identity and access control, security isolation, and data security protection.

4.6.6.2 Self-Detection
With this architecture, NEs can promptly obtain intrusion information, and analyze and report the information to NetGraph in real time. NetGraph uses big data and AI analytics to perform quick analysis based on historical rules, achieving **second-level** single-domain detection. NetGraph then reports the detection result to the security O&M center to detect security events across network domains. In addition, NetGraph and the security O&M center can automatically learn attack features and normal network behaviors and can detect unknown types of attacks.

4.6.6.3 Self-Assessment

In this architecture, NetGraph can evaluate operation users and NEs on the network in real time and perform dynamic policy control based on the evaluation results. In addition, NetGraph can evaluate the network impact of the solution for repairing risky network configurations and the solution for responding to and rectifying network security events and then select the optimal solution.

4.6.6.4 Self-Recovery

With this architecture, preset policies and online orchestrated policies can be used to automatically respond to and recover single-domain and cross-domain security events. In addition, the response and recovery modules of NetGraph and the security O&M center have the automatic and dynamic learning capability, and can automatically generate and execute response and recovery solutions based on the real-time network status.

REFERENCES

1. TM Forum, "IG1251 Autonomous Networks reference architecture v1.0.0," [R/OL], (2021-11-20) [2022-09-25].
2. T. Sun, Y. Zhou, X. Duan, et al., "Digital Twin Network (DTN): concepts, architecture, and key technologies," *Acta Automatica Sinica*, 2021, 47(3): 14.
3. S. Ji, S. Pan, E. Cambria, et al., "A survey on knowledge graphs: representation, acquisition, and applications," *IEEE Transactions on Neural Networks and Learning Systems*, 2021, 33(2): 494–514.
4. Z. Li, X. Jin, W. Li, et al., "Temporal knowledge graph reasoning based on evolutional representation learning," *Proceedings of the 44th International ACM SIGIR Conference on Research and Development in Information Retrieval*, 2021: 408–417.
5. X. Li, M. Lyu, Z. Wang, et al., "Exploiting knowledge graphs in industrial products and services: A survey of key aspects, challenges, and future perspectives," *Computers in Industry*, 2021, 129: 103449.
6. C. Misa, W. O'Connor, R. Durairajan, et al., "Dynamic scheduling of approximate telemetry queries," *19th USENIX Symposium on Networked Systems Design and Implementation (NSDI 22)*, 2022: 701–717.
7. W. Cerroni, C. Buratti, S. Cerboni, et al., "Intent-based management and orchestration of heterogeneous openflow/IoT SDN domains," *2017 IEEE Conference on Network Softwarization (NetSoft)*, IEEE, 2017: 1–9.
8. China Mobile Research Institute, "A digital twin network approach for 6G wireless network autonomy white paper," [R/OL], (2022-04-13) [2022-09-25].
9. F. Tao, H. Zhang, Q. Qi, et al., "Theory of digital twin modeling and its application," *Computer Integrated Manufacturing Systems*, 2021, 27(1):15.
10. M. Salem, P. Imai, P. Vajrabhaya, et al., "A perspective on Autonomous Networks from the world's first fully virtualized mobile network," *IEEE Wireless Communications*, 2021, 28(2): 6–8.
11. Q. Zhou, A. J. G. Gray, and S. McLaughlin, "ToCo: an ontology for representing hybrid telecommunication networks," In: Hitzler, P., et al., *European Semantic Web Conference*. Cham: Springer, 2019: 507–522.
12. Y. Xu, and A. Bernard, "Quantifying the value of knowledge within the context of product development," *Knowledge-Based Systems*, 2011, 24(1): 166–175.

13. W. Tong, P. Zhu, et al., *6G: The Next Horizon: From Connected People and Things to Connected Intelligence*, Beijing: China Machine Press, 2021.
14. Y. Ouyang, L. Wang, A. Yang, et al., "The next decade of telecommunications artificial intelligence," *Telecommunications Science*, 2021, 37(3): 36.
15. B. Zhang, J. Zhu, and H. Su, "Toward the third generation of artificial intelligence," *Scientia Sinica Informationis*, 2020, 50(9):22.
16. J. Sifakis, *Autonomous Systems - An Architectural Characterization*, Cham: Springer, 2019.
17. ETSI, "TS 128 313-2021, 5G; self-organizing networks (SON) for 5G networks (V16.1.0; 3GPP TS 28.313 version 16.1.0 Release 16)".
18. Z. Pu, J. Yi, Z. Liu, et al., "Knowledge-based and data-driven integrating methodologies for collective intelligence decision making: A survey," *Acta Automatica Sinica*, 2022, 48(3): 17.
19. Software Science and Engineering/National Natural Science Foundation of China, Chinese Academy of Sciences, "Research on the development strategy of software discipline: software science and engineering," Science Press Beijing, 2021.
20. J. Tao, and Y. Chen, "Current status and consideration on brain-like computing chip and brain-like intelligent robot," *Bulletin of Chinese Academy of Sciences*, 2016, 31 (7): 9.
21. M. P. Barrett, "Framework for improving critical infrastructure cybersecurity version 1.1," 2018.
22. S. Rose, O. Borchert, S. Mitchell, et al., "Special publication 800-207 zero trust architecture," *National Institute of Standards and Technology, US Department of Commerce*, 2020: 800–207

CHAPTER 5

Key Technologies of ADN

O VER THE PAST 30 YEARS, ICT has progressed significantly and profoundly changed the way we live and work. With the deepening of digital transformation, its influence is gradually expanding to various industries. This is particularly true in fields that are closely related to human life, property, development, and security and that have higher application values, such as autonomous driving, government decision-making, and healthcare. The digital transformation relies on increasingly intelligent, reliable, and flexible communications systems, promoting the development of ADN but also posing higher requirements on new information infrastructure.

Chapter 4 Reference Architecture of ADN describes the ANE layer, NetGraph layer, and AI native NE layer in detail. Each layer performs its own functions and cooperates with other layers to jointly define the basic features of ADN, such as hierarchical autonomous closed loop, distributed digital twin, distributed knowledge management, lifelong learning and self-evolution, and human-machine/machine-machine collaboration. With these features, ADN – aligned with customers' high-level objectives – uses data-driven, E2E machine learning models to achieve self-fulfilling, self-healing, and self-optimizing, and to enable autonomous network functions such as self-adaptation, self-learning, and self-evolution, thereby achieving the ADN vision and objectives.

To achieve these challenging objectives, ADN needs to innovate in fundamental theories and make breakthroughs in key technologies. ADN is a systematic project that involves many technologies. This chapter describes some of the emerging key technologies from the perspective of reference architecture association.

1. Trustworthy Network AI

With the wide application of AI technologies in the communications network – regarded as a national strategic infrastructure that must be highly reliable – AI faces increasingly more challenges in terms of trustworthiness. Such challenges include potential security issues caused by AI instability and limitations on AI applications in the communications field due to the lack of explainability. Trustworthy network

DOI: 10.1201/9781032662879-6

AI has therefore become a key technology and foundation for building the ADN cognition and trustworthiness architecture.

2. Distributed Network AI

The distributed AI architecture described in Section 4.5 enables AI computing power and algorithms to be embedded into components such as NEs, NetGraph, and ADN agents, to implement localized AI learning, application, generalization, and training. All this requires the support of distributed AI technologies, including distributed AI with central coordinated computing power, distributed AI with swarm intelligence, and distributed AI in federated learning mode.

3. Network Digital Twin

Digital twin is a basic enabling technology for the ANE, NetGraph, and NEs in the ADN architecture. It creates virtual images of physical network entities in digital mode and provides ADN with verification and test capabilities based on historical or real-time data and both modeling and simulation capabilities. In this way, automatic network pre-evaluation, efficient closed-loop management, and agile iteration can be completed in a twin environment.

4. Network Simulation Technology

Traditionally, the network simulation technology is mainly used in the offline network planning and design phase. In terms of ADN, the cross-domain, single-domain, or even intra-NE automated closed-loop framework requires networks and devices to have autonomous decision-making capabilities. The online network simulation technology provides important technical assurance for the correctness and effectiveness of decisions.

5. Digitalization of Network Knowledge and Expertise

The evolution of the ADN architecture also transforms the network O&M mode – from traditional manual O&M to network self-management with humans out of the loop. To achieve this transformation, knowledge mainly used by humans in the current system needs to be converted into that used by machines. Digitalization of knowledge and expertise is a key prerequisite and basis for the conversion. By doing so, we can continuously enable the autonomous driving of networks.

6. Human-Machine Symbiosis

In the future, both the ANE and NetGraph need to possess human-machine collaboration and symbiosis capabilities. Human-machine symbiosis, as the long-term objective of ADN, means that humans and machines understand and cooperate with each other to jointly complete tasks and reinforce each other in turn. In addition, the ANE and NetGraph must be able to learn from each other and evolve together to adapt to the uncertainty of the internal and external environments of the continuously evolving network and the complex ever-changing service requirements.

7. NE Endogenous Intelligence

ADN is a comprehensive and intelligent network architecture paradigm, in which NE endogenous intelligence plays a key role. Section 4.4 defines the AI native NE architecture based on the goal of building AI native NEs. Due to the limited computing and storage resources of NEs, heavy service traffic, and high requirements on privacy, reliability, and real-time performance, key technologies – such as hardware acceleration, lightweight real-time AI, and embedded real-time awareness – need to be implemented on AI native NEs.

8. Network Endogenous Security

The progress and application of big data, cloud computing, and AI technologies have greatly improved our capabilities of analyzing and using data. However, new challenges, such as data "black holes," data security, AI model inexplainability, and platform monopoly, have also emerged. The contradiction between privacy, security, and sharing becomes more obvious, and new cybersecurity threats are arising. As described in Section 4.6, networks must feature endogenous security, and multiple key technologies – such as automatic detection, automatic defense, automatic response, and dynamic trust assessment – must be studied and realized.

5.1 TRUSTWORTHY NETWORK AI

The industrialization of AI is accelerating as its value becomes more apparent. AI technology has become an indispensable driving force behind the development of various industries. However, AI faces many more commercial risks and challenges. Developing trustworthy AI and promoting the transparency, visibility, security, controllability, fairness, and justice of AI have become a global consensus and have been proven to be the only way for the healthy development of AI in the future.

Trustworthy AI refers to AI technologies that are explainable, stable, fair, and secure and that can be trusted by humans. Trustworthiness is a measure of the possibility that AI technologies are beyond expectations and out of control in applications. The lower the possibility, the higher the trustworthiness of AI. Highly trustworthy AI should have three characteristics: transparent and traceable processing; definite, predictable, easy-to-understand, and unbiased decisions; and strong anti-attack and anti-failure capabilities of models.

Currently, there are three main routes for the AI academia and industry to explore trustworthy AI: (1) explainable AI; (2) hybrid AI architecture; and (3) root trustworthy AI. Route 1 explains the opaque decision-making process of the current AI technology after reasoning. Route 2 leverages the strengths and avoids the weaknesses of multiple AI technologies or architecture combinations to enhance the overall trustworthiness of the system. Route 3 attempts to establish trustworthiness as supporting points for AI technologies from the perspective of AI theories and completely resolve trustworthiness issues from the root. This route will be the ultimate solution to trustworthy AI.

5.1.1 Background and Motivation

In recent decades, AI has made many breakthroughs – from Deep Blue to AlphaGo – and its integration into various industries is accelerating. As the application of AI technology increases in both breadth and depth, AI industrialization is facing new challenges in some fields that pursue ultimate precision. For example, how can AI ensure safety in autonomous driving, how can it ensure accuracy and resist attacks in aerospace and national defense applications, and how can it balance laws and ethics. Similar fields include financial investment, intelligent escort, and medical diagnosis (called highly sensitive or high-risk fields). AI applications in these fields may affect enterprise development, endanger life and health, or involve national security. Once a problem occurs, the impact is often unacceptable.

5.1.1.1 Communications Network and Trustworthy AI

As 5G networks become more popular, they coexist alongside 3G and 4G networks, giving rise to increasingly complex networks and emerging requirements. Manual O&M faces severe challenges and cannot relieve the burden on CSPs. AI-centric solutions have come into telecom networks and enabled various service scenarios, making telecom operations enter human-machine collaboration or human-machine collaborative innovation. In addition, these solutions play an active role in telecom network planning, construction, maintenance, and optimization. Typical scenarios include data center temperature control, intelligent shutdown of base stations, holiday traffic prediction, and user package recommendation.

Although AI technologies have been successfully applied to all phases of telecom networks, they are not omnipotent. Some scenarios in telecom networks cannot be handled by using AI technologies at the current stage. Service scenarios of telecom networks can be roughly classified into two types: (1) low-risk scenarios, such as advertisement recommendation and prediction by category; (2) high-risk scenarios, such as network assurance for major events and construction of highly sensitive and secure networks. AI technologies are currently used mainly in low-risk scenarios, whereas manual methods and mature traditional technologies (such as automation) are still used in high-risk scenarios. Unlike in low-risk scenarios, the impact of service failures in high-risk scenarios is usually uncontrollable and unacceptable to customers, CSPs, and telecom enterprises. Currently, AI decision-making cannot be assured in high-risk scenarios. For example, the Olympic Games – an international sporting event – has unparalleled requirements on telecom networks, such as high reliability, high performance, high precision, and high security requirements. In terms of network construction, communications trunk lines and branches are involved in cities and stadiums in different Olympic competition areas. There are requirements for network and device monitoring and attendance, and hierarchical engineering assurance and emergency measures. In terms of delegation array and performance array assurance at the opening or closing ceremony, to ensure second-level precise control and uniform formation, a large-scale lighting display involving tens of thousands of light emitting diode (LED) screens is coordinated through a network to update massive amounts of data within a short period of time. In terms of security, attacks – such as unauthorized control of stadium electronic devices, interference/damage of Internet broadband and broadcast system communication, Olympic website hacking, and ticket sales and printing interruption – need to be monitored, defended against, and recovered. Similar communication assurance scenarios for major events also include international joint conferences. The most mature "old" technologies or manual assurance measures are usually used in the most critical phases, while AI technologies only play an auxiliary role.

At ADN L5, telecom networks will have full-lifecycle closed-loop automation capabilities that feature self-learning, self-adaptation, and self-evolution, achieving autonomous driving. During the evolution from L3 to L4 or L5, more system management authority may be granted to machines, depending on whether AI technologies are highly trustworthy. In the future, L5 ADN may face the co-existence of 3G, 4G, 5G, and 6G. The network environment becomes complex and changeable, emergencies are unpredictable, and there is an unprecedented increase in data complexity and magnitude. Service scenarios involve cloud, network, and edge, as well as various types of tasks across different industries and fields. Decisive factors and noise interference are numerous. The complexity and difficulty of L5 ADN present numerous trustworthiness challenges to the application of AI technologies:

- In high-risk scenarios, AI technologies or solutions must be highly reliable, stable, and secure.

- In addition to solving deterministic problems, AI must be able to cope with unknown environment changes.

- Telecom networks cannot accept "black-box" AI. Therefore, AI must be highly explainable, and its decision-making must be traceable.

- In telecom networks, AI may be fooled by specific noise and make incorrect decisions, causing serious consequences. Therefore, AI must be highly robust.

- Knowledge and user data in the network keep increasing, and the complexity gradually increases. Therefore, AI must have high performance and availability.

5.1.1.2 Root Cause of Untrustworthy AI

The untrustworthiness or low trustworthiness of AI is usually reflected in two aspects: (1) The uncertainty, security vulnerability, and black-box property of AI make services unstable, unreliable, and opaque. For example, the data and decision rules used in the AI decision-making process are neither recorded nor standardized, and the results cannot be traced or audited. While the accuracy of DNNs can reach 99.99%, it cannot reach 100%. Dozens of methods are available in the industry to fool deep learning models, leading to misidentification by models. (2) AI lacks common sense and cognitive capabilities, meaning that machines cannot understand humans' real intents, values, morals, ethical constraints, laws and regulations, policies, and customs. As a result, machines cannot make reasonable decisions based on comprehensive interests or work in a people-oriented manner. For example, the AI network assurance service cannot realize the urgency of network dependence of a major event; AI judges may be unable to take human ethics into account; AI customer service agents may be unaware of racial discrimination.

The root causes of untrustworthy AI mainly include AI uncertainty, security vulnerability, and black-box property brought by AI theories or disciplines.

> **AI uncertainty:** The basic principles of machine learning include the induction approach and probability theory. Incomplete induction and probability randomness make the prediction results random or even distorted.

AI security vulnerability: Since AlphaGo defeated Lee Sedol, deep learning has led AI to a new wave of development, with breathtaking model precision. However, even if the Big Three of deep learning won the Turing Award (the computer field equivalent of a Nobel Prize) for their achievements in deep learning and neural networks in 2018, they cannot confidently say that a neural network algorithm can achieve 100% accuracy. That's because deep learning is data-based, requiring large amounts of training data. In addition, its precision is affected considerably by fluctuations of the data quality. The effect based on mature data is good, whereas that based on new data of new tasks is poor. For example, simple occlusion in image recognition can make the prediction result deviate significantly. The strong dependence on data and lack of data anomaly detection methods make it easy for deep learning to be fooled by malicious samples, thereby generating the wrong result.

AI black-box property: Machine learning can summarize and quickly find complex rules from large amounts of data. However, humans do not fully understand these rules, especially those that involve complex numerical representations. Deep learning simulates the working mode of brain neurons and generates results after complex computing. We do not know what results will be generated and cannot truly understand the working mechanism of thousands or even millions of nodes and parameters. When verifying AI models in labs, we often face problems concerning difficult data simulation and full verification. One of the main reasons for this is that AI algorithms lack the logic of causal reasoning as well as transparent and scientific theoretical bases from input to output.

To sum up, AI in its current implementation cannot fully meet the requirements of L4 or L5 ADN. The next-generation AI theories, technologies, frameworks, and solutions applicable to L4 or L5 ADN need to be explored to overcome the theoretical and technical untrustworthiness of the current AI.

5.1.2 Technology Insights

The trustworthiness challenges posed by AI applications have become the focus of global attention. To achieve harmonious coexistence between trustworthiness and AI technologies, developing trustworthy AI has become a global consensus and its importance has risen to the national strategic level. The AI academia and industry have invested in the research and exploration of trustworthy AI, providing a strong driving force for AI development.

In September 2016, Google, Facebook, IBM, Amazon, and Microsoft jointly announced the establishment of Partnership on Artificial Intelligence to Benefit People and Society (Partnership on AI for short), which is a non-profit organization. One of its visions is to research and develop best practices of AI technologies (from the perspectives of fairness, transparency, privacy security, and human-machine collaboration).

In July 2017, China released *New Generation Artificial Intelligence Development Plan*, which pointed out that AI laws and regulations, ethical norms, and policy systems should be established to form AI security assessment and control capabilities. At the 36th session of Xiangshan Science Conferences (XSSC) in November 2017, He Jifeng, academician of

Chinese Academy of Sciences and chairman of the Key Laboratory of New Generation Artificial Intelligence Standards and Applications of the Ministry of Industry and Information Technology (MIIT), proposed the concept of trustworthy AI for the first time, emphasizing that AI technologies must be trustworthy, including security, explainability, fairness, and privacy protection.

In 2018, IBM developed multiple AI trustworthiness tools to assess and test the fairness, robustness, explainability, accountability, and value consistency of AI products during R&D.

On April 8, 2019, the European Commission released the official version of *ETHICS GUIDELINES FOR TRUSTWORTHY AI*, proposing seven requirements for trustworthy AI: human agency and oversight; technical robustness and safety; privacy and data governance; transparency; diversity, non-discrimination, and fairness; societal and environmental well-being; and accountability.

In June 2019, the G20 proposed the G20 Artificial Intelligence Principles and provided guidance on the development of trustworthy AI in five key initiatives, for example, facilitating public and private investment in R&D to spur innovation in trustworthy AI and creating a policy environment that will open the way to the deployment of trustworthy AI systems.

On July 9, 2021, China Academy of Information and Communications Technology (CAICT) and JD EXPLORE ACADEMY jointly released *White Paper on Trustworthy Artificial Intelligence*, which proposed four rules for measuring AI: stability, explainability, privacy protection, and fairness. Developing trustworthy AI is no longer limited to defining the status of AI technologies, products, and services. Instead, it is gradually extended to a systematic methodology, involving all aspects of how to construct trustworthy AI.

Currently, the AI academia and industry are researching the low trustworthiness problem of existing AI technologies. There are three approaches:

Approach 1: Provide strong evidence for the untrusted performance (such as black-box decision-making process and lack of evidence for trustworthiness) of current AI models and algorithms. This approach focuses on the resolution of the AI black-box property, explores the decision-making process of different algorithms, and provides trustworthy decision-making evidence to achieve explainability and ease of acceptance.

Approach 2: Use engineering or systematic methods to maximize the strengths and minimize the weaknesses of different AI technologies or architectures to enhance the overall trustworthiness of the system. This approach uses innovative architecture methods and integrates the advantages of AI technologies and traditional software engineering to enhance AI trustworthiness in the short and medium term.

Approach 3: Establish reliable new AI theories and technologies based on the "root" (theoretical and scientific foundations) of AI to completely solve the trustworthiness problem.

Based on the preceding three approaches, there are three main technical development routes: explainable AI, hybrid AI architecture, and root trustworthy AI. The next section describes these three routes.

5.1.3 Key Technical Solutions

This section focuses on the three technical development routes (explainable AI, hybrid AI architecture, and root trustworthy AI) of trustworthy AI.

5.1.3.1 Route 1: Explainable AI

1. Classic Definition of Explainable AI

Explainable AI (originated from IBM) is a set of processes and methods that enable humans to understand and trust the results and outputs of machine learning algorithms. It is used to describe the expected impacts and potential biases of AI models, as well as the accuracy, fairness, transparency, and results of models in AI-driven decision-making. Explainable AI is critical to building trust and confidence when organizations put AI models into production.

Explainable AI aims to enable humans to interpret model outputs and understand the basis of models in the decision-making process (how to make decisions, why decisions need to be made, and what decisions are made), so as to establish a trust relationship between humans and AI. In short, it makes AI explainable and trustworthy. Explainable AI is in stark contrast to the "black box" concept in machine learning, as shown in Figure 5.1.

Black-box AI system

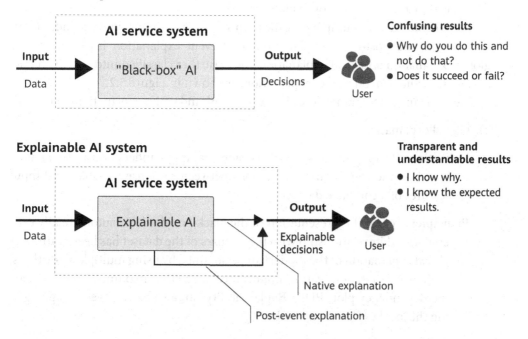

FIGURE 5.1   Comparison between explainable AI and black-box AI.

Note: The preceding figure is designed based on DARPA's idea of explainable AI. For details about this ideal, visit the official website of DARPA.

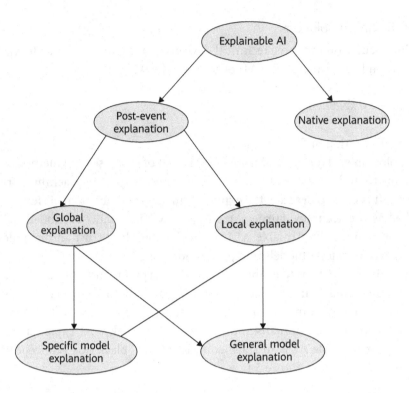

FIGURE 5.2   Classification of explainable AI.

2. Classification and Principles of Explainable AI

Explainable AI has multiple classification modes. Common types include native explanation and post-event explanation. Post-event explanation is classified into global explanation and local explanation and is further classified into specific model explanation and general model explanation, as shown in Figure 5.2.

The following parts mainly describe global, local, and native explanations of models.

(1) Global explanation

Definition: The logic behind model decision-making is understood and explained based on the conditional interactions between response variables and input features of a complete dataset.

Principle: A general representation of the black-box model is automatically generated, and its relationship with the features of the dataset has been trained. A global explanation of the model can be obtained by using multiple algorithms, such as permutation feature importance, activation maximization, and partial dependency plot (PDP). Explainability can also be achieved by aggregating the local explanation results.

Typical explanation algorithm: The principle of the permutation feature importance algorithm is to disrupt a feature and destroy its relationship with the corresponding model inference result, and then calculate the inference error

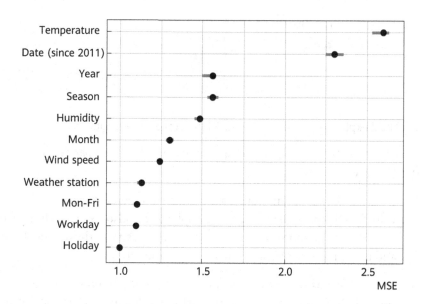

FIGURE 5.3   Permutation feature importance – impact of climate on bicycle rental.

Note: The preceding figure and the bicycle rental case are quoted from *Interpretable Machine Learning* written by Christoph Molnar from Germany.

to find the impact of the feature on model inference. If a feature has little impact on model inference, the model inference result will not be significantly affected after the feature is disrupted. For example, a model predicts the number of rented bicycles based on features such as weather, season, and humidity. After all features are disrupted and errors are calculated, a feature importance chart is obtained, as shown in Figure 5.3. In this example, the permutation feature importance algorithm is used to calculate the feature importance in the SVM model. (The farther left the black points are in the figure, the greater the global impact of the features is on the model.)

Advantages and disadvantages: Global explanation can better reflect the overall behavior of the model, but various aggregation policies also cause information loss and inaccuracy.

(2) Local explanation

Definition: Explanations are provided for decisions made on specific results or instances of a dataset. The explanations may vary significantly depending on the instances considered.

Principle: For local explainability, the internal structure and assumption of the model can be ignored. Instead, you need to pay special attention to a single data point, understand the prediction decision of the data point, view the local area in the feature space near the data point, and try to understand the model decision at the data point based on the local area. Typical algorithms

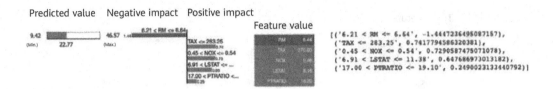

FIGURE 5.4   Local explanation extracted by LIME from the Boston dataset.

Note: **The local explanation and figure are quoted from** *A historical perspective of explainable Artificial Intelligence* **[30].**

calculate local explanations based on the cooperative game theory ("shapely value"). Other methods for local explanation also exist, such as using local gradient of the model or searching for samples near the sample to be parsed and using the samples to train surrogate models.

Typical explanation algorithm: Local interpretable model-agnostic explanations (LIME), an explainable algorithm irrelevant to the model itself, uses a simple model to explain a complex one. For a black-box model that needs to be explained, a desired sample is obtained and disturbed to generate a new sample point, and a simple surrogate model is obtained through fitting on the new dataset. This ensures that the prediction results of the simple surrogate model and the black-box model based on the local dataset are similar and allows the local surrogate model to be explained. Figure 5.4 shows the local explanation of a house price prediction dataset in the Boston region using LIME. On the left side of the figure, a linear regression model is used to explain the predicted house price (unit: USD 1000). On the right side of the figure, the local explanation is provided. A disadvantage of LIME is that the sampling method used to train an explainable model is not applicable to a high-dimensional feature space or scenarios where the decision boundary of a black-box model is complex. To mitigate this disadvantage, the author of LIME proposes a rule-based anchor algorithm (Anchors), which we will not describe here.

Advantages and disadvantages: Local explanation is more accurate than global explanation, but cannot fully describe the overall behavior of a model.

(3) Native explanation

Definition: Models or algorithms have the capability of self-explanation.

Principle: The complexity of models is restricted. Specifically, a simple model structure is used, and the model context is clear and can be explained.

Typical explanation algorithm: Simple models, such as linear model, decision tree model, Bayesian network, and knowledge graph are offered, but will not be described here.

Advantages and disadvantages: Self-explanation is better. However, the application scenarios of models are limited to some extent, and the model performance deteriorates.

3. Exploration and Development of Explainable AI

In recent years, AI giants – including IBM, Google, Microsoft, Huawei, and Tencent – have been seeking technical solutions for explainable AI and launched a rich and powerful set of development tools for explainable AI. For example, IBM has launched the explainable AI360 toolbox; tf-explain implements explainability methods as TensorFlow 2.x callbacks to ease neural networks' understanding; Facebook has announced Captum for the deep learning framework PyTorch to explain neural networks' decisions; Baidu PaddlePaddle has offered the explainability algorithm library InterpretDL; and Huawei's open-source framework MindSpore provides a visualized explanation tool MindInsight, which helps solve the explainability problem faced by the production network.

Explainable AI is the first step toward trustworthy AI. The increasingly complex models make it difficult to determine simple and explainable rules, and eventually explainability cannot be achieved. From another perspective, if AI decision-making rules are simple and easy to understand, does that mean that AI will not require any explanations in the future?

5.1.3.2 Route 2: Hybrid AI Architecture

1. Principles of Hybrid AI Architecture

The hybrid AI architecture is a short- and medium-term feasible solution that CSPs and enterprises around the world provide in the context that trustworthy AI technologies are unavailable and mission-critical services must be as trustworthy as possible. This architecture comes from an academic report [1] by Prof. Joseph Sifakis – "Autonomous Systems – An Architectural Characterization." Hybrid is the core of the architecture.

The hybrid AI architecture integrates model-based and data-based technologies to strike a balance between trustworthiness and performance. When the model-based technology is applied, detailed risk analysis is required to identify various harmful events. Therefore, the model-based technology must have a detection, isolation, recovery (DIR) mechanism and be trustworthy. The data-based technology advocates that machines will gradually replace humans for situational awareness and adaptive decision-making to deal with complex uncertain scenarios without compromising high performance. This is the key to addressing the complexity of L5 ADN. Based on the hybrid AI architecture, R&D engineers can design two modes in order to enable autonomous systems to dynamically and intelligently make choices in the runtime, meeting different trustworthiness and performance requirements. Figure 5.5 shows the hybrid AI architecture.

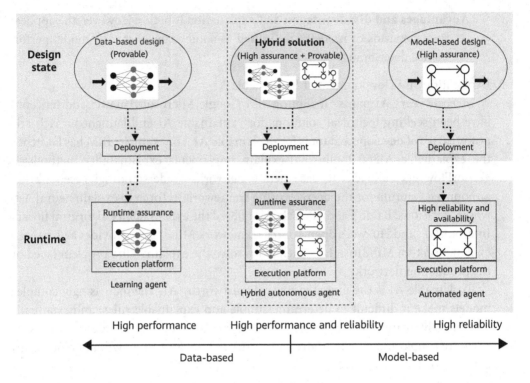

FIGURE 5.5   Hybrid AI architecture.

Note: This figure is based on Joseph Sfakis' speech entitled "Autonomous Systems. An Architectural Characterization" at the Institute of Electrical and Electronics Engineers (IEEE) World Congress on Services 2019. It is not the original picture in the speech – instead, it is adjusted to facilitate the introduction of the hybrid AI architecture. Interested readers can refer to the original speech [1].

2. Technical Application

To implement a service scenario based on the hybrid AI architecture, consider the following key points, as shown in Figure 5.6.

First, analyze and select a service scenario.

The hybrid AI architecture is mainly used to balance trustworthiness and performance. Before starting, identify whether the service scenario has high-risk requirements (high trustworthiness) and non-critical requirements (high uncertainty). Specifically, consider the following two aspects: whether the service has extreme requirements for the success rate (high trustworthiness or availability) and whether the surrounding environment of the service is complex and changes frequently. In cases where these two conditions are met, using the hybrid AI architecture is a good choice. In high-risk or high-uncertainty scenarios, model- or data-based design is more suitable to meet the requirements for high trustworthiness or performance.

Second, design and verify a scenario process.

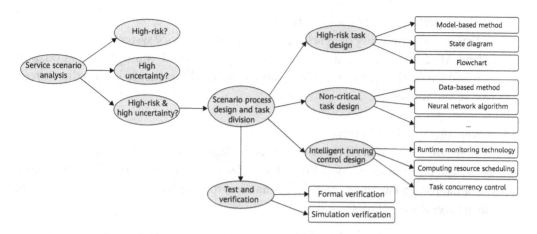

FIGURE 5.6   Key points for applying the hybrid AI architecture.

Perform process design for the service scenario, divide the service into multiple subtasks (of a suitable size) based on the cohesion and decoupling principles, and design subtasks according to their quality attribute requirements (high-risk or non-critical tasks). The following three key points should be considered:

Key point 1: High-risk task design

Carry out as detailed an analysis and design as possible for high-risk tasks. Any harmful event may cause fatal exceptions to high-risk tasks. Therefore, you need to fully consider various service states and exceptions in order to ensure that the service system runs in a predictable state. Model-based design methods are used for this purpose, while state diagrams or flowcharts can be used to show various service state and exception transitions in detail. This helps you quickly learn about the system status and formulate appropriate DIR measures to restore the system to a reliable running state.

Key point 2: Adaptive design for non-critical tasks

For uncertain task scenarios where the surrounding environment is complex and changes frequently, it is difficult to achieve comprehensive analysis and design. In this case, you can use data-based methods, such as DNN, to meet the requirements of services for adaptive environmental changes and high performance.

Key point 3: Intelligent running control design

In service scenarios where high-risk tasks and non-critical tasks coexist, it is key to determine the execution time point of the two types of tasks in the runtime. Generally, to ensure that high-risk tasks can be executed as designed, they must have a higher priority than non-critical tasks. However, if the service scenario of a non-critical task is more important, its priority may also be higher. We need to focus on the use of three key technologies: runtime monitoring technology, to capture system status information in real time for next-step decision-making; computing resource scheduling technology, to properly allocate and use limited resources; and task concurrency control and priority scheduling technology.

Third, perform full test and verification.

Due to the complexity of hybrid service scenarios, service systems implemented by hybrid AI technologies need to be fully tested and verified. Multiple formal verification and simulation verification methods can be used together to ensure the correctness of system design.

3. Advantages and Disadvantages

Based on the current AI theories and technologies, the hybrid AI architecture integrates the advantages of model-based and data-based designs and may solve some explainability, robustness, and performance problems of AI to some extent. The advantages are as follows:

- You can select a model-based or data-based design based on your service scenario.

- High-risk tasks are strictly implemented based on models without errors, and decisions can be explained and proved.

- Non-critical tasks are implemented based on data, allowing decision-making errors and featuring quick implementation and high performance.

However, this architecture also introduces some new problems, meaning we need to continuously explore solutions. First, a difficulty is raised in terms of model selection. Different models need to be deployed in different scenarios, instead of using a common AI model for all scenarios. The scenario judgment rules depend on humans' decisions. Second, the formal verification technology for complex systems remains a challenge in the industry. The introduction of AI makes formal verification more difficult. Formal verification depends on accurate data modeling and simulation and requires semantic awareness capabilities and dynamic system abstraction to ensure the controllability and repeatability of factory verification.

5.1.3.3 Route 3: Root Trustworthy AI

The trustworthiness issue of AI lies in its root. In an attempt to completely resolve the trustworthiness issue from the root, the academic community is trying to establish trustworthiness support points for AI theories and technologies. In this regard, there are currently many exploration routes and different opinions in academia. Two of the most influential technologies are dual-, single-, and three-space models and cognitive graphs.

1. Dual-, Single-, and Three-Space Models

Zhang Bo emphasized the necessity of the third generation of AI in *Towards the Third Generation of Artificial Intelligence* [2]. Robust and explainable AI theories and methodologies need to be established in order to develop secure, trustworthy, and reliable AI technologies. Based on knowledge-driven and data-driven designs, knowledge, data, algorithms, and computing power are employed together to construct more powerful AI. The solutions of dual-, single-, and three-space models are also provided.

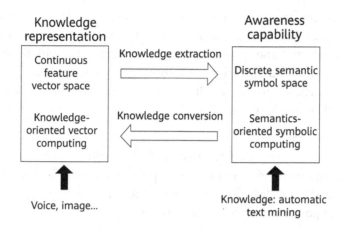

FIGURE 5.7 Dual-space model.

(1) Dual-space model

The dual-space model is a brain-like model, as shown in Figure 5.7. It consists of a symbol space and a vector space. The symbol space simulates cognitive behavior, whereas the vector space simulates awareness behavior in the brain. If the two spaces can be integrated technically, AI can theoretically achieve a similar intelligence level as humans. In this way, problems of unexplanability and poor robustness in current AI are fundamentally resolved.

The key technologies in the dual-space model include knowledge representation and reasoning, AI awareness, and reinforcement learning.

Knowledge representation and reasoning: A large part of human thoughts comes from common sense in memory, that is, knowledge. To reach the same level of intelligence as humans, AI needs a large number of knowledge corpuses for training. The knowledge needs to be automatically extracted from massive unstructured texts with uneven quality (such as encyclopedias, news, and books) and converted into knowledge representations that can be understood by machines. Searching for answers and evidence from massive knowledge based on questions is a knowledge reasoning process and provides the basis for explanability. Knowledge evaluation and scoring can make knowledge reasoning more robust and eliminate uncertainties to some extent.

AI awareness: Currently, AI lacks the capability of perceiving things – this is one of the reasons for its vulnerability and uncertainty. For example, deep learning may identify an image of "a child holding a toothbrush" as "a child holding a baseball bat." According to the dual-space model theory, the information in the vector space can be pushed to the symbol (semantic) space through knowledge guidance in order to achieve the purpose of awareness.

Reinforcement learning: Continuous learning is the basis for human growth. To achieve intelligence, AI needs to interact with the environment so that it can continuously acquire new knowledge. Reinforcement learning simulates humans' learning behavior and learns the most favorable information through trial-and-error and continuous interaction with the environment.

The dual-space model simulates the working mechanism of the brain and requires mature brain science to support it. However, we know little about how the brain works, and there is a long way to go.

(2) Single-space model

The single-space model is based on deep learning, as shown in Figure 5.8. All processing is performed in the vector space to improve the computing speed. The characteristics of deep learning determine that the single-space model has the defects of poor explainability and robustness.

The characteristics of the single-space model determine that it needs vector representation and deep learning as the key support.

Vectorization of symbolic representation: Knowledge is usually represented in the form of discrete symbols of natural languages. For computing in the vector space, the symbolic representation of knowledge needs to be converted into vector representation. Some examples of mature conversion methods currently available include Word2Vec and GloVe. In vector representation of knowledge, "words with similar semantics also have similar vectors" is a defining property. Based on this, methods such as deep learning can be used to perform efficient data computing. They can also be widely applied to text processing work such as machine translation, with remarkable accuracy.

Improved deep learning: addresses the poor explainability and low robustness of single-space models. The unexplainability of deep learning models is due to a difference between the feature space of machine inference and the space that can be understood by humans. An effective way to address unexplainability of deep learning is to associate the feature space of machine inference with the semantic space of humans. Fellow Zhang Bo provided a method to integrate humans' prior knowledge into the training of deep learning models, so that

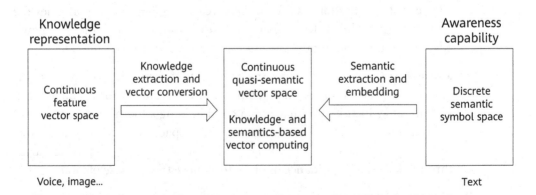

FIGURE 5.8 Single-space model.

features have a clearer semantic connotation and decision-making can be traced. For example, in a joint image-text analysis scenario, topic information that can be understood by humans is extracted from texts for neural network training, and collaborative training based on texts and images is performed to guide neural network training in order to obtain semantic features. The mathematical formula can be expressed as $L(x, y, s) = -\log p(y \mid x, h) + \lambda L_I(\varphi(x), s)$, which means that an explainable regular constraint is introduced to the objective function of the neural network training. $-\log p(y \mid x, h)$ is the task loss function, and $\lambda L_I(\varphi(x), s)$ is the explainable regular constraint. Under the guidance of text data, the explainable regular constraint can be utilized through the information complementarity between different modalities of data to improve the explainability of deep learning models. (The case comes from Zhang Bo's *Towards the Third Generation of Artificial Intelligence*.) There are two roadmaps to improve robustness: (1) Adversarial defense based on sample input, which attempts to reduce the damage that adversarial attacks cause by denoising, augmenting, and performing adversarial detection on training samples in the model training phase. (2) Adversarial defense based on model enhancement, which aims to train a more robust deep learning model by modifying the network structure, model activation function, and loss function in order to improve the defense against adversarial attacks. Ensemble is a typical defense method that has emerged in recent years.

The single-space model is based on deep learning and can fully utilize available computing power, achieving exceptional performance. However, the model faces some fundamental defects. As yet, it is unknown how much of an effect algorithmic improvement will have in overcoming such defects.

(3) Three-space model

The three-space model is a combination of the dual-space model and single-space model, aiming to achieve high-performance computing, explainability, and robustness. Figure 5.9 shows the principles of the three-space model.

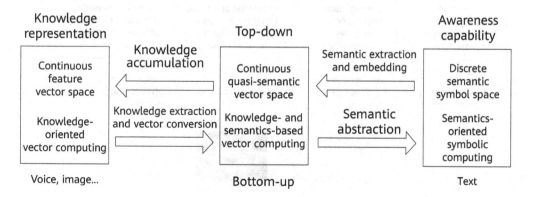

FIGURE 5.9 Three-space model.

The three-space model is a comprehensive route proposed to deal with the risks of uncertainty during the development of the dual-space and single-space models. In addition to learning from the brain-like working mechanism as much as possible, the three-space model also gives full play to the advantages of computing power – it is therefore expected to build more powerful, trustworthy AI.

2. Cognitive Graph [3]

In March 2020, Prof. Tang Jie of Tsinghua University proposed the concept of cognitive graph in the report *The Next Decade of Artificial Intelligence* [4]. According to the report, the key achievements of AI are mainly in awareness. AI has approached or surpassed humans in terms of language recognition, text recognition, and video recognition. However, it is still difficult for AI to complete decision-making analysis and semantic understanding. That is because the human brain has inference paths and nodes in the process of solving problems and can understand the entire process. On the contrary, AI systems, especially deep learning algorithms, regard the process as a black box and lack cognition on the process. The next hop of AI will focus on solving the cognitive problem, as shown in Figure 5.10.

According to Baidu Encyclopedia, cognitive graph aims to develop a next-generation cognitive engine for knowledge graph, cognitive reasoning, and logical expression based on cognitive psychology, brain science, and human knowledge, evolving AI from perceptual intelligence to cognitive intelligence. Cognitive graph, a research branch of computer science, aims to understand the essence of intelligence, make major technical breakthroughs from perceptual intelligence systems to cognitive intelligence systems, and establish explainable and robust third-generation AI.

Cognitive graph includes three core technologies: knowledge graph, cognitive reasoning, and logical expression, as shown in Figure 5.11.

Knowledge graph is an information expression structure, which is called knowledge domain visualization or knowledge domain mapping map. It can express various pieces and types of information in a form closer to human cognition

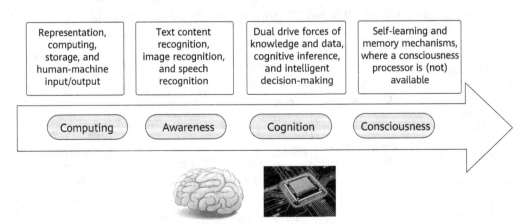

FIGURE 5.10 Next hop of AI.

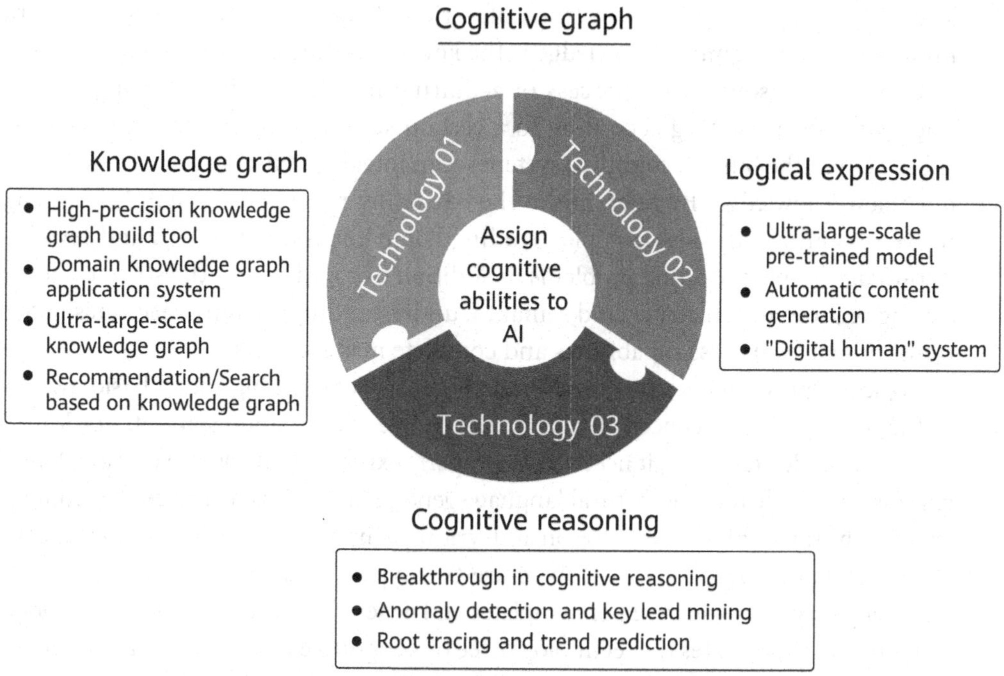

Cognitive graph
Knowledge graph
High-precision knowledge graph build tool
Domain knowledge graph application system
Ultra-large-scale knowledge graph
Recommendation/Search based on knowledge graph
Technology 01
Technology 02
Technology 03
Assign cognitive abilities to AI
Logical expression
Ultra-large-scale pre-trained model
Automatic content generation
"Digital human" system
Cognitive reasoning
Breakthrough in cognitive reasoning
Anomaly detection and key lead mining
Root tracing and trend prediction

FIGURE 5.11 Core technologies of cognitive graph.

Note: This figure is from the speech entitled *Cognitive Map, The Next Treasure of Artificial Intelligence* by Prof. Tang Jie from computer science at Tsinghua University, at MEET 2021.

Area
Population
China
Beijing
Area
Longitude
Latitude
...
UK
Country
Japan
Population
Tokyo
Latitude
Area
Longitude
Area
USA
Population
Area
Washington
Latitude
Longitude
Area

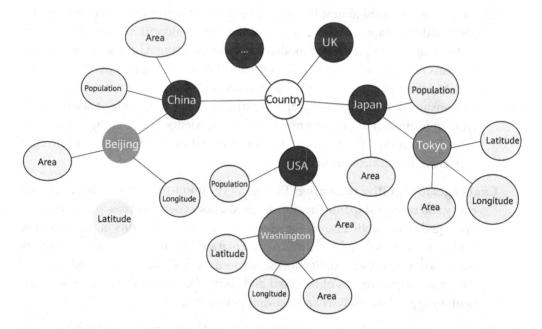

FIGURE 5.12 Knowledge graph example.

(see the example in Figure 5.12). According to the dual-channel theory of cognitive science, the human cognitive system contains a memory bank. Similarly, knowledge graph usually works as the memory bank of AI. Developing a complete large-scale knowledge graph to store knowledge of various languages, common sense, world knowledge, and cognitive knowledge is the key to building cognitive AI.

Cognitive reasoning is a process of acquiring new knowledge by using existing knowledge for reasoning according to a certain strategy. The reasoning system – a subsystem in the human cognitive system – can integrate existing knowledge to produce new knowledge. By referring to the reasoning process of human brains, cognitive reasoning can solve complex reading comprehension problems and few-shot knowledge graph reasoning problems in addition to coordinating the structured reasoning process and unstructured semantic understanding, helping machines obtain multi-modal awareness capabilities and complete massive tasks.

Logical expression is a science that studies the form of thinking and its basic law. One of the main problems concerning AI is that people cannot understand it. For knowledge to be understandable, it needs to be properly expressed. In cognitive graph, logical expression mainly refers to natural language generation. It aims to ensure that computers have the same ability of expression and writing as humans and achieve good explainability for knowledge. Currently, there are two types of natural language generation technologies: generation based on templates and generation based on neural networks.

Figure 5.13 illustrates the technology tree of a cognitive graph. For an introduction to and details about cognitive graph, see *Cognitive Graph of Artificial Intelligence* [3].

Cognitive graph involves various subject foundations and theories. The three core technologies of cognitive graph (i.e., knowledge graph, cognitive reasoning, and logical expression) involve many challenges.

Challenges to knowledge graph: Knowledge graph aims to obtain large-scale and high-quality data at a lower cost by using smarter algorithms, thereby forming better judgment or prediction models and implementing AI at the cognitive level. In terms of data quality and scale in the big data era, there are massive amounts of data or even data noise, and large numbers of storage and network resources are consumed. In knowledge graph construction, due to the wide variety of data types, it is difficult to extract knowledge. In knowledge graph storage, there is no recognized unified standard for data models and query languages, resulting in high costs and difficult promotion.

Challenges to cognitive reasoning: The lack of common-sense knowledge, as well as entity and relationship information, leads to a poor cognitive reasoning effect. The poor quality of public knowledge graph data causes the results of cognitive reasoning based on rules, distributed representation, and neural networks to deviate significantly. Complex application scenario data, such as medical and financial data, and large amounts of repeated and contradictory information make it difficult to apply data analysis and reasoning methods.

Challenges to logic expression: The template-based logic expression technology usually leads to inflexible results due to a fixed format, meaning it cannot comply with the diversity of language expressions. The deep learning-based logic expression technology has more flexible expressions, but the results are random and difficult to control.

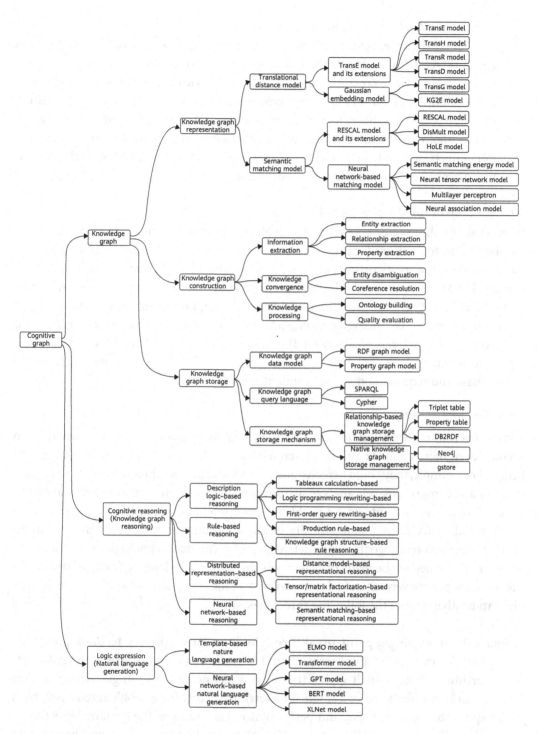

FIGURE 5.13 Cognitive graph technology tree.

Conclusion: A Challenging Road of Exploration

Root trustworthy AI aims to fundamentally solve the trustworthiness problem and is therefore undoubtedly the most difficult road of exploration. This road heads in a new direction, crossing uncharted territory with many forks along the way. However, the exploration may have unexpected gains. Root trustworthy AI is still in its initial stage. To achieve its vision, extensive research along with many theoretical and technological breakthroughs and innovations need to be made. This requires the joint efforts of AI scientists and field experts around the world and will take generation after generation to see it to its conclusion.

5.1.3.4 Comparison of Three Technical Routes

In general, the three routes represent the evolution of trustworthy AI technologies from the short term to medium term and then to the long term. There are different phases of the development of trustworthy AI. Table 5.1 compares the three routes, but in summary: Explainable AI is an enhanced solution with high technology maturity for AI trustworthiness. The hybrid AI architecture is a practical solution approaching high trustworthiness based on systematic technology convergence, but its design and use are complex. Root trustworthy AI, which represents a new direction and involves uncharted territory, is committed to building a new generation of highly trustworthy AI. This route is still in the initial phase and requires continuous exploration.

5.1.4 Technology Prospects

Today's telecom network systems are extremely complex. In the future, they are likely to become even more complex and may even have a certain sense of autonomy like human beings. For example, they could perceive and understand customer requirements or intents; perceive and comprehensively analyze surrounding environments; analyze and make decisions on requirements, intents, or problems, and provide optimal policies; and execute policies and verify results automatically or through human-machine collaboration. To achieve these autonomy goals, a qualitative leap of computer technologies is needed, and AI technologies need to be made fully trustworthy. During the long exploration and evolution process, the convergence of telecom network autonomy and trustworthy AI technologies can be divided into the following three phases:

Phase 1: Make single-point breakthroughs in trustworthy AI technologies. This phase focuses on technical research and breakthroughs in a single (or a few) trustworthiness dimension. It applies trustworthy technologies to a single telecom service scenario in order to solve a single (or a few) trustworthiness problem requiring high explainability, robustness, and performance. For example, the explainable AI technology focuses on solving high explainability. In the future, there will be different technological innovations and breakthroughs in other dimensions of trustworthy AI.

TABLE 5.1 Comparison of Three Trustworthy AI Routes

Dimension	Explainable AI	Hybrid AI Architecture	Root Trustworthy AI
Technical approach	Provides enhanced measures based on problems and post-event explanations. However, the trustworthiness problem of algorithms is not solved.	Based on pragmatism, integrates the advantages of different AI technologies to meet service scenario requirements.	Establishes a trustworthy foundation from the root to solve the trustworthiness problem completely.
Application scenario	Solves the problem of opaqueness and "black box" in the AI decision-making process, which leads to the breakdown of human-machine interaction because humans cannot understand the AI decision-making process. Application scenarios include AI-assisted medical diagnosis, financial decision-making, and autonomous driving.	Balances the requirements for high explainability, robustness, and assurance in specific service scenarios to achieve high trustworthiness to some extent. Application scenarios include key service provisioning (such as financial service provisioning) and dynamic computing resource scheduling (such as network assurance).	Attempts to solve the high trustworthiness problem of AI in all scenarios of service applications. This route is oriented to all scenarios, with no or few restrictions.
Application scope	Focuses on explainability in trustworthy AI.	Strikes a balance between multiple dimensions of trustworthy AI.	Aims to provide highly trustworthy AI technologies from the root.
Maturity	Mature	Not mature enough, incurring many problems during application	Under theoretical exploration
Availability	Available	Available	Not available in the short term
Application difficulty	Easy to learn and use	Models need to be analyzed and established based on different scenarios. The system implementation is complex, formal verification is difficult, and the overall difficulty is high.	Expected to apply to all scenarios through artificial general intelligence (AGI). The difficulty is unknown.
Development space	It is in the high-speed development period and has a large space for evolution. We need to improve or develop new machine learning technologies in order to obtain more explainable models and combine advanced human-machine interaction technologies in order to transform models into explanatory dialogs that are meaningful to and can be understood by humans.	It is the main exploration path in the industry in the short and medium term. We need to solve the universality and replicability problems in different scenarios and simplify verification technologies.	As a next-generation AI, it features multi-path exploration, large development space, and high uncertainty.

Phase 2: Implement trustworthy convergence of systematic technologies and AI.
This phase focuses on achieving the trustworthiness objectives of telecom network systems. Systems will not only rely on the trustworthiness of AI technologies; they will also adopt systematic and structured methods (such as technology combination and conditional trade-offs) in order to enhance their trustworthiness. For example, the hybrid AI architecture technology implements model-based and data-based conditional trade-offs for service scenarios of different importance levels to improve system performance, explainability, and reputation. Aiming to realize the goals of self-adaptation and self-evolution in L4/L5 ADN, we are expected to combine systematic technologies with AI in order to implement online lifelong self-learning and self-verification of services, automatic extraction and evaluation of knowledge models, and self-evolution of system software while also meeting the requirements for high trustworthiness and reliability in the telecom field.

Phase 3: Achieve root trustworthy AI for telecom networks. Innovate and create a highly trustworthy next-generation AI technology from the root to provide self-explanation, self-transparency, self-traceability, attack defense, high performance, and high availability. This will be the ultimate approach for solving the untrustworthiness problem caused by AI in telecom network systems.

Although ADN is rapidly evolving from L2 to L5, with L2/L3 ADN considered as being mature already, a long journey awaits us in exploring next-generation trustworthy AI technologies, solving trustworthiness from the root, and achieving the goal of phase 3. The most efficient technical means to solve the trustworthiness problem is undoubtedly root trustworthy AI. However, it takes a long time from basic research to AI theoretical research and then to AI technology exploration and trial commercial use. Realizing effective technical achievements that can be used for ADN in the short term is difficult. Explainable AI technologies play a key role in solving some trustworthiness problems and are the first choice for dealing with opaque and unexplainable decision-making in telecom networks. However, problems in trustworthiness dimensions, such as robustness and high performance, have not been effectively solved, and explorations are still underway. ADN is expected to reach L4 or even junior L5 by 2025, yet trustworthy AI technologies are not ready. Because of this, L4/L5 ADN construction still needs to rely on explainable AI technologies in the short and medium term – the hybrid AI architecture technology will also be one of the effective methods. Although, to some extent, explainable AI and hybrid AI architecture technologies can solve the trustworthiness problem in simple scenarios in the short and medium term, in complex environments and uncertain scenarios of telecom networks, they still face various problems, such as high costs of algorithm-by-algorithm reconstruction for explainability, complex hybrid design, and difficult verification. In the long run, we still need a new generation of trustworthy AI from the root to comprehensively solve the trustworthiness problem faced by L4/L5 ADN in an efficient and cost-effective manner. Although this road is difficult, reaching the ultimate destination will be made possible through the joint efforts of AI scientists and field experts around the world.

5.2 DISTRIBUTED NETWORK AI

From the birth of the Internet to the popularity of the Internet Plus, and then to the explosive success of the IoT era, each transformation is accompanied by the exponential growth of components (such as PCs, mobile communications devices, and intelligent terminals, which are collectively referred to as NEs) connected to the network. In addition, with the development of deep learning technologies, the scale of model parameters supported by AI algorithms is increasing – for example, the number of model parameters in the industry has increased from hundreds of millions to hundreds of billions in recent years. More and more information can now be identified by NEs and used for model training. The number of datasets that can be used for model training is also increasing rapidly, with the size of a single dataset reaching the TB level. Given such large amounts of data and large-scale parameters, a single device will take a long time to complete model training or may lack the computing power necessary to even complete the training. Consequently, the concept of distributed AI needs to be introduced. This section reviews the emergence and development of distributed AI technologies, discusses their applications in the telecom field, and explores their prospects for future evolution.

5.2.1 Background and Motivation

As described in the introduction, traditional AI encounters many problems – such as insufficient computing power, long task time, and even task failure – due to the sharp increase of data volume and model scale. Why can distributed AI solve these problems? What capabilities does distributed AI need to have? Before answering these two questions, we need to understand the concepts of distribution and distributed AI.

Distribution or distributed computing is a research direction in computer science. It studies how to divide a task that requires huge computing capabilities into many sub-tasks, allocate these sub-tasks to different computers (or other devices with computing capabilities) for processing, and combine the computing results to obtain the final result.

Distributed AI is a computing paradigm. It combines distributed computing and AI technologies to eliminate the need to transfer large amounts of data, distributes the computing power required by AI computing to different nodes, and provides source analysis, computing, and data reprocessing capabilities (e.g., the NetGraph system in ADN delivers training tasks to NEs and a swarm network is constructed based on the swarm intelligence theory).

Compared with a standalone AI system, a distributed AI system has the following advantages:

- It is more adaptable and can take a wider variety of measures for emerging situations (e.g., elastic scaling of storage and computing resources based on requirements).

- It is more cooperative. A distributed AI system enables distributed nodes to cooperate with each other in order to solve more problems than a single system can solve and has faster improvement efficiency.

- It is cheaper. Typically, multiple computers with lower specifications cost less than a centralized AI system with higher specifications and its associated sensors.

- The development process of a distributed AI system can be divided into multiple parts, which are developed by experts in each knowledge domain in parallel.

- It runs more efficiently. If the synchronization performance is good, the computing speed of parallel tasks is faster than that of sequential tasks.

- It has better scalability. New components can be developed and easily integrated with the distributed AI system.

- The most important part of a distributed AI system usually has redundancy, and agents used for backup exist in different locations.

- The results of a distributed AI system can be crossed and combined to achieve better results than those of non-distributed AI systems.

The basic idea of the distributed and distributed AI concepts is to divide the original large data and model into multiple small blocks and distribute the centralized computing power to multiple devices or edge nodes. However, division only is not enough; the following key problems also need to be solved or partially solved at the minimum:

- How to compute on a large scale?

- How to split a model?

- How to implement multi-agent system collaboration?

- How to address insufficient datasets during the multi-agent game and training evolution?

- How to organize multi-agent decision-making and intelligent system decision trees in order to adapt to complex application scenarios, such as industrial, biological, and aerospace fields?

- How to adapt to the IoT and small smart devices in order to combine more computing devices and units?

- How to learn collaboratively when device data is secure?

5.2.2 Technology Insights

Based on the focus, distributed AI can be classified into distributed AI with central coordinated computing power (focusing on large-scale computing of AI applications), distributed AI with swarm intelligence (focusing on intelligent collaboration of edge computing power), and distributed AI in federated learning mode (focusing on data isolation between distributed nodes in security scenarios).

Distributed AI with central coordinated computing power represents an algorithm or system in which an NE with coordination capabilities (referred to as Master, e.g., the NetGraph service) coordinates computing power of a cluster NE (referred to as Worker) for machine learning or deep learning. It aims to improve performance with scalable computing power and ultimately apply to larger amounts of training data and larger machine learning models.

This type of distributed AI mainly solves the following problems: the volume of computing is too large, the amount of training data is too large, and the scale of models is too large.

In scenarios where a single NE has no computing power (such as air conditioners in equipment rooms) or the NE computing power is insufficient (such as mobile communications devices), the most common method is to aggregate data to the data center (centralized storage) through data reporting (uplink) or data collection (downlink). Then, the NetGraph service fragments data (or models) and distributes the fragments to each NE with computing power under collaborative management for model training. After a unified model is generated, it is delivered to the NE side for real-time inference. Figure 5.14 shows an example of this for a campus service.

Distributed AI with swarm intelligence prioritizes efficiency and marginalizes computing power. That is, NEs have high computing power and can communicate with each other through networks at a high speed (e.g., NEs in swarm networks). This type of distributed AI can take advantage of groups to find new ideas to solve complex problems without centralized control.

The emergence of AI-driven application scenarios forces the computing power on the edge to be improved (e.g., image rendering and beautification computing scenarios). In addition, the requirements for shortening the processing delay have become unprecedentedly high. Considering the cost and delay, solutions with centralized computing power (e.g., clouds or big data platforms) may not be effective processing methods in more and more scenarios in the future. Instead, the best choice may be edge computing, which provides

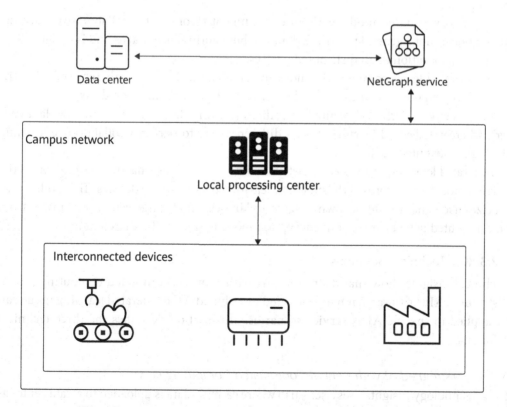

FIGURE 5.14   Uploading campus data to the data center.

the necessary computing power and minimizes the service delivery delay. AI therefore needs to be introduced into edge computing.

Swarm intelligence is a typical application scenario of introducing AI into edge computing. So what is swarm intelligence? It is defined as the collective behavior of decentralized or self-organizing systems composed of many individuals with limited intelligence who communicate with each other according to agreed principles. Swarm intelligence is inspired by nature, for example, the extensive division of labor and collaboration among bees, the way birds communicate when flying in flocks, and similar patterns in ant colonies. All this reflects the wisdom of groups. Swarm or collective intelligence consists of multiple decentralized and self-organizing agents (autonomous entities that perform tasks). The term collective intelligence was originally coined by Howard Bloom (1995) in the study of complex adaptive systems.

Distributed AI in federated learning mode prioritizes security and marginalizes computing power. It is applicable to scenarios where NEs do not exchange data (for data security) but collaborate with each other for learning. It can effectively help multiple organizations correctly use data and perform machine learning modeling while also meeting the requirements of user privacy protection, data security, and government regulations. Its design objective is to carry out efficient machine learning among multiple participants or compute nodes while also ensuring information security during big data exchange, protecting terminal data and personal data privacy, and guaranteeing legal compliance.

Federated learning enables data to be retained on devices so that user privacy can be better protected.

It provides a shared model with an environment favorable for collaborative learning. This model is not a general pre-trained model, but continuously learns and is updated during the collaboration of all distributed devices.

In federated learning mode, the model is retained on the device, thereby reducing the dependency on the central cluster and shortening the communication delay.

Traditionally, machine learning centralizes training data (in a machine or data center), whereas federated learning allows different users to perform collaborative learning through distributed devices.

Federated learning enables each distributed device (such as smartphones) to obtain the current model and improves the model by learning data from the devices. The model summarizes itself and updates its own weights and biases. Finally, the weights and biases from all distributed devices are sent in encryption mode to update the shared mode.

5.2.3 Key Technical Solutions

Technical insights show that distributed AI with central coordinated computing power, distributed AI with swarm intelligence, and distributed AI in federated learning mode can be applied to specific ADN service scenarios. This section describes the three technical solutions.

5.2.3.1 Distributed AI with Central Coordinated Computing Power

5.2.2 Technology Insights uses a scenario where campus data is uploaded to a data center as an example of distributed AI with central coordinated computing power. The prerequisite for this scenario is that model training and inference have different requirements for computing power. Scenarios that require high computing power are usually training scenarios (e.g., derive a model that is closely matched with the real scenario from the valid features of massive datasets). However, inference often uses real-time or quasi-real-time data, without the requirement for high computing power. Therefore, the entire service scenario can be abstracted as a process of collaboration between the NetGraph and NEs. The distributed AI capability is reflected in the distributed cluster task of the NetGraph that is generalized in the following structure:

- **Task:** minimum computing unit in the distributed cluster task. In a job structure, each task has a unique index.

- **Job:** worker node (running on an NE in ADN). Each job indicates a complete training target, in which tasks are split for the same training target.

- **Cluster:** worker node cluster (mapped to an NE cluster in ADN), which manages multiple jobs. Generally, a cluster corresponds to a dedicated neural network. Different jobs have different targets, such as gradient calculation, parameter optimization, and task training.

- **Master Server:** main control service (mapped to the NetGraph service in ADN), which interacts with remote distributed devices and drives and coordinates multiple jobs to run.

- **Client:** client (each NE that initiates AI jobs in ADN), which is used to start AI jobs and communicate with the remote service cluster using RPC.

Different policies are used during task division based on service scenarios, including distributed data training, distributed model training, and hybrid model training.

Distributed data training is mainly used in scenarios where models need to be trained using large amounts of data. As shown in Figure 5.15, a complete model training program

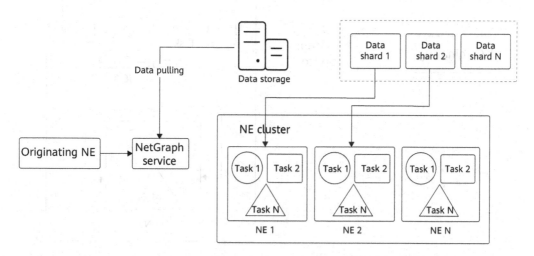

FIGURE 5.15   Distributed data training.

is stored or run on each node (each server), and the data is divided into data subsets and then allocated to multiple nodes. Each node performs training based on the data subset it receives.

Each node trains a submodel based on its own data subsets and communicates with other nodes based on a specific rule (e.g., exchanging submodel parameters or updating parameters). Finally, the cluster ensures that training results from each node can be effectively integrated to obtain a global machine learning model. For example, each node trains a submodel to obtain node parameters, and a final model is generated based on the average parameter values of a plurality of nodes.

Distributed model training, also called parallel task or distributed task in the distributed field, is mainly used in large model training scenarios. As shown in Figure 5.16, a large model is split into submodels that are allocated to different nodes for training.

Unlike distributed data training, distributed model training stores and runs only some model training programs (not a complete model training program) on each node. Submodels depend strongly on each other, for example, the output of node 1 is the input

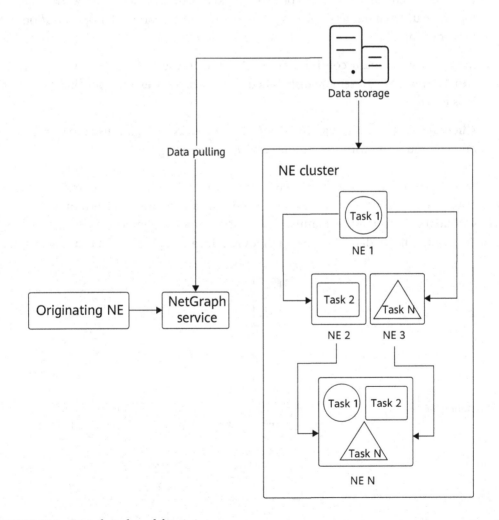

FIGURE 5.16 Distributed model training.

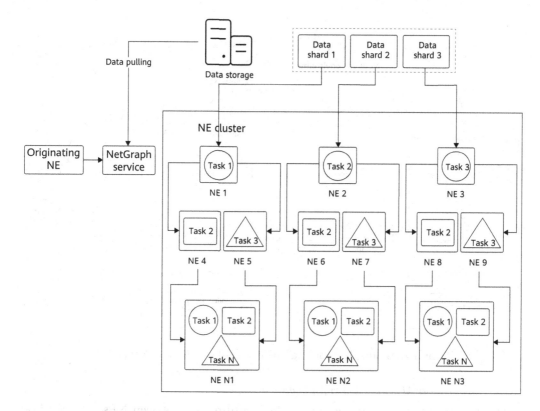

FIGURE 5.17 Hybrid distributed model training.

of the submodels of nodes 2 and 3. Therefore, nodes need to communicate with each other about intermediate computing results.

Hybrid model training combines distributed data training and distributed model training and is mainly used in scenarios where large-scale data training and large model training coexist. As shown in Figure 5.17, a model is split into multiple submodels (assume that there is a multi-GPU cluster system) that are allocated to different GPUs on a single node. Then, data is divided, and each node trains a part of the data. Finally, model parameters are synchronized to obtain global parameters and a global model.

The hybrid model training process shows that:

- Parallel or distributed model training implemented by a single node or multiple nodes involves model splitting, parallel computing, and distributed computing.

- Distributed data training is implemented between multiple nodes, and technologies such as data splitting and distributed data storage and management are involved.

- Distributed model training on a single node requires multi-process communication on the node.

- Distributed training between multiple nodes requires cross-node and cross-process communication.

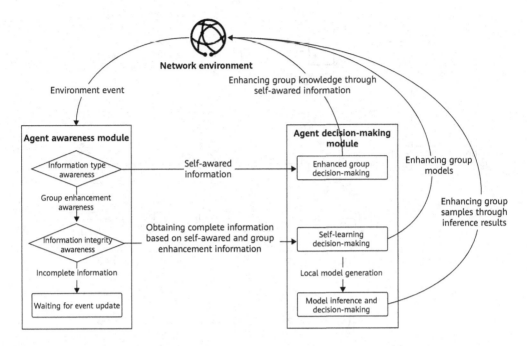

FIGURE 5.18   NE awareness and decision-making model of swarm intelligence.

5.2.3.2 Distributed AI with Swarm Intelligence

Swarm intelligence, a natural mechanism for coordination between NEs, is carried out through indirect communication. When a task is executed in the environment, an NE deliberately propagates the information it perceives to trigger another event. In this way, the entire series of tasks is performed until the final target is achieved. A single NE usually consists of two parts: awareness module and decision-making module. Figure 5.18 shows the collaboration relationship between them and the group network [5].

Imagine a community surveillance system consisting of multiple smart cameras. Each camera supports dynamic image recognition (belonging to the AI domain) and is preset with images of abnormal events (such as hiding a person's face, carrying tools for suspected criminal purposes, and climbing doors and windows) before delivery. Due to the large area and complex terrain of a community, no camera can independently capture complete information about a specific monitored object (especially if there are many monitored objects that move frequently). Nor can each camera determine which monitored objects have abnormal behaviors and generate corresponding alarms. In this case, the swarm intelligence algorithm is useful. First, each smart camera determines the monitored object locally (e.g., whether the behavior features of the monitored object in the field of view are abnormal). Then, the locally collected data, together with the locally generated model and inference results (as enhanced samples), are sent to the shared network center (in centralized mode, such as the surveillance center) or synchronized to other cameras (in decentralized mode) on the entire intelligent network in real time. In the former case, the network center aggregates the inference results returned by each intelligent node, trains an enhanced model, and delivers the model to each node. In the latter case, each intelligent

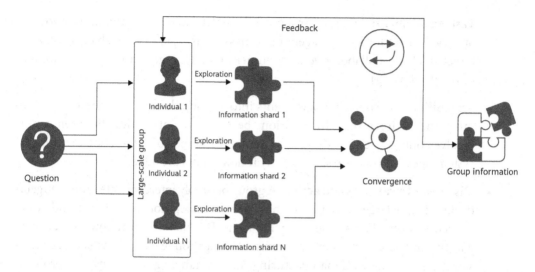

FIGURE 5.19   Swarm intelligence process construction model.

node performs local retraining after receiving the inference results synchronized by other nodes, thereby achieving information sharing and accuracy improvement.

Based on the preceding example, the swarm intelligence operation process can be summarized as shown in Figure 5.19. It consists of three steps [6]:

Exploration: Each individual in a group independently explores the current problem to obtain part of the information about the problem (local inference result).

Convergence: The information explored by all individuals is converged in a certain way (the converged inference results are used to enhance samples for retraining to generate a new model).

Feedback: The group information generated by the convergence activity is fed back to each individual in a certain way to stimulate the individuals to continuously explore (the model is delivered again to enhance the inference capability).

1. Advantages of Swarm Intelligence Compared with a Single Complex Agent [7]

According to the preceding example of a swarm intelligent network formed by smart cameras, we can conclude that swarm intelligence offers the following advantages:

• **Improving performance through parallelization:** Swarm intelligence systems are ideal for parallelization because group members run based on their own rules and can perform different operations at different locations at the same time. This feature makes groups more flexible and efficient for complex tasks because individual agents (or their groups) can independently solve different parts of the complex tasks.

- **Task enablement:** An agent group can complete some tasks that are impossible or very difficult for a single agent (e.g., mass transport of heavy objects, dynamic target tracking, collaborative environment monitoring, and large-scale autonomous monitoring).

- **Scalability:** Incorporating new agents into a group does not require reprogramming the entire group. In addition, because the interaction between agents involves only adjacent individuals, the total number of interactions within the system does not increase significantly if new agents are added.

- **Distributed awareness and action:** A group of simply interconnected mobile agents deployed in a large search space has greater exploration capabilities and wider awareness scope than a single complex agent. This makes swarm intelligence more effective in tasks, such as exploration and navigation (e.g., in disaster rescue missions), nanorobot-based manufacturing, and human diagnosis using microrobots.

- **Stability and fault tolerance:** Due to the decentralized and self-organizing attributes of swarm intelligence, the failure of a single unit does not hinder the completion of a given task. If one or more individuals fail or exit a task, the group can adapt to changes in population size through implicit task reallocation without any external operation.

2. Problems to Be Solved for Swarm Intelligence

The swarm intelligence method is based on systems with individual redundancy. There are still many problems and shortcomings in applying the swarm intelligence theory to a multi-agent system. In current research, the following are the main problems that exist:

First, conflicts often occur when a threshold model is used to assign self-organizing tasks. Some tasks attract many individuals, while others do not receive any attention.

Second, the swarm intelligence method is based on group behavior. A system using such a method is difficult to design and formally analyze and often produces a suboptimal solution. Because group behavior relates to the interaction between individuals and between individuals and the environment, it is difficult to predict the accurate behavior of individuals and the entire system.

Finally, the swarm intelligence method performs distributed control based on large numbers of simple individuals. However, a multi-agent system sometimes needs to solve complex problems, making it difficult to apply the swarm intelligence method to a multi-agent system, especially a heterogeneous multi-agent system (e.g., a system consisting of non-peer-to-peer intelligent NEs).

In swarm intelligence, each individual has part of the information for solving problems. After the information of each individual is processed, the information that can be identified by the group is formed and shared within the group, achieving an effect of 1+1>2. However,

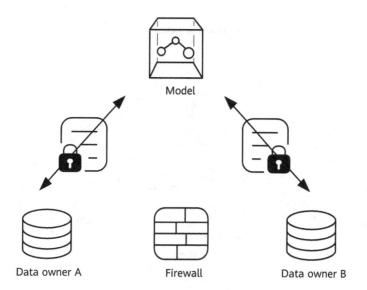

FIGURE 5.20   Data relationship of a federated learning model.

there are service scenarios where multiple NEs need to work together without data or other information shared between them, for example, collaborative analysis between banks and user centers. In this case, distributed AI in federated learning mode is required.

5.2.3.3 Distributed AI in Federated Learning Mode

1. Technical Features of Federated Learning [8]

    As shown in Figure 5.20, federated learning has the following technical features in terms of data usage, service interaction, and model sharing compared with other distributed AI technologies:

    • Data of all parties is stored locally with network isolation, preventing privacy disclosure and violation against laws and regulations.

    • In the federated learning system, each participant has the same identity and status (equivalent in the network structure).

    • The modeling effect of federated learning is the same as or similar to that of using a centralized dataset. (Each participant interacts only with a single model as if it were their own private model.)

    • The participants combine the data to establish a virtual common model that is a system of shared benefits.

    Figure 5.21 shows an evolution by mapping the preceding model to the ADN scenario.

2. Technical Classification of Federated Learning [8]

    Based on the distribution of the feature space and sample space of the participants' datasets, federated learning can be classified into horizontal federated learning, vertical federated learning, and federated transfer learning.

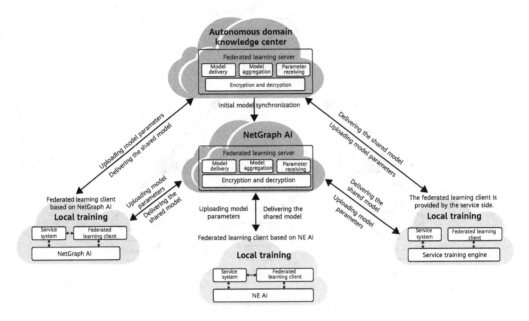

FIGURE 5.21   ADN federated learning scenario.

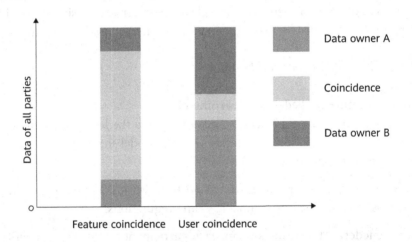

FIGURE 5.22   Horizontal federated learning feature and user coincidence.

The essence of horizontal federated learning is sample combination, which is applicable to scenarios where participants have the same business form but serve different customers, that is, scenarios with high feature coincidence but low user coincidence (as shown in Figure 5.22). For example, banks in different regions have similar businesses (features are similar) but serve different customers (samples are different).

The essence of vertical federated learning is feature combination, which is applicable to scenarios with high user coincidence but low feature coincidence (as shown in Figure 5.23). For example, shopping malls and banks in the same region serve residents in this region (samples are the same) but provide different services (features are different).

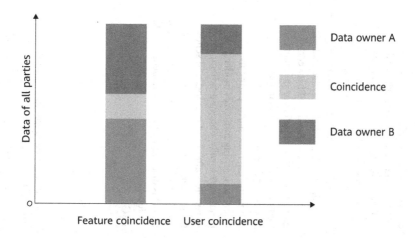

FIGURE 5.23   Vertical federated learning feature and user coincidence.

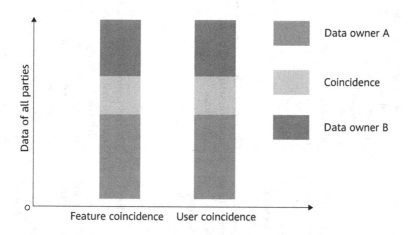

FIGURE 5.24   Federated transfer learning feature and user coincidence.

Federated transfer learning aims to leverage transfer learning in order to overcome the problem of insufficient data or feature coincidence while also protecting privacy (as shown in Figure 5.24). It is further promoted based on the concept of federated learning so that collaborative modeling can be performed on any data distribution and any entity to learn a global model. It can be applied not only to the space of two different samples but also to two different datasets.

5.2.4 Technology Prospects

The preceding sections describe some of the different application scenarios of distributed AI with central coordinated computing power, distributed AI with swarm intelligence, and distributed AI in federated learning mode. This section compares the three types of distributed AI from different dimensions, such as problems to be solved and data processing solutions (as described in Table 5.2), helping you better understand their application scenarios.

TABLE 5.2 Comparison between the Three Types of Distributed AI

Dimension	Distributed AI with Central Coordinated Computing Power	Distributed AI with Swarm Intelligence	Distributed AI in Federated Learning Mode
Key problems	Scenarios with large amounts of computing and data	Scenarios where edge facilities are scattered (and even moving), the computing power of a single facility is weak, and there is no central control	Scenarios where conflicts between user privacy protection, data security, and collaborative training need to be solved, and data silos need to be broken
Data processing	The training data is divided into multiple shards, and multiple compute nodes use their own data shards to train the same model in parallel. The central server dynamically determines whether the shards are balanced.	Most data comes from real-time collection.	For each modeling node involved in federated learning, data is stored locally (so that the data is not equal or balanced between nodes). Model parameters or gradients are trained locally and then shared in encrypted form to update models.
Training mode	Data is mainly processed in parallel mode. Each node uses different data to calculate gradients and update the shared parameters, and the resulting new model is sent back to each node.	Different training modes are used based on swarm intelligence algorithms.	Each modeling node participating in federated learning initializes model parameters locally, obtains gradients or parameters after local training, and sends the gradients or parameters to a trustworthy third party for model update. Then, the new model is distributed to each modeling node for local update.
Communication mechanism	Multi-point interface (MPI), Nvidia Collective Communication Library (NCCL), Huawei Collective Communication Library (HCCL), and Google Remote Procedure Call (gRPC)	Different communication mechanisms are used based on the environments where swarm intelligence facilities are located. For example, Wi-Fi communication can be used for campus cameras.	gRPC
Architecture characteristics	The central server has absolute control over compute nodes and their data, and the compute nodes receive only instructions from the central server.	In a distributed architecture without central control, each edge compute node is adaptive to environment data and can share data and models among multi-agent networks.	Compute nodes have absolute control over data, and even the central server cannot operate the data on the compute nodes. In addition, the compute nodes can stop computing and communication and exit the collaborative learning process at any time.

Future of Distributed AI in the Telecom Field [9]

By 2030, there is expected to be an increasing number of smart devices around the world, including personal and household devices, various sensors across urban areas, unmanned ground vehicles, and smart robots. All these smart devices need wireless connectivity to achieve unattended task coordination and cooperation, requiring the communications system to provide higher throughput, higher reliability, and lower latency and jitter. The convergence of communications and computing platforms enables us to make full use of the awareness and learning capabilities of networks. The communications system will intelligently and automatically configure resources, provide users with highly intelligent and personalized services, and achieve almost perfect performance.

In higher-speed telecom networks, AI can empower robots semantic awareness capabilities to help them understand semantic instructions, raising their awareness and positioning capabilities closer to human levels. In addition, AI can implement intelligent information source coding, improving the communication capability of robots from the current bit level to the semantic level.

AI can also be applied to synthetic network slicing to build heterogeneous networks, for example, integrated terrestrial and non-terrestrial networks.

In typical high-speed networks, AI can coordinate complex multi-layer heterogeneous networks to provide optimal coverage for users.

5.3 NETWORK DIGITAL TWIN

In recent years, various industries have actively promoted digital and automated transformation to achieve service agility, improve operations efficiency, and significantly reduce costs. In addition, all-new smart cities and digital governments are being propelled as top-level national strategies in order to build data infrastructure and widely apply digital technologies to government management services, enabling digital and intelligent government operation. In the communications field, CSPs and equipment vendors have been exploring, researching, and deploying automation in network management and service provisioning for many years. As of yet, however, they have been unable to effectively solve problems such as high network energy consumption, high O&M costs, and low efficiency. With the development of 5G, IoT, and cloud computing technologies along with the emergence and exploration of new network services, the network scale is expanding, the network load is increasing, and the increasingly complex network poses more and more challenges to O&M. In addition, the high reliability requirements for network operations and the high costs associated with faults and O&M trial-and-error severely restrict the efficiency and innovation of network operation. To address these challenges and problems, it has been proposed to apply the digital twin technology to networks. Through network digital twin construction, key capabilities such as precise awareness and online simulation for physical networks are developed, helping networks achieve low trial-and-error cost, intelligent decision-making, and efficient innovation while also supporting the realization of full-lifecycle network autonomy.

5.3.1 Background and Motivation

In the ADN era, networks have become increasingly digital and intelligent. For example, 6G is deeply integrated with AI in the design phase, unlike the AI function add-on mode in the 5G era. The in-depth integration of networks and AI poses higher requirements on data awareness, quality, and sharing and collaboration. The specific challenges are as follows:

First, the status of traditional networks cannot be detected in a comprehensive, real-time, and refined manner. They can only be managed and controlled within the scope supported by long-period statistics at the surface level. In addition, the data quality is poor; for example, some data is missing, the sample set is unbalanced, and the data is not labeled. Due to limited data storage resources, most of the data stored in the network is historical data generated within half a year, resulting in poor timeliness. To sum up, the data infrastructure, acquisition mechanism, and sharing mechanism in today's networks cannot meet the requirements of ADN for real-time and accurate data.

Second, in terms of data sharing and collaboration, future networks need to quickly identify and adapt to complex and changeable dynamic environments through closed-loop interaction between digital and physical domains, cognitive intelligence, and automated O&M. In addition, cross-scenario and cross-domain data and data models need to support the sharing and interaction mechanism in order to implement full-scenario, full-lifecycle autonomy, including planning, construction, maintenance, optimization, and operations.

A digital twin network can interact and map with physical network entities in real time. As a digital image of physical network entities, the digital twin network has the same NEs, topology, and fitting behavior models as the physical network and can accurately duplicate the physical network and its mechanisms, providing a digital verification environment close to the real network for network O&M optimization and policy adjustment. The digital twin technology is used to implement real-time interaction, digital analysis, verification, and control between physical and digital networks through real-time data awareness and online real-time computing, driving ADN to realize the following key capabilities:

1. Real-time holographic digital images enable online simulation and verification, substantially reducing trial-and-error costs. In a digital twin network, various network management systems and applications can efficiently analyze, diagnose, simulate, and control the physical network based on data and models. In addition, the behavior of the digital twin network can be recorded and managed (e.g., traced and played back), completing pre-verification without affecting network operation.

2. AI and knowledge drive network intelligence and self-evolution. Compared with traditional simulation platforms, AI models are trained based on a digital twin network and their pre-verification results are more reliable. In addition, the digital twin network can be independently constructed and expanded. It can also be combined with

AI technologies to explore new service requirements that have not been deployed on the live network and verify their effect. This enables such networks to achieve self-evolution.

3. The development mode has changed from service scenario-based development to twin data-based development. Traditionally, network functions are developed based on service scenarios and features. In the future, network functions will be developed based on digital twin data.

5.3.2 Technology Insights

The concept of digital twin dates back to 2002, when Dr. Michael Grieves, a professor at the University of Michigan, introduced the Product Lifecycle Management (PLM) concept prototype [10] to the industry. Although this concept was not formally proposed, the key elements of digital twin were included in the PLM concept prototype, including physical object space, virtual object space, and information flows between them, as shown in Figure 5.25.

Since its emergence, the digital twin technology has been successfully applied in multiple industries, such as city construction, aerospace, and production workshops. In 2017, 2018, and 2019, the digital twin technology was selected as one of Gartner's top 10 strategic technologies [11]. It is becoming a new engine for national digital transformation, a new direction for multinational enterprises' business layout, and a new focus for global information technology development.

There is no unified definition for the digital twin model and implementation framework. Both industry and academia are trying to define the general or dedicated model framework. Gartner has proposed four elements for building a digital twin model in the IoT digital twin technical report: model, data, monitoring, and uniqueness. International Organization for Standardization (ISO) has released a draft framework standard for digital twin systems oriented to manufacturing and proposed a reference framework that consists of a data collection domain, a device control domain, a digital twin domain, and a user domain. The draft will soon become the first international standard in the digital twin field. In academia, Tao Fei, a professor of Beihang University, has proposed a typical five-dimensional digital twin model [12]. In this modeling concept, the twin system

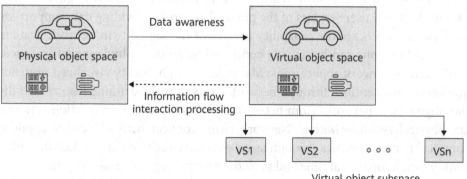

FIGURE 5.25 PLM conceptual model.

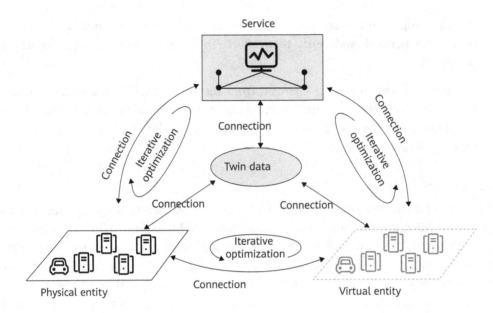

FIGURE 5.26   Five-dimensional conceptual model of digital twin.

is represented by *{PE, VE, Ss, DD, CN}*, where PE indicates physical entity, VE indicates virtual entity, Ss indicates service, DD indicates twin data, and CN indicates connections between these parts. For details about the model elements, relationships between them, and the overall modeling concept, see Figure 5.26. The model system has been put into practice in intelligent production workshops.

5.3.3 Key Technical Solutions

Currently, there is no unified and clear definition for network digital twins in the industry. In reference [13], network digital twins are defined as a network system consisting of physical network entities and virtual twins that can interact and map with each other in real time. In addition, four core elements of network digital twins are defined: data, model, mapping, and interaction. Data is the cornerstone of building a digital twin network. A unified data-sharing repository is constructed as the single data source of the digital twin network to efficiently store historical and real-time data, such as the configurations, topology, status, logs, and user services of the physical network, providing data support for the network twin. Models are the capability sources of the digital twin network. Data models with rich functions can be flexibly combined to create multiple model instances for use with various network applications. Mapping is a high-fidelity visualized presentation of physical network entities through network twins. It is the defining feature that distinguishes digital twin networks from network simulation systems. Interaction is the key to virtual-physical synchronization. Network twins connect network service applications and physical network entities through standard interfaces to collect and control physical network information in real time and provide prompt diagnosis and analysis.

Based on related concepts and practices in the industry and the objectives of ADN, this book defines the network digital twin and its key features as follows:

Objective: Design open models, an elastic data foundation and pipes, real-time data awareness, real-time online computing (trend prediction, online simulation, and knowledge self-update), and open twin interfaces to support hierarchical network autonomy and collaborative autonomy.

Definition: Network digital twin is a collection of technologies and architecture mechanisms, including twin models, a data foundation and pipes, real-time data awareness mechanism, real-time online data computing mechanism, open interfaces, and hierarchical architecture.

Key Constraints and Quality Attributes

- **Model composition:** A digital model of telecom networks is not a new concept. Traditional telecom network systems have many information management models, and many standards that define and restrict how to construct these models. Note that network digital twins are not only a 1:1 mappings of traditional physical network entities, but also a superset of the mappings. For example, in the time dimension, a twin model can gain insight into the future network trend in addition to expressing the real network status. In terms of breadth, a model includes not only traditional network components, but also other contexts that affect network quality, including traffic, crowd flow, and weather. This is necessary to meet the high-level requirements of future network autonomy. For example, base station parameters can be intelligently adjusted based on contexts such as weather and crowd flow to meet the requirements for ultimate service experience in scenarios like large gatherings and peak hours.

- **Real-time performance:** This is one of the key features of a network digital twin, which provides support for online real-time computing and service closed-loop management of upper-layer twin applications. Services at different layers have different requirements on twins in terms of real-time performance. The management and control units require a real-time performance ranging from hundreds of milliseconds to subseconds. Upper-layer closed-loop management can be implemented in offline mode (including dynamic deployment of ML models).

- **Uniqueness:** Uniqueness is one of the main differences between the network digital twin and the data layer of a traditional system (including the NMS). An NMS has many data silos and redundant data, meaning that large amounts of data need to be converted when data traverses different network functional units. For example, when the inventory system data is transferred to the performance analysis system, the latter converts the data based on its own model. In the future, the network digital twin will be the only source of system data at each layer, significantly reducing data redundancy, inconsistency, and conversion overheads caused by the same data (such as inventory data) traversing different network functional units.

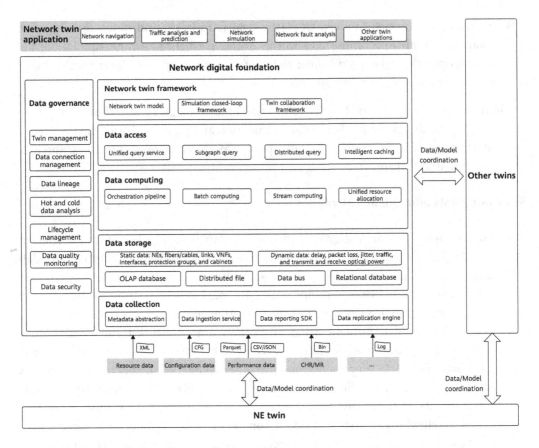

FIGURE 5.27   Network digital twin reference implementation.

Based on the definition, key features, and design principles of the network digital twin, this book provides a reference implementation, as shown in Figure 5.27. The key components are as follows:

Data collection: provides a real-time data awareness mechanism to meet real-time awareness requirements between upper- and lower-layer systems. In addition, it provides interfaces that can map the physical world to meet real-time closed-loop management and control requirements.

Data storage: provides heterogeneous data storage capabilities for network object data, time series indicator data, and log text data to support large-scale data storage and scenario-specific real-time data association and retrieval.

Data computing: provides real-time data analysis, computing, and inference capabilities to support real-time trend awareness, big data computing, and AI inference, as well as ADN online simulation and real-time data interaction.

Data access: provides real-time and flexible access to scenario-specific data in order to meet the requirements for real-time consumption of upper-layer twin application data and quick innovation of twin applications.

Network twin framework: provides unified models for pan-network domains, environment state, and knowledge interaction to support quick innovation of ADN applications based on twin models. In addition, it provides a data and model-sharing mechanism to meet the requirements for multi-agent system autonomy and upper- and lower-layer collaborative autonomy.

Data governance: provides global data governance capabilities to ensure the E2E quality and security of data in addition to providing data lifecycle management.

Future network digital twins must possess key capabilities such as real-time twin data awareness, real-time online simulation, and cross-domain twin collaborative autonomy. Based on service requirements and reference implementation, there are four technical challenges, which are summarized below:

Real-time awareness: In the future, many applications built on twins will have high requirements for real-time performance, such as real-time online network simulation and dynamic network congestion awareness. These applications require real-time online computing and analysis in addition to large amounts of data for analysis. Therefore, we need to make breakthroughs in fine-grained collection using traditional collection methods and address the bottlenecks of computing, bandwidth, and storage resources caused by the required higher real-time performance.

Modeling complexity: Modeling based on large-scale network data must ensure rich model functions while also taking into account model flexibility and scalability. These requirements further increase the difficulty in building efficient and hierarchical basic models and functional models.

Real-time computing: In the ADN era, many real-time analysis applications frequently access twin data, and any computing delay will affect the timeliness of upper-layer applications. Therefore, the network twin technology needs to support real-time computing of massive data and fully utilize system software and hardware resources in order to provide ultimate computing power.

Twin collaboration: Future networks will become intelligent and consist of multiple network agents. Each agent can complete its own service closed-loop management and autonomy as well as collaborate with other agents to support the collaboration and autonomy of the entire network. This poses difficulties and challenges in terms of data negotiation between twins, data sharing between systems, and standardization.

In the following parts, we discuss the key technologies for overcoming these challenges based on the technical challenges of network digital twins and the technical trends in the industry.

1. Real-Time Awareness Technology of Network Digital Twins

The real-time performance of awareness depends on factors such as the data collection method, bottom-layer transmission protocol, and data encoding mode.

Data collection is the basis for building a twin data warehouse. A digital twin network is a digital mirror of the physical network. As such, the more comprehensive and accurate the data is, the higher the fidelity of restoring the physical network through the digital twin network. Data collection should be target-driven, meet the objectives of digital twin network applications in terms of type, frequency, and method, and be comprehensive and efficient. When data modeling is performed on a specific network application, the required data can be efficiently obtained from the data-sharing warehouse at the network twin layer.

The industry is awash with network data collection methods. For example, there is SNMP, which is mature and widely used; NETCONF; NetFlow, which can collect original code streams; sFlow; and network telemetry, which supports the push mode at the data source end. Different data collection methods have different characteristics and are applicable to different application scenarios.

Selecting an appropriate interface protocol can help improve the transmission efficiency and reliability. For example, reference [13] recommends selecting different interface protocols at different network layers to meet the requirements for scalability, real-time performance, and reliability.

In addition to the protocol layer, efficient data encoding can be further considered to significantly reduce the amount of transmitted data. There are two types of encoding: lossless compression and lossy compression.

A common encoding method for lossless compression is the difference method, that is, difference function or difference operation. The difference results reflect the changes between discrete magnitudes, and the original function f(x) is mapped to f(x+i) – f(x). In many scenarios, differential encoding can be used for network O&M data. For example, in the case of bit error counting, the difference method records only the increment, and then the prefix sum method can be used to quickly restore the data.

A common lossy compression method is using AI models to capture joint probability distribution of data and using AI model–based inference to replace actual data query and statistical calculation. This method may introduce certain errors. The relative error rate of AI models is a key indicator. Common performance indicators in a network include bit error rate and delay. These indicators or their combinations are referred to as time series, and periodic indicator features can be captured using mathematical models. Common time series models include Long Short-Term Memory (LSTM) and Transformer.

2. Modeling Technology of Network Digital Twins

Network twin modeling involves a great deal of complex work. It must have good compatibility to express objects at all levels of the entire network, meet openness requirements, and provide model policies to support twin multi-data sources, heterogeneous storage, and real-time twin representation.

First, we need to answer the following questions: (1) What is the object of network twin modeling? (2) Which scenarios exist and what data is required to support these scenarios? The objects of network twin modeling include the following data:

Network service provisioning data: includes inventory data related to objects such as NEs, boards, physical ports, logical ports, timeslot resources, wavelength resources, and Virtual Local Area Network (VLAN) resources. A digital model of telecom networks is not a new concept. Traditional telecom network systems have many information management models and many standards that define how to construct these models.

Network service assurance data: includes network alarms and performance indicator data.

Physical simulation data: includes building, equipment room, electrified cable distribution, and air conditioner data, supporting equipment room planning, network planning, and online deployment simulation.

Network simulation data: includes physical mechanism data of optical components, electrical components, and RF components related to network communication, supporting online and accurate real-time simulation of network communication.

External environment data: includes other contexts that affect network quality, including traffic, crowd flow, and weather, so as to meet high-level requirements of future network autonomy. For example, base station parameters can be intelligently adjusted based on contexts such as the weather and crowd flow to meet the requirements for ultimate service experience in scenarios like large gatherings and peak hours.

AI and knowledge-derived data: includes O&M knowledge (fixed expertise and new knowledge that is continuously generated) and AI models that support intelligent network decision-making.

System target behavior data: includes definition data of service self-fulfilling, self-healing, and self-optimizing targets, supporting target-based autonomy of twins.

Then, we need to understand what modeling mechanisms and languages are needed to represent the above data.

There are many practices and references in the industry about twin modeling languages. This book analyzes and compares several mainstream modeling languages, as described in Table 5.3.

To meet the requirements of E2E lifecycle management and collaborative autonomy in the future, modeling languages must be sufficiently open and scalable. Table 5.4 provides a reference design of the network twin model based on the preceding requirements.

3. Real-Time Computing Technology of Network Digital Twins

In the future, service closed loops will be completed in milliseconds to subseconds. To ensure highly reliable automatic closed loops, real-time online simulation involving large amounts of data access and computing becomes a must. Therefore, the real-time computing capability of digital twins becomes a key technical indicator.

TABLE 5.3 Digital Twin Modeling Languages

Modeling Language	Function Description	Common Field	Model Type	Maintenance Organization/Vendor
DTDL	Be able to describe twin status attributes, telemetry, commands, components, and relationships, as well as inherit features.	IoT	Information model	Microsoft
ECSchema	Be able to describe twin attributes, telemetry, relationships, and components, as well as inherited features. Main characteristics: integrated but multi-plane and multi-layer, comprehensive, flexible, and easy to expand	Infrastructure	Information model	Bentley
OPC UA	OPC Unified Architecture (OPC UA) is an open international standard specification developed for secure and reliable data exchange in industries such as industrial automation. It was released by the OPC Foundation in 2008, based on which the international standard IEC62541 was formulated.	IoT	Information model	OPC Foundation
Modelica	Open, object-oriented, and equation-based unified physical system modeling language for multiple domains, supporting component modeling for objects such as mechanical and hydraulic objects. Main characteristics: multi-domain unified modeling, equation-based non-causal modeling, object-oriented physical model, continuous discrete hybrid model, and separation of knowledge and computing platforms	Industrial field	Behavior model Information model	Modelica Association

Real-time online computing of twins includes two key capabilities: efficient converged data computing and ultimate computing power based on software and hardware.

Efficient converged data computing: The closed-loop delay ranges from milliseconds to subseconds, whereas the simulation time ranges from milliseconds to

TABLE 5.4 Abstraction Relationship Definition of Network Twin Model Reference Design

Relationship Abstraction	Relationship Definition	Description	Source	Sink
Generalization	E2E	Subclass-Parent class	Router	Device
	Inherit Extent	Inherit	Router	Device
Reification	instanceOf IsA	Type instance	XXX NE	Router
	Has	Instance type	Router	XXX NE
Unidirectional association	connectTo Peer, linkTo	Connect to	OSPF interface 1	OSPF interface 2
	Trigger	Trigger/Generate	Interface 1 down	Alarm 1
	happenOn	Occurred in	Alarm 1	Board 1
	measureOn	Measure	CPU usage	Board 1
	affectedBy	Affected by	ETH_LOS	BD_BAD
	Cause	Cause	BD_BAD	ETH_LOS
	carriedOn bearing InverseCarriedOn	Carried on	Tunnel	PW
Aggregated to the whole	aggregation	Aggregation	E2E Ethernet service 1	Sap1
		Aggregation	Trunk 1	Interface 1
	memberOf	Member	Interface 1	Trunk1
	protectOf	Mutually protected	Interface 1	Interface 2
Combined to the whole	Contain Composition	Contain	Board	Port

hundreds of milliseconds. In addition, the simulation process involves large amounts of data and many computing steps. For example, if the route distribution protocol is used for simulation in 1:1 mode, the simulation time may be at the minutes level, which cannot meet the requirements for low-delay closed-loop in the future. Currently, the industry proposes a method of fitting the simulation operation process by using a mathematical model. This can significantly reduce the simulation operation time. For example, the GNN method is used to implement simulation computing of network routes, achieving millisecond-level inference on large-scale networks.

Ultimate computing power based on software and hardware: In the future, intelligent computing will use data analysis and AI-powered computing as the mainstream computing modes. How to use the underlying computing power effectively to achieve the ultimate efficiency of upper-layer intelligent computing is the key.

To meet the requirements of large-scale analysis and computing and AI-powered intelligent computing in the future, underlying chips provide a series of support technologies, including Single Instruction Multiple Data (SIMD), vectorized computing, and AI-dedicated computing technologies. These technologies reconstruct chip instructions to meet specific computing requirements, such as column-oriented batch processing (SIMD and vectorized computing) and targeted acceleration for AI training and inference.

Facing the computing requirements of current network twin applications, the twin computing engine will help upper-layer applications automatically obtain the maximum underlying computing power in the future, including computing power orchestration and automatic computing power acquisition.

Computing power orchestration: Applications do not need to be aware of how the underlying hardware computing power is implemented. The bottom layer of the digital twin provides flexible pipeline orchestration capabilities to design the data computing process.

Automatic computing power acquisition: The twin base is automatically generated based on code. It then automatically orchestrates underlying hardware computing power to implement distributed parallelism, instruction-level parallelism, and breakdown and allocation of AI-powered computing.

4. Collaboration Technology of Network Digital Twins

Future networks will become intelligent and consist of multiple network agents. Each agent will complete its own service closed loop and autonomy as well as collaborate with other agents to support the collaboration and autonomy of the entire network. How does a network digital twin implement data and model negotiation between twins? How can automatic discovery, automatic synchronization, and model adaptation be implemented for the data? This book breaks down twin data collaboration and sharing as follows:

Automatic Data Discovery and Synchronization: Various models with virtual-physical interaction (modeling of physical space and sharing of status and environment data), and data sharing, automatic discovery, and automatic synchronization between different systems are involved in automatic data discovery and synchronization. Large amounts of physical resource, status, and environment data may be reported, synchronized, or changed for running instances, and the status of instances may change. All this requires full automation and real-time performance. In addition, the data changes will trigger automatic changes and adaptive adjustment of upper-layer applications.

Target-based Model and Behavior Collaboration: The unified collaboration capability oriented to autonomy intent requires target-based collaboration between different twins. This involves model information sharing and interaction as well as behavior understanding and collaboration. Related technologies involve unified target description metalanguage, model behavior collaboration engine and framework, and key implementation mechanisms that support target breakdown, conflict adjudication, and collaboration.

5.3.4 Technology Prospects

This section describes the basic concepts of digital twins and network data twins, analyzes the closed-loop timeliness and data availability differences of network systems at different layers, and provides a reference implementation of network digital twins.

The following key technologies are introduced:

Real-time awareness technology of network digital twins:

The increasing scale of network status data conflicts with the higher requirements for real-time awareness. This book points out the bottleneck of the current data collection technology and proposes technologies such as improved data encoding to overcome this conflict.

Modeling technology of network digital twins:

Digital twin models are analyzed and compared, several elements for future network twin model modeling (model expression openness, real-time representation, heterogeneous data access, and upper-layer application interface call) are proposed, and a reference for network twin model design is provided based on modeling requirements.

Real-time computing technology of network digital twins:

SIMD, vectorized computing, AI-dedicated chip technologies, and the latest framework technologies for big data and AI-powered computing are analyzed, and technical suggestions and directions are provided for mainstream computing scenarios of ADN AI+big data analysis.

Collaboration technology of network digital twins:

Automatic data discovery, automatic data synchronization, and target-based collaboration technologies are proposed to implement autonomous collaboration between twins in future ADN.

As a key enabling technology of ADN, the network digital twin acts as a data and model hub. With the industry and academia continuing to explore and promote business scenarios, technologies related to the network digital twin will gradually become mature. In the future, as the application of digital twin increases and becomes more complex, and twin cognition capabilities gradually advance, the following technical directions need to be further analyzed and discussed:

Multi-model integration technology:

Network configurations and service information, including basic NE configurations, environment information, running status, and link topologies, can help us accurately describe physical networks in real time. In addition, there are many applications oriented to complex scenarios, such as online network simulation. The overall model framework needs to take into account how to integrate these simulation mathematical models, AI models, and network object models in order to meet the requirements of different twin application scenarios and combined functions in the future.

Network twin cognition technology:

As ADN develops toward adaptive, self-learning, and self-evolution, network twins need to possess cognitive capabilities. Data update and closed-loop feedback can be used to implement twin adaptation, self-learning, and self-evolution.

5.4 NETWORK SIMULATION TECHNOLOGY

Real-time network applications, such as AR/VR, telemedicine, and remote control, are increasing year by year. In addition, more and more enterprises are adopting remote office as part of their operations. In these scenarios, users have stricter and more flexible resource management requirements on the network, posing significant challenges to CSPs' network resource management. The traditional O&M mode, which is human-dominated and time-consuming, cannot meet the fast-growing service requirements.

In the future, machines – rather than humans – will perform network management. Building a real-time, efficient, and accurate simulation network can accelerate machine cognition and enable machines to learn human O&M methods. Machines can independently execute the optimization solution, simulate troubleshooting measures, and perform upgrades on the simulation network without changing the physical network or affecting the services running on it.

5.4.1 Background and Motivation

Simulation is a digital technology that abstracts a real system as a model and conducts experiments on the model.

Network simulation establishes models for network devices and links on a physical network to simulate network trafficor behaviors, including network planning, changing, troubleshooting, and optimization, and predict changes in the network topology, traffic, and configuration to check whether policies function as expected, as shown in Figure 5.28.

Network simulation is classified into non-real-time offline simulation and real-time online simulation based on scenarios.

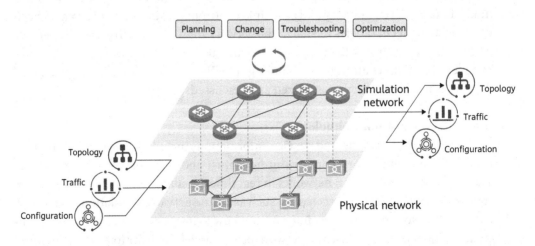

FIGURE 5.28 Network simulation principles.

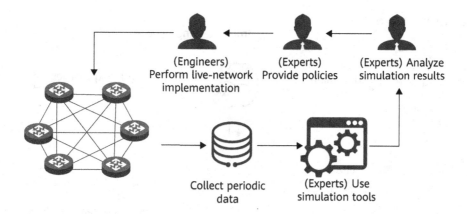

FIGURE 5.29   Offline simulation workflow.

Offline simulation is mainly used for long-duration network activities, such as network planning, optimization, and prevention, covering periodic data collection, simulation tool use by experts, simulation result analysis by experts, policy provision by experts, and live network implementation by engineers. Figure 5.29 shows the offline simulation workflow. This type of simulation is implemented at a low frequency and does not require high real-time performance. Simulation tools are mainly used to assist experts in verifying the effectiveness of policies and reduce implementation risks on the live network.

Online simulation is mainly used in scenarios where network changes are performed in real time, for example, network troubleshooting and emergency recovery. It includes network mirroring, exception awareness, policy generation, policy verification, and network implementation. The simulation system generates network mirroring in combination with network data. When a network exception is detected, the analysis system generates a response policy, the simulation system verifies the feasibility of the policy, and the control system implements network changes, as shown in Figure 5.30. As the level of network automation increases, customers expect services such as network troubleshooting and self-service application to be implemented in minutes or even seconds. Therefore, the real-time performance requirement for the simulation system becomes increasingly strong.

In the ADN era, the network structure becomes more and more complex, and the requirements for network automation become higher and higher. Traditional simulation technologies face the following challenges:

- **Real-time performance challenges:** Users require service provisioning and dynamic network optimization to be performed within minutes. However, this timeframe is insufficient for CSPs to transfer live-network data to the lab for simulation and then send the simulation results back to the NetGraph center.

- **Systematic challenges:** Customer service may involve multiple network domains, such as access, datacom, and transport. A single simulation technology cannot meet service requirements.

The following sections systematically review the network simulation technology and describe the corresponding countermeasures for the preceding challenges.

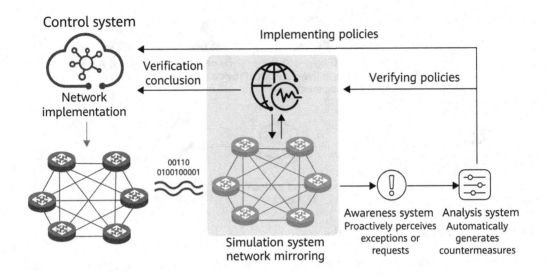

FIGURE 5.30   Online simulation workflow.

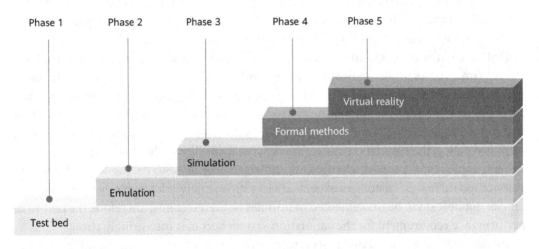

FIGURE 5.31   Network simulation phases.

5.4.2 Technology Insights

The network simulation technology has been developed for a long time and has witnessed significant changes in its precision, efficiency, and coverage scenarios. The development process of this technology can be divided into five phases, as shown in Figure 5.31.

5.4.2.1 Review of Network Simulation Technology

1. **Phase 1:** Test Bed

     The common method is test bed. Generally, a mirroring environment that is consistent with the target system is set up in the lab to analyze and study the target system.

This method is costly but reliable and is mainly used in the network integration verification lab to simulate the response capability of network hardware in extreme environments such as high temperature, cold temperature, and humidity. It mainly tests the network hardware and performance and simulates faults.

2. **Phase 2:** Emulation

The common method is hardware simulation. This method simulates a test environment similar to or even the same as the target environment, connects the devices, applications, and products/services to be tested in the environment, verifies their performance, stability, or functions based on the network scenario, and predicts the bearer capabilities. The principle is to use software to simulate hardware. This method has high requirements on understanding hardware principles and engineering.

Typical software is Open Network Emulator (CrystalNet) [14] launched by Microsoft in 2018. It simulates the entire Azure network infrastructure to search for network terminal faults and malware. CrystalNet requires that the simulation environment include the actual production configuration, software, hardware, and topology, so as to perform similar network operations to obtain the simulation results. It consists of the orchestrator, device virtualization sandbox, and virtual links.

3. **Phase 3:** Simulation

The common method is logic simulation, with which software is used to simulate some functions of the hardware network. If other influencing factors are in the ideal state, network events such as what-if events can be simulated to observe the network status and response. This method is based on ideal conditions and therefore cannot simulate device exceptions.

Typical software is Cisco's OPNET simulation tool [15], which helps customers design, construct, analyze, and manage network architecture, device configurations, and network routing. It includes a three-layer modeling mechanism, provides a complete device simulation model library, and uses the discrete event-driven simulation mechanism for calculation, making simulation much more efficient.

4. **Phase 4:** Formal Methods

The common method is formal modeling, which uses mathematical methods to prove or refute the correctness of the system relative to the expected algorithm of a formal specification or attribute [16]. Formal verification requires a strict formal description for product specifications and implementation. Formal modeling and verification overcome the shortcomings of delay-based verification and reduce the simulation difficulty by using mathematical methods. However, whether the model abstraction is comprehensive becomes a bottleneck. As the network becomes more and more complex, the model that represents it also becomes more and more complex.

5. **Phase 5:** Virtual Reality

Virtual simulation uses a virtual system to simulate another real system or physical environment. It can provide an immersive experience for participants, who can also obtain a perceptual and rational understanding of objective things from the virtual environment with qualitative and quantitative integration. Immersive, interactive, and conceptive are the three basic features of VR. When applied to the network field, VR combines people who use the network, machines (network devices) in the physical network, and environments (environment factors) related to network devices in the same virtual space for converged display. The virtual space contains factors related to users, networks, and environments. User factors include user track, network access point, user experience, and user preference. Network factors include device size, space location, connection relationship, and signal coverage. And environment factors include crowd density, atmospheric temperature, area attributes, and holidays. Through the combination of people, machines, and environments, holographic stereoscopic simulation centered on user experience is constructed.

5.4.2.2 Network Simulation Evolution Trends

Based on the five phases of simulation technology development, network simulation has displayed three development trends: digital, systematic, and online, as shown in Figure 5.32.

From physical to digital: The simulation digital evolution process spans from test bed simulation to software-based hardware simulation and finally to converged simulation by combining the network, people who use the network, and network-affecting environment in a digital space.

From single to systematic: Simulation has evolved from single-technology simulation to multi-technology and multi-condition converged simulation, from single-component simulation to integrated system simulation, and from single-NE service simulation to multi-layer network service simulation.

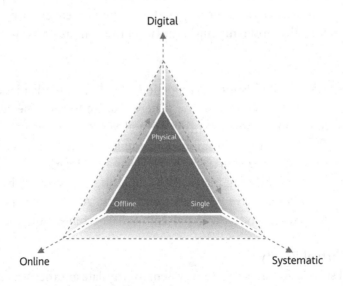

FIGURE 5.32 Network simulation evolution trends.

From offline to online: With the ongoing construction of computing power networks and the application of AI technologies, simulation that originally required in-depth participation of lab experts is gradually replaced by machine-based simulation. Machines are deployed in customers' production and O&M processes to automatically determine various network conditions, perform real-time simulation, and implement real-time closed-loop management.

5.4.3 Key Technical Solutions

Physical simulation, analog simulation, and function simulation have been widely used in the industry and are not described here. The following part mainly describes the application practices and exploration of digital simulation and virtual simulation in the network field.

5.4.3.1 Key Technology 1: Real-Time Simulation Using the Digital Modeling Technology

The digital modeling technology breaks the traditional simulation process down into three parts, as shown in Figure 5.33. The time-consuming simulation calculation is stripped from the process, and simulation modeling is performed based on feature relationships. During inference simulation, the feature relationships are matched in the model, and multiple matching results may exist. Finally, the simulation results can be obtained by performing multi-objective decision-making.

1. Offline Simulation Modeling

    Offline simulation modeling is necessary for real-time simulation. Figure 5.34 shows the working principle of offline simulation modeling.

    A massive amount of historical data is used for unsupervised training to learn the relationships between NE parameters. Through large-power computing and continual learning, the offline simulation model can mine the change relationships

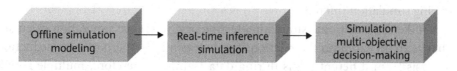

FIGURE 5.33   Working principle of real-time simulation.

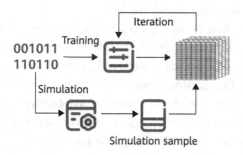

FIGURE 5.34   Offline simulation modeling.

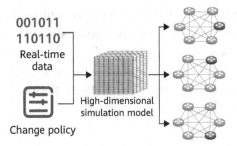

001011
110110

Real-time
data

Change policy

High-dimensional
simulation model

FIGURE 5.35   Real-time simulation inference.

between NEs and between NEs and parameters from data. At the same time, a simulation module is integrated into the system to simulate the data sample at a specific threshold. The simulation result is used as a positive sample to continuously modify the relationship model. In this way, a vector body with tens of thousands of dimensions is obtained. Each vector that forms the vector body represents a variation relationship between an NE and its peripheral NEs and between an NE and its related parameters. The vector body is called a high-dimensional simulation model.

2. Real-Time Simulation Inference

Inference refers to the process of using known knowledge in the knowledge base according to a certain strategy in order to draw a conclusion step by step from the initial evidence. Real-time simulation inference is a key step in digital simulation, the working principle of which is shown in Figure 5.35.

In the offline simulation modeling phase, the historical data of a network is used for long-duration training to construct the known knowledge combination of the network. When a simulation task is executed, real-time network snapshots are injected into the high-dimensional simulation model. In this case, users only need to enter the change policy that needs to be simulated. The simulation result is then provided during simulation inference.

Unlike the traditional simulation technology, inference simulation calculates the change trend based on the relationships between NEs and performs deduction and analysis from different paths during data training. Therefore, multiple simulation results may exist.

3. Simulation Multi-Objective Decision-Making

The modeling method of the digital simulation technology has many advantages. However, compared with the traditional white-box simulation, the result is not unique. This means that a new technology needs to be introduced in order to make decisions on multiple results, that is, simulation multi-objective decision-making. Figure 5.36 shows the working principle of simulation multi-objective decision-making.

When multiple simulation results exist, experts may find it challenging to identify which simulation result is correct. The graph attention mechanism needs to be introduced in order to simulate expert judgment.

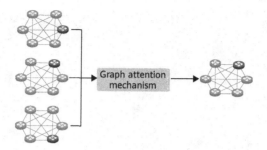

FIGURE 5.36   Simulation multi-objective decision-making.

As the name implies, the graph attention neural network is a neural network structure that runs on a graph. This network introduces the attention mechanism based on the graph neural network. The attention mechanism focuses on local information.

We analyze the simulation results and implement weighted aggregation of neighbors by learning the neighbor weights of NE-level parameters. Based on the weight superposition, we can calculate a weight for each simulation result. The simulation result with the highest weight is the most possible simulation result.

5.4.3.2 Key Technology 2: Building Virtual Simulation with People, Machine, and Environment Combined

The traditional network simulation technology considers user requirements on the network and the impact of the environment on the network only in general terms and does not conduct proactive awareness and management. As a result, the network always lags behind service requirements. Using the simulation technology is crucial to detect user requirements and environment changes in advance, analyze their impact on the network, generate countermeasures, and dynamically adjust the network. This is why we try to break through the boundary of a pure network and incorporate network-related users, environment information, and the network into a virtual system, which is called "Virtual Simulation with People, Machine, and Environment Combined".

1. People

   People refer to the users who are using or are about to use the network and have ultimate awareness of the network quality. To ensure user experience, the traditional approach involves planning network construction and configuring network resources based on experience. This approach cannot adapt to environment changes and causes redundant resource configuration. There are different exploration paths for human track awareness in the industry, such as wireless triangulation, ultra-wideband (UWB) tracking, and facial recognition. These approaches have their own advantages and disadvantages and apply to different scenarios.

   Virtual simulation does not need to identify user identities and characteristics or collect large amounts of user information. Instead, it only needs to detect user access

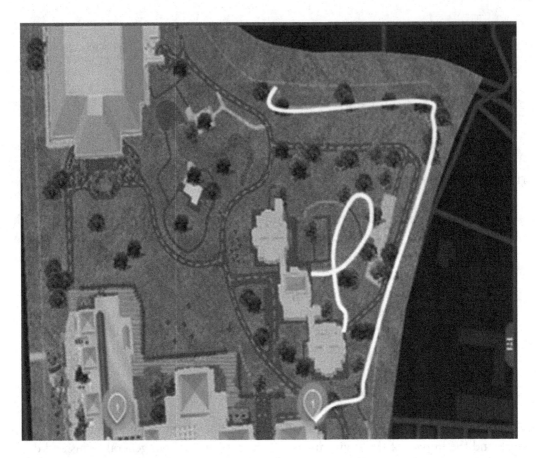

FIGURE 5.37   Re-ID technology.

terminals on the network. We choose the person re-identification (Re-ID) technology [17] to meet our requirements. This technology does not collect, store, or associate specific user characteristics, and marks each user as a random ID. As shown in Figure 5.37, user IDs are repeatedly identified under different cameras to construct user tracks.

With anonymized user tracks and network traffic, the network simulation technology can predict user experience of abstract user instances at different network access points, providing input for network optimization.

Typical applications include VIP user assurance, emergency assurance in user gathering areas, and the like.

2. Machine

Machines refer to physical devices that are virtualized in the simulation environment, as shown in Figure 5.38. Information about exposed ports, such as network cables, fiber ports, and locations, is recorded in the system to associate the impact of the environment on devices (e.g., device footprint and power consumption). Digital simulation is performed on the impact of devices on the environment, such as heat dissipation and ray coverage.

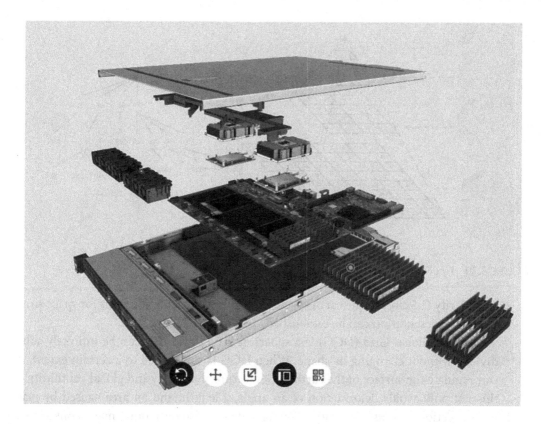

FIGURE 5.38   Network device virtualization.

Virtual simulation of NEs can be combined with physical simulation, analog simulation, function simulation, and digital simulation to associate internal and external network information and eliminate network impacts caused by external changes.

For example, when a port on the network is faulty, the virtual simulation system can map the physical port of a board. Maintenance engineers can quickly identify the fault point through smart terminals (such as mobile phones and VR devices).

Another example involves misoperations causing a fiber to become loose, or high device temperature resulting from a faulty heat dissipation system causing the network to deteriorate. In such cases, it is difficult to locate the fault on the network. After the virtual simulation system is introduced, the root cause of the fault can be quickly identified.

3. Environment

The environment here refers to the environment information that affects the network, such as weather, temperature, holidays, crowd flow, and vehicle flow. Environment simulation has a major impact on the network. While related technologies have been explored and applied in single-point service fields, there is no unified environmental representation system. To deal with this problem, the GeoSOT technology [18] is introduced to combine people, machine, and environment information in one expression space and assign a unique one-dimensional code to the minimum

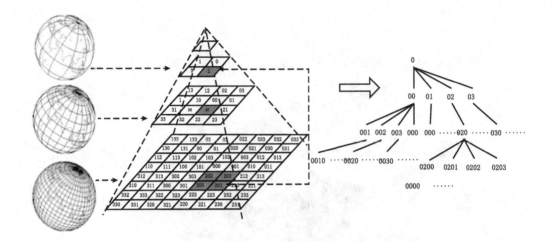

FIGURE 5.39 GeoSOT.

granularity (1.5 cm³) in the earth space. In this way, a calculation basis for space simulation representation can be established, as shown in Figure 5.39.

Discrete Global Grid (DGG) is a spherical fitting grid that can be infinitely subdivided without changing its shape. When DGG is subdivided to a certain extent, it can simulate the surface of the earth. DGG features hierarchy and global continuity – this not only avoids deformation of an angle, a length, and an area caused by planar projection and discontinuity of spatial data but also overcomes many constraints and uncertainties of GIS application. That is, image data of any resolution (different precisions) obtained at any location on the earth can be expressed and analyzed in a standard manner, and multi-resolution operations can be performed at a definite precision. This has become a new research hotspot in international GIS academia. The regular hierarchical subdivision structure gives the grids with different spatial resolutions strict transformation relations and provides a unified expression mode for the fusion of geographical phenomenon data with uneven distribution and unequal scale.

Along with the improvement of the simulation real-time performance, the network simulation technology will be closely combined with the network digital twin, and more application practices will emerge in the virtual simulation field. Many vendors have started research in scenarios such as E2E network SLA quality assurance, wireless network rate improvement and energy saving, and integrated visualized operations of communications networks. The development of virtual simulation technologies will lead to disruptive changes to CSPs' intelligent O&M.

•

5.4.4 Technology Prospects

Real-time high-performance simulation depends on high-speed physical computing power, efficient computing models, and distributed computing frameworks. William Nordhaus, a winner of the 2018 Nobel Prize in economics, proposed in *The Progress of Computing*: "Computing power is the amount of information that a device can process per second based on internal status changes." The pre-trained simulation model provides a model

FIGURE 5.40   Predicting network traffic based on vehicle flow.

basis for efficient computing, and the model quantization technology uses the hardware acceleration function to accelerate model execution. With cost reductions, large amounts of computing power will be used to perform refined real-time simulation, providing customers with precise capacity expansion, fault identification, and energy saving, while also significantly reducing TCO. Real-time simulation will be used more and more widely.

As an example, imagine that in the future, when you are about to drive to a scenic spot, the CSP analyzes the real-time traffic on the road leading to the scenic spot (as shown in Figure 5.40), automatically invokes the real-time network simulation technology to predict the number of tourists in the next hour, and then predicts that the egress traffic of the scenic spot network is about to be saturated, and the Internet access experience of users will decrease significantly. The network analysis system quickly calculates optimization policies and utilizes the online simulation system to verify the policies in the virtual mirroring network, ensuring that the policies can resolve network congestion and network experience does not deteriorate. The simulation system instructs the control system to deliver policies for resource adjustment. When you enter the scenic spot, the virtual simulation system analyzes and simulates the tour path based on the user track. In combination with the network traffic simulation technology, the virtual simulation system predicts that users will gather in a certain area and the self-media interaction service will increase rapidly, as shown in Figure 5.41. In this case, the uplink network traffic needs to be increased. The system automatically invokes the real-time digital simulation technology to predict whether the increase in uplink network traffic will affect service experience such as shopping and calling in the scenic spot. Simulation analysis shows that there is no impact. The system delivers optimization policies to increase uplink traffic of base stations and improve user experience.

With the support of real-time network simulation and virtual simulation technologies, ADN will make network changes more reliable, network control more intelligent, and user experience more friendly.

FIGURE 5.41   Predicting network traffic based on pedestrian track.

5.5 DIGITALIZATION OF NETWORK KNOWLEDGE AND EXPERTISE

CSPs' network O&M is currently driven by customer complaints related to network problems. It relies heavily on human expertise for manual analysis, decision-making, and loop closure with assistance from OSSs, NMSs, or tools. In the future, network access will increase by hundreds of times, and network applications will be deployed on a far greater scale. As such, manual network management and O&M will no longer be able to cope with the challenges brought by the increasing network scale and complexity. On top of that, the efficiency of manual operations in fault management, configuration automation, performance monitoring, and cybersecurity will lag significantly behind the development of networks. To address these challenges, digitalization of network knowledge and expertise is proposed to construct an intelligent network O&M solution.

5.5.1 Background and Motivation

Massive connections, growing network scale, and on-demand service provisioning on cloud – these are just some of the challenges that face traditional network O&M. As such, it needs to transform to a new one that has the following capabilities:

Network prediction and awareness: Network O&M can deeply analyze massive network data, proactively analyze the network status, predict network exceptions, promptly provide root cause analysis results, and resolve problems before customers complain.

Autonomous decision-making: Under certain conditions and O&M personnel's supervision, the network can make O&M decisions in specific networking and service scenarios, speed up the response to and close the loop on complex and uncertain problems, and improve network energy efficiency.

Automated execution: Process automation will transform inefficient and repetitive manual operations into ones that can be automated. O&M personnel will change from "in the Loop" to "on the Loop," and will focus more on process and rule management and design.

Digitalization of network knowledge and expertise is the key to improving these capabilities. Both CSPs and network device vendors alike have accumulated vast amounts of expert knowledge and experience throughout their years of network O&M in terms of network optimization policies, management rules, fault propagation chains, and troubleshooting methods. Such knowledge and experience are recorded in device and NMS O&M manuals, network O&M specifications, and expertise cases in different forms like natural language, rules, and cases. Closed-loop network automation requires that such scattered knowledge – which is understandable to human beings – be injected into computers to form a centralized knowledge repository that can be understood and used by computers. With assistance from AI technologies, computers can play a key role in automatic network analysis, decision-making, and closed-loop management. Currently, methodologies and technologies such as knowledge graph are applied to telecom networks, promoting intelligent incident management and closed-loop processing in addition to achieving good results in knowledge application. Digital management and application of unstructured and semi-structured knowledge and experience will play a huge role in reducing costs, increasing revenue, improving quality and efficiency, and finally achieving business success.

Most senior network O&M experts have accumulated around 20 years of experience in the O&M field. If such experience is not consolidated, it will be lost when those experts leave their positions. Digitalizing expertise – tacit network knowledge – is therefore an important task. For example, there is a lack of experience in complex aspects of network O&M such as network planning, construction, maintenance, and optimization. This means that O&M personnel need to find management knowledge from natural language documents such as product documentation, experience repositories, and O&M specifications. Digitalizing such explicit network knowledge will enable intelligent capabilities of the O&M system.

5.5.2 Technology Insights

In 1955, scholars represented by McCarthy and Minsky proposed the basic idea of symbolic AI in the Dartmouth AI summer research project: "It may be speculated that a large part of human thought consists of manipulating words according to rules of reasoning and rules of conjecture." According to this idea, they proposed an inference model based on knowledge and expertise. In the late 1970s, the emergence of expert systems successfully transformed AI from theoretical research into practical application. As shown in Figure 5.42, the expert system solves problems in a specific field by simulating domain knowledge and expertise – primary factors in the success of the first-generation AI. An example of this is Deep Blue, which summarizes the rules of chess from 700,000 games and numerous endgames with only 5 or 6 pieces remaining played by chess masters. While playing against chess masters,

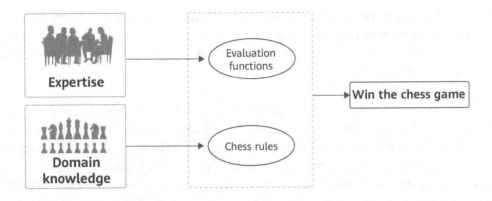

FIGURE 5.42   Expert system.

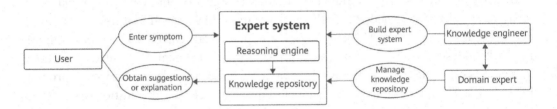

FIGURE 5.43   Knowledge engineering.

Deep Blue introduces the masters' expertise into programs by debugging 6000 parameters in "evaluation functions." In 1997, Deep Blue defeated the then-world chess champion Garry Kasparov in a symbolically significant moment for expert systems.

The expert system is the first milestone of knowledge engineering, which – in essence – enables machines to use human experts' knowledge to solve problems, as shown in Figure 5.43. Knowledge engineering builds the human experts' knowledge into reasoning capabilities and integrates them into computer systems. This, in turn, helps humans solve practical problems. The success of expert systems, however, is phased and limited. Just like chess has clear rules and boundaries, an expert system solves problems in a closed field and remains impervious to changes in the external environment changes. Yet the environment of telecom networks is constantly changing – users make calls and access the Internet randomly. This poses a challenge to expert systems in terms of planning, construction, maintenance, and optimization of the changing telecom networks.

With the dawn of the Internet big data era, new challenges are emerging as a result of more and more open issues, such as Internet search. Because expert systems rely heavily on manual input, it is difficult for them to satisfy the scale and coverage of knowledge. As such, the concept of knowledge graph is proposed. Knowledge graph uses a large-scale semantic network to express the world, thereby making it possible to cope with various entity concepts and semantic relationships that may be encountered. This essentially meets the application requirements of knowledge engineering openness, and in turn leads to the emergence of data-driven methodologies. Obtaining and extracting knowledge from massive data is an inevitable direction in the evolution of big-data-based knowledge engineering represented by knowledge graph [19]. Therefore, knowledge graph becomes the second milestone on the evolution roadmap of knowledge engineering.

The success of knowledge graph on the Internet has the following characteristics:

- Massive data from the Internet provides enough input for knowledge extraction.

- The Internet is a general field where knowledge tends to be presented in a fairly flat structure, making it easy to build knowledge graph.

- The Internet has a high tolerance for knowledge application errors.

- Internet knowledge offers a shallow application based on many simple facts.

In contrast to the general Internet field, the vertical telecom field has the following characteristics:

- A telecom network has limited data, and telecom faults may recur after a long period of time.

- The knowledge of the telecom field has a deep structure.

- Telecom networks are intolerant to errors.

- Telecom knowledge is necessary to tackle complex problems on network planning, construction, maintenance, and optimization.

Both the traditional expert system technology and the big data knowledge engineering technology represented by knowledge graph are based on symbolic knowledge – also called explicit knowledge. As AI technologies have continued to advance, deep learning, reinforcement learning, and large-scale pre-training models have become the new underpinnings of intelligent applications, which can solve problems that symbolic knowledge systems cannot. For example, AlphaGo Zero can defeat chess masters simply by learning the rules of chess and then teaching itself how to play without requiring any human expertise. Data-driven AI is a technology that extracts different features from data, learns the features, identifies the nonlinear relationships between the features, and finally forms them into tacit knowledge in order to solve problems. Essentially, tacit knowledge is a nonlinear pattern between the input and output of data. The experience that network experts amass after 20 years in the industry is regarded as a type of implicit knowledge. Although such experience can be used to solve efficiency problems, it is prone to reliability risks and requires manual monitoring and verification. Consequently, the application of tacit knowledge cannot be automated. In addition, the data volume of a telecom network is small, and configuration and fault data occur at low frequencies, making it impossible to provide sufficient features to feed machine learning in a short period of time.

5.5.3 Key Technical Solutions

In the telecom networks of the future, network knowledge and expertise will be digitalized to continuously enable ADN. This digitalization methodology will build an automated and intelligent O&M system and promote the development of human-machine collaboration. Talent transformation will be accelerated as machines will replace humans in performing repetitive, trivial, and heavy workloads. At the same time, new O&M positions will emerge, such as network strategists, orchestration engineers, and data analysts. Humans will play an important role in intent design, exception handling, and key decision-making, producing greater benefits with the assistance of machines. More human intervention in feedback, intent, and decision-making, as well as AI online training and incremental learning capabilities, will promote the iterative optimization of AI algorithms. In turn, this will make machines smarter and enable them to share more O&M work. A bidirectional positive cycle is thus achieved, and the O&M process is transformed from being passive, isolated, and closed to being proactive, closed-loop, and open, enabling automatic and intelligent O&M capabilities. Digital network expert and knowledge representation and acquisition are key technology research directions [20] to achieve this vision.

5.5.3.1 Digital Network Expert

Telecom networks are complex. The wireless domain has a mixture of different generations of protocols, and the fixed domain runs different link and routing protocols. All domains and network layers have evolved towards multi-modal convergence. As humans become evermore reliant on networks, telecom networks play an increasingly important role in infrastructure, and requirements on network reliability become higher, making it necessary for network devices to remain always online. Specifically, network planning, configuration, and policy optimization must be reliable and must be provided with reliable methods for design verification. Currently, such network reliability is guaranteed by network O&M experts involved in planning, policy formulation, construction, and maintenance. The routine work and knowledge of these experts are not digitalized, nor are their learning and growing processes. Expert activities are carried out manually and fail to use expertise effectively, resulting in the inability to cope with the increase of network scale and complexity. Against this backdrop, we propose the vision of digital network experts, as shown in Figure 5.44, to digitize network knowledge and expertise.

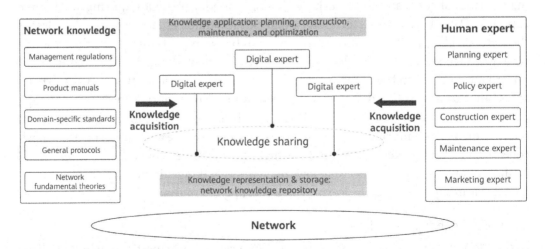

FIGURE 5.44   Vision of digital network experts.

Digitalization aims to build a series of digital experts for the telecom network O&M system to continuously accumulate and share network knowledge, and intelligently and automatically solve problems in network planning, construction, maintenance, and optimization. To explain how digital network experts intelligently diagnose network faults, predict network performance, and issue tickets, we will explore several dialog-based scenarios.

1. Digital network experts proactively monitor severe network faults and provide rectification suggestions.

   Digital network expert: A critical network alarm has been generated for the fault on N012 in A12. N012 is a bearer NE with multiple VIP services, and immediate rectification is required. Two plans are available. Plan A is to trigger the minimum-service system self-recovery API, with a success rate of 70%. Plan B is to trigger the restart API, with a success s rate of 100%.

   O&M engineer: How long does it take to complete the two plans? And what are their impacts?

   Digital network expert: Plan A does not affect services, and the recovery time is 3 minutes. Plan B affects accessed users and the recovery time is 10 seconds. At present, there are only a few non-VIP users who are online.

   O&M engineer: Start plan B, now.

   Digital network expert: OK. Restarting N012... N012 restarted, and eight non-VIP users are online again.

   O&M engineer: Got it.

2. Digital network experts automatically dispatch tickets.

   O&M engineer: I need the latest data for network running indicators.

   Digital network expert: According to network status monitoring, the latest upgraded NE N012 generates a lot of capacity alarms.

   O&M engineer: Any suggestions? Is version rollback necessary?

   Digital network expert: Rollback is not required. Another site that had such capacity alarms on similar NEs after upgrade changed the default capacity threshold.

   O&M engineer: Start remote configuration to change the capacity threshold of N012.

   Digital network expert: OK. Issuing a ticket to perform remote configuration on N012...

3. Digital network experts predict faults in advance.

   O&M engineer: What's your advice about network optimization?

   Digital network expert: The network is running properly. But the weather trend shows that strong thunderstorms will occur in A12 next week, meaning that power outages may occur in this area.

   O&M engineer: Check the power backup of all sites in A12 immediately.

Digital network expert: The core site S23 in this area is short of backup power and is prone to power outage. Do you want automatic scheduling of the power backup vehicle to S23?

O&M engineer: Yes. Perform automatic scheduling.

Based on our vision for digitizing network knowledge and expertise, we will present our proposed technical solutions from the context, modules, and working principles of digital network experts.

First: context of digital network experts

In addition to automatic fault diagnosis, automatic ticket dispatching, and fault prediction, digital network experts also play their roles in network planning, deployment, design, and optimization, as shown in Figure 5.45.

Through the accumulation of network knowledge and continual learning of expertise and network data, digital experts are able to provide intelligent capabilities.

Digital experts need to master the following types of network knowledge: (1) network planning, to support semantic intent-based intelligent planning; (2) network construction, to implement site configuration check and automatic generation; (3) network maintenance covering all fault scenarios, to achieve quick fault demarcation, locating, and rectification; and (4) network optimization, to continuously improve network performance and capabilities.

Because designers cannot preset all scenarios for digital experts, these experts must have continual learning capabilities on external environments (like thunderstorms and electromagnetic forces) and internal environments (like system hardware aging, faults, and system defects) so that networks can operate effectively. Nor can designers preset all events and changes – for example, unexpected network aggregation events – for digital experts. Furthermore, the complexity of network maintenance and troubleshooting is beyond the programming capabilities of developers, meaning that digital experts need to use learning algorithms and neural networks for continual learning.

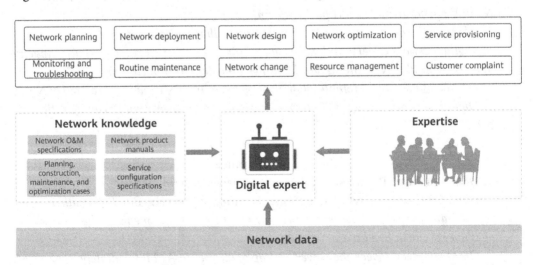

FIGURE 5.45   Context of digital network experts.

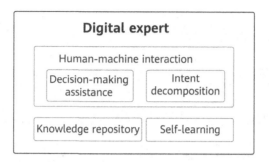

FIGURE 5.46   Modules of a digital network expert.

Second: modules of digital network experts

We expect that digital experts, integrating network knowledge and expertise, will replace humans for repeated work and accumulate expertise in the future. The functional modules of such experts consist of a knowledge repository, a self-learning module, and a human-machine interaction module, as shown in Figure 5.46.

Knowledge repository: stores network knowledge and expertise, the quantity and quality of which are key factors in solving problems.

Self-learning: records human experts' behaviors, operations, and results in their routine work (covering network planning, construction, maintenance, and optimization), and automatically learns procedural and heuristic knowledge based on the network image status. It can monitor the flow of information on the network and conduct continuous learning according to the status changes of the flow. In this way, self-learning extracts new knowledge in addition to integrating and optimizing existing knowledge.

Human-machine interaction: communicates with human experts through unstructured natural languages, obtains new tasks and goals through intent decomposition, provides suggestions to aid human experts' decision-making process, and supports decision-making authorization of human experts within a limited scope.

Third: working principles of digital network experts

Based on the three modules described above, we give four interactions in terms of network knowledge learning, expertise learning, human-machine interaction, and intelligent decision-making, as shown in Figure 5.47.

Interaction 1: Digital experts analyze network and environment data, extract and generate knowledge through the self-learning module (by means of summary and induction, assumption and verification, and analogy and association), and store the knowledge in the knowledge repository.

Interaction 2: O&M personnel and digital experts share knowledge and expertise through Q&A exchanges and other methods. In this way, O&M personnel learn about the network situation and trend from digital experts, and digital experts extract expertise from O&M personnel through the self-learning module, generate new knowledge, and store it in the knowledge repository.

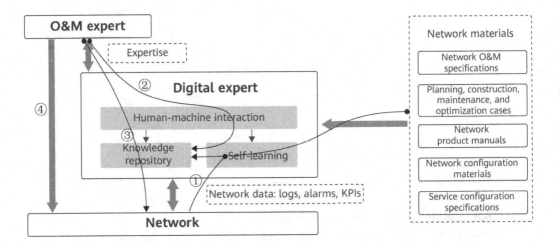

FIGURE 5.47   Working principles.

Interaction 3: O&M personnel provide valuable suggestions through digital experts' human-machine interaction modules. Digital experts use the decision makers to understand the suggestions, convert them into executable commands with the help of the knowledge repository, and issue the commands to networks through the manager or controller.

Interaction 4: In emergency scenarios, O&M personnel can take over responsibilities from digital experts and directly operate networks.

A digital expert is a logical unit that can be integrated into the OSS, network ADs, or NetGraph system based on its category. For machines to understand different knowledge categories and complex knowledge levels, the self-learning module and knowledge repository should be based on unified knowledge representation for digital modeling. This does not mean that there should be only one knowledge representation. Instead, different knowledge categories can have their own knowledge representations based on their inputs, for example, from expertise, network data, or network materials, as shown in Figure 5.47. These different inputs might have different acquisition approaches. Due to the characteristics of the telecom field, knowledge engineering technologies used in the Internet field cannot be directly used for knowledge representation and acquisition. Applying such technologies in the telecom field involves a number of challenges, as listed in Table 5.5.

5.5.3.2 Network Knowledge Representation Technology
Knowledge representation technology, proposed from the concepts of semantic network in 1956 and general problem solver in 1959, has been studied for a long time in the field of AI. It has involved a continuous evolution of standards including knowledge repository for reasoning and solution, rule-based expert system, and RDF/OWL/labeled property graph (LPG)/RDF*. There are many knowledge repositories in existence today that are based on knowledge representation, for example, WordNet, DBpedia, FreeBase, and YAGO. Telecom networks require a knowledge repository constructed based on knowledge representation,

TABLE 5.5 Challenges of Applying Traditional Knowledge Engineering to Telecom Networks

Characteristics of the Internet Field	Characteristics of the Telecom Field	Challenge of Applying Knowledge Engineering to Telecom Networks
Closed system, not affected by environments	Open network system, substantially affected by environments	Knowledge acquisition is difficult.
Single scenario, with single-dimension problems to solve	Complex scenario, with multi-dimension problems (like network planning, construction, maintenance, and optimization) to solve	Knowledge representation is difficult.
Flat knowledge structure	Complex knowledge structure, with large network hierarchy	Knowledge representation and acquisition are difficult.
Fact-based knowledge with simple vocabularies	Intensive network domain knowledge	Knowledge representation and acquisition are difficult.
Large-scale user data	Limited network data and occasional fault data	Knowledge acquisition is difficult.

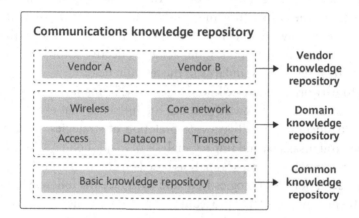

FIGURE 5.48   Telecom knowledge repository.

as shown in Figure 5.48. Common concepts like OSI model, network topology, NE, link, port, protocol, packet loss, delay, and jitter belong to the basic knowledge repository of the telecom field. ODN, optical network terminal (ONT), and PON are access network concepts, IP and router are datacom network concepts, OTN is a transport network concept, 3G/4G/5G and base station are wireless network concepts, and NFV and 5GC are cloud core network concepts. All these concepts, as well as their entities and relationships, belong to the domain knowledge repository. The different approaches and processes that different vendors adopt for interface, model, and protocol configuration, maintenance, and optimization belong to the vendor knowledge repository.

In the telecom field, the characteristics of knowledge are as follows: First, there are many sources of knowledge, including static data (like specifications documents and product manuals), dynamic data generated during network running (like logs, alarms, and KPIs), and expertise. Second, knowledge is hierarchical, with applications, platforms, services, and hardware infrastructure being connected and affecting each other. Third, the network is always running, and the network topology, NE and link status, and infrastructure health change over time. Network knowledge representation defines the structural framework of knowledge and serves as the basis for extracting, converging, modeling, computing, and applying network knowledge. A good network knowledge representation scheme ensures the integrity and stability of a network knowledge system and guarantees the application of knowledge-aware network services – after all, the quality of such a scheme determines the quality of knowledge-aware applications. Knowledge representation is primarily the symbolization of facts, concepts, relationships, logic, and processes. However, its application in downstream tasks is low because of the difficulty involved in manually constructing symbolic knowledge into a complete knowledge system. This problem leads to a branch of research into knowledge representation learning. Based on knowledge translation not being deformed, knowledge representation learning embeds discrete symbolic knowledge into continuous vector spaces and evolves toward technologies such as representation spaces, scoring functions, and encoding models. This, combining the characteristics of telecom services (e.g., the mesh structure, measurable status, and strong data time sequence), necessitates a telecom knowledge representation system to meet the overall requirements of knowledge management and application, achieve effective knowledge mounting, and form knowledge representation standards in the telecom field.

In addition to network and device knowledge and CSP management regulations, digital experts also need to learn knowledge about the influence that external environments have on networks, including intelligent interpretation of strategies, impact analysis and prediction of natural disasters, and impact analysis of major holidays. This is necessary so that they can perform network impact analysis based on environment changes. Traditional knowledge representation technologies RDF and LPG face the following challenges: (1) it is difficult for them to express tacit, procedural, and domain knowledge in a formal manner; (2) expertise is inevitably subjective, and may be inconsistent in different experts; and (3) it is difficult to express knowledge comprehensively, and is prone to deficiency. In order to address these challenges, we need a variety of knowledge representation techniques. In terms of the current knowledge representation technology, statistical modeling and symbolic modeling are two research directions. Symbolic models can be used to represent the structure and relation characteristics of network knowledge. Another kind of knowledge that cannot be explicitly represented by digital symbols is expertise, which therefore belongs to tacit knowledge. It may be possible to represent expertise using statistical models instead. The representation technology of a certain type of telecom knowledge can be measured from the four attributes described in Table 5.6.

There are two types of digital techniques for knowledge representation: symbolic knowledge representation and vector space-embedded knowledge representation.

First, we will discuss symbolic knowledge representation.

Symbolic knowledge representation has undergone first-order logic, rule-based system, RDF, and LPG. Table 5.7 lists their advantages and disadvantages.

TABLE 5.6 Key Attributes of the Telecom Knowledge Representation Technology

Key Attributes of Knowledge Representation	Requirements
Representational accuracy	The ability to represent all kinds of required knowledge, involving declarative, procedural, and structural knowledge.
Acquisitional efficiency	The ability to acquire new knowledge easily using automatic methods, with low requirements on humans' dependency and capabilities.
Inferential adequacy	The ability to manipulate the representational structures to produce new knowledge corresponding to existing structures.
Inferential efficiency	The ability to direct the Inferential knowledge mechanism towards the most productive directions by storing appropriate guides.

TABLE 5.7 Symbolic Knowledge Representation Classification

Knowledge Representation Classification	Technology	Advantage	Disadvantage
Logical representation	First-order logic	Helps express reasoning logic.	Difficult to build, with low reasoning efficiency.
Rule-based representation	Rule-based system	Helps express reasoning logic.	Incapable of automatic learning, with low reasoning efficiency.
Semantic network	RDF	Natural representation, which is easy to understand and extend.	Time-consuming reasoning, with poor scalability.
Property graph	LPG	Easy to understand and extend, high execution efficiency, and large-scale inference.	Weaker knowledge representation capability than RDF.

In terms of functions, knowledge in the telecom field is classified into declarative knowledge, structured knowledge, procedural knowledge, and expertise. Declarative knowledge represents "what it is," structured knowledge represents "what it has," procedural knowledge represents "how to do it," and expertise represents intuitive experience. Different knowledge representation techniques are applicable to knowledge of different functions.

Declarative knowledge (concepts, facts, and objects) represents factual and conceptual network knowledge, such as physical objects (e.g., NEs, links, and ports), protocol rates (e.g., PON, DSL, GE, and WDM), and physical attributes (e.g., optical power attenuation in optical transmission). This class of knowledge is suitable for RDF. However, RDF offers low knowledge retrieval efficiency and poor multi-hop reasoning performance when there is a large amount of domain knowledge. As such, further study is required for RDF extension or fusion.

Structural knowledge (relations between concepts, and between concepts and objects) represents structured network knowledge, such as hierarchical network representation, topology structure, and connections between different types of ports. In the network planning phase, structural knowledge includes rules such as site selection policies and route planning policies. This class of knowledge has structured characteristics, and nodes in a structure have many network-related attributes. It is therefore suitable for LPG. However, LPG has limited semantic representation and weak representation accuracy compared with RDF. As such, further study is required for LPG extension or fusion.

Procedural knowledge (rules, policies, procedures, and processes) represents network process knowledge, including the service provisioning and configuration delivery processes in the network construction phase and the fault recovery, version upgrade, and device update processes in the network maintenance phase. This class of knowledge is suitable for logical representation, rule-based system, and event graph.

Expertise is heuristic knowledge (expert intuition, quick thinking, and black box process). Instead of being based on logical or mathematical theoretical deduction, this class of knowledge is summarized during problem solving and then guides problem solving by means of subjective strategies and procedures. Because heuristic knowledge is subjective experience based on objective phenomenon that experts observe for a long time during network planning, construction, maintenance, and optimization, it lacks logical deduction processes and is difficult to explain. Therefore, it is suitable for vector space-embedded knowledge representation.

Second, we will discuss vector space-embedded knowledge representation.

Symbolic knowledge representation performs well in representing explicit and discrete knowledge, but it falls short in expressing tacit knowledge with sparse data. It also achieves low calculation efficiency and cannot solve the knowledge integrity problem effectively. Distributed knowledge representation based on vector space learning embeds entities and relationships in a knowledge graph into low-dimensional continuous vector spaces to complete semantic computing in vector spaces, thereby improving computing performance [21]. Moreover, tacit knowledge can be mined in vector space – something that is beneficial to the construction, reasoning, and fusion of the knowledge repository. This research direction is called knowledge representation learning.

In one-hot representation, no learning process is involved, and the representation process is fast and simple. It assumes that all represented objects are independent of each other, resulting in the loss of large amounts of valid information in a telecom network. Specifically, in one-hot representation space, all vectors that represent objects are orthogonal, and the semantic similarity based on a Euclidean distance or a cosine distance is 0. For example, although a Gigabit-Capable PON (GPON) port and an Ethernet PON (EPON) port are two different types of ports, they are both PON ports and have high semantic similarity. One-hot representation loses this feature, impacting data representation sparseness. Compared with one-hot representation, knowledge representation learning is dense, meaning that the vector dimension is low. This enables semantic information between telecom network objects to be fully represented and enhances computing efficiency.

In essence, representation learning attempts to simulate the human brain, which can discern observable and discrete entities in the real world having obvious characteristics. Neurons in the human brain represent these objects by activating and inhibiting states, forming an implicit world that the human brain understands. In this implicit world, the state of a single neuron is meaningless, but the accumulation of tens of billions of neurons will cause qualitative changes: thoughts and memories emerge, accurately representing the outside world. Inspired by these neurons, representation learning uses distributed representation vectors to simulate them. By means of continuous representation of the neural network for discrete objects, representation learning possesses a relatively high intelligence level and learning capabilities.

In the hierarchical telecom network structure, a network consists of NEs, NEs consist of boards, and boards consist of ports. This hierarchical conceptual relationship is more suitable for distributed knowledge representation learning that is oriented to entities and relationships in a knowledge repository. By embedding network knowledge into low-dimensional vector space (to simulate how a human brain memorizes knowledge), a computer can realize semantic representation of knowledge entities and relationships in vector space. Symbolic knowledge representation is based on one-hot representation. It cannot represent semantic information and thus has poor representation capabilities. It has high representation complexity, low computing performance, weak representation correlation, and poor scalability. Conversely, the distributed knowledge representation learning can improve computing efficiency, alleviate sparse data, and enhance semantic relationship expression. Telecom network knowledge is heterogeneous, for example, lifecycle knowledge in network planning, construction, maintenance, and optimization, along with documents, specifications, cases, and configuration references. Representation learning integrates the heterogeneous information into a complete space. With the representation learning model, heterogeneous objects can be projected into a semantic space, making it possible to establish a unified knowledge representation space for telecom networks and realize information convergence of the network knowledge repository. Knowledge representation learning matches the network's hierarchical characteristics, supports information fusion of the heterogeneous network knowledge, effectively alleviates sparse data, and improves the computing efficiency. This direction of study is therefore of great significance to the construction and application of the telecom network knowledge repository and is worth further research.

Over the past few years, knowledge representation learning has continued to develop, and academia has proposed many models to learn the representation of entities and relationships in the knowledge repository, including translation (Trans series) models, bilinear models, and neural network models. The following describes two typical models.

First, the TransE model is a representation that embeds knowledge into vector space. In his 2013 paper proposing TransE, Antoine Bordes considers the relationship r as a translation from the head entity h to the tail entity t in the low-dimensional vector space, that is, $h+r \approx t$. In *TransE*, *Trans* stands for Translate and E stands for Embedding. The TransE model supports entity prediction, relationship prediction, triplet classification, and semantic vector analysis. The TransH model proposed in 2014 introduced a hyperplane to embed the complex relationship of 1-n, n-1, and n-n. Hyperplane projection was upgraded to spatial projection, and projection vectors were upgraded to a projection matrix in the TransR model proposed in 2015. TransD dynamically constructs a projection matrix using projection vectors, reducing parameters and calculation workload. Compared with TransR, TransD improves the calculation efficiency.

Second, the bilinear model uses vectors to represent entities, uses matrices to represent relationships, and captures the internal interaction of triplets through user-defined scoring functions. The semantic interaction between entities and relationships is depicted through bilinear transformation of the entities and relationships. Entities are low-dimensional vectors learned from neural networks, and relationships are linear or bilinear mapping functions. This model can learn semantic representation from bilinear objectives. The latent factor model (LFM) uses relationship-based bilinear transformation to describe the second-order relationship between entities and relationships and uses a simple and effective approach to describe their semantic relationship, achieving good collaboration and low calculation complexity. A later distance multiplication (DistMult) model explores a simplified form of LFM, significantly reducing model complexity and improving the model effect.

5.5.3.3 Network Knowledge Acquisition Technology

Essentially, rules of physics, chemistry, and electronic signals apply on networks, and data generated on networks is sporadic and a fragmented presentation of these rules. Intelligent O&M attempts to obtain the fragmented data and use it to restore the operation rules of the entire network. Due to the incomplete nature of the fragmented data, traditional information systems face major challenges in forming the operation rules through data-driven methods.

Network experts familiar with physics and networking can observe and analyze the fragmented data to detect, locate, and solve problems, and can automatically calculate physical constraints through simulation. This means that future network knowledge needs to integrate live network data, network knowledge, and simulation data.

The basic form of knowledge is symbolic or vectorized entities and relationships. Network knowledge acquisition involves obtaining network object entities and the relationships between them. The knowledge acquisition process can be divided into the following types of technologies: knowledge entity discovery, knowledge relationship acquisition, and knowledge completion. To explain the knowledge entities and relationships, we will use an example. In an optical transmission network, the receive optical power of an optical transmission board has two indicators: overload point and receiver sensitivity. Signals can be received properly only when the optical power is between these two indicators. If the optical power exceeds the overload point, the optical module is at risk of being burnt. To regulate the receive optical power of an optical transmission board, we need to add or adjust an attenuator and configure it according to such factual knowledge as the physical distance between devices. In this example, we can obtain some entities and relationships, as shown in Figure 5.49.

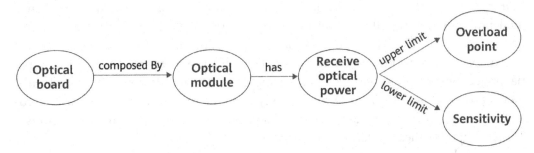

FIGURE 5.49 Entities and relationships obtained from the description of the receive optical power.

1. Knowledge entity discovery

The main techniques of knowledge entity discovery are entity recognition and entity disambiguation.

Entity recognition discovers and recognizes entities from text. There is a large amount of network knowledge in product documents, technical manuals, O&M cases, and specifications, where the names of network resource objects, network performance indicators, and network alarms can be identified only through the automatic entity identification technology. As tacit knowledge, expertise helps identify network entities from the language description of human experts through the natural dialog between network digital experts and human experts.

Entity disambiguation maps reference fragments in a document to entities in a structured knowledge repository. In 2015, the deep semantic relatedness model (DSRM) proposed entity disambiguation by modeling entity semantic relatedness. In 2016, EDKate proposed the joint embedding of entity and text. In the following year, the paper *Deep Joint Entity Disambiguation with Local Neural Attention (DJEDLNA)* proposed a neural attention model over local context windows for entity embedding learning and differentiable message passing for inferring ambiguous entities. Then in 2018, Le developed an E2E neural architecture with relation-wise and mention-wise normalization, by regarding relations between entities as latent variables. The continuous development of entity disambiguation is essential to supplement unstructured documents to the structured knowledge repository.

2. Knowledge relation extraction

Human knowledge is passed on through forms such as books, so too is network knowledge. Network expertise is transferred through language communication or documents. Unlike knowledge engineering experts, network experts cannot record knowledge in the form of knowledge representation, yet network documents accumulate a wealth of network knowledge. Knowledge relation extraction involves extracting relational facts from plain text. Network knowledge relations include inheritance relation, inversion relation, upper- and lower-level relation, composition relation, causal relation, conditional relation, co-reference relation, and time sequence relation. Take the following network fault rule as an example: "An IN_PWR_ABN alarm is reported when the receive optical power of an optical module falls outside the range between the overload point and the receiver sensitivity." From this text, we can extract the knowledge relation shown in Figure 5.50. The optical power overload point and sensitivity are the optical module's attributes. The receive optical power exceeding the overload point is the condition attribute of an overload event, and that falling below the sensitivity is the condition attribute of a low-load event. Events and alarms are generated (happenOn) on optical modules and NEs, and there is a triggering relationship between events and alarms.

happenOn and *trigger* in Figure 5.50 are typical knowledge relations in the telecom field. In 1992, Hearst proposed the template-based syntax pattern to automatically extract the hypernym-hyponym relation from text. The hypernym-hyponym relation

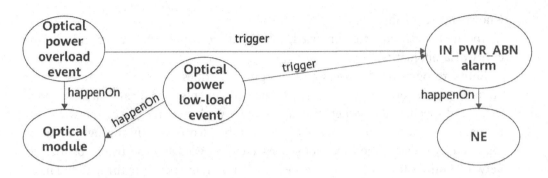

FIGURE 5.50   Knowledge relation extraction.

can be understood as an *is-a* relation. For example, in the hypernym-hyponym relation of board and control board, board is a hypernym, and control board is a hypo-
nym. Template-based extraction requires manual customization, involving a heavy
workload and producing a low recall rate of relation extraction. To address this problem, neural network-based relation extraction has been developed rapidly. In 1999,
Craven et al. proposed weak supervision for relation extraction. Then in 2009, Mintz
et al. adopted classifier models to train and predict relation classification. In 2016,
Fudan University developed the attention mechanism to obtain semantic relations.
A couple of years later, in 2018, Stanford University proposed graph neural networks
(GNNs) to extract semantic relations. All these technologies are collectively referred
to as neural relation extraction (NRE), which requires huge amounts of training data
and involves manual labeling that is cost-ineffective. Distant supervision is proposed
to automatically obtain training data. It aligns text with existing knowledge graphs
and automatically labels large amounts of training data, for example, the triplet of
alarm, happenOn, and NE. It assumes that all texts, including NEs and alarms, are
training samples of the *happenOn* relation. Although automatic labeling speeds up
the labeling of large numbers of samples, it inevitably labels some samples incor-
rectly. By introducing adversarial noise, adversarial learning implements CNN- and
RNN-based relation extraction, reducing incorrect relations caused by distant supervision. (RNN stands for Recurrent Neural Network.) Overall, there is active research
into NRE, motivating the research on knowledge relation acquisition in the future.

3. Knowledge graph completion

Knowledge graph completion (KGC) is a task that adds new triplets to a knowledge graph and predicts missing entities and relations based on the existing entities
and relations in the graph. Through graph completion, KGC identifies new relations.
In Figure 5.51, for example, three new trigger relations are generated for fan speed
threshold-crossing alarms: board fault alarm, fan fault alarm, and board temperature
threshold-crossing alarm.

The industry's research on KGC involves the following: knowledge representation-based completion, path search-based completion, reinforcement learning-based
completion, reasoning rule-based completion, and meta learning-based completion.

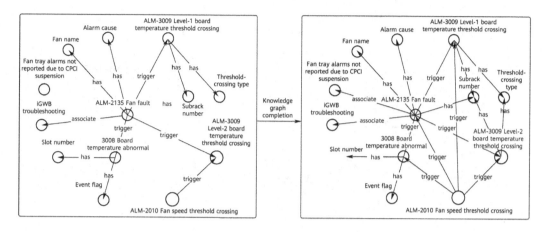

FIGURE 5.51   Knowledge graph completion.

Research on knowledge representation-based completion involves learning the low-dimension embedding representation of the nodes and relations in a graph and then using the similarity reasoning method to predict the potential relations between nodes in order to complete the missing triplets (head node, relation, and tail node). Despite this, knowledge representation-based completion cannot obtain the required relations from multi-hop reasoning. To complete the missing relations, path search-based completion adopts the path ranking algorithm (PRA) to compare the degree of association between path vectors and prediction relation vectors. The knowledge graph, however, is not perfect, which impacts the effect of path search-based completion. Reinforcement learning-based completion introduces multiple reward functions to make pathfinding more flexible and effective. Reasoning rule-based completion takes a different approach than path search-based completion, instead completing relations by means of reasoning rules. It combines such rules with the low-dimensional vector space embedding method, and combines the inference model with the neural network model, effectively reducing the computing space of reasoning. Meta learning-based completion solves the problem of long-tail relation completion with only a small amount of training data.

5.5.4 Technology Prospects

With the improvement of machine cognitive intelligence, machines' tacit knowledge will be a significant supplement to human knowledge system, and the machines' cognitive ability will assist human beings to widely expand their cognitive ability. Humans and machines are good at different things: Humans tend to deal with vague and fused knowledge or meta knowledge, and make decisions, whereas machines tend to deal with clear, single, and factual knowledge, and perform value-irrelevant operations or static associations. And humans are open, whereas machines are closed. We can therefore conclude that human-machine collaboration is vital. As the cognitive intelligence of machines improves, their tacit knowledge will supplement the human knowledge system to a significant extent, and their cognitive ability will help expand humans' cognitive ability.

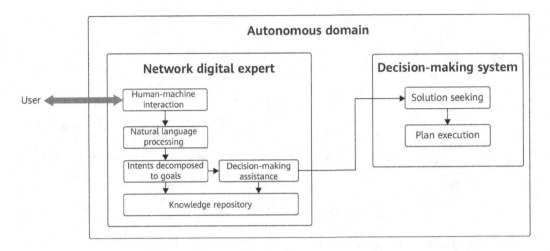

FIGURE 5.52   Digital expert-assisted decision-making.

5.5.4.1 Prospect of Network Digital Expert

The breakthroughs in intelligent technologies lead to expert-assisted decision-making capabilities of network digital experts. These experts can identify and decompose expert intents based on natural language processing and deliver the decomposed goals to the intelligent decision-making system for solution and plan execution, as shown in Figure 5.52.

In the telecom field, expertise, fault rules, and O&M guides – which are tacit knowledge understood by humans – need to be converted into explicit knowledge involving concepts, entities, relations, and rules that can be understood by machines. Such conversion is performed through digital methods like knowledge presentation. With the continuous accumulation of digital knowledge, network digital experts can dynamically respond to real-time environmental changes on telecom networks, intelligently assist decision-making, and finally achieve zero manual intervention. When knowledge engineering is applied to telecom networks, it is necessary to solve the problems of knowledge representation and knowledge acquisition.

5.5.4.2 Prospect of Knowledge Representation

Knowledge representation learning is of great significance in the telecom field. Compared with traditional knowledge representation based on discrete symbolic logic, knowledge representation learning provides a feasible solution for unified and accurate representation of semantic information in telecom networks. It also significantly improves automatic knowledge acquisition, fusion, and reasoning capabilities. Using cognitive science to summarize human knowledge types helps classify network knowledge. The tree-structured relation indicates the hierarchical classification between entities, such as networks, subnets, NEs, boards, and ports. A grid relation specifies a spatial relation in the real world, for example, the spatial relation of a physical topology, a base station, a site, or a cabinet. The sequence relation denotes a partial sequence relation between entities, for example, events that occur in sequence in a telecom network. A directed network relation illustrates the association or causal relation between entities, for example, the fault propagation chain in a telecom network. Because of the complex relations between different telecom knowledge, it is necessary to study different types of knowledge representation learning technologies. With the technical trend being the gradual fusion of symbolism and connectionism, knowledge representation learning is an effective supplement to knowledge graph symbol representation and is worth further exploration in the telecom field.

5.5.4.3 Prospect of Knowledge Acquisition

Given that the network environment is full of uncertainty, ADN needs to continuously learn, adapt to, and generate new knowledge in order to establish a network knowledge repository, persist on status, action, and result learning, and enrich its knowledge range. An example is Google's self-driving cars, which, despite having driven millions of miles, are still considered unsafe on public roads. In contrast, humans can drive relatively well after only a short time spent on learning because they have enough knowledge before learning how to drive, they understand basic traffic rules, and they have experience in riding bicycles or motorcycles. This research, which continuously learns and accumulates knowledge based on existing one, is called lifelong learning. The telecom network system is an artificial system that embodies human knowledge. Human learning never really starts from scratch, nor does learning in the network field. Instead, communication networks are continuously evolving, and traditional and emerging network technologies coexist for some time. Learning new knowledge of next-generation networks based on the existing network knowledge is in line with the characteristics of continuous evolution and is also a research direction of knowledge acquisition technologies.

5.6 NETWORK HUMAN-MACHINE SYMBIOSIS TECHNOLOGY

A complex telecom network involves many technologies, service scenarios, and configuration parameters and requires quick response, relying on ADN because humans cannot respond quickly enough. However, ADN is yet to reach a sufficient level of maturity, meaning that reliance on humans will continue for a long time. Network planning, construction, maintenance, and optimization depend on the experience, value, awareness, and action capabilities of human experts. Humans mentioned here include network planning personnel, operation personnel, O&M personnel, and vendors' service personnel.

Network planning is a creative activity that requires humans' awareness and analysis of many factors, like the traffic trend of enterprise and individual customers in the next few years, the attitude of community residents on new base stations, and the suitable route for laying new optical cables. These factors are difficult for machines to obtain and need to be provided by humans.

ADN cannot cover all possible scenarios in the R&D phase. In the O&M and optimization phase, machines may not know how to handle unexpected complex faults or network attacks. Furthermore, when multiple network optimization objectives conflict, machines may not know which objective takes precedence. In such cases, human experts can assist the machines in decision-making and transfer knowledge to the machines.

TABLE 5.8 Evolution of Human-Machine Relationships

Phase	Human-Machine Interaction	Human-Machine Collaboration	Human-Machine Teaming	Human-Machine Symbiosis
Machine's Role	Tool	Assistant	Teammate	Symbiote
Machine's Intelligence	None	Algorithms, logics, and rules	+Artificial intelligence +Cognitive intelligence	+Brain-like intelligence
Human-Machine Interaction Form	GUI Explicit interaction	+Intuitive interaction (e.g., voice interaction)	+Multimodal interaction (e.g., tactile interaction)	+Brain-computer interaction Implicit interaction

The construction, capacity expansion, and maintenance of network infrastructure, which cannot be remotely controlled by AI, still require manual operation on site. Capacity expansion and maintenance tasks need to be completed through human-machine collaboration.

5.6.1 Background and Motivation

5.6.1.1 Human-machine Relationship Changes in ADN

In ADN's different phases, the autonomous system plays different roles and has different human-machine relationships, as listed in Table 5.8.

The system in the initial phase (approximately ADN level 2 or lower) runs according to the preprogrammed rules. That is, for users' deterministic input, the system provides definite output according to the programs. In this phase, the system is an auxiliary tool that executes human instructions, and human-machine interactions are explicitly performed in traditional GUI mode.

A middle- and high-level system features higher autonomy to achieve a cooperative relationship, similar to a team of humans to some extent. In a specific environment, the human-machine cooperation is goal-driven, two-way active, mutually enhanced, and self-adaptive. The system has developed from an auxiliary tool to a teammate who cooperates with humans, and plays the role of "intelligent assistant+human-machine cooperation teammate." The human-machine relationship is evolving into a teammate relationship, forming a "human-machine teaming" cooperation. This relationship, in different stages, presents different characteristics.

1. Human-machine collaboration

   Humans are in the dominant position, and machines are assistants, cooperating with humans to efficiently complete routine and regular work.

   In this phase, ADN performs some analysis and decision-making under the control of humans, provides decision-making suggestions or automatically executes behaviors based on preset rules, and supports human-machine collaboration. Machines at this level do not understand human intents but intelligently assist humans. In this relationship, AI is an enhancement of human intelligence. It has algorithm-, logic-, and rule-based inference capabilities to improve the efficiency of specific tasks, such as information search, data mining, data analysis, and automatic execution of repetitive tasks.

2. Human-machine teaming

Machines have cognitive capabilities such as awareness, understanding, analysis, and reasoning, and are humans' teammates. Each person and smart machine is considered a team member who plays a unique role in the team, striving to achieve the team's common goal.

In this phase, ADN starts to understand human intents, perform analysis and decision-making independently, and support humans' decision-making. Machines are becoming teammates to collaborate with humans. **Human-machine teaming in ADN is an entire system, in which, ADN (or its intelligent agent) senses and understands humans' intents, make decisions independently to some extent, and collaborates with humans to complete network planning, construction, maintenance, and optimization tasks.**

ADN needs to fully understand humans' intents and automate most scenarios – this, however, will take some time to realize.

3. Human-machine symbiosis

Human-machine symbiosis is a long-term goal that aims at human-machine's mutual understanding and collaboration to co-accomplish tasks, promote each other, and evolve together.

ADN's human-machine symbiosis, in addition to team collaboration, must be able to learn from each other and evolve together at runtime in order to adapt to the continuously evolving network technologies, uncertain running environments, and complex and changeable service requirements.

When a machine has self-growth and self-evolution capabilities, a human's response speed and the breadth and depth of human knowledge lag far behind those of the machine, meaning that humans will become the bottleneck. Human-machine symbiosis helps people better understand the world, or better interact with smart machines of the future, and is, therefore, a future-oriented relationship model. At this time, machines are human-like in cognitive behaviors and have the ability of self-growth and self-evolution. This means that machines can:

- Sense the real world and respond to the environment in real time with continuously enhanced adaptability.

- Identify different types of problems, design problem-solving processes, and solve problems by themselves.

- Imitate humans during autonomous learning processes, including learning human actions.

- By means of human-like intelligent behaviors, implement continuous interaction with human-machine-environments in the real world, steady autonomous learning, and autonomous intelligent growth and evolution.

  From human-machine interaction, collaboration, teaming, and finally symbiosis, the human-machine cooperation capability of a higher level is enhanced based on that of a lower level.

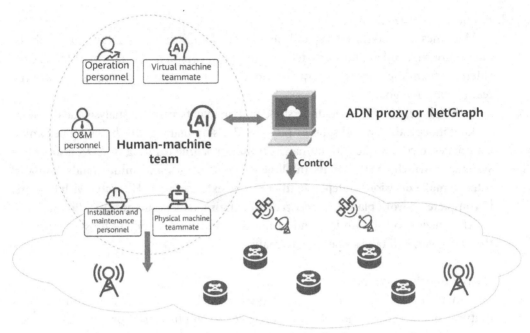

FIGURE 5.53   ADN's human-machine teaming.

5.6.1.2 Examples

Assume that, in the future, a CSP builds ADN, which provides an AI O&M expert named Smartee. John is an O&M expert, and Leo is a device installation and maintenance engineer. Figure 5.53 shows the schematic diagram.

Scenario 1

John: There is a large concert in the sports center of city A from 8:00 p.m. to 10:00 p.m. on Saturday, attracting xx thousand people. Evaluate the surrounding wireless network resources.

Smartee: Based on the number of people and our user occupation rate, the base station resources near the sports center can meet requirements, but we need to temporarily adjust the power-saving mode. This will cause extra power consumption. Please check. (The N sites are marked on the screen.)

John: OK.

Smartee: From 18:00 to 22:00 this Saturday, the power saving mode of the N sites near the sports center will be adjusted to high throughput, and will be restored after that time. Configuration plan ready.

In this scenario, John is the proposer of the task, and Smartee is the partner. Through natural language, Smartee obtains information such as the task, time, location, and number of people, understands John's intents, and processes John's requirements. When finding that the power saving mode needs to be adjusted and may be inconsistent with the previous power saving intent, it confirms with John by voice and image and takes measures after receiving a reply.

Scenario 2

Leo receives a ticket from Smartee, asking him to replace an aged optical module for an NE at a site. He takes spare parts and tools to the site and finds that there are dozens of optical modules installed on the NE. Leo then uses smart AR glasses to connect to Smartee and communicate with it in natural language.

Li: *Smartee, I'm in position.*

Smartee: *It is planned to replace the optical module on optical port 2 in slot 3, next to which an orange indicator blinks. Check the spare optical module, with the model as X.*

   Leo finds the optical port and takes out a spare optical module.

   Smartee (uses the AR glasses to scan the QR code on the optical module): The optical module model is correct. I will now switch services to the standby channel. Perform the replacement after the orange indicator turns off.

   Following the prompts, Leo removes the optical fiber and optical module and then inserts the new optical module and the original fiber. Then, the yellow indicator turns on.

Smartee: *The indicator of the optical module is normal, but the receive optical power at the peer site is low. Check that the optical fiber is securely connected and the optical connector is clean.*

   Leo removes the optical fiber, cleans the optical connector carefully, and reinserts the optical fiber. The indicator turns green.

Smartee: *The indicator of the optical module is normal, and the receive optical power at the peer site is as expected. Replacement complete. Switching back service... Switchback successful. Take your belongings and close the cabinet door before you leave. Thank you!*

In this scenario, Smartee takes the dominant in the service process and Leo cooperates to complete the spare parts replacement. During the replacement, a small incident occurs (the optical connector is dirty). Smartee immediately detects and issues instructions to correct the problem based on its awareness capability and intelligence, eliminating the need for Leo to revisit the site, and ensuring proper service running in the replacement process. In this way, Li's workload is significantly reduced. Leo can perform device maintenance safely after simple training. In the past, the personnel in the network O&M center cooperated with Leo by phone. They cannot see Li's operations and may not detect the abnormal receive optical power at the peer end in time.

Scenario 3

Smartee detects abnormal network traffic flowing to the CSP's cloud data center, but is not sure whether it is a fault. Therefore, Smartee asks John for help.

Smartee: John, I found that the VM traffic destined for tenant Y in data center X was three times higher than the historical normal value, and the packet loss rate increased to 20%. I'm not sure what the problem is and need your help. (The traffic curve and packet loss rate are displayed on the screen. The curve shows a sharp increase and is still growing.)

John: Please check whether the traffic complies with the known DoS attack features.

Smartee: No known DoS or DDoS attacks are found, but the traffic proportion of the TCP destination port xxxx is greater than 80%. (A pie chart is displayed on the screen, identifying top 5 traffic compositions (grouped by destination TCP port)).

John: I'll check... (A few minutes later) According to security experts, this is a DDoS attack that appeared recently. Redirect traffic from TCP destination port xxxx to the AntiDDoS server for cleaning.

Smartee: OK. AntiDDoS configuration updated. The network traffic recovers to normal. Will this problem, if encountered later, be handled in the same way?

John: Yes, handle it in the same way.

In this scenario, Smartee finds a problem that it does not know how to handle and seeks help from human experts. The latter gets new information through other channels and tells Smartee how to deal with such a problem. This realizes human-to-machine teaching.

John's analysis may also be this way:

John: I'll check... This port is used by tenant Y to provide network services. Tenant Y is conducting a large-scale network promotion activity today. The traffic exception time complies with the promotion time, and it seems that the traffic is valid. The promotion will end in half an hour, and no action is required. Ask the customer service specialist to promote our on-demand capacity expansion service to tenant Y.

Smartee: Got it.

After half an hour, the network traffic returns to normal as expected.

In this scenario, John determines that the problem is caused by a promotion activity and does not take any action. Although Smartee is not taught new knowledge, a human-machine takeover occurs.

In the preceding examples, Scenario 1 and Scenario 2 illustrate human-machine teaming, and Smartee in Scenario 2 has higher autonomy. Scenario 3 denotes human-machine symbiosis.

5.6.1.3 Form Evolution of ADN Machine Teammates

Machine teammates may be physical (e.g., a physical machine or robot, like a sweeping robot or an unmanned aircraft) or virtual (e.g., a running AI program, like J.A.R.V.I.S, a private AI assistant of Iron Man in the movie *Iron Man*). Virtual machine teammates can control external systems with awareness and execution capabilities to achieve awareness and perform actions. For example, J.A.R.V.I.S can control Iron Man's private studios and armor.

ADN's machine teammates first appear in the form of virtual machine teammates, which may be parasitic applications in ADN agents (such as NetGraph), or independent software systems. The ADN system needs to provide a "body" for these virtual machine teammates using an ANE, NetGraph, NE, network connection, and the like. The "body" is shared by multiple virtual machine teammates.

CSPs can independently purchase, train, use, and discard different virtual machine teammates. For example, operators use different machine teammates for dedicated network planning, troubleshooting, and optimization. The machines can be upgraded independently without affecting each other, thereby facilitating the independent evolution of the system functions. Different virtual machine teammates can be introduced to maintain different autonomous domains, realizing service diversity, and achieving "survival of the fittest" for similar types of agents. System administrators can grant different permissions to each virtual machine teammate in order to restrict their behavior boundaries. The burden on humans will increase as they encounter more and more machine teammates at the same time. For example, humans need to control information transmission between multiple machine teammates and determine their different answers to the same question.

In the future, physical machine teammates may emerge, helping humans maintain network hardware infrastructure or which, themselves, are network infrastructure. These physical machine teammates can be deployed in hard-to-reach places and collaborate with humans remotely.

5.6.2 Technology Insights

Human-agent teaming or human-autonomy teaming or human-machine teaming is a system that consists of multiple individuals and agents. Agents have certain autonomy and can work together with humans through communication and interaction to achieve common goals.

Human-machine symbiosis represents the interdependence of humans and machines, which evolve synchronously over time and become smarter.

At the 2021 World Robotics Conference under the theme "The Future Era of Human-Machine Integration," Shi Yuanchun, a professor at Tsinghua University, Wang Yongtian, a professor at Beijing Institute of Technology, Zhou Zongtan, a professor at National University of Defense Technology, and Hu Chengwei, a researcher at China Aerospace Science and Technology Corporation, pointed out that the ultimate state of the human-machine relationship is human-machine integration and human-machine symbiosis. The relationship is as follows:

1. Human-machine symbiosis is a long-term goal that aims at human-machine's mutual understanding and collaboration to co-accomplish tasks, promote each other, and evolve together.

2. Technically, human-machine collaboration (human-machine teaming) and human-machine integration (human-machine symbiosis) proceed step by step. In human-machine integration, a machine is not subordinate to a human; rather, they are equal parties.

3. With the further development of high-performance computing and AI technologies, the first problem in the future era of human-machine integration and human-machine symbiosis is: humans' response speed as well as their breadth and depth of knowledge will significantly lag behind those of machines, and humans will become a bottleneck of human-machine interaction. The brain-computer interface provides an approach to realize human-machine integration. It is hoped that in the future, the non-invasive brain-computer interface can enable ordinary people to get what they think, reaching a slightly advanced stage of human-machine integration. Human-machine integration and human-machine symbiosis also need to address the issue of how machines understand humans.

5.6.2.1 Elements of Human-Machine Teaming

We can use human-human teaming to simulate the elements of human-machine teaming and analyze the conditions that must be met for an effective human-machine team.

An effective human-human team has common goals or tasks and its team members have a sense of independence and the ability to act independently and undertake tasks. To promote the understanding of the goals and tasks and the understanding between team members, as well as build trust, team building is required to share knowledge and experience with each other. In addition, team members need to communicate closely, support each other, and ensure overall progress and risk control.

The requirements for an effective human-machine team are similar to those for a human-human team. *Human–Autonomy Teaming - Definitions, Debates, and Directions* [22] defines the elements as follows:

Autonomy: Agents must have a high level of autonomy to form teams with humans.

Agents can form a team with humans only when they have capabilities similar to human cognition, learning, self-adaptation, and independent execution and can independently complete certain tasks in specific scenarios.

Proactive closed-loop interaction: Agents must be capable of proactive communication, and the interaction between team members must be closed-loop to ensure that they have received and understood each other's information.

Communication mechanisms help form shared situational awareness, shared mental models, and goal alignment, significantly improve team efficiency, and accelerate the process for humans to consider agents as teammates.

Intent understanding: Humans and agents must be able to understand each other's intents through communication.

Intent is the understanding of goals, sub-goals, and actions, and communication aims to guarantee consistent understanding of them.

Common cognition: Humans and agents share team experience, knowledge, awareness, and situational awareness to achieve common cognition.

Only common cognition can form a common understanding in a dynamic context environment, ensuring consistent objectives and synchronous actions in specific situations. It allows members of a human-machine team to understand and predict the team's needs, actions, and possible problems.

Common cognition does not require every bit of information to be shared with every team member. An effective human-machine team needs to know two points: (1) The information that needs to be shared with teammate. (2) The suitable time to share the information. Both points are equally important.

Mutual takeover: Humans and agents must be able to supervise each other, be a backup of each other, and take over services from each other.

Humans and agents monitor each other's performance to infer their goals, plans, and needs and detect errors in their decisions or actions.

Humans and agents back up each other, proactively provide information that teammates are expected to need, or provide support and feedback when teammates make mistakes or encounter difficulties during task execution.

Humans and agents take over teammates' tasks that they have difficulties handling.

5.6.2.2 Future Technical Subjects of Human-Machine Teaming

In 2019, the Future Directions in Human Machine Teaming Workshop [23] sponsored by the United States Department of Defense proposed several key technical topics required by human-machine teaming in the next 5–20 years. These topics are split into four research trajectories: human's natural intelligence, machine's artificial intelligence, human models of machines, and machine models of humans. Table 5.9 lists the technical topics.

The preceding planning shows that, in addition to the technologies for machine teammates, human-machine teaming also involves research on neuroscience such as the thinking mode, learning capability, attention, and brain operation mechanism of human teammates. This part is beyond the scope of the computer and telecom fields.

The preceding research and planning will last 5–20 years and will be oriented to specific tasks in the short term, and to basic theories and general scenarios in the long term. Put simply, general human-machine teaming is a lengthy process. ADN's human-machine teaming or human-machine symbiosis is task-oriented, whose research focuses on the preceding short-term topics.

TABLE 5.9 Technical Topics of Human-Machine Teaming

Research Trajectory	Short-Term (5–10 Years)	Long-Term (10–20 Years)
Human's natural intelligence: research to better understand human cognitive capabilities in the context of complex and dynamic situations. The following studies are involved: Communication Robust unsupervised learning Active learning and curiosity Task learning and generalization Task control and multithreading Integrated cognition in complex and dynamic environments Systems that decode neural signals for human-machine interactions	New experimental paradigms to understand natural language in real-world situations Studies to understand human mechanisms for regulating learning rates and memory retrieval Studies to understand the effects of human's curiosity on learning Studies of neural representations of overlapping tasks and generalization to novel tasks Research examining generalizability of models based on laboratory findings Development of minimally invasive sensors to collect detailed real-time measures of neural activity	Development of natural language models that represent real-world complexity and uncertainty Identifying the factors that determine memory replay and the content and timing of replay events Understanding real-time interactions between systems that support episodic memory and systems that form general knowledge about events and situations Development of computational models that can actively seek information through directed questioning of human teammates Understanding the fundamental mechanisms that allow humans to learn from single instances Development of computational models of situations where multiple goals must be achieved by sequencing and combining task representations Theoretical frameworks to explain how multiple cognitive processes interact across extended timescales Development of machine interfaces that use theory-driven computational neuroscience models to decode brain activity
Human models of machines: research to understand what humans must know and learn about machines and their internal structure in order to effectively interact with them, including what is required in human-machine teaming to establish and maintain trust. The following studies are involved: Real-world team experiments Legible and predictable machine behaviors Explainable AI Trust	Designing real-world experiments to examine how humans react to a variety of human-machine teaming arrangements and variations in machine capabilities Researching how to make machine behavior legible and predictable beyond manipulation and motion Developing machines that can dynamically explain their behavior for simple human-machine teaming tasks Studies in simple human-machine teaming domains to examine the effect of variations in machine explanation, legibility, and related capabilities on human trust	Developing theories and corresponding implementations of legible and predictable machine behaviors Designing machines that can produce explanations for human-machine teaming tasks Developing new theories to describe the impact of machines on human trust for human-machine teaming domains

(Continued)

TABLE 5.9 (Continued) Technical Topics of Human–Machine Teaming

Research Trajectory	Short-Term (5–10 Years)	Long-Term (10–20 Years)
Machine's artificial intelligence: research to improve intelligent machine capabilities in order to enable effective human–machine teams. The following studies are involved: Perception Communication (grounding the meaning of a communication to context and environment) Models of the environment and the machine's own capabilities Reasoning, problem solving, planning, and task expertise Learning Integrated architectures	Research on how cognitive processing can aid perceptual processing and enable machines to track humans throughout different types of tasks Studies on multimode human-machine dialogs to avoid ambiguity Research on human-machine interaction and interactive task learning where humans teach machines new tasks through demonstration and language and correct machines' behaviors Research on a common model of cognition for perspective-taking, joint attention, and cooperation Research on new cognitive architectures that integrate knowledge from cognitive science, AI, and cognitive neuroscience	Designing machines with the ability to build internal models of their environments and predict future states Building machines that can communicate with contextual understanding of the specific environment and the specific context of the utterance Designing machine agents with real-time models that can be used to reason about, and even predict, the world around them Developing the theoretical framework to enable machine reasoning, problem solving, planning, and task expertise Building machines that can learn and adapt their behaviors directly from human instruction, including imitation, demonstration, and language Developing integrated cognitive architectures that create machine reasoning and provide machine models for human teammates
Machine models of humans: research to understand and realize the internal representations and processing of a machine required for reasoning about human teammates. The following studies are involved: Understanding which aspects of human behavior need to be modeled Understanding human perception abilities Understanding human motor control abilities Understanding human reasoning and planning abilities Building dynamic models	Designing real-world teaming experiments for specific tasks to test which levels and types of human behaviors, human perception, human motor control, and human reasoning and planning abilities are needed for effective human-machine teaming Building personalized models of human teammates for specific tasks	Developing theories for what levels and types of human modeling are needed for effective teaming Developing theories for what levels of human perception are needed on teaming tasks Building dynamic models of human teammates that extend across a range of tasks

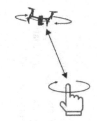

Human-machine team collaboration

Drones cooperate with humans for video shooting

Human-machine learning

Humans teach drones command gestures
Drones teach beginners gesture skills

Human-machine takeover

Humans take over drones to avoid obstacles

FIGURE 5.54   Human-machine teaming or human-machine symbiosis scenarios.

5.6.3 Key Technical Solutions

As shown in Figure 5.54, human-machine teaming or human-machine symbiosis involves the following aspects:

- **Human-machine team collaboration:** Human-machine teams share task contextual situational awareness, communicate with each other, break down complex tasks, and track tasks.

- **Human-machine learning:** Two-way learning is implemented during system running. Machines learn new skills from and provide suggestions to humans.

- **Human-machine takeover:** Humans and machines back up each other in tasks for error-proofing.

Figure 5.55 provides the key technologies of ADN's human-machine symbiosis from the preceding three aspects.

5.6.3.1 Human-Machine Team Collaboration

Figure 5.56 shows the principles of ADN's human-machine team collaboration.

Instead of simply using machines as tools, human-machine team collaboration regards machines as teammates, and machines can understand and track team goals and make decisions independently. To achieve human-machine team collaboration, machine teammates need to have several more capabilities in addition to the intelligent agent capabilities.

First, data and knowledge models for team collaboration, including (1) human knowledge, like humans' capabilities and preferences; (2) team knowledge, team rules, teammate roles, and workflows; and (3) a network digital twin that contains teammate status information. In addition to the network information itself, the network digital twin also includes the areas that human teammates are responsible for, the locations, and the tasks that are being executed.

Second, situational awareness sharing. Team members need to share information about the system status and trends.

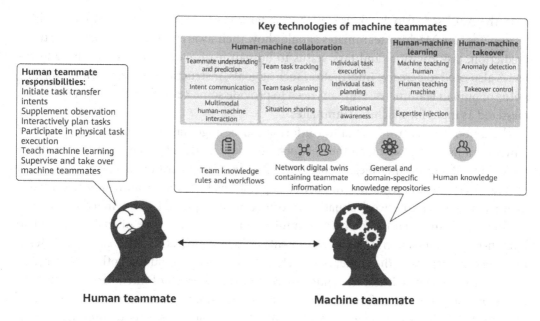

FIGURE 5.55   Key technologies of ADN's human-machine symbiosis.

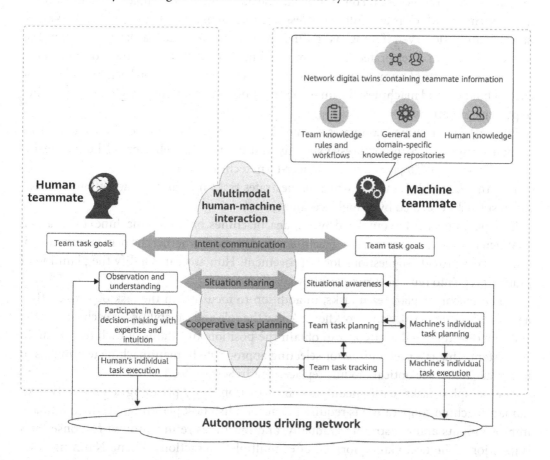

FIGURE 5.56   Principles of ADN's human-machine team collaboration.

In the ADN scenario, humans can observe far less network information than machine teammates can. Machine teammates should show their awareness of network status, trend prediction, task division, and task status to human teammates. In turn, machine teammates also need to perceive information such as goals, instructions, locations, and working status of human teammates. Humans need to provide some key information that they have mastered as input for machine teammates.

The amount of network situation information is huge, far exceeding the capacity of human brains, and pushing all the network situation changes to all human teammates is impossible. Based on the roles, scenarios, and current tasks of human teammates, ADN should display key information and action suggestions to human teammates in a suitable manner, and provide network situation information as required by human teammates.

Third, human-machine intent communication. Team tasks are often transferred to human-machine teams in the form of intents. When cooperating with each other, team members must transfer their intents to each other and understand each other's intents.

Recent years have witnessed major progress in the research of intent-driven networks in the industry, but the definition and translation of complex intents are awaiting study. The latest definition of intent in IETF draft-irtf-nmrg-ibn-concepts-definitions-09 [24] includes operational goals and outcomes, but the outcomes have complex logic and ambiguous semantics, which is difficult to express in a formal manner. For example, "Maximize network utilization even if it means trading off service levels (such as latency, loss) unless service levels have deteriorated 20% or more from their historical mean." To understand the complex intents of humans, machines need to rely on the common background knowledge of humans and machines, the understanding of human language logic, and the ability to perceive situations.

Higher-level machine teammates should also understand the hidden information that human teammates do not express explicitly and predict the behaviors of human teammates. This is a challenge as well as a longer-term technical goal.

Fourth, team task planning, which orchestrates tasks into multiple workflows consisting of subtasks executed by a single teammate.

Task planning may be completed by humans, machines, or human-machine cooperation.

When humans plan team tasks, machines need to check whether the plan is correct and, if necessary, provide suggestions for improvement. Humans can solidify the planning of routine tasks into reusable team workflows.

When machines plan team tasks, in addition to focusing on the task objectives, they need to follow team rules and workflows, know the role and capabilities of each teammate, and rely on situational awareness to obtain the position and status of each teammate in the system. This is a prerequisite for selecting appropriate human/machine teammates to undertake tasks. See optical module replacement in Section 5.6.1.

For complex tasks with incomplete information (e.g., planning a new network), human-machine cooperation is required to accomplish task planning, in which humans improve inputs and constraints gradually, and machines return prompt responses and suggestions. The task plan is formed after multiple interactions. Zheng Nanning et al. [25] proposed that for some tasks with highly complex algorithms, humans' intuitive reasoning can provide a reasonable initial iteration position so that it can avoid the local minimum problem to a great extent.

During the planning of team tasks, each teammate needs to be told what to do, when to do it, and under what conditions to do it, but not how to do it. Machine teammates need to further break down their tasks.

Jessie Chen et al. [26] pointed out that the transparency of machine decision-making is critical to maintaining the trust of a human-machine team. Machine teammates need to express their decisions to relevant humans, as well as the references and expected results of the decisions. If machine teammates perform or participate in team task planning, they should tell human teammates why they do so, helping to enhance human trust in it.

The challenge here is team task planning for uncertain goals and conditions.

Fifth, team task tracking. After humans and machines reach a consensus on team task planning, machine teammates should track the task status until the task is completed or canceled. They need to execute their tasks as planned, report the results, and remind humans to execute tasks promptly. When external conditions change or a phase fails, the team needs to be triggered for task replanning. Task tracking depends on situational awareness. Team tasks can last for a long time and involve multiple roles, to maintain a business intent.

Sixth, multimodal human-machine interaction, which is required by processes such as situational awareness, intent interaction, and team task planning.

In order to make the collaboration of a human-machine team efficient and natural, the human-machine interaction mode must go far beyond the scope of existing visual human-machine interfaces. The technology of transmitting video, audio, and somatosensory information from machine teammates to human teammates is relatively mature. What urgently needs to be developed is a more natural human-to-machine input technology, involving natural language, gestures, body movements, handwriting plus sketches, and even expression and eye contact.

Machine teammates need to be equipped with multiple sensors, like video sensors, audio sensors, pointing devices, locating devices, keyboards, and writing devices, in order to observe the status of human teammates and obtain human inputs. Many of these hardware technologies are mature. Network installation and maintenance personnel work in a complex environment and need to move frequently, requiring that such devices be highly portable. Currently, the accuracy and speed of computers' recognizing voice and gesture instructions, and handwritten text, are poor. They are mainly used in some specific non-critical applications (such as smart speakers and mobile phones). In the future, natural interaction needs to be drastically improved, especially in environments with complex background.

Brain-computer interface is one of the future human-machine interaction technologies, which arose in the 1990s, but it is still in the initial stage of development and cannot be put into commercial use in a short term.

Seventh, understanding and predicting teammates. Interactions between humans are often based on background, common sense, and environmental context, use multiple channels (visual, auditory, and tactile) simultaneously, and rely on historical memory. A person may define a certain type of knowledge in a previous dialog and then use it in a later dialog, or reference in a dialog a concept that was defined half a year ago and use pronouns (he, she, it, this, that...) to indicate an entity in the current environment or mentioned earlier. When someone points to a port and asks, "Here's a yellow light blinking. What's going on?" a machine teammate needs to use knowledge reasoning to associate the inputs of multiple channels (body movements, languages, and sketches) with knowledge (yellow indicates minor faults) to understand the true meaning of its human teammate: The port the person points to is faulty, and the person wants to know the cause and impact of the fault. Further, the machine teammate should observe and learn the habits of the human teammate and predict the next action of the human teammate in order to provide timely assistance or advice. When the person raises a yellow light problem, the machine teammate should predict that the person's next course of action might be to deal with the fault. Understanding and predicting humans require cognitive theories. For details, see Section 3.2.

5.6.3.2 Human-Machine Learning

In a human-machine system, humans are the source of wisdom and provide valuable input to help machines quickly master response knowledge. That is, humans train machines to improve machine skills. Meanwhile, humans are subject to physiological restrictions, and human knowledge storage and information processing resources are limited. As the system evolves, humans become the bottleneck in the human-machine interaction process, requiring machines to provide efficient methods to enhance human capabilities.

Machines learn from humans: Machines acquire ADN domain knowledge, expertise, or human teammates' habits to have self-learning and evolution capabilities. Figure 5.57 shows the machine-to-human learning mode.

Supervised learning and semi-supervised learning still exist in human-machine teaming. Due to the human training cost of supervised learning being high, developing unsupervised learning capabilities (like imitative learning and generative learning) will become a trend in the future.

- **Supervised learning:** Machines learn with assistance from humans, and humans train machines by labeling results and content. It is generally used in scenarios such as fault prediction, in which a certain number of labeled samples are provided to machines for learning and training.

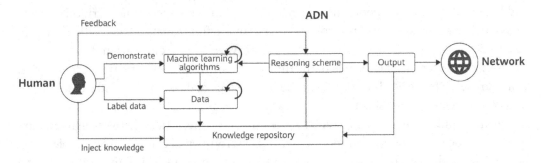

FIGURE 5.57   Machine-to-human learning.

- **Semi-supervised learning:** In scenarios where some sample data has no learning value, iterative human-machine collaboration provides an initial subset of manually labeled data for machine learning algorithms from a large-scale unlabeled data set. The algorithms process the data and provide prediction with certain confidence while sending low-confidence prediction results to labeling personnel to request labeled data. This process is repeated until the algorithms are trained to reach the expected precision.

- **Unsupervised learning:** Manually labeled data is not required. It is generally used for alarm clustering, performance data dimension reduction, and anomaly detection.

- **Imitative learning:** Machines can directly learn from human demonstrations without labeled data. Humans only need to show actions, and machines can learn by themselves. For example, during dialog-based O&M, a machine can generate a human-like dialog by imitating a user's expression. Note that a machine's imitation capability is based on its understanding of transactions. Therefore, imitation learning depends on the understanding capability of machines. That is, machines can build and use mental models that are synchronous with humans through abstraction and analogy, in order to understand human intents, goals, and behaviors.

- **Generative learning:** A machine learns from the samples generated by itself or the cases constructed by humans. When the case data constructed by humans is insufficient, the machine can generate numerous samples – many of which may seldom even occur in real scenarios – based on rules for practice. In the natural language processing (NLP) and cybersecurity fields, more diversified samples can be generated based on the generative adversarial network (GAN) to meet the requirements of deep learning and applications.

The applications should jointly use these machine learning methods to analyze specific problems based on data characteristics and application requirements. When the knowledge to be learned can be easily described using formulas, theorems, or code, the "simple and rough" method of injecting knowledge into machine teammates in a certain way may be the most efficient.

Machine-to-human learning, however, should be interactive. To optimize their learning models, machine teammates need to provide a visualized interface to display their learning results and obtain feedback from humans. The models of system self-learning should also be acknowledged by human mentors. Humans, as mentors, can decide whether apprentices can graduate.

Machine-enabled humans (humans learn from machines): Machines' auxiliary functions make up for the lack of humans' physiological capabilities, enhance human intelligence, experience, and responsiveness, and improve human learning and intelligence.

- During site planning and design, the desktop virtual reality technology is used to establish a vivid, virtual, and interactive three-dimensional space for geographical terrains and network structures on a network by means of three-dimensional modeling and rendering. This improves the site survey efficiency and accuracy of ADN.

- When a user uses a complex system for the first time or locates or diagnoses a complex issue, the system processing logic is modeled based on technical research like simulation, virtual reality (VR), simulator, and graphics and images to simulate a demonstration for practice – this effectively improves the quality and effect of user learning. In addition, repeated trial and error helps accumulate experience and improve human learning efficiency.

- In hardware installation and maintenance of large-scale and complex equipment, VR not only simulates scenarios but also displays an immersive aspect of the real environment and O&M process. At the same time, augmented reality (AR) combines the real environment and virtual objects and overlays them in the same image or space. In addition to providing real-time equipment maintenance information, this improves learning efficiency and ensures learning quality.

With the development of brain-computer technologies, machines have unique advantages in enabling humans, improving humans' cognition, and compensating for humans' physiological limitations. For example, non-intrusive brain-computer interfaces help improve humans' attention and memory during long-duration surveillance, avoiding distraction and fatigue. During troubleshooting, the brain-computer interfaces can detect O&M personnel's cognitive fluctuations, identify their knowledge requirements, and provide support quickly based on the operation context. In addition, such interfaces can detect O&M personnel's emotional fluctuations and help relieve their pressure.

5.6.3.3 Human-Machine Takeover

The telecom network serves as the infrastructure of modern society. Implementing wrong decisions on it may cause serious economic loss or even personal injury. Therefore, the collaboration of ADN's human-machine team must be reliable to prevent system breakdown due to individual human or machine errors.

When a machine teammate makes a mistake, human teammates should detect, prevent, and correct the mistake promptly. There are many examples in literature and film where intelligent systems that were designed to serve humans subsequently harmed them, either intentionally or unintentionally. In the science fiction film *2001: A Space Odyssey*, the artificial intelligence character HAL 9000, which controlled the spacecraft generated a misjudgment and killed several crew members. The only survivor had to sabotage and shut down HAL 9000. This illustrates deep concerns about the out-of-control of intelligent systems and the need for humans to take over machine teammates to control the system when necessary.

Conversely, when human teammates make mistakes, machine teammates should also provide prompt reminders or take over the jobs. Humans inadvertently make mistakes.

Most software and hardware systems can check human input, reject obviously wrong instructions, and give clear prompts. In the network human-machine team or human-machine symbiosis scenarios, machines replace humans in dealing with specific jobs. Humans input intents but seldom involve operation details (e.g., writing code), thereby reducing misoperations by a considerable margin. Machine teammates still need to check and provide reminders about humans' intent conflicts, and provide warnings or require secondary authorization when humans perform potentially dangerous behaviors (such as deleting quantities of services or powering off devices).

The following will focus on humans taking over machines, which has multiple alternatives:

- **Online correction:** If machine teammates do not regard an issue as sufficiently serious, human teammates can pause them, and input some constraints to let the machine teammates reanalyze the decision. For example, to solve a problem in which furniture will block a robot vacuum's path, we can input restricted areas for the robot vacuum. This can be a simple human-machine takeover method.

- **Redundancy or design diversity:** There may be multiple machine teammates with different implementations. When one machine teammate is abnormal, the system automatically or manually switches to another machine teammate. This method is simple, but involves high costs.

- **Intrusive takeover:** In certain key scenarios, humans serve as backups of machines. For example, a self-driving car provides a manual driving mode. This method has high requirements for humans and is applied to critical scenarios.

Machine teammates may make mistakes in any phase of awareness, analysis, decision-making, and execution. For telecom networks, analysis and decision-making can be conducted by humans, and awareness and execution– weaknesses for humans – can be achieved by means of redundancy design.

Figure 5.58 illustrates the technical principles of humans' intrusive takeover of machines on ADN. When a machine teammate is abnormal in the analysis and decision-making phase, humans can take over the machine teammate's job.

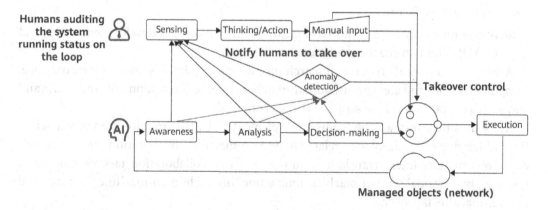

FIGURE 5.58   Humans' intrusive takeover of machines on ADN in the decision-making phase.

- **Prerequisites:** Machines need to continuously present task context information, system-aware states, system decision-making, and execution results to human teammates so that the human teammates can perceive the task status at any time. In this way, human teammates can detect exceptions and take over services when necessary.

- **Step 1:** If a person or machine teammate finds that an error occurs in the machine teammate, the person or machine teammate needs to forcibly switch to manual decision-making. The machine should have a built-in exception detection module. If confidence in the machine decision is low or the decision is abnormal, the machine actively applies for human takeover and refuses to execute the incorrect machine decision before the human takeover, thereby avoiding loss. To prevent human-machine contention for control, humans should have the highest privileges so that the authorized person can actively take over the machine in emergency scenarios.

- **Step 2:** The human teammate replaces the machine teammate to complete decision-making, and the machine teammate only executes the decision. Due to the differences between human and machine capabilities, the efficiency of the entire human-machine system may be significantly reduced – the system may even need to run in degraded mode. The undamaged functions of the machine teammate need to be retained in order to reduce the extra workload caused by manual takeover and minimize the impact. If the wrong decision-making behavior has occurred, it is also necessary to find ways to remedy the loss caused by the wrong behavior.

- **Step 3:** Human teammates diagnose and improve the machine teammate, and resume the machine teammate only after checking that the errors on the machine teammate have been corrected. Diagnosis and improvement may be offline, (e.g., retraining the machine teammate, upgrading the software, or even returning the machine to the factory for repair). Machine teammates with the summary and inference capabilities may perform imitative learning to imitate humans' decision-making in human-machine takeover scenarios. For details, see "Human-Machine Learning" in this section.

5.6.4 Technology Prospects

Human-machine teaming and human-machine symbiosis are the development trends and goals of ADN's human-machine relationship.

Achieving these goals requires research on multiple disciplines, such as neuroscience, computer theories and algorithms, human-machine interaction equipment, and ethics and law, which are far beyond the scope of the telecom field.

ADN uses human-machine teams to implement tasks that require human participation, addressing key technologies related to human-machine collaboration, such as knowledge construction, intent translation, human-machine collaboration task planning and tracking, multimodal human-machine interaction, online human-machine learning, and human-machine takeover.

5.7 NE ENDOGENOUS INTELLIGENCE TECHNOLOGY

At the beginning of AI native NE design, we need to consider data- and knowledge-driven services and leverage the advantages of new AI hardware to maximize intelligent service experience. Section 4.4 defines the architecture and describes the key features of AI native NEs. Compared with upper-layer network graphs, NEs are limited in their computing and storage resources and face the challenges of large service data volume, high degree of real-time requirements, and high privacy and reliability requirements in implementing AI native NEs. This section will introduce the research progress of related technologies and possible research directions in the future.

5.7.1 Background and Motivation

According to the ADN vision of "building a self-fulfilling, self-healing, and self-optimizing, autonomous network," there is a big gap in the intelligent capabilities of NEs, in terms of the following aspects:

- **Weak detection on silent faults:** If an IP fault occurs, the port remains normal but forwarding becomes unavailable, which cannot be effectively detected or identified by the management and control units.

- **Weak real-time awareness:** More than 90% of customer complaints on government and enterprise private networks are caused by intermittent disconnections, and more than 30% of labor resources are used to handle intermittent disconnections. Locating such problems is industrially difficult, but it has high degree of real-time requirements – as such, reliance on the management and control units is ineffective.

- **Insufficient resource digitalization:** Take dumb optical cable resources as an example. Most ODN resources depend on manual input and cannot be released after disassembly, meaning they unnecessarily occupy ports. In addition, resource data on the NMS cannot be updated in real time.

- **Weak self-healing and self-optimization capabilities:** Due to the aforementioned problems, self-healing and self-optimizing lack foundation and are therefore weak.

By embedding key capabilities such as real-time AI inference, real-time service awareness, and adaptive control, AI native NEs process local data locally to implement small closed-loop management, minimizing data interaction and latency between NEs and management and control units. This addresses the challenge of thousands-fold growth of intelligent data in the future, provides millisecond-level awareness, and therefore substantially enhances resource detection, high reliability, and self-optimizing capabilities.

Based on the target architecture described in Section 4.4.3, a next-generation NE consists of the hardware system and software system (system software layer, embedded real-time awareness layer, and adaptive control layer). This section focuses on the hardware system, system software layer, and embedded real-time awareness layer.

- **Hardware system:** Provides computing resources for traditional services, data/knowledge processing, and AI models/algorithms. The core of the hardware system lies in fully utilizing resources by means of software and hardware collaboration to provide real-time assurance for upper-layer services.

- **System software layer:** Shields hardware infrastructure differences at the bottom layer and provides development framework and runtime capabilities for the top layer. Special attention is required on the lightweight and efficient execution of the frameworks and models.

- **Embedded real-time awareness layer:** Provides lifecycle governance capabilities for data collection, preprocessing, storage, analysis, and distribution. As a key basic capability for NE resource digitalization, the embedded real-time awareness layer needs to consider how to reduce the data volume to be processed. Based on such a capability, this layer can then provide the modeling and simulation capabilities of NEs and services in order to support problem solving of core services and self-verification before result delivery, thereby ensuring system reliability.

5.7.2 Technology Insights

Currently, NE intelligence mainly focuses on single-point AI features, performing single-point AI algorithm optimization in common NE scenarios, (e.g., traffic prediction/classification/routing, congestion control, and memory faults) to replace traditional algorithms.

The hardware system reuses existing hardware. Most hardware types are CPUs, but they have low matrix computing efficiency in the neural network and therefore affect the model inference speed. To solve this problem, the industry adopts the CPU instruction set acceleration technology. This is a method of accelerating the instruction set of algorithm code based on the characteristics of the hardware platform architecture. Advanced RISC Machines (Arm) processors, for example, have the following two technical directions:

- Adopting single instruction single data (SISD) to improve algorithm performance, for example, adopting the architecture technologies like branch prediction, interruption, pipeline, multi-thread, and cache to accelerate the implementation of specific functions in the algorithms.

- Adopting simple instruction multi-data (SIMD) to improve algorithm performance. For example, Arm NEON instruction sets improve algorithm execution parallelism through vectorization, thereby improving the algorithm computing performance.

Many acceleration libraries in the industry adopt the instruction set acceleration technology, including multi-thread optimization, memory overcommitment, data quantization, assembly optimization, and the like. These acceleration libraries can be used effectively in embedded devices. Moving toward 2030, the computing requirement will increase by hundreds of times. However, the annual performance improvement rate of a single-core CPU has decreased from 50% to less than 3%. Therefore, CPU-based AI inference solutions are unlikely to be mainstream in the future. Instead, more powerful AI hardware is needed.

The system software layer is responsible for building the AI inference capability. Due to the relatively limited NE resources, problems associated with the inference framework and model lightweight need to be addressed. In terms of inference frameworks, most inference platforms in the industry provide Lite versions (e.g., MindSpore Lite and TensorFlow Lite). In terms of models, the following methods are adopted for model compression:

- **Quantization:** Converts floating-point computing into low-bit fixed point computing and establishes data mappings between specified points and floating points. For example, mapping FP32 to INT8 can implement four-fold parameter compression, accelerating inference while compressing the model.

- **Pruning:** Overparameterization occurs in the deep learning network model. During inference, only a few weights participate in effective computing but have major impacts on the inference result. Therefore, redundant weights, nodes, or layers can be deleted from the network structure in order to reduce the model size and accelerate inference.

- **Knowledge distillation:** Teacher models provide knowledge and guide student model training. In this way, small student models can have the same performance as large teacher models with significantly fewer parameters, compressing models, and accelerating inference.

The preceding three methods have many engineering practices in the industry, but are still difficult to deploy on some ultra-lite devices. In addition, model compression often causes loss of inference precision, affecting the AI inference effect.

The embedded real-time awareness layer builds modeling and simulation capabilities based on the data processing foundation. The following provides two typical modeling modes in the embedded field.

- **Data-driven:** Many experiments offer the input and output experimental data for modeling. This mode does not require deep understanding for the principles of modeled objects. For example, services can be modeled as AI models like neural networks and reinforcement learning.

- **First principle:** By analyzing the mechanism of a controlled object, an equation from input to output is obtained. To use this mode, one needs to be familiar with the principles of modeled objects, for example, using the queuing theory to model traffic services and using graph theory algorithms to model network topology services.

In the NE field, data-driven modeling is common, but most modeling is based on single-point AI features with separated data processing for each AI feature. A unified data processing foundation and embedded modeling simulation platform are not formed. In addition, data-driven modeling poses many problems, such as insufficient generalization capability and lack of explainability.

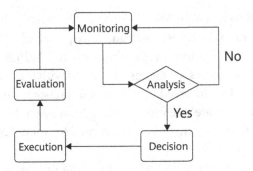

FIGURE 5.59 Centralized SON processing.

The core of the adaptive control layer is to provide the ability to autonomously handle changes and uncertainties in the environment, the layer itself, and its objectives. In the management system, the 3GPP Self-organizing Network (SON) [27] has similar ideas. Figure 5.59 shows the processing procedure.

The monitoring phase collects and analyzes large amounts of management data to determine whether the network has problems that need to be solved. It makes decisions, executes them to solve discovered problems that need to be solved, and evaluates the effectiveness of the solutions.

At present, the industry is seeking good practice on adaptive control as well as its corresponding theoretical guidance in the NE field. It also considers how to integrate the adaptive control loop with the existing service systems and how to ensure the security and reliability of adaptive control decisions.

In summary, NE endogenous intelligence needs continuous exploration to make breakthroughs in key technologies.

5.7.3 Key Technical Solutions

Figure 5.60 provides an overview of key technologies based on the architecture objectives of AI native NEs and the key capabilities that each layer needs to provide.

5.7.3.1 Key Technologies for Intelligent Hardware: AI-dedicated Hardware Acceleration
As mentioned in the previous section, AI inference on CPUs is unlikely to be the mainstream approach in the future and needs to evolve to more powerful AI inference on AI dedicated hardware. Research of AI-dedicated hardware has the following potential directions:

- Digital computing has evolved from general-purpose to dedicated. The hardware architecture is customized so that it has application features in a specific field and can be dedicated to a series of application tasks in that field. Meanwhile, heterogeneous computing (with multiple computing architectures) coexists alongside dedicated computing.

- Analog computing will show advantages in certain areas. Photonic computing will be applied to domains like signal processing, combinatorial optimization, and machine learning, especially to massive MIMO in the wireless domain and to the optical communications domain.

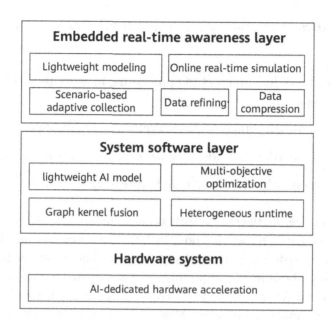

FIGURE 5.60   Overview of key technologies for NE endogenous intelligence.

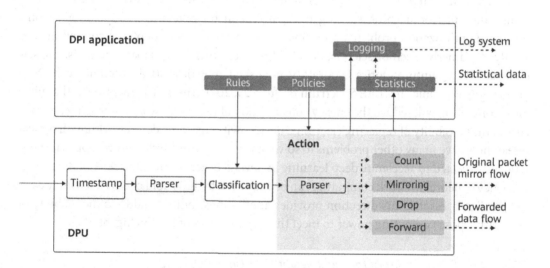

FIGURE 5.61   Intelligent DPI based on DPU acceleration.

In the telecom field, key processes with high resource usage (e.g., data processing and AI inference in AI native NEs) provide key scenarios where the acceleration capability of dedicated AI chips can be fully utilized. Using data processing as an example, a data processing unit (DPU) is a category of newly developed dedicated processor that provides a computing engine for high-bandwidth, low-latency, and data-intensive computing scenarios. As shown in Figure 5.61 [28], the DPU offloads dots per inch (DPI) traffic, and the DPI application delivers the rule library to the hardware to form identification rules. After receiving data, the DPU adds timestamps to it, parses it to match the identification rules, searches for the matching execution policies, and executes the corresponding actions.

A DPU can accelerate the processing of huge data volumes, with the following typical capabilities:

- Network functions, like Ethernet I/O processing, network protocol processing, and network encryption.

- Storage functions, like compression, encryption, and replication.

- Security functions, like encryption, regular expression processing, and hashing.

- Analysis functions, like data analysis and processing.

In terms of inference, AI algorithms such as machine learning can be offloaded to dedicated hardware for hardware acceleration. In future-oriented telecom devices, network hardware needs to be redesigned. Dedicated AI chips will be integrated into communications chips to provide built-in AI computing power. Compared with an external AI accelerator card, dedicated AI chips have lower costs and power consumption in addition to providing faster processing capabilities. Meanwhile, vertical integration based on a full stack of software and hardware is required to achieve ultimate performance.

Analog computing has leveraged its advantages in specific domains, such as photonic computing chips for machine learning, quantum chemistry simulation, and solution to combinatorial optimization problems. In terms of the combination of photonic computing and AI, Ryan Hamerly, a senior scientist at NTT Research Institute in Japan and a visiting scientist at MIT Quantum Optics Laboratory, published an article titled "The Future of Deep Learning Is Photonic" in IEEE Spectrum on June 29, 2021. The article mentioned that photonic computing will reduce the energy consumption of neural network computing and discussed the possibility of replacing electronic devices with photonic devices. Although optical researchers have many other problems to solve in the computing architecture, optics is theoretically expected to accelerate deep learning by several orders of magnitude, and the energy efficiency of neural network computing can be improved by 1000-fold compared with today's electronic processors. This direction provides another possibility to address the inability of general-purpose computing power to meet the requirements of the intelligent world.

5.7.3.2 Key Technologies of the Lightweight Real-Time AI Engine

NE AI is similar to on-device AI, with insufficient resources (computing power and memory) in the deployment environment. The AI model and AI framework should be as small as possible on the premise of guaranteed effect so that as many AI applications as possible can be deployed in the NE environment or with the same resources. In addition, the framework needs to make full use of the computing power of AI chips. NEs face massive amounts of user data and therefore have critical requirements for security, privacy, and efficient data processing. Various NE types with different hardware forms require engine adaptation to shield hardware differences and unify API programming.

In brief, the major challenges faced by the NE AI engine include real-time performance (microsecond-level inference), lightweight (platform size/memory usage/model size), security and privacy, and device fragmentation. The following describes the **lightweight real-time AI** engine, beginning with its key technologies.

First, lightweight AI models.

The AI computing power of network devices keeps improving but remains relatively limited. The increasing capability requirements, such as real-time awareness, real-time inference, and AI trustworthiness, need to be met. If more AI algorithm models can be deployed under limited resources, network devices can be more competitive in terms of intelligence.

Lightweight AI models are classified into two types. One is to compress existing AI models using the following methods:

- **Pruning:** Deletes numerous redundant parameters from models.

- **Quantization:** Quantizes high-precision parameters in a network model into low-precision parameters.

- **Knowledge distillation:** Uses a foundation model to guide small model training and retain valid information of the foundation model.

The other is to redesign more efficient network units in order to reduce the number of network parameters and improve the network running speed, using the following methods [29]:

- **Multiple small convolution kernels replacing one large convolution kernel:** For example, Simonyan et al. proposed that several 3×3 convolution kernels replacing a 5×5 large convolution kernel in a VGGNet network reduces the parameter quantity by 28%.

- **Limiting the number of channels for intermediate features:** For example, Iandola et al. proposed the Fire module in SqueezeNet, which minimizes the calculation workload by reducing the number of channels at the compression layer. Compared with the AlexNet model, the Fire module is nearly 50 times more compressed.

- **Factorized convolutional operation:** For example, Mehta et al. proposed that in ESPNet, a standard convolution is factorized into 1×1 pointwise convolutions and spatial pyramid of dilated convolutions, which is nearly 180 times more compressed compared with PSPNet.

The three methods mainly improve standard convolutional operations in terms of the kernel size, number of input channels, sparse connection between channels, and the like. In practice, manual design reduces Floating-Point Operations Per Second (FLOPS) to some extent, but weakens the effect. In addition, some hardware is not ideal for the Depthwise operator, restricting the application in some scenarios.

Second, multi-objective optimization.

Take an AI feature in the wireless domain as an example. When the predictive gain of the model increases from 95% to 100%, the training overhead needs to increase twofold and the inference overhead needs to increase over 10-fold. As a result, the solution with the predictive gain of 95% is preferred for engineering implementation. Such multi-objective optimization problems are common in design optimization of neural network models for network devices, aiming to strike a balance among multiple objectives like performance, model size, and running memory.

In recent years, the emergence of AutoML brings new possibilities for neural network design, among which the neural architecture search (NAS) algorithm plays an increasingly important role in design and optimization of a lightweight computing model. NAS's basic idea is to gradually abandon humans' long-term accumulated experience in network architecture design and instead rely on the optimization algorithm itself to find the optimal or near-optimal network architecture within a large enough range. Combined with AutoML hyperparameter optimization, NAS can support multi-objective optimization capabilities to a certain extent, like random Pareto multi-objective hyperparameter selection and resource restriction represented as constraint optimization problems.

While realizing lightweight operations, NEs need to have real-time inference capability. Below we will discuss the key technologies of the AI engine for real-time inference. The development of AI chips and computing power poses the following challenges to high performance of the real-time AI framework:

- **Integrated compilation of computational graphs and operators:** Hardware-independent optimization tends to converge. To make full use of hardware computing power, the graph layer needs to be linked with the operator layer for joint optimization, breaking the boundaries between the two layers.

- **Adaption of the model execution mode to scenarios and hardware:** The graph sink mode is mixed with single-operator execution, and the optimal mode varies depending on the hardware.

- **Huge challenges to programmability:** SOC-level heterogeneous programming needs to be supported in order to meet the requirements of multi-chip, single-chip, cross-generation, and cross-model compatibility.

Graph kernel fusion and uniform runtime are two key technologies of the AI engine for real-time high-performance inference.

First, graph kernel fusion.

Take Figure 5.62 as an example. The graph kernel fusion breaks the boundaries of graphs and operators and makes full use of the chip computing power in the following aspects:

- **Unified graph kernel frontend representation:** Shields hardware differences. Users only need to describe computing requirements, and the framework automatically completes hardware performance optimization.

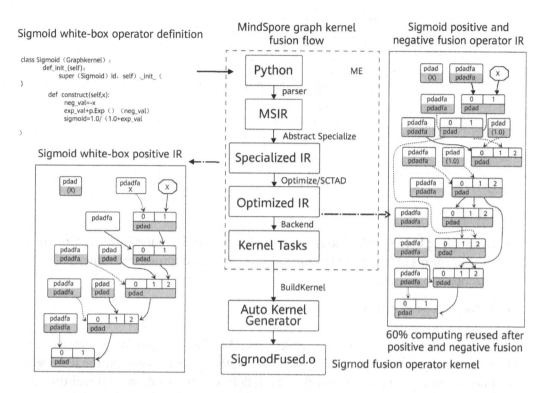

FIGURE 5.62   MindSpore's graph kernel fusion.

- **Unified graph kernel intermediate representation:** Uses MindSpore's intermediate representation to represent the internal logic of operators, breaking the graph kernel information boundaries.

- **Generalized operator fusion capability:** Is applicable to diversified networks. Operators are automatically split, aggregated, and reconstructed based on data dependency, fusion policies, and overhead models, achieving automatic scheduling, splitting, and memory migration by means of the Polly technology.

Second, uniform runtime.

As mentioned earlier in this section, NE hardware will evolve toward heterogeneous computing where multiple computing architectures coexist. Accordingly, to gradually improve the computing power of heterogeneous hardware, the framework runtime will go through the following phases: dedicated runtime, multi-hardware runtime, and universal heterogeneous runtime. As shown in Figure 5.63, the uniform runtime enables different hardware to process computing services; it is best adapted to and presents unified APIs to upper-layer developers, simplifying heterogeneous hardware calling.

The main technical capabilities are as follows:

- **Unified backend architecture:** Adopts the Actor execution mechanism to unify the compilation and execution processes of computational graphs at the backend (which involves memory management, control flow, and design for X (DFX)), avoiding redundant development and reducing maintenance costs.

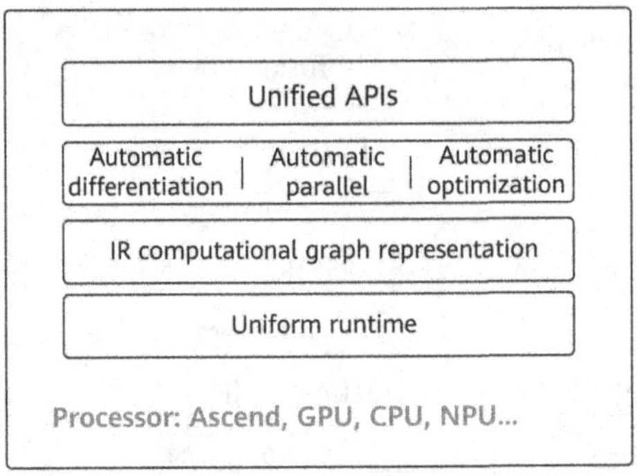

FIGURE 5.63   Uniform runtime context.

- **Decoupling between the framework and hardware:** Separates software from hardware by means of hardware abstraction layer APIs to improve the framework generalization capabilities.

- ActorDAG-based native concurrent execution.

There are other directions in the industry, like AddrNet and product quantization, to reduce computing requirements. Simply put, NE intelligence depends on the lightweight real-time AI engine and needs to consider both lightweight operations and real-time performance during engineering implementation, for example, specifying the inference precision, model size, and running memory to train models.

5.7.3.3 Key Technologies of Embedded Real-Time Awareness

NEs' embedded real-time awareness addresses the following problems:

- **Modeling and simulation of internal devices and services:** NEs and NetGraph form hierarchical awareness and service modeling, which collaborate to significantly reduce the amount of data to be transmitted and achieve real-time NE simulation services.

- **Uncertain changes and real-time data:** NEs usually use AI models for inference, but the inference mechanisms and results are uncertain. To ensure the security and reliability of key NE configurations and decisions, online real-time simulation and verification are required before decision execution.

In terms of reference implementation, NEs' embedded real-time awareness is divided into two layers: data foundation and online real-time simulation engine.

The data foundation provides basic data processing capabilities, like data collection, preprocessing, management, and distribution. Due to the limited storage and computing resources and huge volumes of real-time data, and considering data collaboration with the upper-layer network graphs, the data foundation mainly focuses on how to minimize data processing while also guaranteeing the AI inference effect. The key technologies are as follows:

First, scenario-based adaptive collection.

In the collection phase, data volumes can be reduced by means of on-demand collection and scenario-based collection.

Data collection protocols and interfaces must meet the following requirements: low latency (millisecond-level), low cost (low data volume, on-demand collection, and frequency-based collection), and high reliability (no data loss or disorder), and on-demand collection and scenario-based collection capabilities must be available.

- **On-demand collection:** In this framework, the collection plug-in can be quickly loaded to implement collection feature extension and change, data reporting and collection can be dynamically controlled, and data can be used on demand immediately after being collected.

- **Scenario-based collection:** In this framework, collection items, objects, and granularities are flexibly combined to adopt collection policies in differentiated scenarios for flexible data reporting and on-demand configuration.

Collection policies in differentiated scenarios support flexible data reporting. Figure 5.64 shows an example of scenario-based adaptive collection.

A sampling model can be used for air interface measurement control. For example, a data model that is closely related to a spatial location attribute may learn initial sample distribution curves based on user data distribution features in a time domain and a spatial domain. Such a model is used as an initial sampling model to dynamically control air interface measurement objects and periods. During the running, the sampling model is continuously updated by optimizing the sample distribution curves online in accordance with the sample repetition ratio, thus realizing variable frequency collection. During data collection, differentiated collection control can be performed based on service attribute tags.

Second, data refining.

Another way to minimize data processing is to identify the value of data and process only that with high value.

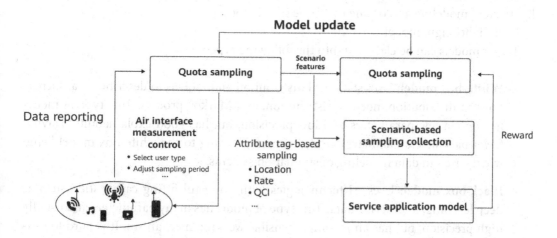

FIGURE 5.64 Scenario-based adaptive collection.

Data determines the upper limit of AI model performance. However, low-value samples, such as redundant, abnormal, and low-information samples, slightly improve AI model performance but increase storage and computing consumption. Evaluating data value and filtering high-value data can lower the resource usage and reduce the impact on AI model performance. Generally, two methods are available for data value evaluation.

- **Static data value evaluation:** Actively learns and evaluates the value of training samples based on the density weight, and removes low-value samples with small differences and representativeness.

- **Dynamic data value evaluation:** Actively learns and evaluates the information of samples based on the minimum confidence. Low-information samples are not transmitted for model training.

Third, data compression.

NE memory resources are limited and cannot store large amounts of data for inference. In addition, most NE data is time series data, requiring chronological analysis on long-term data, and further increasing resource consumption.

- **New compression algorithms:** Support higher compression ratios and faster compression performance, and need to balance the processing performance and storage space based on different AI features.

- **Automatic selection of compression algorithms:** The data types vary in different data processing phases. The data foundation automatically selects compression algorithms for the different data types to achieve optimal compression throughout the AI data process.

In addition to the limited NE resources, the online real-time simulation layer needs to address challenges brought by real-time service changes through key technologies like lightweight modeling and online real-time simulation:

First, lightweight modeling.

Target models can be classified into the following types:

- **White-box model:** Uses statistical distribution and models to describe data, such as Poisson distribution, normal distribution, and Markov process. This type of model has only a few parameters and low precision, but has good explainability. Having fewer parameters facilitates NE deployment, leading to the white-box model being widely used in data modeling of simulation systems.

- **Black-box model:** Uses AI technologies with powerful fitting capabilities, such as deep learning, to describe data. This type of model has many parameters and usually high precision, but has an incomprehensible working mechanism. It is hard to estimate the importance of each feature to the model prediction result and to understand the interaction between these features. In addition, this type of model has disadvantages like high training resource consumption and difficult deployment, which are hot topics in today's research.

Lightweight modeling has the following two research directions:

- **Model compression:** Performs lightweight processing on established models. The AI model for deep learning, for example, is a black-box model. As mentioned earlier in this section, an AI model can be compressed through pruning, quantization, and knowledge distillation.

- **Quick learning:** Optimizes the training process of statistical models with only a few parameters (which is difficult to reduce) by means of optimizing the model update process, and uses a small quantity of data volumes and computing resources to update the models, avoiding cache pressure caused by huge data storage and time consumption caused by model retraining.

Second, online real-time simulation.

Embedded simulation requires online real-time capabilities to accommodate the real-time change of embedded NE services.

Once enabled, embedded simulation is always online. When an NE service sends a request for obtaining the status, the embedded simulation returns the model running status. When an NE service sends a request for updating the status, the embedded simulation adjusts the model parameters and status based on the input data, and then corrects the prediction result. In addition, the prediction duration of embedded simulation can be dynamically adjusted to be a forward-looking long-term stable prediction or a short-term prediction with a small deviation. The predicted running speed of embedded simulation is faster than real time, requiring efficient scheduling, queue algorithms and structures, and high-performance pseudo-random algorithms.

5.7.4 Technology Prospects

In addition to in-depth collaborative optimization of software and hardware and embedded real-time awareness, NEs need to have adaptive control capabilities, whose engineering implementation is one of the future research directions. The third-generation AI proposes knowledge and data convergence, and NEs will introduce domain knowledge to it to make up for deficiencies in data driving. Continuous exploration is required in NEs' adaptive control layer to implement a complete AI native NE architecture.

5.8 NETWORK ENDOGENOUS SECURITY TECHNOLOGY

Networks have been developing rapidly in recent years: Fixed networks have evolved from 40 to 100 Gbit/s and then to 200 Gbit/s, and mobile networks have evolved from 3G to 4G and then to 5G. Such development has driven a boom in the digital economy. At the same time, cybersecurity attracts more attention, especially for basic telecom networks, even affecting national security. Many countries have enacted relevant laws and regulations to bolster the security capabilities of CSPs and device vendors.

5.8.1 Background and Motivation

As mentioned in the Introduction, guaranteeing cybersecurity has become a very important task for CSPs, enterprises, and countries. Section 4.6 describes ADN's endogenous security architecture. According to Section 4.6.3, a network must have security capabilities to automatically detect, defend against, and respond to security events. Its security capabilities can be self-adaptive and self-growing to achieve cybersecurity autonomy.

5.8.2 Technology Insights

Recent years have witnessed the significant development of cybersecurity technologies and theories. Section 4.6.3 introduces three theories that are widely recognized and adopted in the industry: IPDRR, CARTA, and zero trust. The three theories point out that the core of future cybersecurity is as follows: No trust in any communications entity, real-time assessment, automatic detection of intrusion events, automatic recovery, and self-learning and self-adaptation.

Following the preceding theories, the industry focuses on security detection, response and recovery, and trust assessment technologies to quickly detect and recover from attacks. The research directions are as follows:

Security detection: Traditional detection technologies based on attack signatures are mature, but cannot detect new attacks. Therefore, AI technologies are introduced to establish behavior baselines of detected entities and detect their abnormal behaviors.

Response and recovery: Responding to and recovering from an attack mainly rely on manual operations with low efficiency, posing a challenge to the research of automatic response and recovery capabilities.

Trust assessment: Based on the concept of "zero trust," communications entities and users cannot be trusted permanently with only one-off authentication. Instead, dynamic and real-time risk assessment is required. Currently, the industry mainly studies risk assessment technologies for operation users, focusing on the risks of user terminals and the changes of user operations.

5.8.3 Key Technical Solutions

As described in Section 4.6.6, ADN needs to have the characteristics of self-defense, self-detection, self-assessment, and self-healing. Achieving this goal involves multiple key technologies, as shown in Figure 5.65.

5.8.3.1 Key Technologies of Self-Defense

ADN adopts the concept of endogenous security and builds its own defense capabilities, involving system security, identity and access control, security isolation, data security, and AI security.

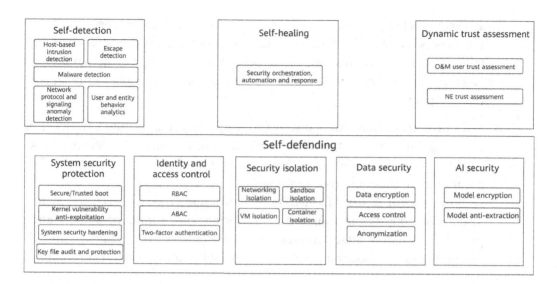

FIGURE 5.65   Overview of key technologies for network endogenous security.

1. System security

Operating systems (OSs) are the basis for service running. Because many attacks target the OS, key technologies such as secure/trusted boot, kernel exploit prevention, system security hardening, and key file audit and protection are required to build a secure and reliable OS running environment.

First, secure/trusted boot technologies ensure that all programs running in the system are trusted and as expected. In the boot phase, layer-by-layer signature verification is adopted to enable secure boot from hardware trusted root, basic input output system (BIOS), and OS to applications, preventing these programs from being tampered with. Furthermore, layer-by-layer measurement is adopted to enable trusted boot from hardware trusted root, BIOS, and OS to applications. This ensures that programs run as expected.

Second, kernel exploit prevention includes technologies like address space layout randomization (ASLR), kernel integrity protection (KIP), kernel control flow integrity, and stack protection.

(1) **ASLR:** Randomizes the layout of linear areas such as heaps, stacks, and shared library mappings of a system to prevent attackers from guessing the location of the code being attacked (called the return-to-libc attack that modifies the returned address to point to an existing function in the memory).

(2) **KIP:** Checks the integrity of kernel code to prevent malicious tampering of OS kernel code and registers as well as malicious code injection.

(3) **Kernel control flow integrity:** Limits control flow transfer during program running, so that the control flow is always within a range limited by an original control flow graph. The control flow integrity mechanism is divided into two phases: First, obtain a control flow graph by analyzing binary or source code programs,

and acquire a list of destination addresses of transfer instructions. Second, at runtime, check whether the destination addresses of the transfer instructions map to those in the list. In this way, the kernel control flow integrity mechanism can detect and prevent control flow hijacking attacks that often violate original control flow graphs.

(4) **Stack protection:** The system inserts verification information into a stack before executing functions. When the functions return values, the system checks whether the inserted verification information is modified. If it is, stack overflow occurs and the program stops running.

Third, system security hardening aims to improve system security. System installation follows the minimum installation and minimum authorization principles to reduce attack surfaces, prevent attackers from using system vulnerabilities for attacks, and provide a secure and stable environment for service running.

Fourth, key file audit and protection audits key system files and controls operation permissions to prevent malicious tampering and unauthorized access, which may cause sensitive information leakage or even implant malicious programs into the device running environment.

2. Identity and access control

Identity and access control technologies include role-based access control (RBAC), attribute-based access control (ABAC), single sign-on (SSO), and two-factor authentication. All these technologies are mature. Traditional network device authentication employs RBAC to assign roles to users and define operations in the roles that the users can perform. In ADN, in addition to user roles, other attributes (e.g., user login time) need to be authenticated. This is because network O&M is strictly regulated on telecom networks and the operation time is predictable, but attackers do not know the regulations and may log in to the system at any time after obtaining the password of an authorized user (such as phishing). In this case, login time authentication can detect exceptions and quickly block attacks. ABAC is required if multiple attributes need to be authenticated.

3. Data security

The world is in a high-speed digitalization process. Almost all data has been informatized, and the data scale increases explosively. All industries are utilizing big data analysis and AI technologies to evolve, heavily promoting the development of the global economy. Data becomes a very important and valuable asset, and data security becomes critical – related regulations have been released in many countries. Because networks transmit data and have large amounts of it, data security is an important goal of ADN.

The objective of data security is to guarantee the confidentiality, integrity, and availability of data. Confidentiality means that data will not be disclosed, with encryption being the most effective method for this purpose. Integrity means that data will not be tampered with, with data signature being the most effective method for this purpose. And availability means that data damage will not affect system running and the original data can be restored, with backup being the most effective method for this purpose. Data can also be protected by means of access control and segmented storage. ADN can take different measures based on the technical costs and data value to ensure data security in the most reasonable way.

4. AI security

With the large-scale application of AI technologies in various industries, AI security issues have attracted more and more attention. AI systems may be the target of specific security attacks, like model theft, poisoning attacks (during AI training, an attacker injects malicious data into a system, causing training misalignment and making the trained model unavailable), and evasion attacks (during AI inference, an attacker adds certain noise to a system, causing inaccurate inference results or controlling the judgment results.) Currently, some countries and organizations have formulated laws and regulations on the security of AI systems, focusing mainly on the impact of AI technologies on natural persons. For example, AI technologies may cause physical or psychological injury to specific groups due to certain characteristics, and generate different criteria for people of different races in terms of employment and education.

In ADN, AI models are important assets and need to be protected through model encryption and anti-extraction protection. According to preliminary analysis, there is a low probability that attackers will use poisoning attacks or evasion attacks against ADN. This is because in addition to being difficult to launch such attacks, other attacks may be more beneficial. Furthermore, AI technologies are mainly used in scenarios such as fault locating, recovery, and network optimization of ADN and do not affect natural persons. Therefore, there are few legal and regulatory risks in this regard.

5.8.3.2 Key Technologies of Self-detection

To ensure system security, NEs and NetGraph have necessary security capabilities in order to provide a secure running environment. However, because they cannot completely defend against all types of attacks, security detection technologies are required to detect attacks and find security risks in real time. Figure 5.66 shows the ADN cybersecurity detection architecture.

In this architecture, security detection agents are deployed on the NE and NetGraph to detect security intrusion events on OSs, network protocols, and O&M users, and report related information to the NetGraph. The network graph processes and analyzes related data, outputs detection results, and reports the results to the network-wide security operations center. The network-wide security operations center provides information such as threat intelligence to threat model libraries for accurate attack detection.

Traditional detection technologies, such as host intrusion detection, malware detection, and VM and container escape detection, are needed. Detection capabilities, such as detecting rogue base stations and BGP hijacking, need to be supported based on different

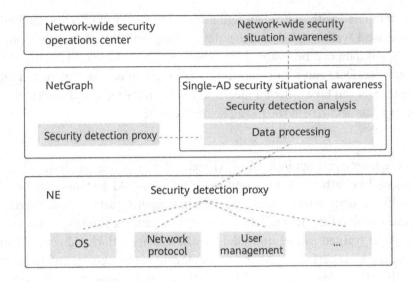

FIGURE 5.66   Security detection architecture.

network characteristics. For scenarios in which traditional detection methods are not suitable, such as advanced persistent threat (APT) attacks, insider threats, and rule bypass, the industry proposes user and entity behavior analytics (UEBA). This technology collects behavior information about users and entities on the network. It then leverages technologies such as big data analysis and AI learning to model user and entity behaviors, establish normal behavior baselines, and compare user and entity behaviors with the behavior baselines to detect abnormal behaviors. In this way, UEBA can find possible attacks on the network. UEBA is able to effectively handle the preceding attack threat scenarios, overcoming the disadvantages of traditional security detection technologies.

The UEBA technology, which is related to the entities to be analyzed and scenarios, is still in the initial application phase in ADN. In the future, experts need to conduct in-depth research to apply the technology in the ADN field.

5.8.3.3 Key Technologies of Self-healing

Self-response and self-closed-loop of cybersecurity incidents are some of the objectives of cybersecurity autonomy. The key technology for achieving this objective is security orchestration, automation and response (SOAR). The SOAR system can integrate the security capabilities of different systems or components in a system through playbooks based on certain logical relationships to implement automatic closed-loop handling of one or one type of threat event. The SOAR system provides a graphical orchestration configuration interface and a flexible response orchestration engine. When a threat event triggers SOAR, the response orchestration engine automatically takes actions according to the event handling process defined in the matched playbook. During the execution, the SOAR system can interact with external systems. Humans can also participate in decision-making to take different actions. Figure 5.67 shows the SOAR functions. The SOAR engine integrates many original actions and provides graphical orchestration capabilities to orchestrate response playbooks after a security event occurs.

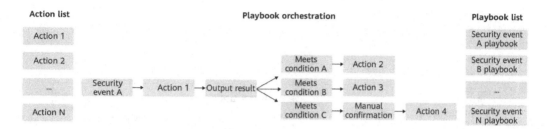

FIGURE 5.67   SOAR functions.

For some new and unknown attacks, the SOAR technology can be adopted to manually orchestrate response policies online, determine the impact on the networks, and execute the policies. However, the current SOAR capability cannot meet the self-response requirements. In the future, the SOAR system must have self-learning and self-adaptation capabilities. It must be able to automatically analyze attack characteristics and historical event processing information, conclude possible handling measures and their impact on the network, and select the optimal measures to execute.

In ADN, both the NetGraph and the network-wide security operations center will have certain SOAR capabilities, but with different responsibilities. The NetGraph is responsible for responding to security events in a single network domain in a closed-loop manner. The network-wide security operations center conducts unified collaboration for security events that need to be recovered across multiple network domains.

5.8.3.4 Key Technologies of Dynamic Trust Assessment

Networks have begun to evolve from bordered to borderless networks. The traditional border-based defense concept is outdated, gradually being replaced with the zero-trust-based cybersecurity concept. The core of zero-trust is "never trust, always verify," meaning that we cannot trust the peer end, regardless of whether it is a natural person, a device, or a system. Continuous risk assessment must be performed on the peer end and dynamic policy control must be executed based on the assessment result to ensure the security of the entire network.

Figure 5.68 shows the dynamic trust assessment architecture of ADN.

ADN mainly performs continuous risk assessment on network O&M users, NEs, and peer systems. Based on the assessment result, ADN further conducts dynamic policy-based access control.

Risks of O&M users need to be evaluated from three aspects: access terminals, login behaviors, and operation behaviors.

1. Assessment of O&M user access terminals

   ADN needs to evaluate a terminal's security awareness, for example, whether security configuration is performed, whether the terminal is infected with viruses, and whether non-compliant software is installed. ADN also needs to evaluate the terminal's physical environment awareness, for example, whether switchover occurs, whether screenshots are captured, and whether multiple persons watch the terminal.

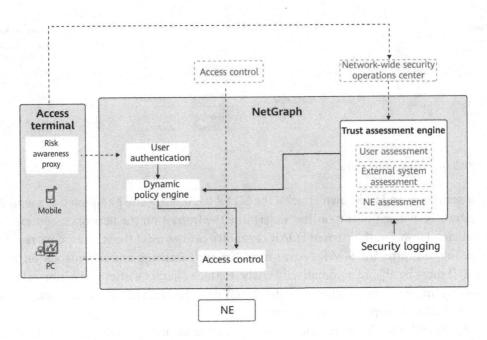

FIGURE 5.68   Dynamic trust assessment architecture.

2. Assessment of O&M user login behaviors

Attackers may use brute force cracking, password guessing, and phishing to attack authorized users. After obtaining the password of an authorized user, attackers can log in to and attack the system and perform unauthorized operations. These behaviors, including the login time, must be assessed in real time because attackers may not log in at the time when authorized users usually do. These behaviors will be used as the basis for user behavior assessment.

3. Assessment of O&M user operation behaviors

Generally, the operations performed by an O&M user on the network are predictable, whereas attackers (both insiders and external attackers) aim to damage or steal information on the network and therefore perform operations that are different from those of authorized users. Technologies such as AI learning can be used to assess user operation behaviors.

Based on the assessment result, ADN can perform dynamic policy control for users, for example, session logout and forcible secondary authentication.

5.8.4 Technology Prospects

Although cybersecurity technologies have advanced leaps and bounds, they still lag far behind ADN's requirements, especially in automatic attack detection, response, and recovery. Many new attacks cannot be automatically detected, and many scenarios require manual intervention for response and recovery. Research on dynamic trust assessment technologies is just starting and applies to limited scenarios. In the future, more AI technologies need to be introduced in the cybersecurity field to achieve cybersecurity autonomy.

5.9 SUMMARY

ADN is a brand-new field that spans multiple disciplines – such as communications science, computer science, control theory, and complex systems – and involves many key technologies. This chapter discusses some key technologies for the ADN reference architecture. Because ADN involves a new network architecture paradigm, further study is needed on in-depth theories and key technologies, including the following: dynamic decision-making management mechanism, high-level objective modeling framework, embodied AI-based decision support system, and semantic communications model in the automation field; goal-driven self-healing decision mechanism and self-healing control dual-closed-loop technology in the self-healing field; uncertainty adaptation technology, goal-driven multi-self-optimizing closed-loop collaboration mechanism, multi-agent distributed collaborative optimization, and cognitive computing-based optimization target decision-making in the self-optimizing field; and dual-system cognitive architecture and collaboration technology, lifelong self-learning, and system adaptive software modes and policies in the autonomy field.

Such a systematic ADN project requires in-depth cooperation between academia and industry to make comprehensive breakthroughs in basic theories and key technologies.

REFERENCES

1. Joseph Sifakis, "Autonomous systems - a rigorous architectural characterization: 2019 IEEE SERVICES Congress," [R/OL], (2019-07-09) [2022-07-13].
2. B. Zhang, J. Zhu, and H. Su, "Toward the third generation of artificial intelligence," *Scientia Sinica Informationis*, 2020, 50(9):22.
3. Institute for Artificial Intelligence Tsinghua University, Beijing Academy of Artificial Intelligence, Tsinghua-Chinese Academy of Engineering K&I, et al., "Research Report of Cognitive Graph," [J], Zhipu AI, Tsinghua, Report of Artificial Intelligence Development (AI TR), 2020, 6.
4. J. Tang, "On the next decade of artificial intelligence," *CAAI Transactions on Intelligent Systems*, 2020, 15(1):6.
5. J. Kaur, "Distributed artificial intelligence latest trends," [R/OL], XENONSTACK, (2022-08-23) [2022-09-25].
6. Tsinghua big data software team, *ruhe gouzao rengong qunti zhineng* [How to Build Artificial Swarm Intelligence], [R/OL], (2022-06-06) [2022-09-25].
7. J. Kaur, "Artificial intelligenc/'e in edge computing," [R/OL], XENONSTACK, (2021-12-05) [2022-09-25].
8. China Mobile Research Institute, "yinsi anquan jisuan zhi lianbang xuexi," [Privacy and Security Computing - Federated Learning], [R/OL], (2021-06-16) [2022-09-25].
9. W. Tong, P. Zhu, et al., *6G: The Next Horizon: From Connected People and Things to Connected Intelligence*, Cambridge: Cambridge University Press, 2021.
10. M. Grieves, "Digital twin: Manufacturing excellence through virtual factory replication," [R/OL], (2015-4-20) [2022-9-25].
11. China Mobile, AsiaInfo Technologies, Huawei, et al., "shuzi luansheng wangluo (DTN) baipishu," [Digital Twin Network (DTN) White Book], [R/OL], (2021-9-29) [2022-9-25].
12. F. Tao, H. Zhang, A. Liu, et al., "Digital twin in industry: State-of-the-art," *IEEE Transactions on Industrial Informatics*, 2019, 15(4): 2405–2415.

13. T. Sun, C. Zhou, X. Duan, et al., "Digital twin network (DTN): concepts, architecture, and key technologies," *Acta Automatica Sinica*, 2021, 47 (3): 569–582.
14. H. H. Liu, Y. Zhu, J. Padhye, et al., "CrystalNet: faithfully emulating large production networks," *Symposium*, 2017.
15. W. Wang, and J. Zhang, *OPNET Modeler yu wangluo fangzhen*, [OPNET Modeler and Network Simulation], People's Posts and Telecommunications Press, 2003.
16. B. Chen, and F. Li, "xingshihua yanzheng fangfa qianxi," [Analysis on Formal Verification Methods], [J], *Computer Knowledge and Technology (academic edition)*, 2019.
17. L. Zheng, Y. Yang, and A.G. Hauptmann, "Person re-identification: Past, present and future," 2016.
18. A. Jin, and C. Cheng, "Spatial data coding method based on global subdivision grid," *Journal of Geomatics Science and Technology*, 2013, 30(3):4.
19. A. Hogan, E. Blomqvist, M. Cochez, et al., "Knowledge graphs," *ACM Computing Surveys (CSUR)*, 2021, 54:1–37.
20. S. Ji, S. Pan, E. Cambria, et al., "A survey on knowledge graphs: representation, acquisition, and applications," *IEEE Transactions on Neural Networks and Learning Systems*, 2021, 33(2): 494–514.
21. Q. Wang, Z. Mao, B. Wang, et al., "Knowledge graph embedding: A survey of approaches and applications,", *IEEE Transactions on Knowledge & Data Engineering*, 2017, 29(12):2724–2743.
22. J. B. Lyons, K. Sycara, M. Lewis, et al., "Human-autonomy teaming: definitions, debates, and directions," [EB/OL], (2021-5-28) [2022-09-25].
23. J. Laird, C. Ranganath, S. Gershman, "Future directions in human machine teaming workshop report," [R/OL], (2020-1-15) [2022-9-25].
24. IETF, "Draft-irtf-nmrg-ibn-concepts-definitions-09," [EB/OL], (2022-3-24) [2022-9-25].
25. N. Zheng, et al., "Hybrid-augmented intelligence: Collaboration and cognition," *Frontiers of Information Technology & Electronic Engineering*, 2017, 18:153–179.
26. J. Y. C. Chen, et al., "Situation awareness-based agent transparency and human-autonomy teaming effectiveness," *Theoretical Issues in Ergonomics Science*, 2018, 19:259–282.
27. 3 GPP, "TS 28.313 version 16.0.0 release 16. Self-organizing networks (SON) for 5G networks," [S/OL], (2020-9-25) [2022-9-25].
28. Institute of Computing Technology, Chinese Academy of Sciences, "Technical white paper of data processing unit," [R/OL], (2021-10-16) [2022-9-25].
29. D. Ge, H. Li, L. Zhang, R. Liu, P. Shen, and Q. Miao, "Survey of lightweight neural network," *Journal of Software*, 2020, 31:8–9.
30. R. Confalonieri, L. Coba, B. Wagner, et al., "A historical perspective of explainable artificial intelligence," *Wiley Interdisciplinary Reviews: Data Mining and Knowledge Discovery*, 2021, 11(1): e1391.

CHAPTER 6

Industry Standards

O VER THE PAST FEW decades, the most effective method for achieving system inter-connection has proven to be the formulation of industry standards. Many organiza-tions, such as 3GPP, IETF, the Internet Research Task Force (IRTF), TM Forum, ETSI, and CCSA, have defined standards that not only lay a solid foundation for network intercon-nection but also promote the prosperity of the network ecosystem. Today, as ADN evolves toward higher levels of autonomy, SDOs need to jointly develop more network intercon-nection standards for ADN.

ADN involves a complex ICT system that includes the business operations layer, service operations layer, resource operations layer, and third-party applications. There are many ADs at the resource operations layer. Each of these ADs, categorized based on technical domains such as wireless, core, transport, fixed access, and bearer networks, has an intel-ligent management and control unit and numerous intelligent NEs. In the ADN industry ecosystem, different CSPs and vendors provide numerous systems and devices, all of which must be interconnected to achieve more effective collaboration and network autonomy. Over the past few decades, the telecom industry has developed numerous standards in order to facilitate network interconnection, proving that standardization is the most effec-tive method for achieving cross-vendor system interconnection in ADN. This chapter describes the standards involved in ADN.

SDOs in various domains participate in developing ADN standards, which can be clas-sified based on the positioning of the organization, or the scope and target domain of the standard.

- **International standards/Chinese standards:** International ADN SDOs include TM Forum, ETSI, IETF, and IRTF. In China, the major organization responsible for defining ADN standards is CCSA.

- **General standards/domain-specific standards:** General standards define ADN con-cepts, general architecture, general levels, interface framework, and key technologies and provide a methodology and framework reference for domain-specific standards.

DOI: 10.1201/9781032662879-7

As the name suggests, domain-specific standards are formulated by organizations specialized in specific domains. For example, 3GPP defines ADN standards for mobile communications networks, whereas IETF defines ADN standards for transport, access, and bearer networks.

6.1 INTERNATIONAL STANDARDS

In recent years, international SDOs have initiated many AN research topics and standards, focusing on defining standards in their own domain and collaborating with each other through the Autonomous Networks Multi-SDO. Through their efforts, they have created an initial AN standards system comprised of general and domain-specific standards formulated from five dimensions: ANL, evaluation system, architecture, interfaces, and key technologies.

International AN standards (see Figure 6.1) are formulated based on the general standards defined by the TM Forum Autonomous Network Project (ANP). ETSI Industry Specification Groups (ISG) Zero touch network & Service Management (ZSM) and TM Forum ANP focus on general AN standards and provide a methodology, top-level architecture, and key technology reference for domain-specific standards.

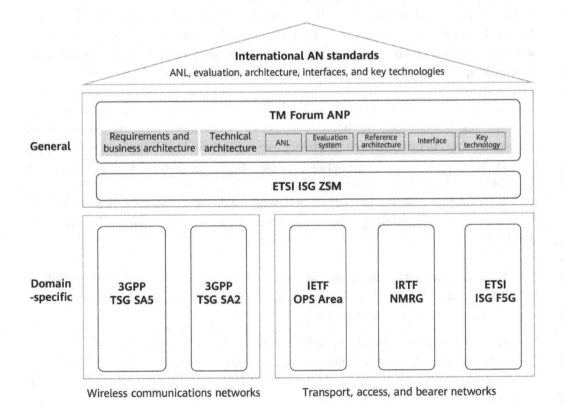

FIGURE 6.1   International AN standards organizations.

- Mobile communications network standards

     3GPP Technical Specification Group Service and System Aspects Working Group 5 (TSG SA5) defined the O&M requirements for AN, as well as a series of standards covering the AN levels, architecture, intents, and closed-loop technologies.

     3GPP TSG SA2 developed standards relating to the overall 3GPP system architecture and services, covering the user equipment, access network, core network, and IP multimedia subsystem (including real-time network and personal data analysis of control-plane NEs).

- Transport, access, and bearer network standards

     The IETF Operations and Management Area (OPS Area) standards working group defined a series of AN standards for NEs and management and control systems.

     The IRTF Network Management Research Group (NMRG) launched research on standardizing many technologies, such as intent-driven technologies and intent APIs.

     ETSI ISG 5th Generation Fixed Network (F5G) defined standards for the requirements, architecture, and AN levels of F5G.

6.1.1 General Standards

General AN standards are mainly developed by TM Forum ANP and ETSI ISG ZSM.

6.1.1.1 Standards Defined by TM Forum ANP

TM Forum is a pioneer in defining AN standards. It initiated the ANP in July 2019 and has since released a series of guidelines and standards about how to fulfill the AN vision. The ANP's standards framework (as shown in Figure 6.2) covers the vision, business architecture, and technical architecture of AN. This framework defines the overall methodologies and reference architecture of AN from a general perspective, providing a reference for different domain-specific standards organizations. Multiple standards development organizations (M-SDOs) collaborate with each other to ensure that they can use the same core concepts when developing domain-specific AN standards.

1. AN business requirements and framework

     TM Forum IG1218 [1] defines the core architecture of AN business requirements. It consists of three layers and four closed loops, as shown in Figure 6.3.

     The three layers are common capabilities of operations that can be utilized to support all scenarios and business needs.

     - **Resource operations layer:** mainly provides network resource and capability automation in each AD.

     - **Service operations layer:** mainly provides the capabilities for network planning, design, rollout, provisioning, assurance, and optimization operations across multiple ADs.

     - **Business operations layer:** mainly provides the capabilities for customer, ecosystem, and partner business enabling and operations for AN services.

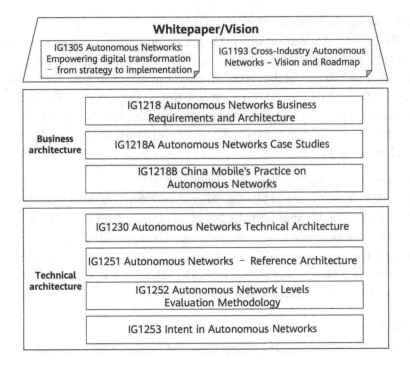

Whitepaper/Vision

| IG1305 Autonomous Networks: Empowering digital transformation – from strategy to implementation | IG1193 Cross-Industry Autonomous Networks – Vision and Roadmap |

Business architecture

- IG1218 Autonomous Networks Business Requirements and Architecture
- IG1218A Autonomous Networks Case Studies
- IG1218B China Mobile's Practice on Autonomous Networks

Technical architecture

- IG1230 Autonomous Networks Technical Architecture
- IG1251 Autonomous Networks – Reference Architecture
- IG1252 Autonomous Network Levels Evaluation Methodology
- IG1253 Intent in Autonomous Networks

FIGURE 6.2 Standards framework of TM Forum ANP.

The four closed loops that fulfill the full lifecycle of the inter-layer interaction are:

- **Resource closed loop:** the interaction of network resource operations in the granularity of ADs.

- **Service closed loop:** the interaction between service and network resource operations that may trigger related resource closed loops in its fulfillment.

- **Business closed loop:** the interaction between business and service operations, which may trigger related service and resource closed loops in its fulfillment.

- **User closed loop:** the interaction across three layers and three closed loops to support the user service fulfillment. The three layers interact with each other through simplified intent APIs.

2. AN technical architecture

TM Forum IG1230 [2] defines the overall AN technical architecture and key AN technologies.

3. AN reference architecture

TM Forum IG1251 [3] defines the AN reference architecture, ADs, and interface reference points. The reference architecture is designed based on the following seven core architectural principles:

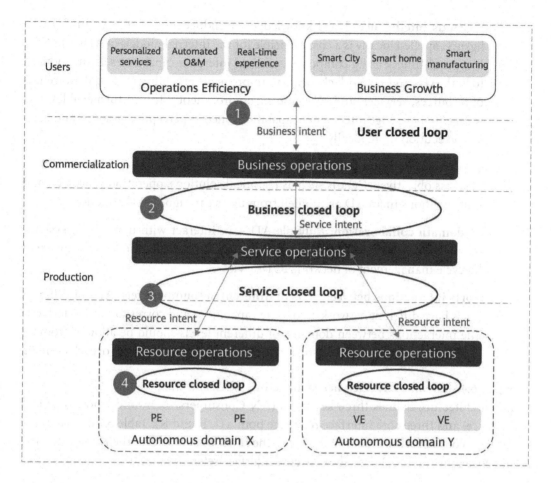

FIGURE 6.3 AN business requirements and framework.

Decoupled operational layers: The overall architecture should comply with the layered architecture pattern. The AN architecture is separated into three layers: business operations layer, service operations layer, and resource operations layer. Each layer runs in self-operating mode and hides the details of domain implementation, operations and the functions within the domain from the consumers.

Intent-driven, open interfaces: Each AD (at any of the three operational layers) of AN should expose standardized interfaces. Where appropriate, those interfaces should now be intent-driven to provide simplified interaction capabilities for upper-layer services through these open APIs.

Closed-loop automation: Automation uses closed-loop mechanisms to ensure service experience by completing workflow steps. It also continuously adapts to ensure goals and objectives are met. The control loop adjusts and adapts itself (through the decision cycle stages of Awareness, Analysis, Decision, and Execution), keeping the system in the desired state without any intervention from outside of a particular loop cycle.

Endogenous intelligence: Local knowledge, or endogenous ("from within") intelligence, applied locally is a core principle for the internal models of ADs and NEs. More real-time sensing components and AI inference capabilities are introduced to both ADs and network elements to improve observability or digital awareness of resources, services, and surrounding environments. This in turn enables data sources to have edge intelligence capabilities such as perception analysis and decision execution more locally.

Single-domain autonomy: Each AD runs in automatic closed-loop mode based on business objectives. Details such as technical solutions, operation processes, and unit functions in an AD are hidden from users through API abstraction.

Cross-domain collaboration: Multiple ADs can interact with upper-layer systems through intent APIs to implement cross-domain collaboration and implement lifecycle management of network/ICT services.

Supports interactions between ADs of different autonomy levels: ADs of different levels have different network autonomy capabilities and corresponding interfaces. The interactions between domains of different levels should be allowed from an architecture perspective, and so too should the evolution (L0 to L5) of each domain.

Figure 6.4 shows the AN reference architecture in IG1251 [3].

This architecture defines three key units (AN Consumers, ADs, and Knowledge and Intelligence) and three core interface reference points (I, F, and K). Table 6.1 describes the functional blocks of ADs. Table 6.2 describes the functional blocks of the Knowledge and Intelligence unit. Table 6.3 describes the core interface reference points.

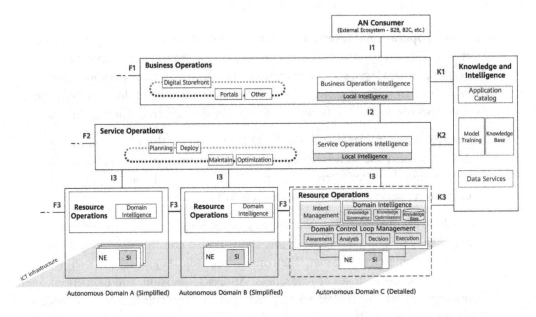

FIGURE 6.4 AN reference architecture.

TABLE 6.1   Functional Blocks of ADs

Functional Block	Description
Intent Management	Intent management unit, which implements external intent API interaction, including the system class (Intent Handler Registration, Capability Release, and other intent entity discovery and connection establishment), intention interaction class (receiving, negotiation, and reporting), and intent instance and lifecycle management.
Domain Intelligence	Provides local knowledge governance capabilities, provides local AI inference based on the local knowledge base, and optimizes local parameters.
Domain Intelligence - Knowledge Governance	Provides local knowledge governance capabilities, including local inference (including local AI inference and knowledge inference) and continuous local model training.
Domain Intelligence - Knowledge Optimization	Provides local AI parameter optimization and knowledge optimization; provides onsite model development and model retraining capabilities. Onsite model development provides lightweight development services to quickly obtain personalized models applicable to sites. Model retraining is performed periodically based on live-network samples to obtain new models in order to ensure model accuracy.
Domain Intelligence - Knowledge Base	Provides local knowledge base and AI asset management capabilities. Assets include models, data, etc. Asset management operations include collecting and releasing AI assets, demonstrating model application results (including intent reports), and model interpretation.
Domain Control Loop	Provides the closed-loop processing capability in an AD, processes external intents by sensing, analyzing, making decisions, and executing, and maintains intents in an AD.
Domain Control Closed-loop Awareness	Provides AD state awareness and information collection for intent execution such as environment information, faults, events, logs, and performance data, analyzes service impacts by correlating collected multi-dimensional original data, identifies incidents that affect services, and predicts risks.
Domain Control Close-loop Analysis	By analyzing the data or context information in incidents or risks generated in the sensing phase, the model inference and analysis techniques are used to further predict the future change trend of the network state, and the decision-making suggestions are proposed.
Domain Control Closed-loop Decision-Making	Based on the decision-making suggestions provided in the analysis phase, a specific rule or human-machine collaboration is used with local knowledge inference to provide required management operations, such as network configuration or parameter adjustment.
Domain Control Closed-loop Execution	Performs management actions and responds with results/feedback to the intent sender (intent owner).
NE	An NE represents the device that is under management.
NE - Site Intelligence	AI inference unit of the NE.

TABLE 6.2   Functional Blocks of the Knowledge and Intelligence Unit

Functional Block	Description
Knowledge and Intelligence	Provides intelligence services for all three operational layers. Includes (AI/ML) model training, data services, knowledge base, and AI/Analytics application marketplace. Works with Localized Intelligence (see the Local Intelligence functional block) where local data and training services are provided by the layered platforms. It does this using 'local-cloud linkages' defined at the K1, K2, and K3 reference points.
Application Catalog	Manages the published AI applications/AI models in a secure catalog. The Application Catalogs contain detailed information on ownership and execution requirements of individual models.
Model Training	Provides an integrated development environment for a one-stop training design environment, model development services, domain model service, federated learning, and knowledge graph. The Training Platform delivers models to the localized intelligence in the operational platforms and (optionally) receives offline data to tune its training algorithms (using K1, K2, and K3 reference points as appropriate depending on the operational layer in question).
Knowledge Base	A repository system that represents knowledge explicitly.
Data Services	Services may include unified data modeling, dataset development and platform and data security dataset enhancement, digital network insight, and simulation.

TABLE 6.3   Interface Reference Points

Reference Point	Description
I1	I1 identifies the reference point for interactions between AN Consumers platform and the business operations layer. Intent-driven interactions are required at this reference point, including the intent delivery interface between the business layer systems and the consumers' application systems, and intent report interface between the business layer systems and its customer application systems.
I2	I2 identifies the reference point for interactions between the business operations layer and the service operations layer. Intent-driven interactions are required at this reference point, including the intent delivery interface between the service layer systems and the consumers' application systems, and intent report interface between the service layer systems and the consumers' application systems.
I3	I3 identifies the reference point for interactions between the services operations layer and the resource operations layer. Intent-driven interactions are required at this reference point, including the intent delivery interface between the resource layer systems and the consumers' application systems, and intent report interface between the resource-layer systems and the consumers' application systems.
F1	F1 identifies the reference point for interactions between ADs at the business operations layer.
F2	F2 identifies the reference point for interactions between ADs at the service operations layer.
F3	F3 identifies the reference point for interactions between ADs at the resource operations layer.
K1	Training sample data collection interface between the business layer systems and the offline K&I training systems. AI inference model delivery interface between the AI offline training systems and the business layer systems.
K2	Training sample data collection interface between the service layer systems and the offline K&I training systems. AI inference model delivery interface between the offline K&I training systems and the service layer systems.
K3	Training sample data collection interface between the resource-layer systems and the offline K&I training systems. AI inference model delivery interface between the offline K&I training systems and the resource layer systems.

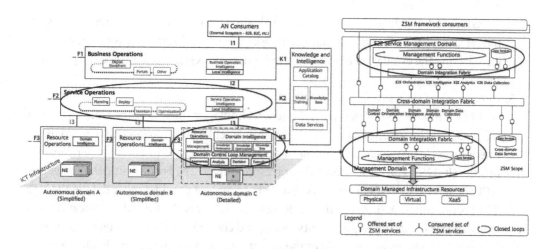

FIGURE 6.5   Mapping between TM Forum IG1251 [3] reference architecture and ZSM's reference architecture.

TM Forum IG1251 [3] maps its AN reference architecture with the reference architecture of ETSI ISG ZSM, as shown in Figure 6.5.

4. AN level evaluation methodology

TM Forum IG1218 [1] defines AN levels to measure customer experience and SLAs. AN levels can be used to develop automated and intelligent networks and services, evaluate the values and advantages of AN services, and help CSPs and vendors evaluate their level of automation and intelligence. Furthermore, IG1252 [4] provides an AN level evaluation methodology, which includes the operation process, task evaluation criteria, and scoring method.

This methodology can be used to evaluate the level of automation for human-machine collaboration from the perspectives of intent/experience, awareness, analysis, decision-making, and execution. TM Forum defines six AN levels.

L0- Manual O&M: The system delivers assisted monitoring capabilities, which means all dynamic tasks have to be executed manually.

L1- Assisted O&M: The system executes certain repetitive sub-tasks based on pre-configurations to improve execution efficiency.

L2- Partial autonomous: The system enables closed-loop O&M for certain units based on pre-defined rules/policies under certain external environments.

L3- Conditional autonomous: Based on L2 capabilities, the system senses real-time environmental changes, and optimizes and adjusts itself to the external environment in certain network domains.

L4- High autonomous: Based on L3 capabilities, the system performs analysis and makes decisions based on predictive or active closed-loop management of services and customer experience-driven networks in more complex cross-domain environments.

L5- Full autonomous: The system provides closed-loop autonomous capabilities across multiple services, domains, and the entire lifecycle.

IG1252v1.1 [4] defines an AN level evaluation procedure and a three-dimensional model (comprised of service domain, network technology domain, and operational flows) for selecting the evaluation object. Section 7.3 uses an example to describe the process.

5. Intent-driven interaction

TM Forum IG1253 [5] defines AN intent technologies, including the concept of intent (IG1253 [5]), intent modeling (IG1253A [6]), intent extension models (IG1253B [7]), intent lifecycle management and interface (IG1253C [8]), and intent manager capability profiles (IG1253D [9]). The open APIs corresponding to TM Forum's intent management API are defined in TM Forum921A [10]. This document provides more details about the TM Forum intent API. According to IG1253 [5], intent is the formal specification of all expectations including requirements, goals, and constraints given to a technical system.

Figure 6.6 shows an example of the intent-driven AN framework. Each operations layer uses different intent APIs at interface reference points I1, I2, and I3 in the AN reference architecture. Note that each arrow shown in the figure represents a bidirectional intent API. This includes the direction of intent setting as well as the direction of intent reporting between intent management functions. All methods proposed on this API are discussed in detail in Chapter 10 in IG1253 [5] and IG1253C [8]. In this example, the intent management function unit at the service operations layer receives intent requests from the business operations layer. Each AD at the service operations layer implements an intent-driven closed loop. To trigger resource operations, the service operations layer delivers requests over an intent API to multiple ADs at the resource operations layer to trigger resource operations. Upon receiving such requests, ADs at the resource operations layer implement the intents through the

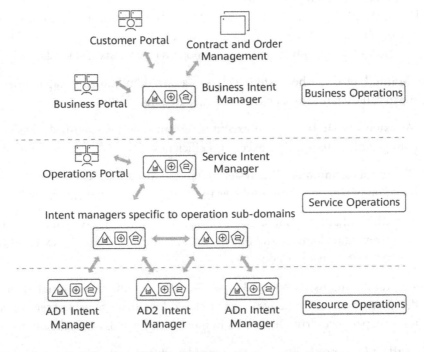

FIGURE 6.6   Example of the intent-driven AN framework.

closed-loop control and management unit. The ADs then report the intent fulfillment status to the service operations layer through the intent reporting API.

The definition of intent (formal specification of all expectations) in IG1253 [5] has become a consensus among SDOs. However, different SDOs use different languages to define intent metamodels. For example, 3GPP uses Unified Modeling Language (UML), whereas IETF uses the Yet Another Next Generation (YANG) model. In addition, TM Forum IG1253A [6] uses RDFS as the basic model language to define an intent common model. Figure 6.7 shows this model's classes, which are intent and intent report. An intent consists of Expectation and Context. Expectation defines the target object and expectation parameters, and Context defines the additional conditions and applicability scope related to the expectation. For details, see TM Forum IG1253A [6].

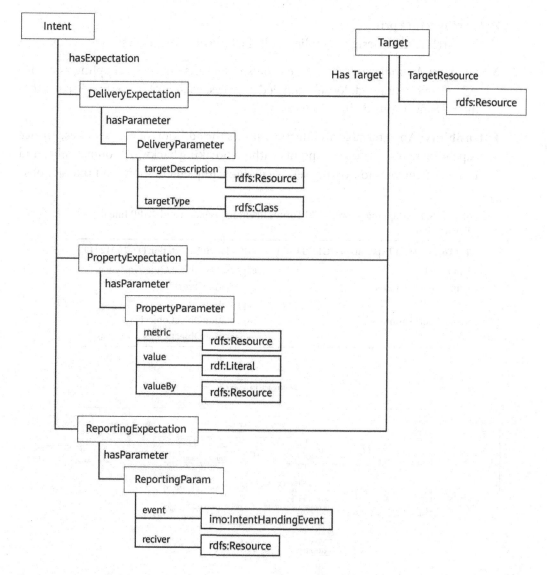

FIGURE 6.7 Classes of TM Forum's intent common model.

The latest version of TM Forum IG1253 [5] maps its intent model to the 3GPP intent model in the appendix, as described in Table 6.4, to help readers understand the mapping between intent models of different organizations.

6.1.1.2 Standards Defined by ETSI ISG ZSM

Similar to the general AN standards system defined by TM Forum ANP, ETSI ISG ZSM focuses on the management domain at the resource operations layer and the E2E cross-domain collaboration management domain and standardizes key enabling technologies for AN. Figure 6.8 shows ZSM's standards framework.

ZSM001 [11] defines user scenarios and requirements, and ZSM002 [12] defines the ZSM architecture principles, requirements, and reference architecture.

1. ZSM architecture principles

   ZSM architecture design complies with the following principles:

   Modularity: A modular architecture avoids monoliths and tight coupling and consists of self-contained, loosely coupled services, each with a confined scope that interacts over well-defined interfaces.

   Extensibility: An extensible architecture allows the addition of new services, service capabilities, and service end-points without breaking backward compatibility and requiring changes to existing service designs, implementations and interactions.

TABLE 6.4   Mapping between TM Forum Intent Expectation and 3GPP Intent Expectation

TM Forum Intent Expectation (IG1253A [6])	3GPP Intent Expectation (TS 28.312 [19])
icm:target	expectationObject.ObjectInstance
icm:propertyParams	expectationTargets
	expectationContexts
icm:deliveryParams	expectationObject.objectType
	expectationObject.ObjectContexts

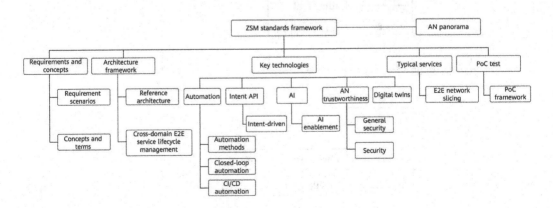

FIGURE 6.8   ZSM's AN standards framework.

Scalability: A scalable architecture allows deployments that can be adapted to satisfy the increasing or decreasing demand of the managed entities and/or to various scales of the geographic distribution of these entities. Based on the principle of modularity, modules can be independently deployed and scaled.

Model-driven, open interfaces: An architecture that is based on a model-driven approach performs the management of services and resources through the use of information models that capture the definition of managed entities in terms of attributes and supported operations. The models are defined independently from the implementation of the managed entities in order to facilitate portability and reusability and to allow vendor-neutral management of resources and services.

Closed-loop management automation: Closed-loop management automation is a feedback-driven process. It seeks to reach and preserve a set of objectives without any intervention external to the specific loop.

Support for stateless management functions: The architecture supports the inclusion of management functions that separate processing from data storage.

Resilience: Management services are designed to, as far as possible, provide and maintain configurable levels of their offered functionalities when facing degradation of the infrastructure and other management services. They also have the ability to return to normal operation when the degradation has been resolved.

Separation of concerns in management: In the ZSM framework, two different management concerns are distinguished: domain management and end-to-end service management across management domains. In practice, there can be a hierarchy of management domains. Inside a management domain, resources and services based on these resources are managed. The complexity of domain resources can be abstracted from service consumers outside of the management domain. The end-to-end cross-domain service management manages end-to-end services that span multiple management domains and coordinates between management domains using orchestration. In this context, end-to-end services may span multiple management domains provided by different administrative entities (e.g., different network service providers or external partners). Decoupling of management domains and end-to-end service management across domains avoids monolithic systems, simplifies the complexity of the overall service, and enables independent evolution of each management domain and of end-to-end management.

Service composability: Management services exposed by the management domains can be combined to create new management services.

Intent-based interfaces: Intent-based interfaces aim to hide complexity and both technology- and vendor-specific details from the user by exposing high-level abstractions.

Functional abstraction: Functional abstraction is defined as the ability to generalize the behavior of related entities, allowing details of multiple variants of those entities to be encapsulated into a single one. Functional abstraction supports several other principles, such as replicability, scalability, and composability.

Simplicity: The architecture has minimal complexity while still meeting functional and non-functional requirements.

Designed for automation: The ZSM framework components and functionalities support the automation of network and service management and the integration of technology evolutions.

2. ZSM architecture requirements

ZSM architecture requirements are defined based on scenarios and architecture principles, for example, resource and service management capabilities, adaptive closed-loop management capabilities, and standard interfaces between management domains. For details, see "Architecture requirements" in ZSM002 [12].

3. ZSM reference architecture

The ZSM reference architecture follows the industry trend and is mapped to TM Forum's AN reference architecture. 3GPP's service-based management architecture is an instance of the ZSM reference architecture.

Figure 6.9 depicts the ZSM framework reference architecture. Every management domain, as well as the E2E service management domain, provides a set of ZSM service capabilities through management functions that expose and/or consume a set of service end-points. The cross-domain integration fabric facilitates providing capabilities and accessing endpoints cross-domain. Some services are only provided and consumed locally inside the management domain. Each of the logical groups of management services contains services with related functionality. The grouping does not imply a particular implementation. ETSI ISG ZSM normatively defines the set of ZSM services visible outside a management domain and the domain integration fabric, which represents one or more management functions responsible for controlling the exposure of services beyond domain boundaries and for controlling access to the management services exposed by the domain. The domain integration fabric may also provide further integration services to the management functions inside the management domain. In addition to providing access to ZSM services, a management domain and the E2E service management domain can also consume ZSM services provided by other management domains. ZSM framework consumers (such as digital store fronts that provide automation of consumer and business management, BSS applications, web portals, another ZSM framework instance, or even human users via additional user interfaces) can consume ZSM services provided by the E2E service management domain and the management domains.

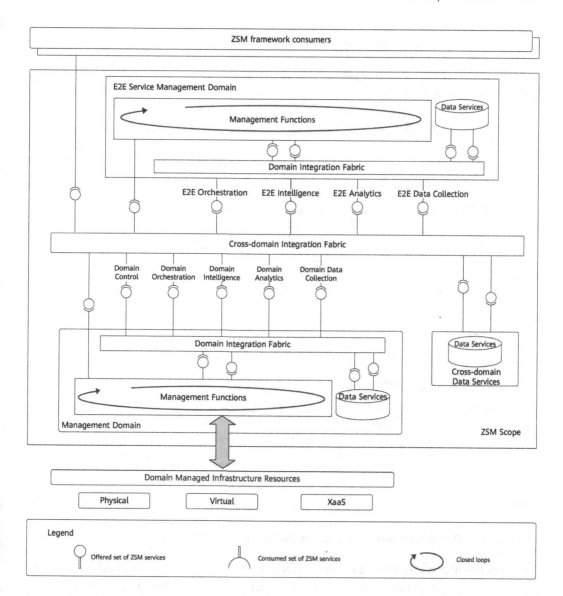

FIGURE 6.9   ZSM reference architecture.

ZSM002 [12] further defines the logical function services in each architecture building block. Figure 6.10 shows an example of the capabilities in a ZSM management domain. For the definitions of other components, see ZSM002 [12].

6.1.2 Mobile Communications Standards

Mobile communications standards are defined by 3GPP. To take responsibility for mobile network management services between CSPs and device vendors, 3GPP established the SA5 working group. It defines function and service standards related to 3GPP-compliant system management, orchestration, and charging, and O&M standards related to 5GC, 5G NR, and slicing. In recent years, 3GPP SA5 has initiated a series of AN standards projects

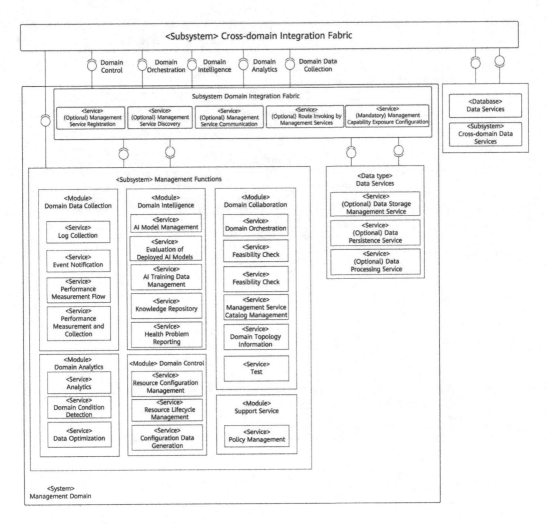

FIGURE 6.10 Definition of management domain functions in ZSM002.

for the entire lifecycle of mobile networks, facilitating industry progress in AN level evaluation, intent simplification, automated O&M, management systems for vertical industries, and other key technologies. 3GPP Release 17 focuses on intent-driven management (IDM) services for mobile networks, management services for communications assurance, and research on enhanced management data analysis and self-organizing network (SON). To date, the industry has reached a consensus on the following standards: level- and domain-based implementation architecture, concepts, use cases, and solutions of AN; definitions of AN capabilities at different levels; closed-loop control of AN; and concepts, scenarios, and solutions of intent-driven networks.

6.1.2.1 3GPP SBMA

3GPP TS 28.533 [13] defines a level- and domain-based management architecture – Service-Based Management Architecture (SBMA). Cross-domain management and single-domain management are the functional components of the SBMA. The fundamental building

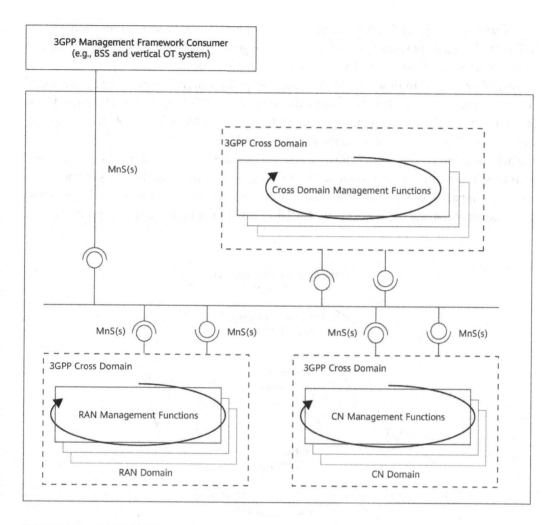

FIGURE 6.11   3GPP SBMA.

block of the SBMA is the Management Service (MnS). An MnS is a set of offered capabilities for the management and orchestration of network and services. An MnS producer offers its services via a standardized service interface composed of individually specified MnS components. A Management Function (MnF) is a logical entity playing the roles of MnS consumer and/or MnS producer. The SBMA instantiates the level- and domain-based ZSM framework, in which the RAN Management Domain and CN Management Domain are management domains, and the Cross Management Domain is either a service management domain or part of a management domain. Figure 6.11 shows the SBMA.

6.1.2.2 3GPP AN Levels

The 3GPP-defined AN levels are applicable to wireless communications, covering both core network and RAN. In 3GPP Release 16, SA5 released AN standards research findings in 3GPP TR 28.810 [14]. In 3GPP Release 17, SA5 officially released 3GPP TS 28.100 [15], which includes the concepts, use cases, and solutions of AN levels. It also specifies that the complexity of AN depends on its management scope. Figure 6.12 shows the autonomy for different management scopes. 3GPP uses the same general network autonomy process and level evaluation method as TM Forum's AN level specifications.

Workflow is used to describe the necessary steps to achieve certain management and control purposes. A workflow is composed of one or more management and control tasks. 3GPP TS 28.100 [15] uses intents as the input to categorize tasks in an AADE closed-loop workflow at different AN levels, as shown in Figure 6.13.

Each workflow task may be performed by a human or by a communications system either with or without human intervention. The autonomy capabilities of the tasks in the workflow may impact the AN level, which describes the level of autonomous capabilities used in the network management workflow. The labor division of humans and communications

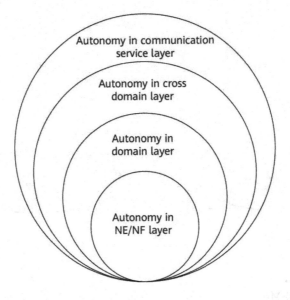

FIGURE 6.12   Autonomy for different management scopes.

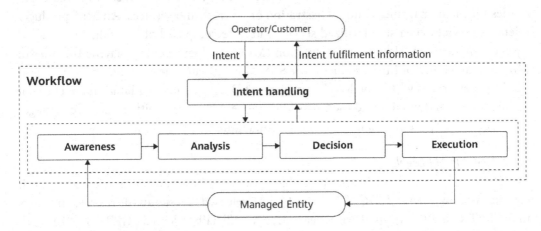

FIGURE 6.13   Categorization of the tasks in the workflow for evaluating AN levels.

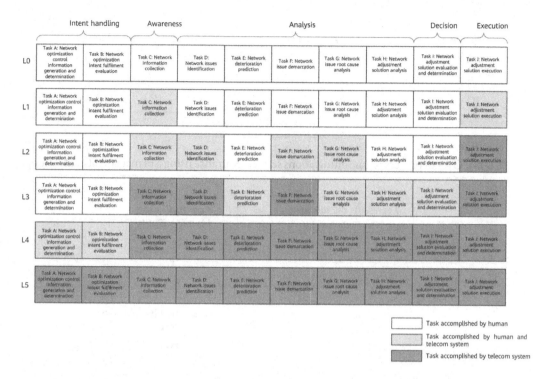

FIGURE 6.14 Classification of generic AN level for network optimization.

systems is an important factor in evaluating the AN level. The tasks that can be performed by a human and those that can be performed by a communications system either with or without human assistance need to be defined for each level. 3GPP's AN levels are defined based on the human-machine labor division and closed-loop workflow according to the AN levels set forth by TM Forum. 3GPP TS 28.100 [15] further defines domain-specific capabilities for each AN level. Figure 6.14 provides an example of network optimization capabilities.

6.1.2.3 3GPP AN Closed-loop Management

In 3GPP Release 16, SA5 defines the concepts of open control loop and closed control loop, related use cases, and requirements and models for closed-loop communications service assurance. For details, see 3GPP TS 28.535 [16] and 3GPP TS 28.536 [17]. In 3GPP Release 17, SA5 launched a project on enhanced closed-loop service assurance – Service Level Specification (SLS). Communication service assurance is enabled by closed control loops which have their own lifecycle. The lifecycle phases for closed control loops are preparation, commissioning, operation, and decommissioning. For communications service assurance one can identify two interactions of management control loops: between the communications service customer (CSC) and the CSP, and between the CSP and the network slice provider (NSP). A control loop consists of four phases: monitor, analysis, decision, and execution, as shown in Figure 6.15.

6.1.2.4 3GPP AN IDM

In 3GPP Release 17, SA5 studied the concept, scenarios, and solutions of IDM to simplify management interfaces. For details, see 3GPP TR 28.812 [18]. IDM can reduce the

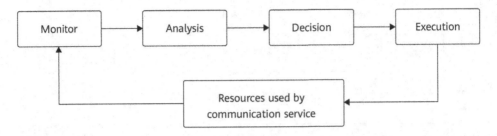

FIGURE 6.15   Overall process of communications service assurance using a management control loop.

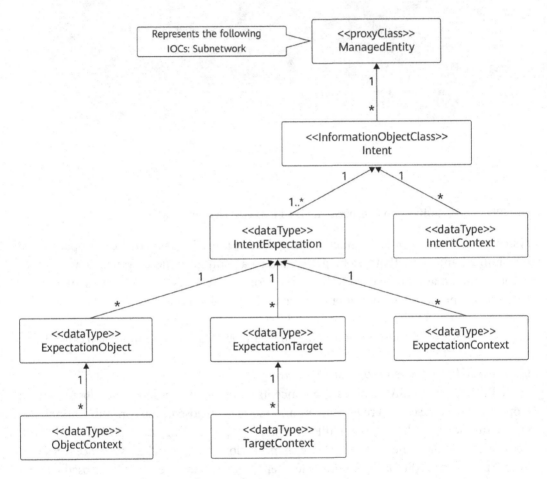

FIGURE 6.16   Relationship UML diagram for intent.

complexity of network and service management through automation mechanisms, allowing its consumers to manage mobile networks and services based on their intents. An IDM service provider translates intents into appropriate network deployment information and automatically implements them.

3GPP TS 28.312 [19] officially defines IDM. The IDM management service manages operations, entities, and information. Figure 6.16 shows the information model.

6.1.2.5 3GPP SON Automation

SON automation plays an important role in enabling CSPs to manage complex 5G networks and especially to maintain optimal performance and efficiency. With the advancement of AI and big data technologies, 5G SON can process vast amounts of management data collected over days, weeks, months, and beyond to perform self-optimizing, self-configuration, and self-healing operations that improve network performance and efficiency. In 3GPP Release 16, SA5 specified the concept, use cases, requirements, and solutions of 5G SON, including automatic neighbor relation (ANR) management, physical cell identifier (PCI) configuration, random access channel (RACH) optimization, mobility robustness optimization (MRO), and energy saving. For details, see 3GPP TS 28.313 [20] and 3GPP TS 28.541 [21]. In 3GPP Release 17, SA5 further studied 5G SON use cases, requirements, and solutions, including 3GPP network function self-setup, centralized capacity and coverage optimization, load balancing optimization, network slice instance (NSI) resource allocation optimization, enhanced MRO, and enhanced handover optimization.

6.1.2.6 3GPP AN Data Analysis Service

In 3GPP Release 17, SA5 TS 28.104 [22] defines the concepts, use cases, requirements, and solutions of the Management Data Analytics Service (MDAS), including the Management Data Analytics Function (MDAF) and corresponding standard interfaces. The MDAS, which is part of the management loop, combines AI and machine learning technologies to implement intelligent and automated network service management and orchestration.

SA2 introduces a control-plane NE – Network Data Analytics Function (NWDAF) – in 5G phase 1 in order to analyze personal data, sessions, and network slice data in real time. Figure 6.17 shows the overall framework of 5G network automation in 3GPP Release 17.

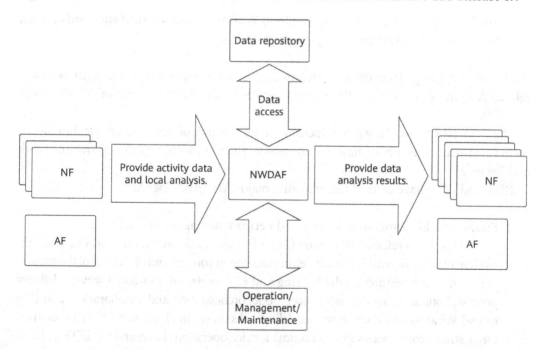

FIGURE 6.17 Overall framework of intelligent 5G core networks.

In addition to accessing network data from a unified data repository (UDR), the NWDAF can also exchange information with an operations, administration, and maintenance (OAM) module, an application function (AF), and a network function (NF). It analyzes the collected data and sends the analysis result to the AF, 5GC NF, and OAM. The NWDAF can be used in a single or multiple domains – use cases include QoS assurance, traffic steering, O&M, and security protection.

6.1.3 Transport, Access, and Bearer Network Standards

International AN standards for transport, access, and bearer networks are defined by many SDOs, including IETF OPS working groups, IRTF NMRG, and ETSI ISG F5G.

6.1.3.1 IETF and IRTF AN Standards

The IETF OPS is an organization responsible for formulating operations and management standards. It is comprised of multiple working groups, some of which have defined AN standards.

- The Operations and Management Area Working Group (OPSAWG) is a joint working group that defined the AN model architecture and related intent model interfaces.

- The Autonomic Networking Integrated Model and Approach (ANIMA) focuses on defining interoperable protocols and procedures for automated network management and control of professionally managed networks.

- The Network Modeling (NETMOD) Working Group defined the interface metamodel and general management interface model related to network management.

- The Network Configuration (NETCONF) Working Group defined standards related to network configuration management protocols.

IETF working groups focusing on different domains are responsible for defining service-related AN interfaces, such as Framework for Abstraction and Control of TE Networks (ACTN).

The IRTF NMRG working group focuses on the research of AN standards technologies, including intent APIs, performance management intent models, and digital twin network architecture.

IETF and IRTF have defined the following major AN technologies:

1. Framework for automating service and network management

   In 2021, IETF released RFC 8969 [23], a framework for automating service and network management with YANG. It defines the design concept and objectives of the model-driven AN architecture: model layering and representation, top-down service delivery process, bottom-up service assurance, model orchestration and collaboration, and E2E cross-layer and cross-domain service delivery. As shown in Figure 6.18, the IETF-defined Orchestrator corresponds to TM Forum's service operations layer, and the IETF-defined Controller and Device correspond to TM Forum's resource operations layer.

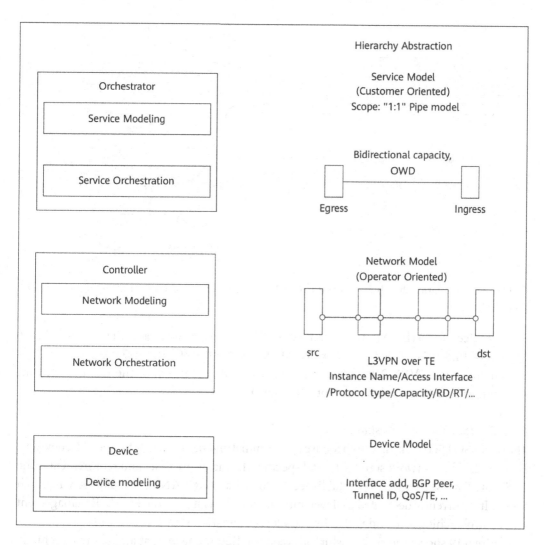

FIGURE 6.18   Framework for automating service and network management with YANG.

2. Research on key AN technologies

In 2015, IRTF NMRG released RFC 7575 [24] – *Autonomic Networking: Definitions and Design Goals*, defining what intent is: an abstract, high-level policy used to operate the network. Its scope is an autonomic domain, such as an enterprise network. It does not contain configuration or information for a specific node. In 2017, IRTF NMRG adopted the concept of IDN and started to define related standards. Formulating IDN standards has become an important area of focus for NMRG, whose work related to AN includes intent classification, digital twin network, and intent-based measurement.

3. Intent APIs

In addition to the concept and definition, IETF defined a series of intent APIs. For example, RFC 8299 [25] released in 2018 defined a Layer 3 Virtual Private Network

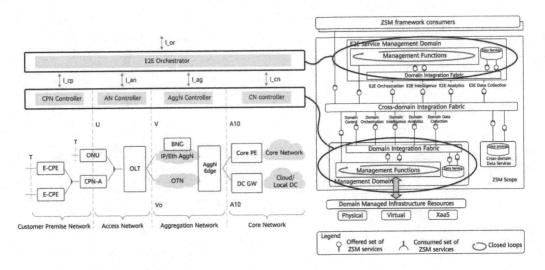

FIGURE 6.19 Relationship between the F5G E2E management and control architecture and the ZSM architecture.

Service Model (L3SM). In the same year, RFC 8466 [26] was released to define a Layer 2 Virtual Private Network Service Model (L2SM). RFC 9182 [27] released in 2022 defined an L3VPN Network Model (L3NM). The definition of the L2VPN network interface model has been accepted by the OPSAWG.

6.1.3.2 ETSI ISG F5G AN standards

The ETSI ISG F5G working group focuses on formulating the standards for the F5G, develops E2E optical fiber network standards, and specifies the major use cases and requirements. The ETSI ISG F5G working group, established in 2020, has taken AN as one of its key research topics. It is currently dedicated to developing standards related to the F5G E2E management and control architecture and will define AN level evaluation standards for the F5G.

Figure 6.19 shows the relationship between the E2E management and control architecture defined by F5G006 [28] and the ZSM architecture. In the ZSM architecture, a management domain uses management functions to manage its services. The F5G domain controllers (CPN Controller, AN Controller, AggN Controller, and CN Controller) are equivalent to the entities of the ZSM Management Domains. The ZSM E2E service management domain is a special management domain that provides E2E management of customer-facing services, composed of the customer-facing or resource-facing services provided by one or more management domains. The F5G E2E Orchestrator is equivalent to an instance of the ZSM E2E service management domain, which manages the F5G E2E services across multiple domains.

6.2 CHINESE STANDARDS

In July 2021, CCSA Technical Working Committee 7 (TC7) held an AN meeting about with China's three major CSPs, vendors, universities, and think tanks, aiming

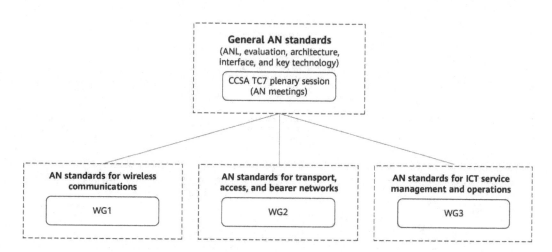

FIGURE 6.20   Organizational architecture of CCSA TC7.

to develop a standards framework for intelligent operations and management of ICT networks. Later that year and the next year, CCSA TC7 held numerous AN meetings to further improve the standards framework from multiple directions, including the architecture, use cases, levels, intents, and key technologies. Standards related to the AN levels include AN level definitions and AN level evaluation methods defined for both general and domain-specific purposes – some of these standards have been submitted for review or approval. CCSA TC610 is an organization dedicated to promoting industry development. It expects to launch an AN project, for which it has already defined the content, objectives, ideas, and plan. Figure 6.20 shows the organizational architecture of CCSA TC7.

The AN meetings held by CCSA TC7 focus on general AN standards, including requirements, use cases, AN levels, architecture, evaluation system, interfaces, and key technologies. CCSA TC7 Working Group 1 (WG1) focuses on AN standards for wireless communications, whereas CCSA TC7 WG2 focuses on AN standards for transport, access, and bearer networks. CCSA TC7 WG3 focuses on AN standards for ICT service management and operations.

The fifth round of CCSA TC7's AN meeting updated the AN standards system, as shown in Figure 6.21.

The standards system for intelligent operations and management of ICT networks consists of many standards series, which are categorized based on the architecture, requirements and use cases, levels, level evaluation methods, interfaces, and key technologies.

6.2.1 General Standards

CCSA TC7's AN meetings have defined general AN standards – some of these standards are in the public consultation stage and have been submitted for review, and the general AN level standards have been submitted for approval. Table 6.5 lists the standards. For details, visit the CCSA website.

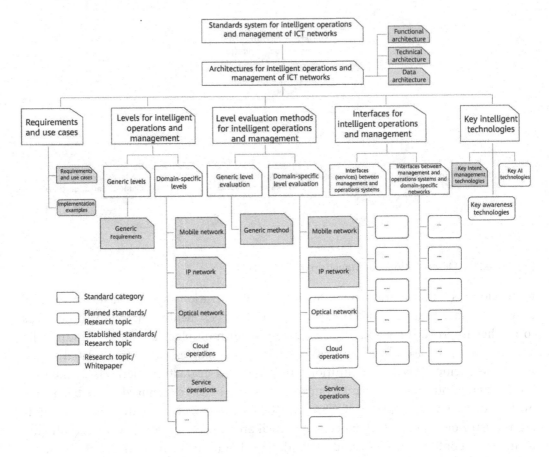

FIGURE 6.21 AN standards system (for intelligent operations and management of ICT networks).

6.2.2 Mobile Communications Standards

CCSA TC7 WG1 defines AN standards for wireless communications, including requirements, use cases, AN levels, and interfaces. The AN level standards have been submitted for approval, and other standards documents are in the public consultation stage and have been submitted for review. Table 6.6 lists the standards. For details, visit the CCSA website.

6.2.3 Transport, Access, and Bearer Network Standards

CCSA TC7 WG2 defines AN standards for transport, access, and bearer networks, including requirements, use cases, levels, and interfaces. The level standards have been submitted for approval, and other standards documents are in the public consultation stage and have been submitted for review. Table 6.7 lists the standards. For details, visit the CCSA website.

6.3 CROSS-ORGANIZATION STANDARDS COLLABORATION

TM Forum believes that aligning cross-organization efforts in terms of the AN concept, vision, architecture, and key topics, as well as discussing the allocation of duties and collaborating on future work will bring benefits to the AN industry. Since September 28, 2020, TM Forum has been regularly holding technical collaboration meetings through the Autonomous Networks Multi-SDO, attracting GSMA, Next Generation Mobile Network

TABLE 6.5   CCSA's General AN Standards

Category	Standards Project Name	Project Type
Architecture	Intelligent operations and management architecture of ICT networks - functional architecture	Industry standards
	Intelligent operations and management architecture of ICT networks - technical architecture	Industry standards
	Intelligent operations and management architecture of ICT networks - data architecture	Industry standards
	AN architecture	Industry standards
AN level	Technical requirements for the levels for intelligent operations and management of ICT networks - general part	Industry standards
	Technical requirements for the level evaluation for intelligent operations and management of ICT networks - general part	Industry standards
Intent	Research on the AN intent translation method and process	Research topics
	Research on AN general intent management technologies	Research topics
Key technology	Technical requirements for AN knowledge management	Industry standards
	Research on AN anomaly and risk management technology	Research topics
	Research on AN trustworthiness evaluation technology	Research topics

TABLE 6.6   CCSA TC7 AN Standards for Wireless Communications

Category	Standards Project Name	Project Type
Requirement and use case	Requirements and use cases of intelligent operations and management of ICT networks - wireless network O&M	Industry standards
	Requirements and use cases of intelligent operations and management of ICT networks -5G RAN energy saving management	Industry standards
AN level	Technical requirements for the level evaluation for intelligent operations and management of ICT networks - mobile communications network	Industry standards
	Technical requirements for the levels for intelligent operations and management of ICT networks - mobile communications network (phase 1)	Industry standards
	Levels for intelligent operations and management of ICT networks - technological research on 5GC network levels	Research topics
Intent API	Core network intent management research report	Research topics
	Technical requirements for wireless intent management services	Industry standards

(NGMN), ETSI Industry Specification Groups Experiential Networked Intelligence (ISG ENI), ETSI Industry Specification Groups Network Functions Virtualisation (ISG NFV), ETSI Industry Specification Groups Open Source Management and Orchestration (ISG OSM), ETSI Industry Specification Groups Multi-access Edge Computing (ISG MEC),

TABLE 6.7   CCSA TC7 AN Standards for Transport, Access, and Bearer Networks

Category	Standards Project Name	Project Type
Requirement and use case	Requirements and use cases of intelligent operations and management of ICT networks - optical network maintenance	Industry standards
	Requirements and use cases of intelligent operations and management of ICT networks - Slicing Packet Network (SPN) maintenance	Industry standards
AN level	Level capability research on intelligent PTN/SPN operations and management	Research topics
	Level capability research on intelligent optical network management, control, and operations	Research topics
	Technical requirements for the levels for intelligent operations and management of ICT networks - IP network	Industry standards
	Technical requirements for the level evaluation for intelligent operations and management of ICT networks - IP network	Industry standards
Intent API	Interface technology research on intelligent operations and management of ICT networks - optical network	Research topics
	Interface technology research on intelligent operations and management of ICT networks - SPN	Research topics

ETSI ISG F5G, ETSI ISG ZSM, 3GPP SA5, CCSA TC7, IRTF NMRG, ITU-T for ITU Telecommunication Standardization Sector Focus Group on Autonomous Networks (ITU-T FG-AN), and IEEE. These meetings have two parts:

1. Meetings for cross-organization management affairs, attended by leaders of each organization.

2. Open technical workshops attended by corporate representatives from each organization. These workshops focus on the following topics:

   • Standards panorama

   • AN O&M use cases

   • General O&M principles

   • Key technologies related to areas such as intent, closed loop, AN level, and autonomy/management domain

Technical experts from around the world gather at the Autonomous Networks Multi-SDO to share their ideas, providing instant and comprehensive information about AN standards activities for industry organizations and helping them to identify the direction for technological collaboration. Through the joint efforts made at the Autonomous Networks Multi-SDO, the industry has reached a consensus on AN level standards. TM Forum and 3GPP have released their own AN level standards, and CCSA has submitted its general level standards for approval. In 2022, SDOs further collaborated with each other in a more fine-grained manner. We hope that more organizations will get involved and share further E2E practical experience for industry partners.

REFERENCES

1. TM Forum, "IG1218 Autonomous Networks business requirements and framework v2.0.0," [R/OL], (2021-07-26) [2022-09-22].
2. TM Forum, "IG1230 Autonomous Networks technical architecture v1.0.0," [R/OL], (2021-01-19) [2022-09-22].
3. TM Forum, "IG1251 Autonomous Networks - reference architecture v1.0.0," [R/OL], (2021-11-20) [2022-09-22].
4. TM Forum, "IG1252 Autonomous Network levels evaluation methodology v1.1.0," [R/OL], (2021-12-17) [2022-09-22].
5. TM Forum, "IG1253 intent in Autonomous Networks v1.0.0," [R/OL], (2021-07-26) [2022-09-22].
6. TM Forum, "IG1253A intent common model v1.0.0," [R/OL], (2021-07-26) [2022-09-22].
7. TM Forum, "IG1253B intent extension models v1.0.0," [R/OL], (2021-07-24) [2022-09-22].
8. TM Forum, "IG1253C intent life cycle management and interface v1.0.0," [R/OL], (2021-01-26) [2022-09-22].
9. TM Forum, "IG1253D intent manager capability profiles v1.0.0," [R/OL]," (2021-01-24) [2022-09-22].
10. TM Forum, "TMF921A intent management API profile v1.1.0," [R/OL], (2022-05-30) [2022-09-22].
11. ETSI, "GS ZSM 001 zero-touch network and service management (ZSM); requirements based on documented scenarios v1.1.1," [R/OL], (2019-10) [2022-09-22].
12. ETSI, "GS ZSM 002 zero-touch network and service management (ZSM); reference architecture v1.1.1," [R/OL], (2019-08) [2022-09-22].
13. 3GPP, "TS 28.533 management and orchestration, architecture framework v17.2.0," [R/OL], (2022-03-22) [2022-09-22].
14. 3GPP, "TR 28.810 study on concept, requirements and solutions for levels of autonomous network v17.0.0," [R/OL], (2020-09-25) [2022-09-22].
15. 3GPP, "TS 28.100 management and orchestration, levels of autonomous network v17.1.0," [R/OL], (2022-03-22) [2022-09-22].
16. 3GPP, "TS 28.535 management and orchestration, management services for communication service assurance; requirements v17.5.0," [R/OL], (2022-06-16) [2022-09-22].
17. 3GPP, "TS 28.536 management and orchestration, management services for communication service assurance, stage 2 and stage 3 v17.4.0," [R/OL], (2022-06-24) [2022-09-22].
18. 3GPP, "TR 28.812 telecommunication management, study on scenarios for intent driven management services for mobile networks v17.1.0," [R/OL], (2020-12-26) [2022-09-22].
19. 3GPP, "TS 28.312 management and orchestration, intent driven management services for mobile networks v17.1.0," [R/OL], (2022-06-15) [2022-09-22].
20. 3GPP, "TS 28.313 self-organizing networks (SON) for 5G networks v17.5.0," [R/OL], (2022-06-16) [2022-09-22].
21. 3GPP, "TS 28.541 management and orchestration, 5G network resource model (NRM), stage 2 and stage 3 v17.7.0," [R/OL], (2022-06-23) [2022-09-22].
22. 3GPP, "TS 28.104 study on enhancement of management data analytics v17.1.0 [R/OL]," (2022-06-15) [2022-09-22].
23. IETF, "RFC8969 a framework for automating service and network management with YANG," [R/OL], (2021-03-31) [2022-09-22].

24. IETF, "RFC7575 autonomic networking: definitions and design goals," [R/OL], (2018-12-20) [2022-09-22].
25. IETF, "RFC8299 YANG data model for L3VPN service delivery," [R/OL], (2019-05-14) [2022-09-22].
26. IETF, "RFC8466 a YANG data model for layer 2 virtual private network (L2VPN) service delivery," [R/OL], (2020-01-21) [2022-09-22].
27. IETF, "RFC9182 a YANG network data model for layer 3 VPNs," [R/OL], (2022-02-15) [2022-09-22].
28. ETSI, "GS F5G 006 fifth generation fixed network (F5G); end-to-end management and control," [R/OL], (2022-09-08) [2022-09-22].

CHAPTER 7

Level Evaluation of ADN

S ECTION 1.5 LEVELS OF ADN briefly describe the ADN levels and the overall level frame-work. Chapter 6 Industry Standards introduce the industry consensus on AN level standards. During the implementation of ADN, how do we leverage these standards to achieve the vision of building self-fulfilling, self-healing, and self-optimizing autonomous networks in each Huawei product domain?

The industry answered this question by proposing the "iterative evolution loop" of AN (see Figure 7.1), which is described in TM Forum's third AN whitepaper [1].

This loop shows how AN capabilities evolve in a three-step iterative manner to facilitate AN evolution from L1 to L5, continuously improving automated and intelligent network O&M capabilities.

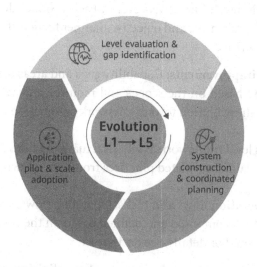

FIGURE 7.1   Iterative evolution loop of AN.

DOI: 10.1201/9781032662879-8

Step 1: level evaluation and gap identification

The automated and intelligent capabilities of AN are quantitatively evaluated, common issues and capability gaps are identified, and improvement measures and implementation plans are formulated accordingly.

Step 2: system construction and coordinated planning

Cross-domain OSSs are centrally planned and upgraded in a more systematic manner, and detailed capability requirements and technical specifications for devices in each network domain are clearly defined. This step helps device vendors improve autonomous capabilities on devices.

Step 3: application pilot and scale adoption

Collaboration between device vendors and OSS vendors is encouraged to introduce advanced automated and intelligent technologies, pilot the technologies at site or operating company level, and promote them on a large scale. Once new applications are deployed, the level is evaluated in an iterative manner.

Comprehensive and objective AN level evaluation needs to be performed during AN implementation in order to accurately assess the level of AN capabilities, analyze and identify gaps, and develop system capabilities in the future based on the assessment result.

Huawei ADN leverages the industry's AN implementation methodology to launch the following level evaluation activities in each product domain on a regular basis:

- **Evaluate the ADN level:** The ADN level in each product domain is quantitatively evaluated in a comprehensive and objective manner to identify gaps between the current level and objectives.

- **Identify areas of improvements:** Capability gaps and areas of improvements for systems are identified based on the scopes and requirements in the level standards in order to promote the evolution towards network automation and intelligence.

Taking TM Forum's level framework as a basis, Huawei defines ADN standards and an evaluation method and launches related practices from the following aspects:

- **Decomposing operation flows and tasks:** Operation flows, sub-operation flows, and operation tasks are decomposed and defined based on the cognitive closed loop proposed by TM Forum. For details, see Section 7.1.

- **Refining the requirements on human-machine division of labor for operation tasks** based on the P (manual), P/S (semi-autonomous), and S (autonomous) categories defined by TM Forum's level framework. For details, see Section 7.2.

- **Specifying the scenarios of evaluation objects** in the level framework as the evaluation scope. For details, see Section 7.3.

- **Designing a level evaluation method (with an example):** An operable evaluation method must be designed to facilitate level evaluation based on the level standards. For details about the evaluation method, see Section 7.4.

7.1 DECOMPOSING OPERATION FLOWS AND TASKS

Evaluating the ADN level in a comprehensive and objective manner is a complex issue. A common method used by many industries to deal with complex issues is the decomposition mean in computational thinking, which decomposes an issue into several sub-issues and then resolves them one by one. For example, the quality of a diamond can be decomposed into the four C's (cut, color, clarity, and carat); the academic performance of a student can be decomposed into the scores of mathematics, English, physics, and chemistry; the autonomous driving level of a vehicle can be decomposed into the automation level of different driving tasks (e.g., acceleration/braking, steering, environment monitoring, and emergency decision-making and handling).

The level of ADN, a far more complex topic than the preceding examples, needs to be evaluated by decomposing the O&M activities throughout the entire ADN lifecycle. Based on industry practices and discussions, TM Forum's IG1252 [2] proposes a three-layer decomposition architecture – **operation flow, sub-operation flow**, and **task** – for AN level standards, as shown in Figure 7.2. This architecture can be used to decompose the issue of evaluating the ANL into many simple issues (e.g., determining whether the fault identification task is automated) in order to provide a more objective evaluation result.

TM Forum's decomposition architecture is used in ADN to further define operation flows and tasks in each Huawei product domain.

The purposes and principles of decomposing operation flows, sub-operation flows, and tasks are as follows:

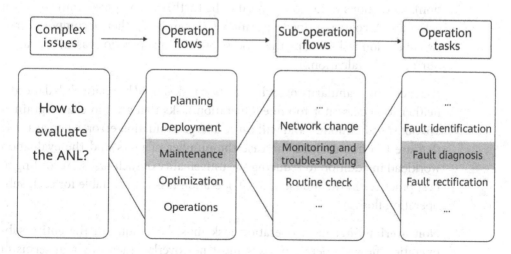

FIGURE 7.2   Decomposition architecture.

First, divide operation flows and sub-operation flows.

Purpose: To identify major network O&M production activities and practices, summarize operation flows (e.g., planning, construction, maintenance, optimization, and operations) and sub-operation flows (e.g., monitoring, troubleshooting, and service provisioning), and formulate level standards accordingly.

Principles: completeness and closed loop

- **Completeness:** Operation flows and sub-operation flows must cover major network O&M production processes and activities that need to evolve toward automation and intelligence.

- **Closed loop:** Each sub-operation flow must cover the cognitive closed loop of intent/experience, awareness, analysis, decision, and execution. For example, demarcation and locating is not a sub-operation flow; rather, it is an operation task of the analysis category.

Second, decompose sub-operation flows into operation tasks.

Purpose: To accurately evaluate the level of a sub-operation flow in a comprehensive and objective manner.

Principles: completeness, balance, and non-overlapping

- **Completeness:** Each sub-operation flow must be decomposed into operation tasks based on cognitive activities (intent/experience, awareness, analysis, decision, and execution) defined by TM Forum. All key operation tasks must be included. For example, in the sub-operation flow of monitoring and troubleshooting, activities of the analysis category are decomposed into different operation tasks (e.g., demarcation and locating, and solution generation). Operations tasks do not need to be further decomposed into cognitive activities. A coarse-grained operation task can be further decomposed into two operation tasks during the process of defining operation tasks, instead of during level evaluation.

- **Balance:** The granularity of each operation task should be relatively balanced – neither too coarse nor too fine. Operation tasks that are too coarse-grained are not specific enough and will cause a large evaluation error, whereas those that are too fine-grained increase the number of tasks and the evaluation workload in addition to reducing the universality of such tasks. According to best practices in the industry, 5–10 operation tasks are suitable for each sub-operation flow.

- **Non-overlapping:** Each operation task must be unique in the entire sub-operation flow – operation tasks must not overlap each other in terms of function.

Table 7.1 describes the recommended ADN operation flows and sub-operation flows defined using the preceding process and principles based on the service conditions in each Huawei product domain.

TABLE 7.1   ADN Operation Flows and Sub-operation Flows

Operation Flow/Sub-operation Flow		Description
Planning	01 Network planning	Formulate a network planning solution based on the customer's business intents, service development objectives, network construction/capacity expansion plan, and network requirements (e.g., capacity) obtained based on analysis and prediction; formulate a network design solution based on the planning solution, live network survey, purchased and selected devices, networking technology requirements, and other factors.
Deployment	02 Design and deployment	Based on the network plan, complete the integration design, data preparation, software and hardware installation, network configuration, commissioning, and optimization; generate an acceptance report; and meet the acceptance criteria and transfer-to-maintenance conditions.
Maintenance	03 Monitoring and troubleshooting	Set monitoring rules based on the customer's O&M policies (such as key assurance areas) and design, deployment, and service provisioning results to monitor network status and quality in real time; quickly detect network faults or potential risks; demarcate and locate the faults or risks; analyze root causes; and quickly restore services, rectify the faults, or eliminate the risks.
	04 Routine check	Based on the maintenance objectives of the live network, perform routine checks and tests on the network infrastructure to quickly detect and eliminate faults or potential risks, thereby maintaining network health. In this way, the network can run securely, stably, and reliably over the long term in order to meet service requirements.
	05 Network change	Based on network change requirements (e.g., service cutover, software upgrade/patch installation, device replacement, and topology adjustment) generated during monitoring and troubleshooting, network optimization, and design and deployment, analyze the impact on user services, formulate change constraints (e.g., those on the time window and service interruption time), design and implement a network change solution (e.g., change time, involved NEs, operation procedure, verification solution, and rollback solution), and handle and verify change requests.
Optimization	06 Network optimization	Formulate and implement a network optimization solution based on the network performance test, customer complaints/feedback, theme analysis, and resource usage to meet users' requirements for service experience and CSPs' requirements for resource usage (e.g., bandwidth and energy consumption).
Operations	07 Service provisioning	Allocate resources, make decisions about resources, and deliver configurations to the network in order to activate services and verify SLAs, fulfilling users' service provisioning or change requests.
	08 Customer complaint	Analyze and handle network faults based on users' network complaints (e.g., key service faults and poor QoE problems), predict the occurrence of complaints, and provide warnings.
Inventory management	09 Inventory data management	Centrally manage the data of active and passive resources during planning, construction, maintenance, optimization, and operations. The operations include centralized data collection, correlation analysis, and checks.

TABLE 7.2   Operation Tasks of Monitoring and Troubleshooting

Operation Task	Description
1. Intent translation	Define network monitoring rules based on monitoring and assurance requirements of VIP services and customers in addition to defining SLA assurance policies for design, deployment, and service provisioning processes. The system performs monitoring based on these network monitoring rules (e.g., based on monitoring areas, monitored objects such as NEs or services, alarm types, alarm severities, KPI types, and alarm reporting policies for abnormal KPIs).
2. Fault identification	Monitor and analyze network running data and external spatiotemporal data to quickly detect faults that interrupt or degrade services.
3. Potential risk prediction	Monitor and analyze network running data and external spatiotemporal data, predict the development trends of network software and hardware statuses, and detect potential risks that may cause exceptions.
4. Demarcation and locating	Demarcate faults based on the fault identification and risk prediction results. The faults need to be demarcated to a specific technical domain in cross-domain scenarios and to a specific NE in single-domain scenarios. Based on the fault demarcation result, further locate the specific software and hardware causes (e.g., configurations, boards, or optical modules) of the faults to generate a rectification solution and rectify services as soon as possible. Analyze the impact of the faults or potential risks on services (e.g., which base stations and users are affected) and notify the involved parties of the impact.
5. Solution generation	Generate alternative rectification solutions (including service restoration) based on the fault demarcation and locating results. The rectification measures include configuration modification, NE restart, board replacement, NE isolation, and more.
6. Evaluation and decision-making	Evaluate the alternative rectification solutions comprehensively (e.g., whether the solutions can rectify the fault, the rectification cost is acceptable, and the solutions have other impacts on the network) and select the optimal one.
7. Solution implementation	Use the optimal solution to rectify faults and eliminate potential risks. For faults or potential risks that can be remotely rectified, deliver rectification operations to the network or isolate faulty hardware (e.g., NEs or links). For faults or potential risks that cannot be remotely rectified, manually replace or re-install boards or optical modules onsite. (Onsite operations such as board replacement are not in the scope of ADN level evaluation.)
8. Service verification	Verify and confirm the execution results once faults are rectified and potential risks are eliminated. For example, check whether services are recovered, poor-QoE problems are resolved, and alarms and KPI anomalies are cleared.

Table 7.2 lists the operation tasks of "03 Monitoring and troubleshooting."

The preceding tables list the general definitions of ADN operation flows, sub-operation flows, and tasks, all of which can be customized and extended for each product domain based on service requirements and scopes.

7.2 REFINING THE REQUIREMENTS ON HUMAN-MACHINE DIVISION OF LABOR FOR OPERATION TASKS

The ADN level framework uses the P (manual), P/S (semi-autonomous), and S (autonomous) indicators to define the types of human-machine division of labor. However, it does not specify the responsibilities of humans and systems, nor does it specify how humans and systems should collaborate with each other. Therefore, it is necessary to describe the division of labor and collaboration more comprehensively. For example, "the system automatically identifies faults based on static rules (e.g., fixed thresholds) defined by O&M

personnel" is a more comprehensive description for P/S (semi-autonomous). As such, after operation flows are decomposed into sub-operation flows and then into operation tasks, detailed requirements on human-machine division of labor for operation tasks must be defined for each ADN level.

The purposes and principles for defining requirements on human-machine division of labor for operation tasks are as follows:

Purpose: To define requirements on human-machine division of labor and human-machine collaboration modes for each operation task from ADN L1 to L5 in order to facilitate level evaluation.

Principles: human-machine division of labor, user perception, and abstraction

- **Human-machine division of labor:** Further define the requirements based on the level framework and human-machine division of labor, instead of on factors such as effectiveness indicators.

- **User perception:** Describe the requirements from a user-perceivable perspective without specifying the technical solutions (e.g., knowledge graph and digital twins) to be used in the system.

- **Abstraction:** The requirements must be abstract, universal, and applicable to different product domains and service scenarios.

Table 7.3 uses the operation flows of "03 Monitoring and troubleshooting" in Section 7.1 Decomposing Operation Flows and Tasks as an example to describe the detailed requirements on human-machine division of labor for operation tasks at each level (except for L5).

7.3 SPECIFYING THE SCENARIOS OF EVALUATION OBJECTS

In the ADN level framework, L1 to L4 are defined as being applicable only to selected scenarios. However, the framework does not specify what those scenarios are. For example, 4G NE disconnection and 5G NE disconnection can be selected for wireless monitoring and troubleshooting. In addition to requirements on human-machine division of labor, scenarios are also criteria for evaluating whether an operation task reaches a certain level.

Independence and completeness are two principles for selecting scenarios.

- **Independence:** The selected scenarios must be in the same dimension. Those selected for the same evaluation object must be independent and unique. For example, 5G base station faults and base station disconnection faults are overlapping scenarios; that is, they are neither independent nor unique.

- **Completeness:** The selected scenarios must cover all related activities and tasks in the sub-operation flow. For example, clock fault diagnosis is not a complete scenario because it only covers activities of the analysis category.

TABLE 7.3 Requirements on Human-Machine Division of Labor for Monitoring and Troubleshooting Operation Tasks

Sub-operation Flow	Task	Requirement at L1	Requirement at L2	Requirement at L3	Requirement at L4
03 Monitoring and troubleshooting	1. Intent translation	Manually configure monitoring rules.	Manually design monitoring rule templates. The system performs monitoring based on the manually selected template.	Manually enter service intents (e.g., monitored areas, VIP customers, and KQIs). The system automatically converts monitoring rules and suggestions, which need to be manually adjusted.	Manually enter service intents (e.g., monitored areas, VIP customers, and KQIs). The system automatically converts monitoring rules and suggestions.
	2. Fault identification	The system collects data (e.g., alarms and KPIs). Manually identify faults.	Manually define rules (e.g., alarm correlations and KPI thresholds). The system automatically identifies faults.	The system automatically identifies faults.	The system automatically identifies faults.
	3. Potential risk prediction	The system collects data. Manually check the items one by one and determine potential risks.	Manually define rules (e.g., health check rules and KPI thresholds). The system automatically performs checks based on the rules. Manually determine potential risks.	The system predicts the network status trend and roughly identifies potential risks (e.g., weak optical signals on a port). Manually confirm the risks.	The system predicts the network status trend and accurately identifies potential risks (e.g., there is a 90% probability that a weak optical signal fault will occur on a port within one week).
	4. Demarcation and locating	Manually use the system to demarcate and locate faults (including connectivity tests, and packet and operation log analysis).	Manually define rules (e.g., correlation rules). The system automatically demarcates and locates faults. Manually confirm the faults.	The system automatically suggests one or more possible causes and sorts them for manual confirmation. The system also automatically provides a list of affected services and the impact degree (e.g., whether it is a mass fault).	The system automatically suggests one accurate cause, the list of affected services, and the impact degree (e.g., whether it is a mass fault).

(Continued)

TABLE 7.3 (*Continued*) Requirements on Human-Machine Division of Labor for Monitoring and Troubleshooting Operation Tasks

Sub-operation Flow Task	Requirement at L1	Requirement at L2	Requirement at L3	Requirement at L4
5. Solution generation	Manually formulate alternative solutions.	The system provides solution suggestions (e.g., suggestions on alarm handling solutions preset in the system before delivery). Manually formulate alternative solutions.	The system automatically generates alternative solutions, which need to be manually adjusted.	The system automatically generates alternative solutions.
6. Evaluation and decision-making	Manually select the optimal solution.	Manually evaluate and determine the optimal solution based on the real-time data provided by the system.	The system performs online evaluation based on real-time data and provides evaluation results. Manually determine the optimal solution.	The system performs online evaluation based on real-time data and automatically determines the optimal solution.
7. Solution implementation	Manually use the system to rectify faults (including emergency recovery) and eliminate risks (e.g., through GUI operations and script import).	The system automatically rectifies faults (including emergency recovery) and eliminates potential risks (except those that must be handled onsite).	The system automatically rectifies faults (including emergency recovery) and eliminates potential risks (except those that must be handled onsite).	The system automatically rectifies faults (including emergency recovery) and eliminates potential risks (except those that must be handled onsite).
8. Service verification	Manually determine whether the faults are rectified and potential risks are eliminated.	The system automatically determines whether faults are rectified and potential risks are eliminated based on real-time data (alarms or KPIs). Manually perform service tests and verification.	The system automatically performs service tests and determines whether faults are rectified and potential risks are eliminated based on real-time data (alarms or KPIs) and service test results.	The system automatically performs service tests and determines whether faults are rectified and potential risks are eliminated based on real-time data (alarms or KPIs) and service test results.

TABLE 7.4   Scenarios Selected for "Mobile 2C - Wireless Network - Monitoring and Troubleshooting"

No.	Scenario Name	Description	Scenario Weight (%)
Scenario 1	Base station disconnection faults	NEs and NetGraph are disconnected and unreachable due to power supply, transmission, or device faults.	20
Scenario 2	Fronthaul/ Optical port faults	RF units and NEs are disconnected and unreachable due to power supply, transmission, or device faults.	20
Scenario 3	Clock faults	Clock faults (e.g., base station clock inconsistency) cause downlink transmission of out-of-synchronization base stations to interfere with uplink transmission of surrounding base stations. As a result, KPIs of many base stations deteriorate.	20
Scenario 4	Cell faults	Faults such as cell capability degradation and cell unavailability occur.	20
Scenario 5	VSWR faults	Some transmit power of the base station is reflected back after passing through the antenna system, causing VSWR faults. Such reflection may occur due to incorrectly made connectors, loose connections, water intrusion, metal fragments, corrosion, scratches on the inner and outer conductors, or small bending radius.	20

The selected scenarios should be high-value ones that focus on O&M challenges and the O&M value in each product domain rather than being too broad. As ADN evolves, such scenarios can be extended and adjusted based on service development and new O&M challenges. The level of automation should not be an explicit criterion for selecting scenarios. For example, "unattended change" is not a suitable scenario.

Table 7.4 uses the evaluation object "mobile 2C - wireless network - monitoring and troubleshooting" as an example to select scenarios. (For details about how to select an evaluation object, see Section 7.4.)

7.4 LEVEL EVALUATION METHOD AND EXAMPLE

The preceding sections describe how to refine the level standards based on the ADN level framework. This section uses a specific evaluation object as an example to describe how to evaluate the ADN level based on the level standards.

Step 1: Select an evaluation object.

In level evaluation for autonomous driving vehicles, evaluation objects are concrete and easy to identify. However, a network is a relatively general concept that can be classified into wireless, transport, core, and other types of networks from a technology or domain perspective. A network can also be classified into individual, home, and government and enterprise services from a service perspective. In addition, level evaluation for ADN needs to be performed based on all operation flows (planning, construction, maintenance, optimization, and operations) and sub-operation flows. As such, we need to determine how to identify and classify evaluation objects before ADN level evaluation.

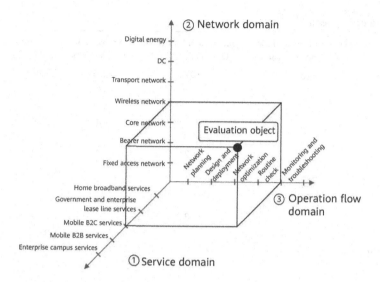

FIGURE 7.3   Model for selecting evaluation objects.

TM Forum's IG1252 [2] describes the industry's three-dimensional model for selecting evaluation objects (see Figure 7.3) – this model is designed based on McKinsey & Company's mutually exclusive collectively exhaustive (MECE) principle. Using this model, we can select an evaluation object from the service domain, network domain, or operation flow domain to ensure the completeness and uniqueness of the objects.

- **Completeness:** All evaluation objects must be identified in order to comprehensively evaluate the ADN level.

- **Uniqueness:** Evaluation objects must not overlap. For example, wireless network and 5G private network are overlapping evaluation objects.
  According to the model shown in Figure 7.3, "mobile 2C - wireless network - monitoring and troubleshooting" is an evaluation object, whereas "monitoring and troubleshooting" is not.
  An evaluation object can cover several selected scenarios (see Section 7.3).

Step 2: Evaluate the level of the scenarios/tasks.
  Evaluate the selected scenarios (see Section 7.3) of the evaluation object "mobile 2C - wireless network - monitoring and troubleshooting" based on the level standards (see Section 7.2) to form an evaluation result matrix (see Table 7.5).

Step 3: Calculate the level of the evaluation object.
  Based on the evaluation result matrix in step 2, calculate the level of the evaluation object using either of the following methods:

Method 1: Based on Table 7.5, first calculate the average of each row, which is the average level of each operation task, and then use these calculation results to calculate the average level of the evaluation object.

TABLE 7.5   Evaluation Result Matrix

Scenario Name	Scenario 1: Base Station Disconnection Faults	Scenario 2: Fronthaul/ Optical Port Faults	Scenario 3: Clock Faults	Scenario 4: Cell Faults	Scenario 5: VSWR Faults
Scenario Weight	20%	20%	20%	20%	20%
1. Intent translation	1	2	2	1	1
2. Fault identification	2	2	4	4	2
3. Potential risk prediction	2	2	2	3	2
4. Demarcation and locating	4	3	3	2	1
5. Solution generation	3	3	3	3	2
6. Evaluation and decision-making	2	2	2	2	2
7. Solution implementation	1	1	1	1	1
8. Service verification	2	2	2	2	2

TABLE 7.6   Levels of Operation Tasks

Operation Task	Level
1. Intent translation	1.4
2. Fault identification	2.8
3. Potential risk prediction	2.2
4. Demarcation and locating	2.6
5. Solution generation	2.8
6. Evaluation and decision-making	2.0
7. Solution implementation	1.0
8. Service verification	2.0

Method 2: Based on Table 7.5, first calculate the average of each column, which is the average level of each selected scenario, and then use these calculation results to calculate the average level of the evaluation object.

The calculation results obtained using method 1 can be used to identify the strengths and gaps from the perspective of operation task. Similarly, the calculation results obtained using method 2 can be used to identify the strengths and gaps from the perspective of scenario. Mathematically, the levels of the evaluation object calculated using both methods are the same. Table 7.6 uses method 1 as an example to calculate the level of each operation task.

The level of the evaluation object equals the average score of each operation task. The final evaluation result of "mobile 2C - wireless network - monitoring and troubleshooting" is **2.1**.

This section uses an example to describe the level evaluation process of Huawei ADN – this process can also be used to evaluate the levels of other evaluation objects.

The evaluation process and requirements can be further refined (e.g., defining scenario weights, providing an evaluation basis, and analyzing capability gaps) for each product domain. Related details are not provided in this book.

REFERENCES

1. TM Forum, "Autonomous Networks: empowering digital transformation," [R/OL], (2021-09-20) [2022-09-15].
2. TM Forum, "IG1252 Autonomous Network levels evaluation methodology," [R/OL], (2021-07-30) [2022-09-15].

CHAPTER 8

ADN Solution

Sɪɴᴄᴇ Hᴜᴀᴡᴇɪ ғɪʀsᴛ ᴘʀᴏᴘᴏsᴇᴅ the concept of ADN at UBBF 2018, it has developed an innovative ADN solution series for various domains over the past 5 years, including wireless, core, access, transport, IP, DC, and enterprise campus networks, as shown in Figure 8.1. Adhering to the concept of Intelligence for ICT, Huawei is committed to systematically applying AI to ICT infrastructure in order to overcome key challenges and fulfill the vision of building an intelligent world. Huawei's ADN solution is designed to improve the level of network intelligence through architecture innovation and overcome numerous challenges, such as increasing O&M complexity, experience assurance for diversified services, and energy saving, facilitating the evolution toward next-level telecom networks and ICT infrastructure.

- IntelligentRAN – Wireless ADN
- IntelligentCore – Core Network ADN
- IntelligentWAN – IP ADN
- IntelligentCampusNetwork – Enterprise Campus ADN
- IntelligentFabric – DC ADN
- IntelligentFAN – All-Optical Access ADN
- IntelligentOTN – All-Optical Transport ADN
- IntelligentServiceEngine – Intelligent O&M

8.1 INTELLIGENTRAN – WIRELESS ADN

Huawei's ADN solution for wireless networks – IntelligentRAN – enables wireless networks to evolve from automatic O&M to intelligent O&M. It focuses on intelligent functions on the RAN side and uses iMaster MBB Automation Engine (MAE) to implement single-domain single-vendor basic O&M in the wireless domain. IntelligentRAN also

DOI: 10.1201/9781032662879-9

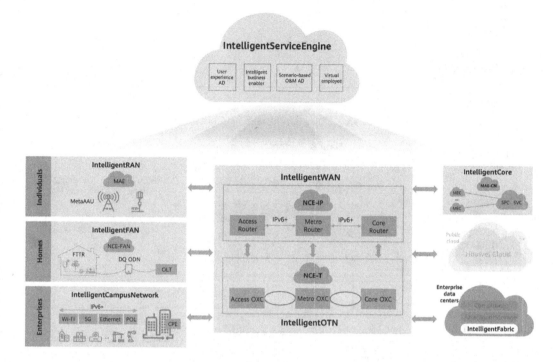

FIGURE 8.1   ADN product and solution panorama.

features the Mobile Intelligent Engine (MIE), providing intelligent use cases in coopera-tion with NEs, and opens up intelligent atomic capabilities to the cloud through an intent API. Figure 8.2 shows the IntelligentRAN solution.

8.1.1 Highlights

With the continuous evolution of wireless networks from 2G, 3G, and 4G to 5G, 5.5G, and 6G, mobile network capabilities will be further upgraded, services will be increasingly diversified, and networks will become more and more complex. In terms of their structure, wireless networks face the following challenges, which will become more prominent in the future:

- **Challenge 1:** how to simplify O&M given the increasing network complexity

- **Challenge 2:** how to handle 100-fold growth of traffic without significantly increas-ing energy consumption

- **Challenge 3:** how to ensure optimal service experience while providing diversified services

To address these challenges, IntelligentRAN integrates intelligent capabilities into wire-less network services, experience, O&M, and energy saving. In doing so, it helps build a wireless ADN that features intelligent and simplified O&M, intelligent network optimiza-tion, and intelligent service operations.

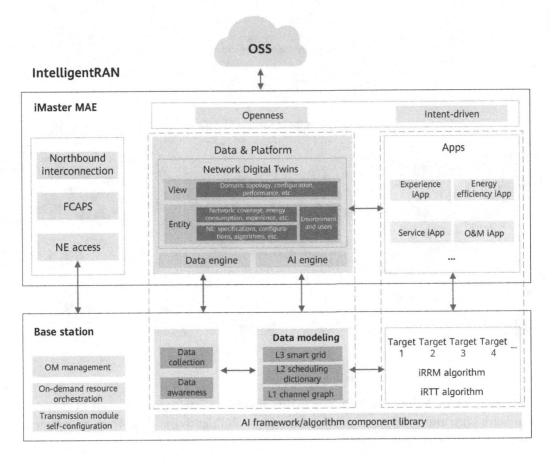

FIGURE 8.2   IntelligentRAN solution.

- **Intelligent and simplified O&M:** Leveraging key platforms and technologies such as the expert knowledge repository, prediction algorithms, and neural network, IntelligentRAN provides intelligent alarm management to accurately identify alarms, quickly locate faults, and predict and prevent faults. With this feature, CSPs can transform their O&M from a responsive approach to a predictive and preventive one, achieving a "zero-trouble" network.

- **Intelligent network optimization:** In the IntelligentRAN solution, intelligent NEs are deployed to implement intelligent resource scheduling, making it possible to optimize user experience and capacity and maximize spectral efficiency on multi-band multi-site heterogeneous networks. Furthermore, the network-level intelligent engine is used to implement intelligent collaboration based on multiple intents and objectives, helping CSPs focus on achieving optimal performance and energy consumption rather than only optimal performance. This not only maximizes the gains from energy saving but also ensures that network performance remains stable.

- **Intelligent service operations:** User-level dynamic simulation is used to implement precise network planning based on coverage, rate, and latency according to differentiated SLA requirements, enabling fast service deployment and provisioning. In addition, based on prediction capabilities, real-time dynamic resource scheduling is implemented to ensure service experience and realize service-oriented network adjustment.

8.1.2 Key Use Cases

IntelligentRAN supports a wide range of use cases. The following describes some of the key ones:

1. Intelligent and simplified O&M

   Prediction-based fault management is implemented to transform O&M from a passive and responsive approach to a proactive one. Because 2C and 2B services on wireless networks must always be online, the traditional approach based on post-event ticket dispatching cannot meet the requirements of these services. iMaster MAE accurately identifies alarms and locates faults by enhancing fault awareness capabilities. It also predicts and analyzes both software and hardware faults as well as performance deterioration (such as high board temperature, optical module faults, and short power backup duration) on the network based on long- and short-period awareness data collected through collaboration between iMaster MAE and NEs. This facilitates fault rectification, achieving a "zero-trouble" network and highly reliable performance.

2. Intelligent network optimization

   Intelligent selection of multi-band carriers based on smart grids is implemented to achieve optimal network performance. A wireless network typically operates over multiple frequency bands, each of which has different characteristics. Coordination between these bands is critical for improving the spectral efficiency of the entire network. In complex multi-band networks, intelligent schemes are used to make multi-band coordination more efficient and combine the advantages of different frequency bands to achieve optimal network performance.

   In addition, multi-intent multi-dimensional collaborative energy saving is implemented to optimize both performance and energy saving. Given that the communications industry and society as a whole are focusing more on reducing carbon emissions, energy efficiency has become an important indicator for mobile communications networks. To achieve such targets, intelligent algorithms and models are introduced to determine optimal policies for saving energy in a dynamic, multi-dimensional, and coordinated manner based on the traffic and environment, achieving network scenario auto-adaptation, one policy for one site, and multi-network coordination. This not only maximizes the gains from energy saving but also ensures a stable network performance in addition to striking an optimal balance between energy consumption and KPIs, transforming networks from being performance-oriented to ones that balance performance and energy consumption.

3. Intelligent service operations

    SLA-oriented precise network evaluation and planning is implemented to facilitate precise and fast service provisioning. Planning networks manually based on expertise cannot meet deterministic requirements in various industries, especially given the wide variety of 5GtoB services with high SLA requirements and complex application environments. In scenarios where public networks are employed for dedicated use, the network coverage and data rate of given areas are accurately evaluated, significantly reducing the cost of onsite measurement and evaluation. In industry-specific network scenarios, SLA requirements of various services on the live network are met by using industry profiles, environment modeling, user-level simulation evaluation, and SLA-based precise planning, thereby improving network planning efficiency.

    Prediction-based slice SLA assurance is also provided to enable service-oriented network adjustment. Traditionally, slice SLA assurance requires exclusive resources, which are often reserved in quantities several times greater than the actual demand. In order to ensure stable service performance, the amount of resources reserved for slice SLA assurance is usually several times more than the actual demand. The prediction capability is therefore introduced to implement adaptive slice SLA assurance, improving resource utilization while also ensuring slice SLA.

8.2 INTELLIGENTCORE – CORE NETWORK ADN

Adhering to the cloud-based O&M transformation paradigm featuring "high network stability, intelligent and simplified O&M, and optimal user experience", Huawei's ADN solution for core networks – IntelligentCore – integrates many innovative core network products and professional service tools to visualize, manage, and trace network-wide data assets. AI technologies, such as data native, intelligent analysis, model training, AI inference, and intent insight, are introduced to provide automation and intelligence capabilities at different network layers (including the telecom cloud base, 5GC, and SVC at the NE layer, and iMaster MAE-CN at the management and control layer). This solution helps CSPs deploy self-fulfilling, self-healing, and self-optimizing core networks that feature full-process automation. Figure 8.3 shows the IntelligentCore solution.

8.2.1 Highlights

Designed to meet the requirements of cloud-based O&M transformation and new 5G services, Huawei's IntelligentCore provides capabilities in network maintenance, operation and delivery, and experience closed-loop management, helping CSPs achieve digital intelligent transformation.

- **High stability of always-online services during network maintenance:** Single-domain fault maintenance of telecom clouds and core network NEs is implemented in a closed-loop manner based on expertise, knowledge graph, AI self-learning, and digital simulation. NE- and module-level fault management capabilities are provided to implement sub-health prediction, precise fault demarcation, and quick self-healing. This ensures that always-online communications services can be provided

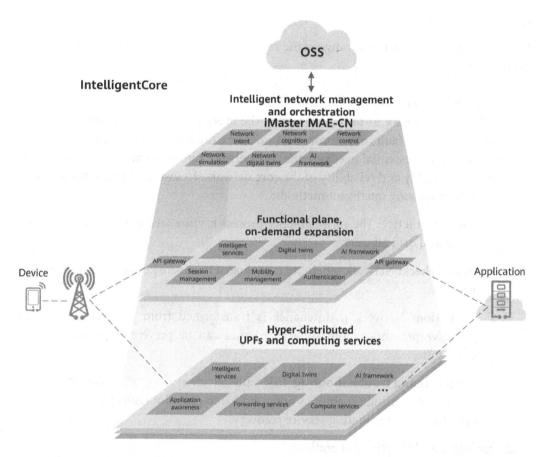

FIGURE 8.3   IntelligentCore solution.

for consumers and enterprise users and enables CSPs to transform their O&M mode of cloud-based infrastructure from passive response to proactive practice, detection, prevention, and remediation.

- **E2E network operation automation:** Intelligent and simplified delivery capabilities are provided for routine operation scenarios, such as upgrade, capacity expansion, migration, and testing. Leveraging the digital twin technology and cloud-based Continuous Integration Continuous Delivery (CICD) tool chain, IntelligentCore exponentially reduces the complexity of routine operations on cloud-based networks. This solution, driven by user intents, also streamlines the delivery process, delivers configurations automatically throughout the entire process based on the pipeline, and ensures hitless and secure change operations.

- **Refined and personalized experience optimization for an experience closed loop:** Native AI is used to achieve personalized user experience-centric network management (service experience standard, experience awareness, and experience closed loop) and provide enterprise-level SLA assurance for customers in different industries, achieving experience monetization.

8.2.2 Key Use Cases

IntelligentCore supports a wide range of use cases. The following describes some of the key ones:

1. High-stability network

   The core network forms a vital part of the overall network and provides services for many users – faults on the core network therefore have a wide impact scope. This means that it is essential to ensure the core network remains highly stable. To ensure the high stability and reliability of the core network, Huawei's IntelligentCore introduces the following intelligent methods:

   - **Routine practice:** The entire practice process is visualized to improve user experience and drill efficiency.

   - **Health check:** Network reliability is evaluated to ensure key resources are always available.

   - **Prediction:** Network maintenance is transformed from passive handling to proactive prevention, and subhealth issues can be prevented without human intervention.

   - **Diagnosis and troubleshooting:** Fast fault detection along with accurate demarcation and locating capabilities are provided to pinpoint faults to the minimum operable units, facilitating service recovery.

2. Intelligent and simplified operations

   Traditionally, network changes (such as upgrade and capacity expansion) are performed manually, involving complex operations and a large amount of manual intervention. Such a manual procedure is inefficient, and the changes may create additional risks. Based on the industry's advanced DevOps concept, Huawei's IntelligentCore implements efficient, secure, and hitless change operations.

   - **Automation:** The E2E tool chain eliminates the breakpoints of manual operations, reduces manual intervention, and improves delivery efficiency in all scenarios, including upgrade, capacity expansion, and migration.

   - **Hitless changes:** The operation simulation capability is used to simulate operations such as dynamic elastic capacity expansion in a low-cost trial-and-error manner, realizing hitless service operation changes.

3. Optimal user experience

   User experience management faces new challenges in different phases of 5G commercial use. Huawei's IntelligentCore transforms network management from network-centric into user experience-centric and value-centric, improving user experience, which is the basis for realizing high levels of user satisfaction.

To improve user experience for key services such as voice over New Radio (VoNR) and video over New Radio (ViNR), native AI is used and the tool chain is optimized. This ensures quick call setup, high voice quality, and zero call drops during communication, reducing the user churn rate.

8.3 INTELLIGENTWAN – IP ADN

Huawei's ADN solution for IP networks – IntelligentWAN – is composed of a set of key components such as intelligent IP network routers and an intelligent network management and control system, iMaster NCE. This system offers Path Computing Element (PCE), intelligent O&M, and open programmability to automatically schedule traffic throughout the entire lifecycle, helping CSPs build next-generation E2E intelligent IP networks. Figure 8.4 shows the IntelligentWAN solution.

8.3.1 Highlights

IntelligentWAN can simplify integration, systematically rectify faults, and provide open programmability for path computing elements, helping CSPs deploy intelligent IP networks.

- PCE and One Connection for Visualization reduce integration complexity by 50%. Multidimensional indicators such as latency and bandwidth utilization are displayed on the network digital map in real time. During path computation and optimization, more than 15 factors are flexibly combined to automatically schedule network traffic throughout the lifecycle.

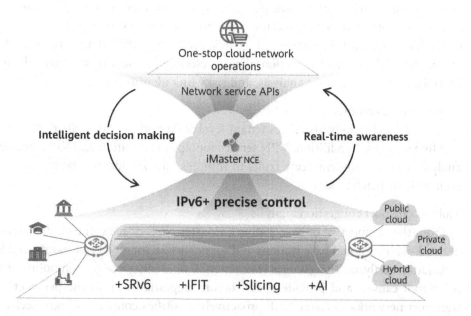

FIGURE 8.4   IntelligentWAN solution.

- "Congestion Free" facilitates "Troubleshooting 0–1–3–5", a fault-oriented closed-loop solution in which "0–1–3–5" refers to the minutes needed for prevention (0), identification (1), demarcation/locating (3), and recovery (5). This solution aims to build a self-optimizing and self-healing IP transport network that can deliver the best possible service experience.

- Open programmability accelerates service rollout with "three 1s." Based on YANG models, iMaster NCE provides E2E open programmability, including device driver programmability, network service programmability, and open APIs for devices and services. These capabilities make it possible to complete prototyping in 1 week, testing in 1 month, and commercialization in 1 quarter. More importantly, CSPs' O&M personnel are empowered to don the IT hat.

8.3.2 Key Use Cases

IntelligentWAN supports a wide range of use cases. The following describes some key ones:

1. Network digital map

   Indicators such as network latency, bandwidth, and utilization are visualized for a topology in real time thanks to technologies such as BGP-LS and Telemetry. Navigation-like path computation and one-stop provisioning in a map make configuration simple and efficient. Network paths are automatically optimized based on SLAs to continuously guarantee user experience.

2. Network risk analysis

   In the big data + three-layer AI architecture (device/network/cloud), devices integrate AI chips for real-time awareness, networks leverage AI models to construct local knowledge repositories, and the cloud provides an AI training platform for federated learning. All this enables risk-centric predictive O&M that features configuration check, device KPI detection, device resource prediction, strong/weak signal analysis, co-routing impact analysis, and risky link identification.

3. VPN service assurance

   The IFIT technology visualizes tenant-level SLAs and provides differentiated private line services. In addition, VPN service topology restoration and KPI association analysis are used to demarcate faults in minutes, quickly identify fault points, and accurately dispatch tickets.

4 Mobile transport congestion analysis

   From the perspective of base stations, iMaster NCE displays the quality trend of network-wide/regional base stations and supports E2E topology restoration and SLA association analysis. This enables iMaster NCE to identify congestion points, determine root causes, and provide optimization suggestions. From the perspective of transport networks, iMaster NCE proactively identifies congestion bottlenecks and guides network planning. By analyzing four typical types of congestion as well as the impact of transport network KPIs on base stations, iMaster NCE proactively identifies bottlenecks on transport networks, providing actionable insights for network planning.

5. Network slicing

As many as 10,000 slices can be planned and automatically deployed with a single click. Network-wide slices are visualized to facilitate management and can be hitlessly scaled up or down with a single click. Automatic management is integrated throughout the entire lifecycle of slices, providing differentiated SLA assurance in the 5G and cloud era.

6. Intelligent incident management

Massive O&M data is used for online training and intelligent algorithms are used to transform O&M from focusing on vast quantities of alarms to being based on "one ticket for one fault." This increases the alarm compression rate to 99%+ and results in much higher ticket dispatch accuracy and O&M efficiency, as well as a better user experience.

7. Agile Open Container (AOC)

Users can define their own service YANG models, and programming is made easy by adopting a building-block approach. New services can be quickly developed and rolled out, achieving the agile development goals of prototyping in 1 week, testing in 1 month, and commercialization in 1 quarter. In addition, standard northbound APIs and southbound device configuration scripts are automatically generated based on YANG models, enabling automatic provisioning of E2E services within minutes.

8.4 INTELLIGENTCAMPUSNETWORK – ENTERPRISE CAMPUS ADN

Huawei's ADN solution for enterprise campuses – IntelligentCampusNetwork – is composed of three main components: CloudEngine campus switches, AirEngine access points (APs), and iMaster NCE-Campus. Providing management, control, and analysis functions for campus networks, IntelligentCampusNetwork delivers full-lifecycle automated network management and intelligent O&M services, leading the industry in implementing L3 ADN. Figure 8.5 shows the IntelligentCampusNetwork solution.

8.4.1 Highlights

IntelligentCampusNetwork provides the following features to help enterprises deploy intelligent campus networks:

- **Zero-wait:** Network management is automated, instead of relying exclusively on expertise. This ensures zero wait time for network provisioning and reduces OPEX by 85%.

- **Zero-intervention:** Terminal access on traditional networks needs to be controlled manually. By automating such access, IntelligentCampusNetwork realizes seamless access for terminals within seconds.

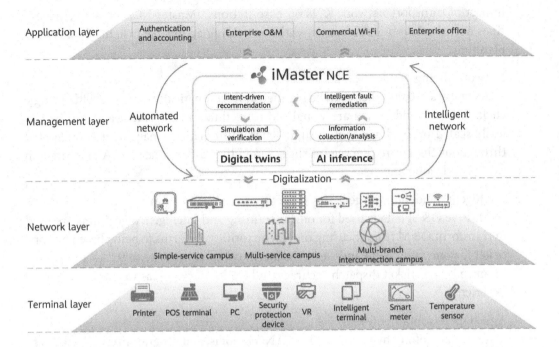

FIGURE 8.5   IntelligentCampusNetwork solution.

- **Zero-interruption:** In terms of network O&M, the passive response approach is transformed into one where optimizations are performed automatically within minutes with no service interruption.

8.4.2 Key Use Cases

IntelligentCampusNetwork supports a wide range of use cases. The following describes some key ones:

1. Intent-driven deployment

    With a scenario knowledge repository and collaborative recommendation algorithm, iMaster NCE-Campus accurately maps service scenarios with networking models and recommends optimal network solutions by analyzing service intents. In this way, networks can be provisioned within minutes, without the need for professional personnel.

2. Intelligent verification

    The connectivity simulation method used by iMaster NCE-Campus to verify network changes is much faster than conventional options, which can take 4 hours to verify a single change that takes only 10 minutes to perform. And if the change is not fully verified, there is a risk that many complaints would ensue. With iMaster NCE-Campus, verification takes just minutes to complete and ensures there are no errors associated with the change.

3. Free mobility

IntelligentCampusNetwork uses natural language to orchestrate free mobility, achieving matrix-based simplified management, cross-vendor deployment through IP-security group mapping, and one-off policy configuration. This delivers consistent service experience to users anytime and anywhere on all-wireless campus networks.

4. Intelligent terminal management

iMaster NCE-Campus supports intelligent terminal management, featuring a conventional terminal fingerprint database and a range of innovative application AI clustering identification capabilities. In this way, iMaster NCE-Campus can accurately identify networked terminals (98% of known types and 95% of unknown types), allocate them to correct networks, and prevent access by spoofed terminals. This reduces the need for manual intervention and assures secure access within seconds.

5. 360-degree network health

Based on network health evolution from various dimensions, iMaster NCE-Campus can proactively identify more than 200 typical problems and reduce potential network problems by 85%.

6. 360-degree user experience

iMaster NCE-Campus can visualize the experience of each user at any time, reducing user complaints by 90%.

7. 360-degree application assurance

Thanks to being able to identify more than 1000 mainstream applications, iMaster NCE-Campus can intelligently detect the application quality and slash the fault locating time from hours to minutes.

8. 360-degree intelligent optimization

During routine network optimization, iMaster NCE-Campus analyzes and predicts future AP loads based on data of the previous 7 days and implements intelligent and automatic network optimization. It also continuously trains terminal profiles and performs differentiated roaming steering for different terminal types based on AI algorithms, such as reinforcement learning. This improves the roaming success rate by 70% and roaming speed by 30%.

8.5 INTELLIGENTFABRIC – DC ADN

Huawei's ADN solution for data centers – IntelligentFabric – is comprised of CloudEngine data center switches and iMaster NCE. IntelligentFabric unifies the computing, storage, and service networks with an all-IP architecture, supports IPv6, and offers unique L3.5 ADN capabilities. Furthermore, this sophisticated future-proof solution supports full-lifecycle automation and network-wide intelligent O&M for data center networks, reducing OPEX by 30% and enabling intelligent upgrades for enterprises. Figure 8.6 shows the IntelligentFabric solutions.

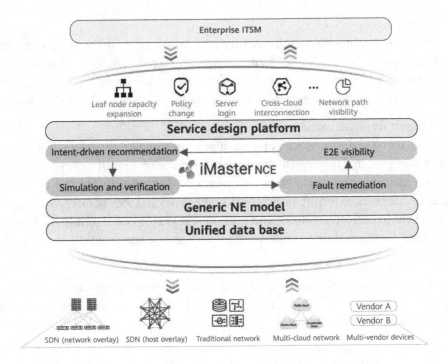

FIGURE 8.6   IntelligentFabric solution.

8.5.1 Highlights

IntelligentFabric provides the following features to help enterprises deploy intelligent data centers:

- **Zero-wait:** The time required to deploy and roll out services is slashed to minutes, significantly reducing the O&M workload and improving O&M efficiency.

- **Zero-error:** Network changes are evaluated for risks to help prevent faults caused by manual errors, thereby maximizing productivity.

- **Zero-interruption:** Network trends are predicted to help prevent network quality deterioration and failures, minimizing the possibility of faults. If faults do occur, they can be quickly and accurately demarcated and located.

8.5.2 Key Use Cases

IntelligentFabric supports a wide range of use cases. The following describes some key ones:

1. Intent-driven planning and deployment

By understanding and translating customers' service and network intents, iMaster NCE automatically selects the optimal network deployment solution, enabling E2E automated service provisioning and automated closed-loop management of intents throughout the lifecycle.

2. Network change simulation and evaluation

Based on network information (device configurations, topology, and resources) on the live network, iMaster NCE evaluates network change risks and eliminates design logic defects and configuration errors through network modeling and formal verification algorithms, thereby ensuring 100% configuration correctness.

3. "1–3–5" intelligent O&M

Telemetry is used to collect network performance data and comprehensively evaluate network health based on service experience in order to proactively identify more than 60 potential risks and over 90 typical faults within 1 minute. Based on knowledge graphs and Huawei's exclusive AI algorithms, fault aggregation, and source tracing are performed to locate root causes within 3 minutes. Thanks to the intelligent decision-making system, the fault impact is analyzed and the optimal remediation solution is recommended, enabling typical faults to be rectified within 5 minutes.

4. Open industry ecosystem

IntelligentFabric integrates seamlessly into enterprises' O&M systems to become a key part of the O&M process, helping achieve automated closed-loop management on the entire data center network. In the northbound direction, iMaster NCE uses the runbook service designer to flexibly orchestrate service flows and seamlessly interconnect with enterprises' O&M systems. In the southbound direction, AOC – Huawei's open programmability platform – implements fast adaptation of devices from multiple vendors, achieving automated provisioning of heterogeneous multivendor and multi-cloud networks within minutes. On top of that, IntelligentFabric opens up all network data services to facilitate integration with the service performance monitoring system, implementing unified O&M of services and networks.

8.6 INTELLIGENTFAN – ALL-OPTICAL ACCESS ADN

The core components of Huawei's ADN solution for all-optical access – IntelligentFAN – include all-optical access networks and iMaster NCE. It leverages digital modeling, cloudification, big data, and AI technologies for all-optical access networks to visualize ODNs and home networks and to enable full-lifecycle intelligent O&M, helping to meet requirements of differentiated application scenarios and superior broadband experience. This solution helps realize single-domain autonomy of all-optical access networks. Figure 8.7 shows the IntelligentFAN solution.

8.6.1 Highlights

IntelligentFAN provides the following features to enable all-optical ADN:

- **Zero-wait service provisioning:** DQ ODN, one-stop fiber to the room (FTTR) planning and acceptance, accurate resource information, and quick service provisioning

- **Zero-trouble service:** intelligent O&M, self-identification, self-diagnosis, and self-optimizing of PON and Wi-Fi faults and experience issues, and guaranteed broadband network experience

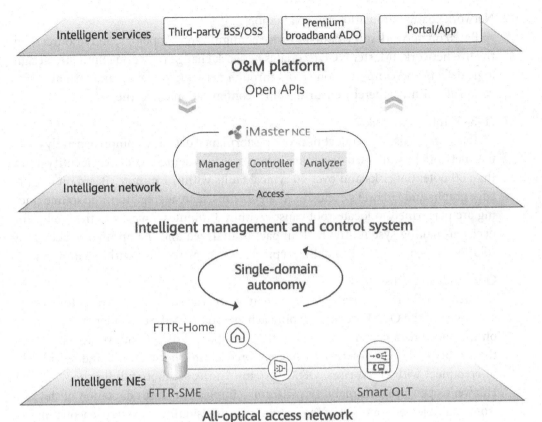

FIGURE 8.7   IntelligentFAN solution.

- **Zero-touch service:** autonomous home network management based on insights into behavior, experience, bottlenecks, and networking, enabling precision marketing and auxiliary operations.

8.6.2 Key Use Cases

1. Visualized management of ODN resources

    The iris solution based on the image recognition and DQ ODN automatically analyzes and restores the ODN topology, achieving visualized management for ODN networks and offering accurate resource data.

2. Remote ODN acceptance and precise locating

    Intelligent boards on OLTs and the optical iris solution enable automatic and remote ODN network acceptance and meter-level optical line locating on iMaster NCE.

3. Automatic identification of poor-QoE home Wi-Fi

    Home Wi-Fi faults make up a large proportion of home broadband faults. Through the intelligent boards on OLTs, IntelligentFAN can capture undistorted traffic features. This solution can also identify faults such as poor Wi-Fi coverage and interference of network-wide subscribers thanks to its unique intelligent Wi-Fi experience analysis algorithm, making it possible to visualize Wi-Fi experience faults.

4. Broadband poor-QoE root cause locating

Segment-based speed tests are used to accurately demarcate poor-QoE faults between STAs and Wi-Fi routers, ONTs, ODNs, OLTs, and bearer networks. In addition, the Huawei-developed spatiotemporal association intelligent diagnosis algorithm is used to align and analyze 110 types of application KPIs and 300 types of network KPIs by time or space. This algorithm is also used to quickly identify more than 30 types of home broadband (HBB) poor-QoE root causes of Wi-Fi network congestion, 100BASE-T cables, and weak optical signals on optical lines. As such, O&M engineers, who would otherwise need to carry out site visits for diagnosis and fault check, can instead remotely optimize and rectify non-hardware faults on iMaster NCE, significantly reducing their workload.

5. Precise identification of potential HBB subscribers

Insights into STAs, home networking, coverage/device capability bottlenecks, and applications help identify potential subscriber requirements and generate labels for potential subscribers. Such insights also help CSPs identify broadband upselling, Wi-Fi networking, and scenario-based potential subscriber requirements, greatly improving the marketing success rate and facilitating the development of HBB.

6. One-stop FTTR acceptance

IntelligentFAN includes an FTTR field service app that can be used to perform one-stop acceptance on more than 10 types of broadband KPIs (e.g., networking, rate, latency, and roaming) and automatically generate acceptance reports to ensure networking standardization – all without the need for further home visits.

7. Proactive FTTR assurance

Two innovative capabilities are provided for the new FTTR "optical+Wi-Fi" networking. One is to remotely manage the network-wide topology and device status, and provide 24/7 playback, thereby enabling the precise moment of network deterioration to be captured. Second, the speed test assurance solution enables O&M personnel to identify potential risks of substandard bandwidth by remotely testing the network speed between STAs, slave FTTRs, the master FTTR, and Internet segments with one click. In this way, network faults can be rectified before they are perceived by subscribers, ensuring a better service experience.

8.7 INTELLIGENTOTN – ALL-OPTICAL TRANSPORT ADN

The core components of Huawei's ADN solution for all-optical transport – IntelligentOTN – include all-optical transport networks and iMaster NCE. It leverages digital modeling, cloudification, big data, and AI technologies to visualize dumb fiber resources, and to create an intelligent, green, and highly reliable all-optical base, providing a premium private line service experience to customers. Figure 8.8 shows the IntelligentOTN solution.

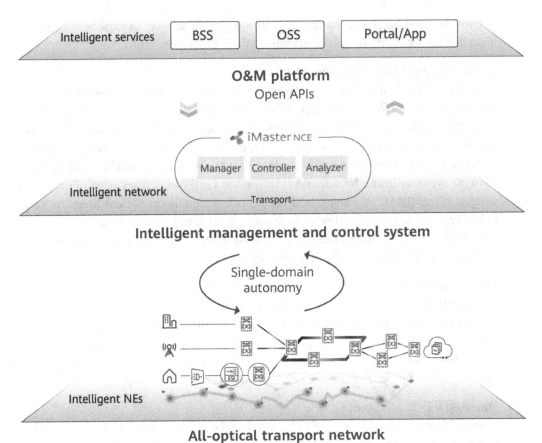

FIGURE 8.8   IntelligentOTN solution.

8.7.1 Highlights

IntelligentOTN provides the following features to enable all-optical transport:

- **Visualization of dumb resources:** Visualizes and predicts fiber health status, locates faults, intelligently identifies optical fibers in the same cable, and provides GIS-based display of optical cable networks, eliminating the problems of managing dumb resources.

- **Intelligent and simplified O&M:** Covers the entire lifecycle of planning, construction, maintenance, optimization, and operations, transforms O&M from passive to proactive; and builds networks with 99.999% reliability, providing ultra-high-bandwidth, low-latency, and highly-reliable transport capacity to customers.

- **Intelligent premium experience:** Provides visualized and manageable SLA performance, automatic provisioning of private line services, and after-sales SLA assurance.

8.7.2 Key Use Cases

IntelligentOTN supports a wide range of use cases. The following describes some key ones:

1. Optical network resource assurance

   Data related to optical network resources, planning, and design is centrally managed and analyzed to implement unified visualization, analysis and prediction, online check, and capacity expansion planning of network resources. This helps customers learn about resource usage, identify potential resource bottlenecks, and accurately expand capacity, realizing zero-wait time to obtain resources and shortening the service TTM.

2. Optical network health assurance

   For optical transmission section (OTS) fiber and optical channel (OCh) performance deterioration faults on WDM networks, intelligent forecast and analysis of optical network subhealth status are performed based on second-level awareness and edge inference capabilities on devices. This achieves visualized and predictable fiber and OCh health status and fault locating, transforms O&M from a passive to a proactive approach, and reduces the potential risks of optical line interruptions.

3. Availability assurance

   IntelligentOTN automatically evaluates and analyzes the availability of optical fibers and services in order to identify potential availability risks and bottlenecks. It also provides optimization suggestions designed to help improve availability.

4. Intelligent identification of optical fibers in the same cable

   Optical NEs use built-in sensors to detect and analyze performance changes in optical fibers caused by scattering (i.e., the Rayleigh, Brillouin, and Raman scattering effects) in real time and automatically identify risks associated with the working and protection fibers in the same cable. In this way, services can be adjusted to eliminate potential incidents.

5. Intelligent incident management

   IntelligentOTN uses three-level intelligent alarm compression (alarm compression, alarm aggregation, and root cause analysis) to significantly improve troubleshooting efficiency, speed up fault detection, diagnosis, and recovery, and enable "one ticket for one fault."

6. Latency map

   A dynamic network-level latency map that offers microsecond-level data in real time makes it possible to perceive and accurately measure private line latency – something that could not have been done before the introduction of this map. Similar to web mapping service applications, the latency map allows CSPs' marketing personnel to evaluate whether the latency and bandwidth between sites meet tenants' requirements. This facilitates the mapping of network resources and marketing of private line services that have differentiated SLAs.

6. Agile service provisioning

   IntelligentOTN supports multiple service scenarios and automatic service configuration even if only the source and sink are specified. Network capabilities are fully exposed through standard ACTN APIs, and iMaster NCE can be quickly and easily integrated with the OSS/BSS to become part of CSPs' private line service production processes, implementing automatic provisioning of private line services and improving the self-service level.

7. Private line SLA

The SLA performance of private line services is monitored in real time. Warnings are generated when the performance indicators exceed thresholds, allowing potential risks to be eliminated and thereby ensuring that contractual obligations are not breached.

8.8 INTELLIGENTSERVICEENGINE – INTELLIGENT O&M

Huawei's intelligent O&M solution – IntelligentServiceEngine – not only implements closed-loop management to meet CSPs' service objectives and domain objectives but also facilitates systematic, scenario-specific digital transformation for CSPs. It consists of various key modules, including the domain knowledge engine, business intelligence engine, hyper-automation engine, domain app development engine, and network and environment digital twins. Based on the digital intelligent transformation practices from its partnership with over 100 CSPs around the world, Huawei has launched three digital intelligent O&M solutions (AUTIN, SmartCare, and ADO) to achieve efficient O&M, deliver a superior experience, and facilitate agile businesses. Figure 8.9 shows the IntelligentServiceEngine solution.

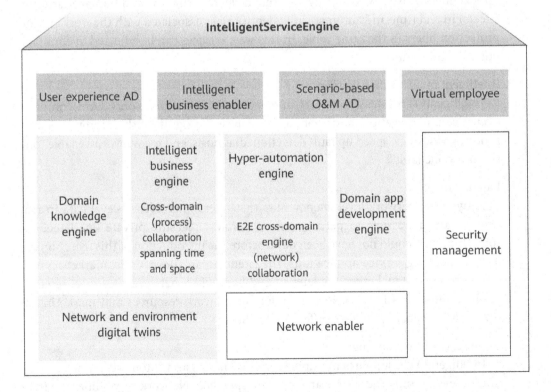

FIGURE 8.9 IntelligentServiceEngine solution.

8.8.1 AUTIN: Intelligent O&M

The commercial use of 5G networks, the large scale and high complexity of networks, and the diverse array of emerging services pose many O&M challenges for CSPs in terms of cost, efficiency, quality, and talent upskilling. CSPs' digital intelligent transformation for network O&M is speeding up due to the COVID-19 pandemic and has become an industry trend.

AUTIN, one of Huawei's intelligent O&M solutions, meets three key O&M requirements: quality improvement, efficiency improvement, and rapid talent upskilling. This solution helps CSPs quickly implement digital intelligent transformation towards Zero-X network O&M.

- **Quality improvement:** In 5GC scenarios, major faults have a large impact scope and take a long time to demarcate and locate. AUTIN intelligently predicts service impacts and risks and automatically diagnoses faults within just a few minutes, significantly cutting the MTTR.

- **Efficiency improvement:** Over 70% of daily operations in a network operations center (NOC) are repetitive, inefficient, and depend heavily on expertise. AUTIN helps NOCs implement integrated, automated monitoring and maintenance, intelligent diagnosis, and self-service, closed-loop management of onsite operations through mobile phones. Faults can be automatically diagnosed and managed in a closed-loop manner, reducing the number of tickets per NE and significantly improving O&M efficiency.

- **O&M talent upskilling:** Automating O&M operations gives rise to the need for O&M personnel to be upskilled. Huawei's open platform and abundant O&M knowledge assets enable orchestratable, O&M application development with minimal coding, simplifying O&M talent upskilling. The systematic Accompanying Service and enablement service for talent upskilling are provided to shorten the O&M application development period from months to weeks.

AUTIN continuously integrates expertise and iteratively optimizes domain-specific automated, digital, intelligent engines to improve its level of automation and intelligence.

8.8.2 SmartCare: Superior Experience

Delivering a scenario-specific, superior user experience is the backbone of development strategies for most CSPs. This goal helps CSPs deploy high-performance networks, achieve business success, and maintain a market-leading position.

- **Scenario 1 – optimal voice over LTE (VoLTE) experience:** CSPs need to shut down their 2G and 3G networks, and deploy a high-quality fundamental VoLTE network. SmartCare performs multi-domain, multi-interface data association analysis and slicing to accurately locate VoLTE experience problems and provide proactive assurance, preventing surges in user complaints. The VoLTE experience assurance solution helps CSPs significantly slash the volume of voice service-related complaints. The convergent data platform associates wireless network, core network, terminal, and registration information to facilitate VoLTE user migration.

- **Scenario 2 – optimal 5G experience:** Quickly increasing the number of 5G users and the volume of traffic is the key for CSPs looking to create a positive 5G business cycle. Algorithms are improved to focus on optimal experience instead of coverage so that more users can camp on 5G networks while also maintaining the optimal rate for these users. SmartCare helps CSPs significantly improve the camping ratio. The convergent data platform and insights into mobile phones, networks, and packages help CSPs target more 5G users and increase the proportion of 5G traffic.

- **Scenario 3 – highest experience ranking:** Network experience ranking is the key to a CSP's brand image. Traditional optimization based on drive tests is inefficient. SmartCare utilizes third-party crowdtest data to perform analysis and device-pipe-cloud collaborative optimization in order to maximize the usage of network resources, help CSPs achieve a high 5G network experience ranking, and improve their market share.

SmartCare's convergent data platform converges and analyzes data from multiple domains. Built-in intelligent operators, out-of-the-box intelligent prediction models, and abundant domain-specific expertise models help CSPs create digital twins to improve network experience and achieve efficient data-driven network operations, superior network performance, and leading business results.

8.8.3 ADO: Business Enablement

ADO is a premium HBB solution. Based on in-depth awareness of user-level service experience indicators, ADO models services for poor-QoE users, causes of poor QoE, and potential users. It provides functions such as Internet access quality analysis, single-user quality query, potential user identification, and VIP experience assurance to support closed-loop poor-QoE rectification and precision marketing.

Superior HBB experience: This solution helps CSPs build a user experience model based on the analysis of user complaints, user experience, user behavior, and Internet access quality, and allows CSPs to add service tags to models. The prediction accuracy for poor-QoE issues is as high as 80%, and CSPs can implement proactive O&M to eliminate potential faults, reduce the complaint rate, and improve user experience.

Grid-based precise operations: To meet differentiated service requirements of individual users, homes, governments, and enterprises, this solution analyzes and predicts the network bearer capability based on grid-based service insights, matches the resource capability of the live network, and allows CSPs to expand capacity and plan the network in advance. In addition, grid-based poor-QoE identification and rectification help realize precise grid-based service development.

CHAPTER 9

Summary and Outlook

H UAWEI HAS ADOPTED ADN as one of its core ICT strategies for 2030, aiming to jointly promote the evolution of ICT networks toward "hyper-automation and intelligent autonomy" over the next decade with all industry partners. Such evolution is a process that depends on fundamental theories in numerous fields and disciplines, a reference architecture adopting new concepts and views, and cutting-edge technologies in multiple fields. This book summarizes and describes those dependencies.

First, fundamental theories of ADN, including network adaptive control theory, network cognitive theory, and user and environmental model theory, are introduced from the perspectives of the driving forces and key elements involved in ADN. The progress and practices of these theories in different fields are also described. Second, a top-level architecture is defined based on the ADN vision, and the components (AN engine, NetGraph, AI Native NEs, distributed AI, and trustworthiness-oriented design) in the architecture are introduced in terms of basic concepts, key design principles, target architecture, modules, and key features. After that, in-depth research on key ADN technologies is provided, covering topics such as trustworthy AI, distributed AI, digital twin, simulation, digitalization of knowledge and expertise, human-machine symbiosis, NE endogenous intelligence, and endogenous security.

The sustainable development of ADN relies on a thriving AN industry. As an emerging industry, AN is not just about technologies; it is also about business success, industry collaboration, standards formulation, and continuous evolution. As such, we propose five key areas of focus for all industry partners to jointly develop the AN industry over the long term.

1. **Cultivate an environment conducive to scientific and technological achievements, and improve the system for applying these achievements practically.**

    Since AN requires cutting-edge technologies in numerous fields and disciplines, its technology and evolution roadmaps remain uncertain.

    - Policy makers should formulate more policies favorable to AN development. In addition, investment of more research resources and talent is needed to further

DOI: 10.1201/9781032662879-10

encourage joint innovation between upstream and downstream players throughout the entire AN industry chain. This will facilitate theoretical research and technological breakthroughs in the future. Furthermore, the "lay eggs along the way"[1] mechanism needs to be improved to progressively apply new AN technologies practically.

- A system for applying scientific and technological achievements practically needs to be built and improved in order to increase research efficiency throughout the entire industry chain and speed up the application of these achievements to the planning, construction, maintenance, optimization, and operations processes in every domain on ICT networks. This will help create a positive cycle of academic research, innovation, and production.

2. **Deliver long-term value to the digital economy, ICT industry, and end users.**

- Digital economy
  AN should invigorate the digital economy and accelerate the digital transformation of various industries. To do so, it must quickly meet new or advanced network requirements in production and life scenarios, such as smart city, smart factory, smart healthcare, interactive residence, and naked-eye 3D.

- ICT industry
  AN must make the ICT industry more powerful with scale advantages. AN capabilities need to be improved in order to develop networks capable of double-digit gigabit speeds as well as unlock the potential of network and ICT infrastructure for the evolution toward digital, intelligent, and green networks.

- End users
  AN should provide networks and services that offer superior quality to end users. For example, it should provide 10 Gbit/s ubiquitous connections that deliver an immersive user experience; provide 99.9999% ultra-high reliability, 5–10 ms ultra-low latency, and 1 million/km^2 ultra-high connection density for production and operations scenarios in vertical industries; provide enterprise customers with on-demand flexible subscription, minute-level provisioning, elastic bandwidth, and visualized O&M services; and provide dedicated, secure, and deterministic networks for both vertical industries and individual consumers, allowing them to enjoy the convenience and benefits of network upgrade.

3. **Promote solid and sustainable development of the entire industry chain by helping CSPs achieve business success.**
   AN has become a goal that CSPs wish to realize as well as a systematic method for CSPs to perform digital transformation. We firmly believe that more CSPs will start planning and deploying AN over the next few years. The key to the solid and sustainable development of the AN industry is helping CSPs maintain their positivity to achieve business success, develop services, and improve O&M efficiency.

According to TM Forum's 2022 AN survey report, 37.1% of the surveyed CSPs believed that they would reach L3 and achieve significant business success over the next 3 years.

All industry partners should continue to develop innovative applications and mature commercial solutions for high-value scenarios (such as 5GtoB, enterprise cloud access, and FTTR) throughout the entire process of planning, construction, maintenance, optimization, and operations. CSPs should accelerate how they introduce and test new AN technologies, products, and solutions, and quickly replicate and promote them after they reach maturity. By doing so, CSPs will be better placed to seize new opportunities that emerge during the digital transformation in various industries and create a positive business cycle conducive to the AN industry.

4. **Encourage efficient collaboration among industry organizations, standards organizations, and industry partners.**

Over the next few years, SDOs will need to further collaborate with each other in order to extend the scope and depth of AN standards from crucial aspects (target architecture, domain-specific levels and evaluation, intent API, and API map). They also need to speed up standards application and promotion. The Autonomous Networks Multi-SDO – a standards collaboration organization – needs to quickly streamline domain-specific standards and set up a standards co-construction and mutual recognition system through top-level design and cross-organization communication.

- In the short term, standards organizations need to work with both upstream and downstream industry partners with a competitive edge on technologies in order to add more details to the level standards for L3, improve the target architecture, and further define key technologies.

- In the medium term, technology pre-research for L4 will be initiated, and new scenarios and functions will be introduced to improve and test the maturity of technologies and standards.

- In the long term, more theoretical research and advanced technology projects will be launched to facilitate the evolution toward L5.

    The next few years will witness the rapid development of the AN industry, where both upstream and downstream industry partners will further and more frequently collaborate with each other. Industry organizations need to streamline the resources and strength of all industry players. This will result in further collaboration between the industry and standards organizations, collaboration among the industry, academia, research institutes, and businesses, and technological collaboration among different vendors. Industry players will be motivated to participate in joint innovation for the large-scale development of AN.

5. **Continue to develop innovative scenarios, services, and networks.**

The solid and sustainable development of the AN industry is impossible without continuous innovation.

- Expand the application scope of AN.

  A wide range of new scenarios are emerging in entertainment, life, and production, including the metaverse, immersive XR, interactive education, home office, precise control, and autonomous driving. The value of network automation and intelligence lies in quickly developing more innovative applications for these scenarios.

- Use AN to enable more new services.

  Over the next few years, computing networks, 5GtoB, industry private networks, FTTR, and other high-value services will develop at scale amid the emergence of multiple new services. AN must underpin CSPs' service innovation and large-scale development. For example, CSPs can use AN to improve business agility in a fast-growing market and industry that require collaborative production in order to deliver consistent quality and differentiated pricing so that they can deliver services of differentiated quality, laying a solid foundation for a healthy digital ecosystem in the telecom industry.

- Empower new networks.

  The communications network is evolving toward 6G/F6G, where it will be an air-ground integrated and comprehensive digital economy infrastructure with advanced intelligence, ubiquitous high-speed connections, and high energy efficiency. AN needs to keep up pace with network evolution and expansion. It needs to be integrated into the planning and operations of new networks to develop native and endogenous autonomous capabilities.

The digital world is on the horizon – ADN will undoubtedly become a crucial element of it. With integrated sensing capabilities and cognitive intelligence, ADN will transform into a "higher form of life" with great physical strength, acute senses, and a flexible mind. It will evolve toward L5 that features advanced intelligence, full autonomy, and high energy efficiency, facilitating the sustainable development in a fully intelligent world.

NOTE

1 "lay eggs along the way" is an idea proposed by Mr. Ren Zhengfei, CEO of Huawei. It means taking the initiative to apply newly incubated technologies in different fields.

Glossary

Acronym or Abbreviation	Full Expression/Description
3GPP	3rd Generation Partnership Project
3GPP TSG SA2	3GPP Technical Specification Group Service and System Aspects Working Group 2
3GPP TSG SA5	3GPP Technical Specification Group Service and System Aspects Working Group 5
5G	5th-generation mobile communications technology
5GtoB	A solution that uses 5G technologies to build basic information networks, enable various industries, and achieve business success in the industry.
6G	6th-generation mobile communications technology
AADE	awareness, analysis, decision, execution
ABAC	attribute-based access control
ACTN	Framework for Abstraction and Control of TE Networks
AD	autonomous domain
ADN	Autonomous Driving Network
AENS	average energy not supplied
AF	application function
AGPS	assisted Global Positioning System
AI	artificial intelligence
AI Native	Artificial Intelligence Native
AN	Autonomous Networks
ANE	Autonomous Network engine
Anima	Autonomic Networking Integrated Model and Approach
ANP	Autonomous Networks Project
ANR	automatic neighbor relation
AOC	Agile Open Container
API	application programming interface
App	Application
APT	advanced persistent threat
ARM	Advanced RISC Machines
AS	autonomous system
ATO	automatic train operation
AutoML	automated machine learning

B/S	browser/server
B2B2X	Business to business to everything (B2B2X) is a business model evolving from B2B. This business model provides various services to end users (X) through smartphones and Internet sensors.
B2C	business to consumer
BA	business architecture
BAZ	business autonomous zone
BGP	Border Gateway Protocol
BIOS	basic input output system
BSP	board support package
BSS	business support system
C/S	client/server
CARTA	continuous adaptive risk and trust assessment
CBD	central business district
CCSA	China Communications Standards Association
CCSA TC7	CCSA Technical Working Committee 7
CCSA TC7 WG1	CCSA TC7 Working Group 1
CICD	Continuous Integration, Continuous Delivery
Cloud Native	Cloud Native
CNN	convolutional neural network
CPE	customer-premises equipment
CPS	cyber-physical system
CPU	central processing unit
CSC	communication service customer
CSP	communications service provider
CT	communications technology
CXO	chief x officer
DARPA	Defense Advanced Research Projects Agency
DC	data center
DevOps	development & operations
DFX	design for X
DGG	discrete global grid
DIR	detection, isolation, recovery
DistMult	distance multiplication
DJEDLNA	deep joint entity disambiguation with local neural attention
DKRL	description-embodied knowledge representation learning
DNN	deep neural network
DPI	dots per inch
DPU	Data Processing Unit
DSL	digital subscriber line
DSRM	deep semantic relatedness model

DSV	delivery service vendor
DT	digital twin
DTN	digital twin network
DTO	digital twin organization
E2E	end-to-end
ECA	event-condition-action
EDNS	expected demand not satisfied
EMS	element management system
EPON	Ethernet passive optical network
ETSI	European Telecommunications Standards Institute
F5G	5th Generation Fixed Network
FLOPS	floating-point operations per second
FOCALE	Foundation, Observation, Comparison, Action, and Learning Environment
FTTR	fiber to the room
FTTx	fiber to the x
GAN	generative adversarial network
GANA	Generic Autonomic Network Architecture
GE	Gigabit Ethernet
GeoSOT	Geographical Coordinates Subdividing Grid with One Dimension Integral Coding on 2n-Tree
GIS	geographic information system
GPON	gigabit-capable passive optical network
GPU	Graphics Processing Unit
gRPC	Google Remote Procedure Calls
GSMA	Global System for Mobile Communications Association
HAL	hardware abstraction layer
HAT	human-agent teaming
	human-autonomy teaming
HCCL	Huawei Collective Communication Library
HMS	human-machine symbiosis
HMT	human-machine teaming
IBO	in-building operator
ICT	information and communications technology
IDM	intent driven management
IDS	intrusion detection system
IEC	International Electrotechnical Commission
IEEE	Institute of Electrical and Electronics Engineers
IETF	Internet Engineering Task Force
IID	independent and identically distributed
IoT	Internet of Things
IP Native	Internet Protocol Native
IPDRR	Identify, Protect, Detect, Respond and Recover

IPS	intrusion prevention system
IRTF	Internet Research Task Force
ISG ENI	Industry Specification Groups Experiential Networked Intelligence
ISG MEC	Industry Specification Groups Multi-access Edge Computing
ISG NFV	Industry Specification Groups Network Functions Virtualisation
ISG OSM	Industry Specification Groups Open Source Management and Orchestration
ISG ZSM	Industry Specification Groups Zero touch network & Service Management
ISO	International Organization for Standardization
ISV	integration service vendor
ISV	independent software vendor
IT	information technology
ITU	International Telecommunication Union
ITU-T	International Telecommunication Union-Telecommunication Standardization Sector
ITU-T FG-AN	ITU-T for ITU Telecommunication Standardization Sector Focus Group on Autonomous Networks
KIP	kernel integrity protection
KPI	key performance indicator
KQI	key quality indicator
L2M	Lifelong Learning Machines
L2SM	Layer 2 VPN Service Model
L3NM	Layer 3 VPN Network Model
L3SM	Layer 3 VPN Service Model
LED	light emitting diode
LFM	latent factor model
LIME	Local Interpretable Model-Agnostic Explanations
LPG	labeled property graph
LSTM	long short-term memory
MAC	media access control
MAE	MBB Automation Engine
MAPE-K	Monitor-Analyze-Plan-Execute over a shared Knowledge
MDAS	management data analytics service
MEC	mobile edge computing
MECE	mutually exclusive collectively exhaustive
MIE	Mobile Intelligent Engine
MIMO	multiple-input multiple-output
ML	machine learning
MnF	Management Function

MnS	management services
MPI	multi-point interface
MRO	mobility robustness optimization
MTTR	mean time to repair
NAS	neural architecture search
NCCL	Nvidia Collective Communication Library
NCE	Network Cloud Engine
NE	network element
NETCONF	Network Configuration
NetGraph	Network Graph
NETMOD	Network Modeling
NF	network function
NFV	network function virtualization
NGMN	Next Generation Mobile Network
NIST	National Institute of Standards and Technology
NLP	natural language processing
NMRG	Network Management Research Group
NP	network processor
NRE	neural relation extraction
NSI	network slice instance
NSP	network slice provider
NWDAF	Network Data Analytics Function
OAM	operation, administration, and maintenance
OCh	optical channel
ODN	optical distribution network
OLT	optical line terminal
OMC	operation and maintenance center
ONAP	Open Network Automation Platform
ONT	optical network terminal
OOD	out-of-distribution
OPEX	operating expense
OPS Area	Operations and Management Area
OPSAWG	Operations and Management Area Working Group
OS	operating system
OSS	operations support system
OTS	optical transmission section
OTT	Over the top (OTT) is a service mode that offers services directly to users via the Internet.
OWL	Web Ontology Language
PCI	physical cell identifier
PDP	partial dependence plot
PLM	product lifecycle management
PON	passive optical network

PRA	path ranking algorithm
PUE	power usage effectiveness
QoS	quality of service
RACH	random access channel
RAN	radio access network
RBAC	role-based access control
RDF	resource description framework
RDFS	resource description framework schema
RNN	recurrent neural network
RPA	robotic process automation
RSRP	reference signal receiving power
SAE International	Society of Automotive Engineers International
SBMA	Service Based Management Architecture
SDN	software-defined networking
SIMD	single instruction multiple data
SISD	single instruction single data
SLA	Service Level Agreement
SLS	Service Level Specification
SNMP	Simple Network Management Protocol
SOAR	Security Orchestration, Automation and Response
SOC	security operation center
SoC	system on a chip
SON	self-organizing network
SRCON	Simulated Reality Communication Networks
SSO	single sign-on
STA	static timing analysis
STU	situation-task-user
TA	technical architecture
TAZ	traffic autonomous zone
TCO	total cost of ownership
TM	terminal multiplexer
TM Forum	TeleManagement Forum
TR	technical report
TS	technical specification
TTM	time to market
UBBF	Ultra-Broadband Forum
UDR	unified data repository
UEBA	user and entity behavior analytics
UML	Unified Modeling Language
URLLC	ultra-reliable low-latency communications
UST	user-situation-task
UWB	ultra-wideband
ViNR	Video over New Radio

VIP	very important person
VLAN	virtual local area network
VM	virtual machine
VoNR	Voice over New Radio
VPN	virtual private network
VPWN	virtual private wireless network
VR/AR	virtual reality/augmented reality
WDM	wavelength division multiplexing
XR	extended reality
YANG	Yet Another Next Generation
ZSM	Zero-touch Network and Service Management